AN ANNOTATED BIBLIOGRAPHY OF INDIAN ENGLISH FICTION

Volume - I

Compiled by

V. INDIRA SAMBAMURTHY

ATLANTIC

ATLANTIC PUBLISHERS AND DISTRIBUTORS

Published by
ATLANTIC PUBLISHERS AND DISTRIBUTORS
B-2, Vishal Enclave, Opp. Rajouri Garden, New Delhi-27
Phones : 5413460, 5429987
e-mail : info@atlanticbooks.com
web : www.atlanticbooks.com

Sales Office
4215/1, Ansari Road, Darya Ganj, New Delhi-02
Phones : 3273880, 3285873, 3280451
Fax : 91-11-3285873

ISBN 81-7156-944-7 (Vol. I)
ISBN 81-7156-956-0 (Vol. II)
ISBN 81-7156-957-9 (Vol. III)
ISBN 81-7156-998-6 (Set)

Typeset at
APD Computer Graphics, Delhi

Printed in India at
Mehra Offset Press, Delhi

PREFACE

Originally started under a U.G.C. senior fellowship, contains about 10,900 entries, both primary and secondary, of about 8100 books and articles by scholar-critics and about 2800 entries of primary sources. The book envisages to be a Reference Guide for scholars who intend to do research in the field of Indian English Fiction. The enormous amount of scholarship that has enriched the field during the last twenty-five years sustains the usefulness of this Bibliography.

This Annotated Bibliography follows the M.L.A. style sheet (Third Edition, New Delhi : East-West Press, 1991) in its presentation of the materials. However the following guidelines may help scholars to browse through the materials more easily :

The Order in which the materials are presented is :

Part I : General

- A. Reference Works
- B. Special Issues & Periodicals
- C. General Works (Books)
- D. General Works (Articles)
- E. General Works (Dissertations)

Part II : Individual Authors

Entries on authors are presented in the following pattern :

- A. Primary Sources
  - Books
  - Articles
  - Interviews
- B. Secondary Sources Critical Works :
  - Books
  - Articles
  - Reviews
  - Dissertations

2. Cross-references :

(a) A book or an anthology which brings together a single author's own writings or articles of various writers by an editor is entered in the appropriate section on books. At the end of the annotation of the book/anthology numbers of each author's separate critical articles are given as cross-references ("See ....").

For example :

378. Naik, M.K., ed. *Aspects of Indian Writing in English*, Madras : Macmillan, 1979.

Annotation

See 590, 857, 1009, 1144, 1189, 2049, 2161, 3283, 3637, 5540, 6566.

Separate entries are made for individual essays in the appropriate section along with the annotations.

(b) Each article in the anthology/book of essays is given with the author's name followed by the title of the article, the name of the editor/author of the book, and then the title of the book, page numbers, and reference number of the book.

e.g.

1189. Singh, Amritjit, "Contemporary Indo-English Literature: An Approach." Naik, *Aspects* 1-14. ref. : 378.

However, in the case of those authors who have edited only one anthology, the name of the editor alone is given in the cross reference.

e.g.

319. Kaul, R.K. and Jaidev, eds. *Social Awareness in Modern Indian Literature*, Shimla : Indian Institute of Advanced Study, 1993.

Annotation

See 808, **1288**, 1614, 4110, 6439.

1288. Yadav, Kumkum. "Gandhian Influence on Indo-English Novelists." Kaul & Jaidev 167-176, ref. : 319.

3. If a novel is published several times, the first publication date followed by the dates of subsequent editions, is given.
4. Some novelists who earlier regarded as Indian English writers (Ahmeḍ Ali, R.P. Jhabvala, etc.) and later on migrated to other countries (either to their homeland or to a third country) are treated here as Indian English writers, on the basis of their earlier work and also the critical tradition.
5. General Reference Works such as *Contemporary Novelists*, and *World Authors* are not entered with the editors of these books, but with the titles.
6. Articles and essays which have a bearing on the creative work of the novelists are included under 'Primary Sources'.
7. Autobiographical works and titles on them are included if they have a bearing on the work of that novelist.
8. If an author's book contains only one or two articles on the central theme of this Bibliography, bibliographical details are given when the article is entered. In such cases the book is not entered.
9. With all the assiduous trials, some books are not available. In such cases the entries are given (from secondary sources) and no annotation is given.
10. Similarly annotations are not given to the articles published in dailies, weeklies, seminar papers, editorials, etc. Articles based on critical theories (post-colonial theories etc.) are also not annotated.
11. Some dissertations do not contain dates of obtaining the degrees.
12. The entries of 1997-99 are written without annotations as they are later additions and to re-annotate them would take two years by which time the work already done will become outdated.

V. INDIRA SAMBAMURTHY

ACKNOWLEDGEMENTS

I would like to express my profound gratitude to Prof. M. Nagabhushana Sarma, Professor of English and Theatre Arts, Osmania University (Retd.) who has motivated me to take up this work and guided me althrough the project. He has been a great source of inspiration to me althrough my career. I owe a special indebtedness to him for his professional advice and generous assistance at every stage in the preparation of this book.

I am thankful to the U.G.C. for having given me the opportunity to work on this major project by offering me a Post-Doctoral fellowship.

I take this opportunity to thank all the scholars (from India and abroad) working in the field of Indian English fiction for their ready response for my queries.

My grateful thanks are due to the librarians and the staff of the Central Institute of English and Foreign Languages, Hyderabad for allowing me to make use of the library facilities. A special mention need be made of Mr. Narendra Kumar who has helped me to secure rare materials connected with my work. I am also thankful to the librarians of Osmania University (Hyderabad). Indo-American Center for International Studies (Hyderabad), University of Hyderabad, British Library (Hyderabad), National Library at Calcutta, Delhi University, Sahitya Academy (Delhi), Dhvanyaloka (Mysore) and State Central Library (Hyderabad) who made this compilation possible with their unfailing assistance.

I am grateful to M/s Atlantic Publishers and Distributors, New Delhi for readily agreeing to undertake the publication of this work.

V. INDIRA SAMBAMURTHY

LIST OF JOURNALS BEING CONSULTED

1. *ACLALS Bulletin* (Kampala, Uganda).
2. *Abstracts English Studies* (Calgary, Canada).
3. *Agra University Journal of Research* (Agra).
4. *Aligarh Journal of English Studies* (Aligarh).
5. *Alternatives* (Boulder, Colarado)
6. *Ariel* (Calgary, Canada).
7. *The Aryan Path* (Bombay).
8. *The Atlantic Monthly* (Boston, U.S.A.).
9. *Bansthali Patrika* (Rajasthan).
10. *Bhavan's Journal* (Bombay).
11. *Books Abroad* (Oklahoma, U.S.A.).
12. *Book Review* (New Delhi).
13. *Chandrabhaga* (Cuttack).
14. *Chelsea Review* (Nutley, New Jersey).
15. *Choice* (Chicago, Illinois).
16. *College English* (Urbana, Illinois).
17. *Commonweal* (New York).
18. *Commonwealth Essays and Studies* (France).
19. *Commonwealth Novel in English* (Bluefield State College, Bluefield).
20. *Commonwealth Review* (New Delhi).
21. *Commonwealth Quarterly* (Mysore).
22. *Contemporary Indian Literature* (Delhi).
23. *Critical Inquiry* (Chicago, U.S.A.).
24. *Critical Practice* (New Delhi).
25. *Critical Quarterly* (Manchester).
26. *Criticism and Research* (Varanasi).
27. *Critique.*

28. *CRNLE Review* (Centre of Research in New Literature).
29. *Cygnus* (Lucknow).
30. *Debonair* (Bombay).
31. *Encounter* (London).
32. *E.L.T. Forum Journal of English Studies* (Tellichery, Kerala).
33. *English Studies in India* (Srinagar, Kashmir).
34. *Essays in Criticism* (Oxford, England).
35. *Guide to Indian Periodical Literature* (Gurgaon, Haryana).
36. *Humanistic Review* (Bombay).
37. *The Humanities Review* (New Delhi).
38. *The Illustrated Weekly of India* (Bombay).
39. *Imprint* (Bombay).
40. *Index India* (Jaipur).
41. *India Abroad* (Delhi).
42. *India Today* (New Delhi).
43. *Indian and Foreign Review* (New Delhi).
44. *Indian Horizons* (New Delhi).
45. *Indian Journal of English Studies* (Lucknow).
46. *Indian Literary Review* (New Delhi).
47. *Indian Literature* (New Delhi).
48. *Indian P.E.N.* (Bombay).
49. *Indian Review of Books* (Madras).
50. *Indian Scholar* (Raipur).
51. *Indian Writing Today* (Bombay).
52. *The International Fiction Review* (Frederiction, Canada).
53. *Jadhavpur Journal of Comparative Literature* (Jadhavpur, Calcutta).
54. *Journal of Asian Studies* (Ann Arbor, Michigan).
55. *Journal of Commonwealth Literature* (Leeds, U.K.).
56. *Journal of English Studies* (Warangal).
57. *Journal of English Association.*
58. *Journal of Indian Writing in English* (Gulbarga).
59. *Journal of Karnataka University* (Humanities) (Dharwar).

60. *Journal of Literature and Aesthetics* (Haripad, Kerala).
61. *Journal of Literary Studies* (Bhubaneswar).
62. *Journal of M.S. University of Baroda* (Baroda).
63. *Journal of School of Languages* (Delhi).
64. *Journal of South Asian Literature* (Michigan, USA).
65. *Kakatiya Journal of English Studies* (Warangal).
66. *Kunapipi* (Aarthus, Denmark).
67. *Kurukshetra University Research Journal* (Kurukshetra).
68. *Language and Style* (Carbondala, Illinois).
69. *Language Forum* (New Delhi).
70. *Library Journal* (New York).
71. *Link* (Delhi).
72. *Listener* (London).
73. *The Literary Criterion* (Mysore).
74. *The Literary Endeavour* (Anantapur).
75. *The Literary Half-yearly* (Mysore).
76. *The Literary Voice* (Punjab).
77. *Literature East and West* (Austin, Texas).
78. *Litticrit* (Trivandrum).
79. *Mahfil* (Chicago, U.S.A.).
80. *Marg* (Bombay).
81. *Miscellany* (Calcutta).
82. *Modern Asian Studies* (London).
83. *Modern Fictional Studies* (Lafayette, Indiana, U.S.A.).
84. *Modern Language Journal* (St. Louis).
85. *Modern Language Quarterly* (Washington).
86. *Modern Review* (Calcutta).
87. *Modern Philology* (Chicago, U.S.A.).
88. *New Literary Review* (Canberra, Australia).
89. *New Delhi* (Delhi).
90. *The New Quest* (Pune).
91. *New York Review of Books* (New York).
92. *New York Times Book Review* (New York).
93. *New Yorker* (New York).

94. *Novel* (Providence, Rhode Island, U.S.A.).
95. *Opinion Literary Quarterly* (Bombay).
96. *Orbit* (Gaya).
97. *Osmania Journal of English Studies* (Hyderabad).
98. *Panjab University Research Bulletin* (Arts) (Chandigarh).
99. *P.M.L.A.* (New York).
100. *Partisan Review* (New Brunswick, N.J.).
101. *Philological Quarterly* (Iowa City).
102. *The Quest* (Bombay).
103. *The Quest* (Ranchi).
104. *Rajasthan Journal of English Studies* (Sikar, Rajasthan).
105. *Rajasthan University Studies in English* (Jaipur, Rajasthan).
106. *Ravenshaw Journal of English Studies.*
107. *Revaluations* (Bhubaneswar).
108. *Review of National Literatures* (New York).
109. *Research in African Studies.*
110. *Saturday Review of Literature* (New York).
111. *Scholar Critic* (Gandhigram, Madurai).
112. *Sewanee Review* (Sewanee, Tennisee).
113. *South Asia Review* (Florida, U.S.A.).
114. *South Asia Review* (London).
115. *Southern Review* (Lousiana State, U.S.A.).
116. *Southern Review* (Adelaide, Australia).
117. *S.A.L.A.* (South Asian Literary Association).
118. *Span* (New Delhi).
119. *Span* (Flinders University).
120. *Spectator* (London).
121. *Studies in English Literature* (Tokyo).
122. *Studies in the Novel* (Denton, Texas).
123. *Style* (Fayetteville, Arkansas).
124. *Thought* (Delhi).
125. *Times Literary Supplement* (London).
126. *Triveni* (Machilipatnam, A.P.).
127. *Twentieth Century Literature* (Los Angeles, California).

128. *The Uttar Pradesh Studies in English* (Agra).
129. *Vagartha* (Delhi).
130. *Viswa Bharathi Quarterly* (Birbhum, West Bengal).
131. *Westerly* (Nedlands, Australia).
132. *World Literature Today* (Norman, Oklahoma).
133. *World Literature Written in English* (Arlington, Texas).
134. *Yale Journal of Criticism.*
135. *Yearly Review* (Delhi).

CONTENTS

PART I
GENERAL

Reference Works

A. BIBLIOGRAPHIES

1. *Abstracts of English Studies* (Quarterly). Calgary (Canada) : Blackwell Publishers, Oxford, U.K. & Cambridge, U.S.A.
2. *Accession List South-Asia (Monthly)*. New Delhi : Library of Congress office. Bibliographies serially published.
3. Agarwal, Narendra K. *English in South-Asia : A Bibliographical Survey of Resources*. Gurgaon/New Delhi : Indian Documentation Service, 1978.
4. Alphonso-Karkala, John B. "Indo-English Criticism : Being a Selection in Larger Bibliography of Indo-English Literature." *World Literature Written in English* No. 18, Nov. 1970 : 7-26.
5. Alphonso-Karkala, John B. and Leena Karkala, comps. *Bibliography of Indo-English Literature : A Check List of Works by Indian Authors in English 1800-1976*. Bombay : Nirmal Sadanand Publications, 1974.

6. *Annual Bibliography of English Language and Literature.* Leeds (London) : Modern Humanities Research Association, 1921 — Annual Publication.

7. *Aspects of Indian Culture III : Indian Literature.* (Select bibliographies). Eds. H.S. Patil and S. Masihul Hassan. New Delhi : Vikas Publications for Indian Council for Cultural Relations. 1972, 1977.

8. *BEPI — Annual Bibliography of English Publications in India : An Integrated Author — Title Subject Index to Scholarly and Significant Publications of the year.* New Delhi : D.K. Trust Publications.

   A successor to *Indian Books : Annual Bibliography* Vols. I-III. 1973-1975. Brought out the listing for 1980 in 1982.

9. Bender, Ernest. "Modern Indian Fiction" appended to his article "The Treatment of Contemporary Literature to an Undergraduate Course in Indian Universities." *Introducing India in Liberal Education* Ed. Milton Singer. Chicago : University of Chicago Press, 1957. 139-152.

10. Bharucha, Nilufer E. and Vilas Sarang, eds. "Bibliography." *Indian English Fiction 1980-90 : An Assessment.* New Delhi : B.R. Publishing Corporation, 1994 : 227-230.

11. Bhatnagar, M. K. "Bibliography." *Political Consciousness in Indian English Writing.* New Delhi : Bahri Publications, 1991 : 188-202.

12. *Bibliography of Doctoral Dissertations Series* (Social Sciences and Humanities). New Delhi : Association of Indian Universities, 1970 — Annual Publication.

13. *Bibliography of Doctoral Dissertations Accepted by Indian Universities, 1857-1970.* New Delhi : Inter-University Board of India, 1975.

14. *Bibliography of Indian English.* Hyderabad : Central Institute of English and Foreign Languages, 1972.
    Part I. Indian English : Indian English Literatre. Lists works relating to poetry, drama, fiction and criticism for the period 1827-1972.
    Part II. Indian English.

15. "Bibliography of *Mahfil.*" *Journal of South Asian Literature* 14.3-4 (1979) : 28-33.
    An Index Guide to the articles and book reviews published in the *Journal of South Asian Literature.*

16. *Book Review Digest* (Annual). Ed. Martha T. Mooney. New York : The H.W. Wilson Company.

17. *The Cambridge Bibliography of English Literature.* Vol. III : 1800-1900, Sec.7, Sub-Section II : Literature of the Dominions -Anglo-Indian Literature. 1067-1088 and Vol. V. Supplement AD 1600-1900, Sec.7, Sub-Section II : 706.

18. CIEFL Doc. Compiled by N.V. Jagga Rao & M. Kanakachari. Ramesh Mohan Library, Hyderabad : Central Institute of English and Foreign Languages.

19. Carl, Uma. "Select Bibliography of Indian English (up to 1978)." *Zeitschrift fur Anglistik Und Amerkanistik* 27.4 (1979): 327-340.

20. *Chronological Bibliography of English Language Fiction* in the Library of Congress through 1950. Ed. R. Glenn Wright. Boston : G.K. Hall & Co., 1974. 8 Vols.

21. Clark, Richard C. "Bibliographical Spectrum and Review Article." Introducing Indian Literature. *Review of National Literatures* 10 (1979) : 208–223.

22. *Cumulative Index to Journal of Literary Studies.* Vols. 1-8. Comp. Muralidhar Das. Cuttack : Department of English, Utkal University.

23. *Cumulative Index to the Literary Criterion.* Comp. M.T. Ramaswamy Gowda. Bangalore : Libra Library Supplies, 1994.

24. *Cumulative Index to Indian Literature.* ed. and comp. K.C. Dutt. New Delhi. Sahitya Academy. 1981

25. Dayal, B. "Bibliography." *Indian Short Story Writers in English.* Ranchi : Jubilee Prakashan, 1985.

26. Dhalla, Kamal H. "A Bibliography of the Indo-English Short Story 1945-1975." *Journal of Indian Writing in English* 7.1 (1979) : 36-41.

27. *Fiction, Drama and Poetry from the Commonwealth : An Annotated Checklist.* London : National Book League.

28. Gopalakrishna, comp. *Theses on Indian Subcontinent 1877-1971.* New Delhi : Hindustan Publishing Corporation, 1977.

29. *Guide to Indian Periodical Literature.* Gurgaon : Prabhu Book Service, 1964 —
A quarterly publication, cumulated annually.

30. Gupta, Brijen K. *Modern India in English Fiction 1800-1970 : An Annotated Bibliography.* Pref. by George Grella. Metuchen, N.Y. : Scarecrow Press, 1973.
Updates and continues Bhupal Singh's *Survey.*

31. Gupta, Brijen K. and S. Kharbas Datta. "Basic Bibliography." *Learning About India.* Ed. Barbara J. Harrison. New Delhi : Educational Resources Centre, 1977.

32. Hartley, Lois. "Checklist on the Indian Novel." *Literature East and West* 7 (1963) : 86- 90.
A partial list of Indian novels in English in print then in U.S.A.

33. Hassan, Masoodul. *Nineteenth Century Literary Works* (A Bibliography of Rare Books Available in India). New Delhi : B.R. Publishing Corporation, 1978.
A sequel to his earlier *Rare English Books in India.* A Bibliography for the period 1800-1897.

34. "IJES Bibliography (Annual)." *Indian Journal of English*

Studies. New Delhi : Indian Association for English Studies, 1960 —

35. *IMPEX*. Reference Catalogue of Indian Books in English. New Delhi : Indian Book Export and Import Co., 1960.

36. *Index India* (Quarterly). Ed. N.A. Gidwani. Jaipur: Rajasthan University Library, 1967 —
Cumulative Indexes (Subject and Author's name) of articles, reviews and dissertations.

37. *Index to the Journal of Indian Writing in English*. Comps. M. Kanakachari and B.Ramachander. Hyderabad : Central Institute of English and Foreign Languages, 1990.

38. *Index to Kakatiya Journal of English Studies*. Comps. M. Kanakachari and B. Ramachander. Hyderabad : Central Institute of English and Foreign Languages, 1990. Index to the Volumes 1-9.

39. *Index to Literary Half-Yearly*. Comp. A.L. McLeod. Mysore : The Literary Half-Yearly Press, 1985.
Index to the Volumes 1-25 (1960-84) of the journal, *The Literary Half-Yearly*.

40. *Indian Book Chronicle* (Monthly). New Delhi : B.P. Lamba, 1976 —

41. *Indian Book Industry* (Monthly). New Delhi : Sterling Publishers.
Provides latest information about books published in India.

42. *Indian Books* (Monthly). Calcutta.
Exclusively meant for indexing new and forthcoming Indian publications in the English language as well as Indian languages.

43. *Indian Books* (Annual). Comp. R.G. Prasoher. Delhi : Researchee Reprints, 1971-1974, 1983 —
Stopped Publication between 1975-1982. Resumed in 1983.

44. *Indian Books.* Comps. H.D. Sharma and L.M.P. Singh. Varanasi : Indian Bibliographical Centre, 1969 —
An annual bibliography of Indian books published in the English Language in India.

45. *Indian Books in Print 1955-57.* Eds. Sher Singh and S.N. Sadhu. Delhi : Indian Bureau of Bibliographies, 1969.
A select bibliography of English books published in India.

46. *Indian Books in Print.* Ed. Sher Singh. Delhi : Indian Bureau of Bibliographies, 1973, 1979, 1982, 1986, 1988, 1990, 1996, 1999.
Published in three volumes — Authors, Titles and Subject Guide.

47. *Indian Literary Index* (biannual). Ed. K.C. Dutt. New Delhi : Sahitya Akademi.

48. *Indian literature in English : Checklists on Commonwealth Literature* No. 5. Comp. Ronald J. Warwick. London : Commonwealth Institute Library Resource Centre, 1979.
A guide to the holdings of the centre.

49. "Indian Literature in English : A Bibliography." *Indian Literature* Jan.-Feb. 1985 :137-140.

50. "Indian Literature Listing." *Indian Literature* (bimonthly). Delhi : Sahitya Akademi 1990 —

51. *Indian National Bibliography* 1958. New Delhi : Central Reference Library, Ministry of Education. Monthly since January 1964. Annual Volume. Extra in two parts.
Part I is a list of books published in Assamese, Bengali, English, Gujarathi, Hindi, Kannada, Malayalam, Marathi, Oriya, Punjabi, Sanskrit, Sindhi, Tamil, Telugu and Urdu. Part II is a list of Government publications, including those of quasi-Government bodies.

52. *Indian National Bibliography* (Annual). Ed. Ananda Ram. Calcutta : Central Reference Library, Department of Culture, Government of India, 1961 —

53. *Indian National Bibliography* (Monthly). Calcutta (Belvedere) : Central Reference Library, Dept. of Culture, Government of India, 1964 —

54. *Indian Review of Books* (Bimonthly). Madras : Acme Books, 1991.

55. Iyengar, K.R.Srinivasa. "Bibliography." *Indian Writing in English.* Bombay : Asia Publishing House, 1983. First published in 1962. 777-832.

56. Jain, Sushil Kumar, comp. "A Checklist of Works by Indians in English or Translations from Modern Indian Languages." Regina : University of Saskatchewan, 1965 (Mimeographed). Part I : Poetry, Part II : Drama, Part III : Fiction.

57. ——, comp. *Indian Literature in English : A Bibliography.* Part III. Windsor (Ontario) : University of Windsor. 1965, 1970, 1972.

First 39 pages published under the title "Indian Literature in English : A Select Reading List" by the Association for Commonwealth Literature and Language Studies. *Bulletin* 5 May 1968 : 1-39. Rpt. by Leeds University in 1969. A selective list of works in English by Indians since 1960 : A few earlier works of "exceptional historical and literary value" are included.

58. ——, comp. *Indian Literature in English : A Bibliography.* (annotated). St. Michael Tenterden (Kent) : Privately published 1967. Available as a University Microfilm Information edition, Ann Arbor, 1977.

A checklist of works of poetry, drama, fiction, autobiography and letters written by Indians in English or translations from Modern Indian Languages into English.

59. ——, comp. "A Select Bibliography of Indian Short Stories and historical Fiction in English." *Indian Literature* 12.2 (1969) : 76-92.

60. Jha, Rama. "Select Bibliography." *Gandhian Thought and Indo-Anglian Novelists.* Delhi : Chanakya Publications, 1983. 182-203.

61. Jones, Joseph J. and Robert E. McDowell. "A Selected Checklist of Commonwealth English Novel." *Studies in the Novel* 4.2 (1972) : 330-332.
Contains a list of Indian English novels and criticism.

62. *The Journal of Asian Studies : A Bibliography.* Ann Arbor (Michigan) : Association of Asian Studies, 1966 —
An annual publication.

63. *The Journal of Commonwealth Literature.* Leeds : University of Leeds, 1965 —
Contains annual bibliographies of Commonwealth Literature, including Indian English. The section on India is compiled by Shyamala A. Narayan.

64. *The Journal of Modern Literature.* Philadelphia : Temple University, 1970 —
Annual Review. Contains bibliography.

65. Kalinnikova, Elena J. "Select Bibliography." *Indian English Literature : A Perspective.* Ghaziabad : Vimal Prakashan, 1982. 220-228.
A bibliography of books, mostly primary sources.

66. Kesavan, B.S. and V.Y. Kulkarni. *National Bibliography of Indian Literature 1901-1953.* 4 vols. New Delhi : Sahitya Akademi, 1962-1974

67. Kumar, Satish. "Bibliography." *A Survey of Indian English Novel.* Bareilly : Prakash Book Depot, 1996 : 306-318.

68. Mahar, J. Michael. *India : A Critical Bibliography.* Tuscon : University of Arizona Press, 1964.

69. McDowell, Robert E. *et al.*, eds. *A Bibliography of Twentieth Century Indo-English Fiction.* Arlington (Texas) : Department of English, University of Texas, 1970 (Mimeographed). Also appeared in *World Literature Written in English News Letter* No. 17 (Supplement) 1970.

70. Modern Language Association of America. *MLA International Bibliography of Books and Articles on the Modern Languages and Literatures.* New York : Modern Language Association, 1921 —
Annual Publication.

71. Mukherjee, Meenakshi. "Select Bibliography." *Twice Born Fiction : Themes and Techniques of the Indian Novels in English.* New Delhi : Arnold Heinemann, 1971. 219-231.

72. Mund, Subhendu. "Indian English Novels of the Nineteenth Century : An Annotated Bibliography." *Ravenshaw Journal of English Studies*, 6.2 (1996) : 71-75.

73. Nifor. *Guide to Indian Periodicals.* Poona : National Information Service, 1955 —

74. Naik, M.K. and Kaveri Bose, comp. "Select Bibliography." *Perspectives on Indian Fiction in English.* New Delhi : Abhinav Publications,1985. 253-277.

75. Naik, M.K. "Select Bibliography." *A History of Indian English Literature.* New Delhi : Sahitya Akademi, 1982.

76. Naqvi, R.A. *Indian Response to Literature in English : An Annotated Bibliography.* Gurgaon : Indian Documentary Service, 1974, 1977.
Contains Bibliography of British, American and Indian English literatures. Has additional section on general criticism.

77. Narasimhaiah, C.D. *Commonwealth Literature : A Handbook of Select Reading Lists.* Delhi : Oxford University Press, 1976. 47-52.

78. Narayan, Gomathi. "Select Bibliography." *The Sahibs and the Natives.* Delhi : Chanakya publications, 1986. 150-165.

79. Nelson, Emmanuel. "Selected Bibliography." *Reworlding : The Literature of Indian Diaspora.* West Port, CT : Greenwood 1992. 169-177.

80. ——. *Writers of the Indian Diaspora : A Bio-Bibliographical Critical Source Book.* Westport : Greenwood Press, 1993.

81. New, William H., comp. *Critical Writings in Commonwealth Literature : A Selective Bibliography up to 1970 with a list of Theses and Dissertations.* Philadelphia : University of Pennsylvania Press, 1977. 230-267, 305-306.
Contains a section on South-Asia (India, Pakistan and Ceylon).

82. *OJES 20.* Comp. Taqi Ali Mirza. Hyderabad : Osmania University Press, 1981.
An index to the articles and book reviews that have appeared in *Osmania Journal of English Studies* from 1961 to 1980.

83. *OJES 24.* Comps. Bala Kothandaraman and Siddiq Ali. Hyderabad : Osmania University Press, 1989.
An index to the articles and book reviews that have appeared in *Osmania Journal of English Studies* from 1961-1988.

84. Pathan, B.A. "Select Bibliography." *Gandhian Myth in English Literature in India.* Jaipur : Aavishkar Publishers, 1987. 164-172.

85. Patil, Z.N. "Bibliography." *Style in Indian English Fiction : A Study in Politeness Strategies.* New Delhi : Prestige Books, 1994 : 250-262.

86. Perkins, Susan, comp. "A Selected Bibliography Useful for a Study of Indo-Anglian Literature." *Introducing India in Liberal Education.* Ed. Milton Singer. Chicago : University of Chicago, 1956. Calcutta : Asiatic Society, 1957. 267-279.

87. Piet, David. "Bibliography : Secondary Sources on Indian Writing in English." *Literature East and West* 15.1 (1971) : 74-82.

88. Raju, Anand Kumar and C.R. Sunder Raj, comp. *Indian Writing in English : A Concise Bibliography of Secondary Sources.* Bombay : Ivon Publishing House, 1981.

89. Raju, Anand Kumar. *American, British and Commonwealth Literature.* Madras : Affiliated East-West Press, 1990.

90. Ramamurti, K. S. "Bibliography." *The Rise of the Indian Novel in English.* New Delhi : Sterling Publishers, 1987. 284-298.

91. Ramaiah, L. S. *Indian English : A Bibliography.* Hyderabad : Central Institute of English and Foreign Languages, 1987.

92. ——. *Indian English : A Bibliographical Guide to Resources.* Delhi : Gian Publishing House, 1988.

93. *Reference Catalogue of Indian Books in Print in English.* 3 Vols. New Delhi : Today and Tomorrow Publishers, 1973-74.

94. *Sahitya Akademi Awards : Books and Writers 1955-1978.* New Delhi : Sahitya Akademi, 1990.

95. Sanyal, Samares C. "Bibliography." *Indianness in Major Indo-English Novels.* Bareilly : Prakash Book Depot, 1984. 269-278.

96. Sarma, G.P. "Bibliography." *Nationalism in Indo-Anglian Fiction.* Delhi : Sterling Publishers, 1990 : 255-277.

97. Shanker, Lakshmi and S. Hamid Hussain, eds. *English Literature and Linguistics.* Bhopal: Council of Oriental Research Publications Division, 1979.
National register of Doctoral Dissertations accepted and in progress in Indian Universities, Vol. 1, Humanities. Has a section on 'Indo-Anglian Literature' 116-136.

98. Sharma, Krishna Dayal. "Select Bibliography." *Protest in Post-Independence Indian English Fiction.* Jaipur : Bohra Prakashan, 1995 : I-XIII.

99. Shulman, Frank J., ed. *Doctoral Dissertations on South Asia,1966-1970 : An Annotated Bibliography*. Ann Arbor : Centre for South and Southern Asian Studies, University of Michigan, 1972.
Contains entries on 1305 Ph.D. theses on Indian and neighbouring countries.

100. ——. "Modern Indian Fiction." *Literature East and West* 4. 2-3 (1957) : 15. Mimeographed Checklist.

101. Singh, Amritjit, Rajiva Verma and Irene M. Joshi. *Indian Literature in English 1827-1979 : An Annotated Bibliography*. Information Guide Series 36. Detroit : Gale Research Co., 1981.

102. Singh, Bhupal. *A Survey of Anglo-Indian Fiction*. London : Curzon Press, 1975. Originally published in 1934 by Oxford University Press, London.
The supplementary appendix contains a note on some Indian writers of English fiction and a survey of some works published in the period 1900-1920.

103. Singh, Surender. "Bibliography." *Princely Life in Indian English Writing*. New Delhi : Reliance Publishing House, 1995 : 147-155.

104. Spencer, Dorothy M. *Indian Fiction in English : An Annotated Bibliography*. South Asia Regional Studies 98. Philadelphia : University of Pennsylvania Press, 1960.

105. Stenvorth, Klaus. "Bibliography." *The Indo-English Novel : The Impact of the West on Literature in a Developing Country*. Wiesbaden : Frans Steiner Verlag 1975 : 139-148.

106. Suneel, Seema. "Bibliography." *Man-Woman Relationship in Indian English Fiction*. New Delhi : Prestige Books, 1995 : 171-174.

107. Tucker, Martin and John Ferres, eds. *Modern Commonwealth Literature*. New York : Fredrick Ungar Publishers, 1977.
Covers 175 authors, of which 20 are from India, including R.K. Narayan, Raja Rao and Khushwant Singh.

108. Venkateswaran, Shyamala. *Indian Fiction in English : A Bibliography* (Mimeographed). Mysore : University of Mysore, 1970.

109. Venugopal, C.V. "Select Bibliography." *The Indian Short Story in English : A Survey.* Bareilly : Prakash Book Depot, 1976 : i-vi.

110. *Who is Who of Indian Writers.* New Delhi : Sahitya Akademi, 1965.

Contains biographical and bibliographical notes on Indian writers.

111. Williams, H.M. "Bibliography." *Indo-Anglian Literature 1800-1970 — A Survey.* Madras : Orient Longman, 1976. 126-131.

112. Wilson, Patrick. *South Asia: A Selected Bibliography on India, Pakistan, Ceylon.* Revised and Edited. New York: American Institute of Pacific Affairs, 1957.

113. *Year's Work in English Studies* (Annual). Published for the English Association by Blackwell Reference. Atlantic Highland, N.J. : Humanities Press, 1919/20 —

B. SPECIAL ISSUES OF PERIODICALS

114. *Banasthali Patrika* 4.12 (1969). Special Number on Indo-English Literature.

115. *Banasthali Patrika* 5.13 (1969). Special Number on Indo-English Literature (Supplement).

116. *Books Abroad* 43.4 (1969). Special Issue on Indian Literature.

117. *Commonwealth : Essays and Studies* 8.1 (1985). Special Number on *Images of India in Commonwealth Literature.*

A major part is devoted to Indian Writers in English.

118. *Commonwealth : Essays and Studies* 9.2 (1987). Special Number on *Orality and Literacy in Commonwealth Literature.*

Contains two articles on R.K. Narayan.

119. *Commonwealth : Essays and Studies* 10.2 (1988). Special Number on Interviews.

Contains an interview with Anita Desai and an article on R.K. Narayan.

120. *Commonwealth : Essays and Studies* 12.1 (Aug. 1989). Special Number on *Liberty/Liberta/Libertes.*

121. *Commonwealth : Essays and Studies* 18.1 (1995). Special Number on *National Identities in the New Literatures.*

122. *Commonwealth Quarterly* 3.9 (1978). Special Issue on Women Writers.

123. *Commonwealth Review* 2.1-2 (1990-91). Special Number. Australian and Indian Literature : Studies in Mutual Response. Published in a book form under the title *Australian and Indian Literature : Studies in Mutual Response.* Eds. David Kerr and R.K. Dhawan. New Delhi: Prestige Books, 1994. Section II is devoted to Indian Writers in English.

124. *Commonwealth Review* 4.2 (1992-93). Special Number. Commonwealth Writing : A Study in Expatriate Experience. Published in a book form under the title *Commonwealth Writing : A Study in Expatriate Experience.* Eds. R.K. Dhawan and L.S.R. Krishna Sastry. New Delhi : Prestige Books, 1994.

125. *Commonwealth Review* 5.1 (1993-94). Special Number on Indian Literature Today : Drama and Fiction. Published in a book form under the title *Indian Literature Today.* Ed. R.K. Dhawan. New Delhi : Prestige Books, 1994.

126. *Commonwealth Review* 5.2 (1993-94). Special Number on Indian Writing Today : Poetry and Fiction. Published in a book form under the title *Indian Literature Today.* Ed. R.K. Dhawan. New Delhi : Prestige Books, 1994.

127. *Commonwealth Review* 6.1 (1994-95). Special Number on Feminism and Literature.

128. *Cygnus* 2.1 (1980). Special Number on Indian Writing in English.

129. *Indian Literature* 13.1 (1970). Special Number on Indian Writing in English.

130. *Indian Literature* 175 (1997). Special Issue on "Women's Writing in English : New Voices."

131. *Indian Writing Today* 4.1 (1970). Special Number on Indo-Anglian Literature.

132. *Journal of Indian English Studies* (Warangal) 4.2 (1972). Special Issue on Indian Writing in English.

133. *Journal of Indian Writing in English* 8.1-2 (1980). Special Double Issue : Foreign Responses to Indian Writing in English. Published in a book form under the title, *Through Different Eyes*. Ed. Kirpal Singh. Calcutta : Writers Workshop, 1984.

134. *Journal of Indian Writing in English* 12.2 (1984). Special Number : Post-Independence Indian Writers in English. Main focus is on the stylistic variations of contemporary Indian Writers in English.

135. *Journal of Indian Writing in English* 13.2 (1980). Special Number : Indian Writers Abroad : Some Expatriate Writing. Focuses on thematic and artistic concerns of the Indian expatriate writing.

136. *Journal of Indian Writing in English* 14.1 (1986). Special Number : American Students' Perspectives on Indian Writing in English.

137. *Journal of Indian Writing in English* 18.2 (1990). Special Number : Proc. of the Workshop on Creative Writing in English, 26 to 29 Feb. 1990, Madras.

138. *Journal of Indian Writing in English* 20.1-2 (1992). Joint Special Number to mark the establishment of NIRIEL (National Institute for Research in Indian English Literature).

139. *Journal of Literature and Aesthetics* 2.2-3 (1982). Special Number on the Modern Experimental Indian Fiction in English.

140. *Journal of Literary Studies* 2.2 (1979). Special Issue on Indo-Anglian Fiction.

141. *Journal of South-Asian Literature* 12.3-4 (1977). Special Issue on Women Writers.

142. *Journal of South-Asian Literature* 22.2 (1987). Special Issue on Indian Writing in English.

143. *Kakatiya Journal of English Studies* 3.1 (1978). Indian English Novel-Special Number.

144. *Kakatiya Journal of English Studies* 18 (1998). Special Issue on Post-Colonial Literatures.

145. *Language Forum* 7.1-4 (1982). Special Issue : Modern Indo-English Fiction. Published in a book form under the title, *Explorations in Modern Indo-English Fiction.* Ed. R.K. Dhawan. New Delhi : Bahri Publications, 1982.

146. *Language Forum* 11.1.4 (1985-86). Special Issue : Comparative Literature. Published in a book form under the title, *Comparative Literature.* Ed. R.K. Dhawan. New Delhi : Bahri Publications, 1987.

147. *Language Forum* 12.1-4 (1986). Special Number on Indian English Literature : 1981-85. Also published in a book form under the title, *Indian English Writing : 1981-1985 : Experiments with Impression.* Ed. R.K. Singh. New Delhi : Bahri Publications, 1987.

148. *Language Forum* 18.1-2 (1992). Special Number on "Quest for Identity in Indian English Fiction." Also published in a book form entitled *Quest for Identity in Indian English Fiction.* Ed. R.S. Pathak. New Delhi : Bahri Publications, 1992.

149. *Language Forum* 19.1-2 (1993). Special Issue on Indianization of English Language and Literature. Also published in a book form under the title, *Indianization of English Language and Literature.* Ed. R.S.Pathak. New Delhi : Bahri Publications, 1994.

150. *Language Forum* 21.2 (1995). Special Issue on Anger in Action : Explorations in Indian Writing in English. Also published in book form under the title, *Anger in Action : Explorations in Indian Writing in English.* New Delhi : Bahri Publications, 1997.

151. *Language Forum* 24.1-2 (1998). Special Issue on "Search for Tolerance in Indian English Fiction.

152. *Literary Criterion* 12.1-3 (1976). Special Number on Indian Writing in English.

153. *Literary Criterion* 20.4 (1985). Special Issue on "Women in Fiction and Fiction by Women." Also published in a book form under the title, *Women in Fiction and Fiction by Women.* Ed. C.D. Narasimhaiah. Mysore : Dhvanyaloka Publications, 1986.

154. *Literary Review* 29.4 (1986). The Writers of Indian Commonwealth.

155. *Literary Voice* 3 Oct 1995. Special Issue on Images of Woman in the Works of Some Major Indian, African and Canadian Novelists.

156. *Literature East and West* 10.1-2 (1966). Indian Literature : Special edition.

157. *Littcrit* 7, 4.2 (1978). A major part is devoted to Indian English Literature.

158. *Littcrit* 9, 5.2 (1979). Special Number on Indian Novel Since the Fifties (all Languages).

159. *Littcrit* 14, 8.1 (1982). Special Number on Indian Writing in English.

160. *Littcrit* 40, 21.1 (1995). Special Number on Modern Indian Literary Criticism in English, Part I.

161. *Littcrit* 41, 21.2 (1995). Special Number on Modern Indian Literary Criticism in English, Part II.

162. *Littcrit* 42, 22.1 (1996). Special Number on Modern Indian Literary Criticism in English, Part III.

163. *Literary Voice.* Book Series 3. Feb. 1996. "Images of Woman in the Works of Some Major Indian, African and Canadian Novelists."

164. *Massachusetts Review* 29.4 (1988). "Deshi-Videshi: South Asian Expatriate Writers and Artists."

165. *Modern Fiction Studies* 39.1(1993). Fiction on the Indian Sub-continent.

166. *Osmania Journal of English Studies* 7 (1969). Special Number : Indian Writing in English.

167. *Osmania Journal of English Studies* 25 (1989). Special Number : Narrative in Indian Writing in English.

168. *Rajasthan Journal of English Studies* 13 & 14 (1981). Special Number : Indian Writing in English.

169. *Ravenshaw Journal of English Studies.* 6.1 (1996). Special Issue on Indian English Literature.

170. *Revaluations* 1.3 (1995). Commonwealth Literature Special.

171. *Review of National Literatures* 10 (1979). Special Issue on India.

172. *Seminar* 384, Aug. (1991). New Writing in English : A Symposium on Modern English Fiction in India.

173. *Studies in the Novel* 4.2 (1972). Special Issue on Commonwealth Literature (Contains a section on Indian English Literature).

174. *World Literature Written in English* 14.2 (1975). Special Issue on South Asian Literature : A section is devoted to Indian Writers in English.

175. *World Literature Written in English* 17.1 (1978). Special Issue : Women Writers of the Commonwealth.

C. GENERAL CRITICAL WORKS

A. General Books

176. Acheson, James, ed. *The British and Irish Novel Since 1960.* New York : St. Martin Press, 1991.
A reader's guide to contemporary novel in England and Ireland. Contains some succinct essays on subjects concerning the modern novelists in English. There are two essays related to Indian English fiction.
See 3566, 7083.

177. Adam, Ian and Helen Tiffin, eds. *Past the Last Post : Theorizing Post-Colonialism and Post-Modernism.* Calgary : University of Calgary, 1990.
A collection of thirteen essays written by different critics. Contains three articles, two on Rushdie and one on Bharati Mukherjee.
See 5000, 6994, 7278.

178. Afzalkhan, Fawzia. *Cultural Imperialism and the Indo-English Novel : Genre and Ideology in the Novels of R.K. Narayan, Anita Desai, Kamala Markandaya and Salman Rushdie.* University Park : Pennsylvania State University Press, 1993.
Discusses how ideology shapes and is shaped by tne use of particular generic strategies of fiction and how far such usage helps the ex-colonized writer to deal effectively with post-colonial, post-independence trauma, and finally, how the choice of genre or mode determines whether or not the native, excolonized writer has been successful in reflecting the ideological strategies of "containment" perpetuated by most Western "orientalist" writers and their texts. Taking the fiction of Narayan, Desai, Markandaya and Rushdie as models discusses the choice of particular literary genres or modes which reveal the ideological affiliations of a writer's text.

179. Agnihotri, G.N. *Indian Life and Problems in the Novels of Mulk Raj Anand, Raja Rao and R.K. Narayan.* Meerut: Shalabh Book House, 1984, 1993.
The book is a critique of the various shades of Indian life as presented by the three front-ranking novelists — Anand, Raja Rao, Narayan — and the peculiar problems they and other Indian novelists faced in their creative work. The approaches of the three novelists to these problems signify three different angles : one as a progressive proletarian, the second one as philosopher and the third as a pure artist. Incidentally there are also general observations on these novelists' use of language and world view.
See 1550, 5303, 6345.

180. Alam, Quaiser Zoha. *The Dynamics of Imagery : The Image in Indian English Literature.* New Delhi : Atlantic Publishers, 1994.
Collecting different types of similies and metaphors employed by Indian English writers, studies the nature and function of imagery in Indian English literature.

181. ——, *Language and Literature : Diverse Indian Experiences.* New Delhi : Atlantic Publishers, 1996.
A collection of essays published in several journals. Contains six essays on Indian English fiction.
See 571, 572, 4047, 4922, 6348, 7909.

182. Albertazzi, Silvia. *Translating India : Travel and Cross-Cultural Transference in Post-colonial Indian fiction in English.* Bologne : Editrice CLUEB, 1993.
Examines the phenomenon of cross-cultural transference in Indian English fictional works including those of Narayan, Jhabvala, Rushdie, Rohinton Mistry, Bharati Mukherjee, Michael Ondaatji, Farruk Dhondy and Hanif Kureishi.

183. Alphonso-Karkala, John B. *Indo-English Literature in the Nineteenth Century.* Mysore : University of Mysore, 1970.

Based on the author's doctoral dissertation on the subject submitted to Columbia University, the U.S.A., in 1964.

184. ——. *Comparative World Literature.* Bombay : Nirmal Sadanand Publishers, 1974.
The book contains seven essays originally written for presentation at conferences during 1967-72, out of which two are related to Indian English Fiction.
See 580, 5312.

185. Amirthanayagam, Guy, ed. *Writers in East and West Encounter : New Critical Bearings.* London/Basing Stoke : Macmillan Press, 1982.
A collection of papers on the subject of new literatures arising out of cultural and linguistic contacts between the East and the West in twentieth century, presented at a conference of writers in Honolulu. Out of several essays there is one essay by R.K. Narayan on "The Man-Eater of Malgudi" in which the author contrasts the pseudo literature — the mercenary and non-durable — with the literature which impinges on society, the truly creative literature which cannot fail to convey the meaning in any of the social contexts.

186. ——, ed. *Asian and Western Writers in Dialogue : New Cultural Identities.* London : Macmillan, 1982.
Published in two parts, the anthology's main focus is on the inter-action of cultures in an international perspective and an interplay of subcultures within national/regional spheres and their influence on contemporary literatures of Asia and the West.
The first part entitled "Literary and Cultural Roles" is concerned with the problems of creativity in a cross-cultural milieu and the second part, "Literary and National Identities" deals with specific national/regional cultural ramifications. Greater emphasis is laid on the

influence of Western culture on Asian literature and culture.
See 731, 990, 1658, 3551.

187. Amrithanayagam, Guy, and S.C. Harrex, eds. *Only Connect : Literaray Perpespectives — East and West.* Adelaide/Honolulu : Centre for Research in the New Literatures in English/East-West Centre, 1981.
This volume brings together twenty four contributions on various aspects of the cross-fertilization that strengthens modern literature. Among articles that focus on individual writers there is one on Raja Rao.
See 6590.

188. Amur, G.S. *A Critical Spectrum.* Aurangabad : Parimala Prakashan, 1975.
The book reflects the author's deep involvement in several literatures — British, American and Indian. lmost all essays presented here are, explicitly or implicitly, of a comparative nature. Out of the twelve essays, there is one on Raja Rao.
See 6351.

189. ——. *Images and Impressions : Essays Mainly on Contemporary Indian Literature.* Jaipur : Panchasheel Prakashan, 1979.
The book is a collection of twelve perceptive critical essays on a variety of subjects — poetry, fiction, art, drama, criticism, etc. These essays have been published in journals and books and some are presented at seminars. Out of these essays two are on Indian English fiction.
See 4325, 6353.

190. ——. *Forbidden Fruit.* Calcutta : Writers Workshop, 1992.
A collection of essays which are published in different journals and anthologies.
See 585, 1552, 3516, 5313, 5314, 5315, 6352.

191. Amur, G.S., *et al.*, eds. *Essays on Commonwealth Literature and Linguistics.* New Delhi : Sterling Publishers, 1984.
The book is a collection of papers presented at a seminar on 21st January 1983 held at Marathwada University, Aurangabad.
The volume consists of three parts. The first is largely theoretical and attempts a few useful definitions while the second and the third deal with problems of translations and comparative studies of literary works in different genres in the Indian languages (includes Indian-English) respectively. Contains an essay on Mulk Raj Anand.
See 1552.

192. ——, eds. *Indian Readings in Commonwealth Literature.* New Delhi : Sterling Publishers, 1985.
The book is a compilation of the articles presented at the seminar conducted by the Department of English, Marathwada University, Aurangabad on 9, 10 and 11 March 1984. It is a companion volume to the earlier publication, *Essays on Comparative Literature and Linguistics.* It consists of two parts. The first part entitled "Perspectives" attempts, from a fairly wide range, to clarify the related concepts of Commonwealth and Commonwealth literature. The second part is devoted to the explication of individual texts and themes from a fairly wide range of Commonwealth writers including those from India.
See 598, 1183, 1251, 5314, 5442, 5568, 6577.

193. Amur, G.S and S.K. Desai, eds. *Colonial Consciousness in Commonwealth Literature.* Bombay : Somaiya Publications, 1984.
The book studies the role of colonialism in India, the Gandhian model of colonial epistemology and the cross-cultural characteristics of the new literatures. Out of

the twelve essays three are related to Indian English fiction.

See 1086, 3087, 3647.

194. Anand, Mulk Raj. *Apology for Heroism : An Essay in Search of Faith*. London : Drummond, 1946. Bombay : Kutub Popular, 1957. New Delhi : Arnold Heinemann, 1975, 1986.

"A brief autobiography of ideas" in which the author critically reviews age-old values of India and outlines the growth of his humanistic beliefs and dignity of man."

195. ——. *Roots and Flowers : Two Lectures on the Metamorphosis of Content and Technique in Indo-English Novel*. Dharwad : Karnatak University, 1972.

Deals with the emergence of the Indian English fiction as a genre illustrating the metamorphosis of content and technique with an illuminating analysis of *Untouchable* (Mulk Raj Anand) and *Kanthapura* (Raja Rao).

196. Ashcroft, Bill, Gareth Griffiths and Helen Tiffin. *The Empire Writes Back : Theory and Practice in Post-Colonial Literatures*. London : Routledge, 1989.

An intensive discussion on the range and nature of post-colonial writing, both creative and theoretical. *The Vendor of Sweets* by R.K. Narayan is one of the several novels selected for a close study.

197. Asnani, Shyam M. *Critical Response to Indian English Fiction*. New Delhi : Atlantic Publications, 1987.

The book is an anthology of critical essays on various aspects of fiction of Indian novelists, both renowned and less renowned.

The book contains twelve essays of which two essays are of general nature while other essays are on individual works and authors. Though the anthology is on fiction one essay on Nirad C. Chaudhuri finds a place in it. It also includes a study on the aesthetics of Anita Desai's fiction.

See 616, 618, 1560, 1561, 2596, 3518, 4328, 5318, 7444, 7445, 7693, 7912.

198. ——. *New Dimensions of the Indian English Novel.* New Delhi : Doaba House, 1987.

The book makes a comprehensive assessment of the major thematic and technical aspects of the contemporary Indian English novelists. Some of the essays have been published earlier in various journals. The book contains twelve essays of which three are of general nature. Other essays are concerned with the literary merits of the works of individual established writers like Mulk Raj Anand, R.K. Narayan, Raja Rao, Bhabani Bhattacharya, etc. and also on those of the later writers like Arun Joshi, Anita Desai, Amitav Ghosh and V.A Shahane who have given a distinct shift to the tradition of the Indian English novel by changing the focus from the socio-political-economic themes to the exploration of the limitless depths of the individual psyche and seeking new techniques to articulate these newly experienced realities.

See 615, 617, 619, 621, 1558, 1563, 2136, 2591, 2592, 2594, 3297, 4048, 4532, 5319, 7442, 7446, 7810.

199. Awasthi, Kamal N., ed. *Contemporary Indian English Fiction: An Anthology of Essays.* Jalandhar : ABS Publications, 1993.

The book is a collection of essays presented in a seminar on Indian English fiction held at Dharmasala from 14 to 16 March, 1990. The book contains fifteen essays by several critics on various authors dealing with a wide variety of aspects.

See 675, 1197, 1705, 2599, 2600, 2611, 2841, 2863, 4049, 4141, 4151, 4624, 5002, 5013, 5686, 6493, 7926.

200. Backman, Sven and Goran Kjellmer, eds. *Papers on Language and Literature : Presented to Alvar Ellegard and Erik Frykman.* Gothenburg Studies in English, 60.

Goteborg : ACTA Universitatis, Gothoburgensis, 1985.
A *festschrift* which contains articles on Narayan and Anita Desai.
See 2715, 5558.

201. Badal, R.K. *Indo-Anglian Literature : An Outline.* Bareilly : Prakash Book Depot, 1975.
Presents a brief outline of Indo-Anglian literature with particular emphasis on Anand, Raja Rao and R.K. Narayan.

202. Baker, Denys Val, ed. *Writers Today.* London : Sidwick and Jackson, 1948.
The volume which discusses some of the major writers of today (up to 1948) includes a critical evaluation of Mulk Raj Anand as a novelist by Jack Lindsay.

203. Baktiyar, Iqbal, ed. *The Novel in Modern India.* Bombay : The P.E.N. All India Centre, 1964.
The book contains papers read at the symposium on the subject, "The novel in Modern India," at the fifth P.E.N. All India Writers Conference at Bhubaneswar in 1959. Dr. K.R. Srinivasa Iyengar's article serves as an introduction making a general survey of the novel in modern India while the other essays trace the progress of the novel in thirteen languages making a reference to important authors and their works from the inception of the novel under Western influence at varying dates from late 19th century up to 1962. Among the thirteen languages chosen, Indian English is one.
See 655.

204. Bald, Suresh Renjen. *Novelists and Political Consciousness: Literary Expression of Indian Nationalism 1919–1947.* Delhi : Chanakya Publications, 1982.
The book traces the nature of the growth of political consciousness among Indians through a critical analysis of the writings of seven significant novelists of the period between 1919 and 1947. Among Indian English

novelists are Mulk Raj Anand, D.F. Karaka, Deven Sharar, Ranjee Shahani (pseudonym for Hasan Ali), Raja Rao and K. Nagarajan. She uses their works to illustrate the nature and growth of the four phases in the development of Indian nationalism.

The book is a modified and revised version of the doctoral dissertation submitted to Harvard University, Cambridge.

205. Bande, Usha, ed. *Mothers and Mother-Figures in Indo-English Literature.* Jalandhar : ABS Publications, 1994.

The book, an anthology of critical essays, studies the concept of the mother and the role played by the mothers and mother-figures in the changing cultural ethos of Indian society as presented in Indian English novels. The theme of the mother and her influence on character, situation and plot are perceived from different angles—archetypal, sociological, cultural, psychological, etc. and from the perspectives of male and female writers.

See 626, 715, 791, 1663, 2213, 2684, 3128, 4720, 5444, 6529, 6600, 7910, 7982.

206. ——, ed. *Victim Consciousness in Indian English Novel.* Jalandher : A.B.S Publications, 1997.

See 1505,1754, 1838, 2180, 3149, 3155, 3588, 4052, 4160, 4739, 5238, 5493, 5569, 6601, 7561,7911, 7986.

207. Bardolph, Jacqueline, ed. *Short Fiction in the New Literatures in English.* Proc. of the Nice Conference of the European Association for Commonwealth Literature and Language Studies. Nice : Fac. des/Letters and Sciences Humaines de Nice, 1989.

Contains articles on R.K. Narayan and Bharati Mukherjee.

See 4939, 5015, 5560.

208. Barfoot, C.C., and Theo D'Haen, eds. *Shades of Empire in Colonial and Post-Colonial Literatures.* DQR Studies

in Literature II. Amsterdam, Atlanta GA : Rodopi, 1993.
Out of nineteen articles three are on Indian English fiction.
See 2642, 7013, 7301.

209. Bauer, Roger and Douwe Fokkema, eds. *Space and Boundaries in Literature/Espaces et Frontieres dans la littirature*. Proc. of the XIIth Congress of the International de Littirature Comparee, Munich, 1988. Vol. 2. Munich : Iudicium, 1990.
Contains an article on Balachandra Rajan.
See 6274.

210. Begum, A. Jameela, ed. *Post-Colonial Preoccupations in Canadian and Indian English Fiction*. Trivandrum : Institute of English, University of Kerala, 1989.
The book is a collection of papers presented at a seminar organized jointly by the Institute of English, University of Kerala and Indian Association for Canadian Studies on 17-18 Nov. 1989. The book brings together the divergent views on Post-colonial preoccupations in Canadian and Indian English fiction particularly the process of decolonization through the studies of individual writers and their works.
See 672,795, 1035, 1071, 1287, 2634, 2686, 2800, 3523, 4121, 4585. 4593. 5029, 5536.

211. Benson, Eugene and L.W. Conolly. *The Encyclopedia of Post-Colonial Literature in English* 2 Vols. London : Routledge and Kegan Paul, 1994.

212. Bennet, Bruce, Ee Teang Hong and Ron Shepherd, eds. *The Writer's Sense of the Contemporary : Papers in South-East Asian and Australian Literatures*. Nedlands: Centre for Studies in Australian Literature, University of Western Australia, 1982.
Contains an article on Salman Rushdie.
See 7261.

213. Bennet, Bruce and Susan Miller, eds. *A Sense of Exile : Essays in the Literature of the Asia-Pacific Region.* Nedlands : Centre for Studies in Australian Literature, University of West Australia, 1988.
A selection of papers presented at a conference in Perth. The essays in this collection explore the theme of exile from a wide range of viewpoints — psychological, linguistic, geographical, etc. The book gives a sense of the new literary cartographers that are being developed in the Asia-Pacific region.
See 934, 994.

214. Berry, Margaret, ed. *Peqasus over Asia : Ventures in East-West Literary Analysis.* Hong Kong : Asia Research Service, 1980.

215. Bevan, David, ed. *Literature and Exile.* Rodopi Perspectives on Modern Literature 4. Amsterdam, Atlanta GA : Rodopi, 1990.
Contains an article on Rushdie and Jhabvala.
See 3567, 7028.

216. Bharucha, Nilufer E. and Vilas Sarang, eds. *Indian English Fiction 1980-90 : An Assessment.* New Delhi : B.R. Publishing Corporation, 1994.
The book is a collection of essays presented at a seminar organized by the Department of English, University of Bombay during March 18-20, 1991.
The anthology makes an exploration of the literary history of the decade and provides a historical perspective. Finds the fiction written between 1980-90 as a literature of self-definition and assimilation into the Indian ethos representing Indian socio-political realities. Feels Indian English as an integral part of Indian environment and is used imaginatively and confidently by the new set of post-colonial writers like Salman Rushdie, Amitav Ghosh, Upamanyu Chatterjee and others.

See 642, 713, 821, 827, 844, 1074, 1098, 1164, 2652, 3148, 3189, 3299, 4933, 4994, 5043, 5455, 6537, 7485.

217. Bhat, Yashoda and Yamuna Raja Rao, eds. *The Image of Women in Indian Literature*. New Delhi : B.R. Publishing Corporation, 1993.
The book is a compilation of papers presented at a National Seminar organized by N.M.K.R.V. College for Women, Bangalore. It gives a historical and critical view of the image of Indian woman as revealed in Indian literature including Indian English fiction.
See 649, 2619, 4545.

218. Bhatnagar, K.C. *Realism in Major Indo-English Fiction*. Bareilly : Prakash Book Depot, 1980.
The book is a study of the works of the three great Indian novelists — Anand, Raja Rao and Narayan — in terms of their treatment of realism. In the preliminary chapter the author discusses "The Aesthetics of Realism", defining the nature and appeal of the realistic novel and the place of poetry as a constituent of the realistic novel. The other chapters deal with the Marxist critique and mystique of realism, and the Indian English novelists' approach to it substantiating them by an in-depth study of the major works of Anand, Raja Rao and Narayan under the subtitles — "Poetic Realism of Protest", "Poetry as Prophecy" and "Myth and Reality of Malgudi" respectively.
See 1574, 5338, 6365.

219. Bhatnagar, M.K. *Political Consciousness in Indian English Writing : A Study of Manohar Malgonkar, Nayantara Sahgal and Bhabani Bhattacharya*. New Delhi : Bahri Publications, 1991.
See 4313.

220. ——, ed. *Indian Writing in English*. New Delhi : Atlantic Publishers. 1998-99. Vol. 1-4 (1998) Vol. 5&6 (1999). Vol. 6 is edited jointly with M. Rajeswar.

221. Bhatnagar, O.P., ed. *Essays in Criticism : Indian Fiction in English.* Jaipur : Rachana Prakashan, 1981.

222. Bhattacharya, P.C *Indo-Anglian Literature and the Works of Raja Rao.* Delhi/Lucknow : Atma Ram & Sons, 1983.

223. Bindella, M.T. and G.V. Davis, eds. *Imagination and the Creative Impulse in the New Literatures in English.* Cross-cultural Readings in the Post-Colonial literatures in English 9. Amsterdam, Atlanta, G.A : Rodopi, 1993.
Contains an article by Silvia Albertazzi : "Passages : The Indian Connections : From Sara Jennette Duncan to Rohinton Mistry."

224. Blaber, Ronald and Marvin Gilman. *Roguery : The Picaresque Tradition in Australian, Canadian and Indian Fiction.* Springwood : N.S.W. Butterfly Books, 1990.
The Last section entitled "Gestures and Suspicions: Indian Reading" offers a capsule view of the use of Picaresque in Indian Writing in English.

225. Blamires, Harry, ed. *A Guide to Twentieth Century Literature in English.* London/New York : Methuen, 1983.
A reference work which is designed to provide a compact and readable guide to the important literatures of twentieth century in English (outside the U.S.A.). Each article contains biographical details and discusses the character and the quality of the work and the writer's achievement.

226. Bock, Hedwig and Albert Wertheim, eds. *Essays on Contemporary Post-Colonial Fiction.* Munich : Max Huber Verlago, 1986.
Contains articles on Jhabvala, Narayan and Anand.
See 1805, 3563, 5534.

227. Breitinger, Eckhard and Reinhard Sander, eds. *Studies Commonwealth Literature.* Tubingen (West Germany) : Gunter Narr, 1985.
The book is a collection of papers presented at the sixth annual conference on Commonwealth Literature and Language held in West Germany. It covers a wide range of topics and approaches and traces divergent strains in Commonwealth literature. Contains two articles on Indian English fiction.
See 1763, 5562.

228. Butcher, Maggie, ed. *The Eye of the Beholder : Indian Writing in English.* Proc. of the Symposium conducted by the Commonwealth Institute, London in 1983 during the festival of India. London : Commonwealth Institute, 1983.
A collection of eleven papers presented at the seminar of which four are on poetry and three are of general nature: one by Nirad Chaudari deals with the impact of English on Indian mind. The papers by Prabhu Guptara and C.D. Narasimhaiah are concerned with the historical development of Indian literature in English. Anita Desai writes about the problems of Indian women writers. Rushdie expresses his novelistic credo. Raja Rao pronounces the Indian concept of the word and its meaning. Mulk Raj Anand narrates the travails he underwent in writing his first novel. Meenakshī Mukherjee outlines the need for new critical strategies in evaluating the Indian English novel.

229. Chadha, Ramesh. *Cross Cultural Interaction in Indian-English Fiction.* New Delhi : National Book Organization, 1988.
The title of the book is misleading. Partly rectified by the inner title which says that 'cross-cultural' is in relation to the novels of Ruth Jhabvala and Kamala Markandaya.
See 3488.

230. Chakravorthy, D.K. *Aspects of Indian Fiction in English.* Calcutta : Sahitya Praksh, 1985.
The book is a collection of essays in which the author interprets and analyses a few well-known works such as *Kanthapura, The Serpent and Rope, The Guide,* etc., mostly meant for the general reader. Though the book is entitled "Aspects of Indian Fiction in English", the essay on autobiographical writings in English finds a place in it. Altogether there are fourteen essays dealing with prominent fiction writers like Anand, Raja Rao, Narayan, Bhabani Bhattacharya and Arun Joshi. Out of the fourteen essays eight are on individual works, two are on short stories and three are on general background of Indian Writing in English.
See 667, 668, 669, 1581, 2144, 2145, 2146, 2147, 2444, 2628, 4059, 4060, 4549, 4550, 5347, 6368, 6369, 7456, 8063.

231. Chandra, Suresh. *Culture and Criticism.* New Literary Series 2. New Delhi : B.R. Publishing Corporation, 1987.
The book is based on the contention that "literature is a part of the cultures of a society and embodies the aspirations, trails and tribulations of a nation". Argues that the writers and their works should be viewed from the point of view of their relation to culture. The book contains studies on Indian and American works. Out of the ten essays five are on Indian English writers. The first one, "Indian English: Its Chroniclers", is of general nature dealing with the Indian variety of English which the author calls "Indolish". The other four are on individual writers.
See 673, 674, 1582, 4063, 4339, 6958, 8064.

232. Chatterjee, Lola, ed. *Woman/Image/Text : Feminist Reading of Literary Texts.* New Delhi : Trianka Publications, 1986.

This book is the product of a seminar on feministic approaches to literature conducted by the English Department, Miranda House, University College for Women, Delhi University, in April 1985.
The book consists of sixteen essays, all concentrating on the close relationship between literary and social structure of consciousness showing how feminism is a political movement working for basic changes in contemporary societies. It also points out that feministic criticism is pluralistic, drawing on the theory and practice of such different schools of thought as Marxism, psycho-analysis, structuralism, existentialism and deconstruction. There are two essays related to Indian-English fiction.
See 5341, 6646.

233. *Contemporary Indian Literature : A Symposium.* New Delhi : Sahitya Akademi Publications, 1957. Revised and enlarged in 1959.

234. *Contemporary Novelists.* Ed. James Vinson. New York : St. Martin Press, 1972. 5ed. edited by Lesley Henderson. Chicago/London : St. James Press, 1991.

235. Coppola, Carlo. *Marxist Influence and South Asian Literature.* 2nd, East Lansing : Michigan State University Asia Studies Centre, 1974.
See 823, 1624.

236. Cowasjee, Saros. *Studies in Indian and Anglo-Indian Fiction.* New Delhi : Indus, 1993.
A collection of papers presented by the author at international conferences between 1975 & 1990. Some of them were published in the proceedings of the conference and others appeared in various periodicals.
See 689, 691, 692, 1595, 1607.

237. Crane, Ralph J. *Inventing India : A History of India in English Language Fiction.* London : Macmillan, 1992.

Examines the fiction written by the British and Indian writers since 1857 to show how they manifest a sense of history and in so doing shape our imaginative response to India. Starting from the historical fiction of Indian Mutiny the author explores the fiction of early 20th century dealing with the East-West conflict, the pre-Independence and post-Independence era. The book provides a sample of fiction that uses history as a metaphor.

238. *Critical Responses.* Dept of English, Osmania University. New Delhi : Sterling Publishers, 1993.
Consists of essays published in *Osmania Journal of English Studies* from 1961 to 1991.

239. Cronin, Richard. *Imagining India.* New York : St. Martin Press,1989.
Conceding the fact that to write about India is an exercise in futility, shows how the English language novel in India is responsible for some of the most exciting and moving literary works of this century, drawing examples from Narayan, Jhabvala, Desai Rushdie and others.
See 693, 2637, 3543, 3544, 4242, 5357, 5358, 5359.

240. D'Haven, Th.L., and A.J. Fry, eds. *Commonwealth Literature : Mostly Canadian.* Papers presented at the fourth literature conference held at the Urige Universiet on 18th June 1985. Amsterdam : Free University Press, 1986.
Contains an article on Salman Rushdie.
See 7015.

241. Das, S. K. and Chandra Mohan, eds. *Comparative Literature.* New Delhi : Stateman Press, 1989.
Contains the essay "Domesticated English : Symbiotic or Syncretic : The Language of African and Indian Fiction Novel."
See 807.

242. Dasgupta, Rabindra Kumar. *East-West Literary Relations.* Calcutta : Papurus, 1995.
The book deals with Indo-English literature and compares it with Western literature.

243. Dass, Veena Noble and R.K. Dhawan, eds. *Fiction of the Nineties.* New Delhi : Prestige Books, 1994.
The book is a collection of twenty five articles by different scholars from India and abroad which mainly deal with the issues of feminism and interpersonal relationships. A reissue of the *Commonwealth Review* Vol. 6, No. 1 (1994-95) in a book form.
See 1210, 2350, 2515, 2528, 2530, 3069, 3242, 3305, 3413, 4214, 4852. 4854, 4868, 4874, 4940, 4945, 6207, 7757, 7761, 7871, 7882, 8023.

244. Dass, Veena Noble, ed. *Feminism and Literature.* New Delhi : Prestige Books, 1995.
Exemplifying that feminism is rapidly developing as a significant critical ideology, and constitutes a major segment of contemporary writing in English, the book comprises twentyeight essays on the theory and practice of feminism. Most of the essays were earlier published in *Commonwealth Review* special issue on feminism and literature 6.1 (1994-1995).
See 627, 696, 892, 1087, 1274, 1663, 2057, 2408, 2616, 2831, 3070, 3184, 3234, 3419, 4065, 5060, 5385, 5777.

245. Davis, A.R., ed. *In Search of Identity : Modern Literature and Creative Arts.* Sydney : Angus Robertson, 1974. 102-118
Contains an essay on Indian English fiction.
See 1120.

246. Davis, Geoffrey V. and Hena Maes-Jelinke, eds. *Crisis and Creativity in the New Literatures in English Cross Cultures.* Amsterdam : Rodopi, 1990.

This book is a collection of papers presented at the 11th annual conference on Commonwealth Literature and Language Studies. Contains a broad-range assemblage of essays on a variety of aspects of the new literatures.
See 4614, 7014.

247. Dayal, B. *Indian Short Story Writers in English.* Ranchi : Jubilee Prakashan, 1985.
Divided into six chapters, the book presents a critical study of the themes and techniques of the Indian short story writers writing in English. In the preliminary chapter Dayal gives the background of the short story and its practice in Pali and Sanskrit. In the following chapters he critically analyzes the stories of the major and minor short story writers from Anand to Usha John, concluding his discussion by assessing the achievement of these writers.
See 699, 700, 1423, 1610, 2149, 5365, 6378.

248. Derrett, M.E. *The Modern Novel In English : A Comparative Approach.* Brussels : Editions de l'Institut de Sociologia, Universite Libre de Bruxelles, 1966.
The book studies the Indian fiction of 1940s and 50s in relation to the earlier history of English writing in India and to the parallel development in various regional languages. The author also examines the sixty and odd novels from the points of view of the Western critic, Indian critic, sociologist and an average reader. She finds that the Indian novelists of English used the fiction of the 19th century as their model.

249. Desai, S.K., ed. *Experimentation with Language in Indian Writing in English* (Fiction). Kolhapur : Shivaji University, 1974.
The book contains six essays dealing with the linguistic studies of English as used by some of the significant Indian writers in English — Raja Rao, Anand, Narayan,

Manohar Malgonkar, Khushwant Singh and Kamala Markandaya. Its chief concern is with the language, with the way in which Indian writers, particularly novelists, try to wrestle with the English language presenting through it an Indian experience. It throws light on several strategies such as using native words or translations of certain characteristic expressions or experiments with English syntax, speech rhythms and so on in adopting the foreign medium and the problems the novelists face in writing dialogues and the solutions they arrived at.

See 1655, 4329, 4633, 5394, 6387, 7955.

250. ——, ed. *Creative Aspects on Indian English.* New Delhi : Sahitya Akademi, 1995.

A collection of papers presented at a seminar organized by Sahitya Akademi in Hyderabad, 9-11 Feb. 1996.

251. Devy, G.N. *In Another Tongue : Essays on Indian English Literature.* Frankfurt : Velag Peter Lang, 1993. New Delhi : Macmillan (India), 1995.

Contains sixteen essays written over fifteen years or so.

252. Dhar, T.N. *History Fiction Interface : M.R. Anand, Nayantara Sahgal,Salman Rushdie, Shashi Tharoor and O.V. Vijayan.* New Delhi: Prestige Books,1998

253. Dhawan, R.K., ed. *Explorations in Modern Indo-English Fiction.* New Delhi : Bahri Publications, 1982.

A republication of *Language Forum* 7.1-4 (1982) (Special Issue on Modern Indo-English Fiction).

The book is a collection of critical essays on varied aspects of Indian-English fiction by several critics presented with a view to trace the emergence of the Indian-English novel to the aesthetic conjunction between the creative self and contemporary history. The scheme of the book is both chronological and interpretative.

The book, containing four parts, deals with a general discussion on themes and methods in the first section and discusses the individual works of the 'pioneers', the 'popularizers' and the 'women writers' under separate headings. Apart from the critical articles on individual writers and their works, there are some articles by creative writers regarding the problems related to their creative process, their use of language, the craft, etc.

See 619, 692, 704, 1052, 1172, 1182, 1290, 1563, 1630, 1745, 2179, 2189, 2228, 2578, 2678, 3503, 3602, 4401, 4579, 4706, 5313, 5702, 5732, 6503, 6569, 7446, 7957.

254. ——, ed. *Comparative Literature.* New Delhi : Bahri Publications, 1987.

A reprint of the special issue of *Language Forum* II. 1-4 (1985-86). Offers studies of various literatures and authors dealing with concepts, aims and methods of comparative literature.

See 1428, 1470, 3534, 5317, 5519, 6595, 7139, 7519, 7814.

255. ——, ed. *Three Contemporary Novelists : Khushwant Singh, Chaman Nahal, Salman Rushdie.* New Delhi : Classical Publishing House, 1986.

The book is a collection of essays by several critics on the three contemporary novelists — Khushwant Singh, Chaman Nahal and Salman Rushdie — who have made a specific use of history of the same period: freedom movement and partition of India. It consists of five sections. The first section is an introduction to the three novelist-historians. The second section deals with the articles by the novelists themselves expressing their views and attitudes about their art. The third, fourth and fifth sections contain articles on the work of the three novelists separately.

See 721, 950, 5150, 5152, 5158, 5161, 6930, 7039, 7189, 7941, 7950, 7957.

256. ——, ed. *Commonwealth Fiction.* 3 Vols. New Delhi : Classical Publishing House, 1988.

In this three-volumed anthology with articles covering all the fictions written in English in the Commonwealth, more than half are devoted to Indian fiction writers in English, spread over the complete first volume and the first section of volume 2. All these chapters on Indian English fiction (twenty four in all including one on Common-wealth fiction which serves as an introduction to the three volumes) follow a particular design. The first section contains a one-chapter article dealing with some broad perspectives on Commonwealth fiction. The four chapters in Section II cover a wide range of general topics on Indian fiction in English with section three dealing with the three major Indian fiction writers in English — Anand, Raja Rao and Narayan with an article on the nature of the hero in these novelists. Section four is concerned with the next generation novelists, namely Khushwant Singh, Manohar Malgonkar and Bhabani Bhattacharya (often comparing them with the earlier novelists). The last section of five chapters is devoted to the work of Indian English women novelists.

In Vol. II, section one deals with contemporary novelists such as Arun Joshi, Salman Rushdie, Namita Gokhale, Amitav Ghosh and Bapsi Sidhwa.

In Vol. III there are three articles, "Third World Fiction", "The Artist as Historian : Some New Writers" and "Gods and Men in the Commonwealth Short Story" which are of general nature.

Vol. I

See 797, 880, 958, 1145, 1745, 2172, 2688, 3635, 3677, 4398, 4598, 4708, 5457, 6441, 6615, 6635, 7513, 7942.

Vol. II
See 3304, 3385, 4099, 7040, 7263, 7864, 7870.
Vol. III
See 721, 832, 1110, 3530.

257. ——, ed. *Indian Women Novelists.* Set I, 5 vols. New Delhi : Prestige Books, 1991.
Set II, 6 Vols. New Delhi : Prestige Books, 1993.
Set III, 7 Vols. New Delhi : Prestige Books, 1995.
The book is an anthology of critical essays comprising three sets, having five, six and seven volumes respectively. All the articles discuss the achievement of Indian women novelists in English and present different interpretations of the individual novels. Articles in Vols. 6 and 7 in Set III (except a few based on comparative method in vol. 6) are on Indian regional languages. Novelists discussed include Anita Desai, Kamala Markandaya, R.P. Jhabvala, Nayantara Sahgal, Rama Mehta, Gita Mehta, Dina Mehta, Shobha De, Attia Hosain, Bharati Mukherjee, Shashi Deshpande, Githa Hariharan, Shouri Daniels, Raji Narasimhan, Meena Alexander, Sarala Barnabas, Namita Gokhale, Jai Nimbkar, Tara Ali Baig, Sumita Jain, Uma Vasudev, Prema Nandakumar, Nergis Dalal, Kamala Das, Mayah Balse and Santha Rama Rau. Entries on individual writers may be found under the respective names.

258. ——, ed. *Indian Literature Today.* New Delhi : Prestige Books, 1994.
Special numbers of *Commonwealth Review* 5.1 (1993-94), Indian Writing Today: Drama and Fiction and 5.2 (1993- 94), Indian Writing Today : Poetry and Fiction are Published in a book form.

259. ——. *50 Years of Indian Writing.* New Delhi : Prestige Books, 199?

260. Dhawan, R.K, P.V. Dhamija and A.K. Shrivatsava, eds. *Recent Commonwealth Literature.* 2 Vols. New Delhi : Prestige Books, 1989P.

The book in two volumes presents Commonwealth literature through different angles. There are some general articles on the nature and tradition of Commonwealth literature, some on separate genres and authors within the Commonwealth and some more are studies of individual works, presented here without any obvious coherent order. Among individual authors and their works discussed Salman Rushdie, Nayantara Sahgal, Anita Desai and Arun Joshi have found a place. Some of the individual works discussed are those of Manohar Malgonkar, Nayantara Sahgal, Narayan, Rushdie, Nergis Dalal, Anita Desai and Rama Mehta. Besides there are some articles of a comparative nature.

Vol. I

See 1586, 1654, 2412, 2737, 2761, 2835, 3510, 3521, 4106, 4351, 4903, 5587, 7212, 7271, 7436, 7465, 7468, 7472, 7845.

Vol. II

See 832, 4913.

261. Dhawan R.K. and L.S.R. Krishna Sastry, eds. *Commonwealth Writing : A Study in Expatriate Experience.* New Delhi : Prestige Books, 1994.

A Reprint of the issue *Commonwealth Review* 4.2 (1992-93). The book contains two sections. The articles of the first section are of general nature defining the experience of expatriation. The other section is devoted to critical studies on individual writers. The fiction of Vikram Seth and Attia Hosain is discussed.

See 2755, 2869, 3444, 3569, 5004, 5005, 5024, 5025, 5035, 5050, 5059, 7765.

262. Dinesh, Kamini, ed. *Between Spaces of Silence.* New Delhi : Sterling Publishers, 1994.

The book is a collection of papers presented in a national seminar on women creative writers, organised by the university of Jodhpur in March 1990.

The book examines various modes of women's writings, discusses their problems and assesses whether women have created a viable identity or not. While it contains some general essays on Indian English writing, other papers study the trends and techniques of individual works and their specific approaches.
See 759, 788, 938, 1150, 2437, 2626, 2646, 2837, 3435, 3583, 4568, 4961, 7500.

263. Dinesh Kamini and R.A. Joshi, eds. *The Novelist and the Political Milieu.* Jaipur : Rachana Prakashan, 1995.
Contains essays presented at a U.G.C. National seminar organized by the Department of English, University of Jodhpur, in March 1991. Besides examining the concept of Nationalism and its concomitant feelings as projected in Indian English fiction discusses the political backdrop during the independence movement which leads people to a search for national self.
See 1291, 2143, 2784, 4349, 5145, 6261, 6421, 6791, 7973, 8021, 8085.

264. Dissanayaka, Wimal and Steven Bradbury, eds. *Literary History, Narrative and Culture.* Honolulu : University of Hawaii Press, 1989.
The book, Vol. 2 of the series of "Literary Studies East and West," is a collection of selected papers presented at a conference on "Literary History East and West" held at Honolulu in April 1988. The articles examine the concepts on literary history and points out how they are vitally connected with questions of meaning that preoccupy modern literary theorists. There is an essay on Anita Desai : "T.S. Eliot's *Four Quartets* and the Fourfold Pattern in Anita Desai's *Clear Light of Day.*"
See 2627.

265. Dodiya, Jagdipsinh, ed. *Contemporary Indian Writing in English.* New Delhi : Atlantic Publishers 1999.

266. Driesen, Cynthia Vanden. *Centering the Margins : Perspectives on Literatures in English from India, Africa and Australia.* New Delhi: Prestige Books, 1995.

267. Durix, Carole and Jean Pierre Durix. *An Introduction to the New Literatures in English.* London/Paris (France): Longman, 1993.

Offers some useful comments on the genesis and development of new literatures. Contains a chapter on the major trends of and techniques in Indian fiction in English from Mulk Raj Anand to the present day.

268. Durix, Jean-Pierre. *The Writer Written : The Artist and Creation in the New Literatures in English.* West Port (U.S.A): Greenwood Press, 1987.

Traces the 'coming of age' of written literatures in Post-colonial societies of the English speaking world exploring the relationship between the writer and his craft, between the artist and society, between the creator and his conception of creation. Discusses major writers from Africa (Wole Soyinka), Australia (Patrick White),Canada (Keri Hulme), and India (Salman Rushdie) from this point of view.

See 6995.

269. Dwivedi, A.N., ed. *Studies in Contemporary Indian Fiction in English.* Allahabad : Kitab Mahal, 1987.

This anthology of critical essays on contemporary Indian fiction in English by several critics analyses and assesses the relative achievements of the contemporary Indian fiction in English while making a comprehensive survey of its origin and growth.

The book contains seventeen articles which are divided into three sections. While the first section entitled "The Origin and Growth of the Genre" contains five articles dealing with the development of Indian English fiction and various aspects of it, the second section is devoted to Anand, Narayan and Raja Rao. The third section,

devoted to "The Other Main Props," contains articles on Bhabani Bhattacharya, Kamala Markandaya, R.P. Jhabvala, B. Rajan, Anita Desai, Arun Joshi, Chaman Nahal and Khushwant Singh.
See 651, 728, 1187, 1195, 1284, 1605, 1627, 2214, 2681, 3108, 3635, 3676, 4072, 4340, 4664, 5156, 5520, 5799, 5800, 6266, 6504, 6633, 7952.

270. ——. *Indian Writing in English.* 2 Vols. Delhi : Amar Prakashan, 1991.
The book, in two volumes, is a collection of critical essays on poetry, fiction and short stories contributed by A.N. Dwivedi to various journals and books. The second volume which is devoted to studies of the genres other than poetry contains twelve essays on fiction of which three are of general nature and the others on individual writers.
Vol. II 727, 728, 729, 2432, 2461, 2650, 4072, 4348, 4562, 4563, 6263, 6264.

271. ——, ed. *Studies in Contemporary Indian English Short Story : A Collection of Critical Essays.* New Delhi : B.R. Publishing Corporation, 1991.
An anthology of critical essays on Indian English short story writers such as Bhabani Bhattacharya, Ramesh K. Srivastava, Sasthi Brata and others.

272. Ezekiel, N., ed. *Indian Writers in Conference : The Sixth PEN All India Writers' Conference.* Mysore 1962. Bombay : The PEN Centre, 1964.
See 743.

273. Galik, M., ed. *Proc. of the Fourth International Conference on the Theoretical Problems of Asian and African Literatures.* Bratislova : Institute of the Slovak Acad. of Sciences, 1983.
See 1675.

274. Garg, Pramila. *The Freedom Movement in Indian Fiction in English.* New Delhi : Ashish Publishing House, 1993.

The book is a comprehensive study of the Indian-English fiction written on the Indian struggle for independence. It attempts to evaluate the creative responses of as diverse novelists as S.M. Ghosh, Anand, Narayan, Chaman Nahal, Raja Rao, Khushwant Singh, Manohar Malgonkar and Kamala Markandaya to the Independence Movement.

Out of the seven chapters in the book, the first and the last provide the background and a final assessment respectively, whereas the other chapters deal with the movement's progress chronologically.

275. George, K.M., ed. *Comparative Indian Literature.* 2 Vols. London : Macmillan, 1984 and 1985.
Gives useful information about essays/books/studies/ written in Indian languages as well as in Indian English.

276. George, K.M. and J. Madeleine and K. Goodman, eds. *Women in Asia and the Pacific: Towards an East-West Dialogue.* Honolulu : University of Hawaii Press, 1985.
Contains an essay on Indian women novelists.
See 851.

277. Gokak, V.K., ed. *Literature in Modern Indian Languages.* New Delhi : Publications Division, Ministry of Information and Broadcasting, 1957.
See 845.

278. Goodwin, K.L., ed. *National Identity in Literature and Language.* London : Heinemann, 1970.
The book is a collection of papers presented at the Commonwealth Literature Conference, University of Queensland, Brisbane, from 9th to 15th August, 1968. The book discusses some generalities about Commonwealth literature such as the development of national attitudes, cultural exchange, quest for identity, etc. Out of the several essays there is only one — "National Identity in Literature and Language : Its Range

and Depth in the novels of Raja Rao" — related to Indian fiction in English.
See 6512.

279. Gooneratne, Yasmine. *Diverse Inheritance : A Personal Perspective on Commonwealth Literature.* Adelaide : University of South Australia, 1980.
Contains essays on Indian-English fiction, in particular the works by Narayan, Jhabvala and Markandaya.
See 3554, 3555, 4574, 5391.

280. Gowda, H.H. Annaiah, ed. *The Colonial and Neo-Colonial Encounters in Commonwealth Literature.* Mysore : Mysore University Press, 1983.
The book is a collection of papers delivered at the seminar conducted by the Post-Graduate Department of English, the Centre for Commonwealth Literature and Research during 21st to 25th Sep., 1981. They deal with the literary aspects of the colonial and the neocolonial relationship. Out of the nineteen essays in the collection two are related to Indian English fiction.
See 806, 1104.

281. Goyal, Bhagawat S. *Culture and Commitment : Aspects of Indian Literature in English.* Meerut : Shalabh Book House, 1984.
With all its very high-sounding title and its claim in the "Preface", the book is a collection of thirtyfive essays of an assorted type largely drawn from Indian English fiction. But there are essays on other sociological aspects of Indian literature and on writers from other languages, especially from Hindi.
See 750, 751, 752, 1642, 2159, 2659, 3235, 4576, 4577, 5146, 5147, 6418, 7690,

282. ——, ed. *Indian Literature in Perspective.* New Delhi : Arnold Heinemann, 1978.
See 5421.

283. Granquist, Raoul. *Report of Workshop on World Literature Written in English, Outside Great Britain and the U.S.A.* Umea (Sweden) : Dept. of English, Univ. of Umea, 1982.
A collection of papers presented at the workshop on world literature conducted by the Department of English, Univ. of Umea on 9-10 June, 1981. Contains an article on R.K. Narayan.
See 5556.

284. Gupta, G.S. Balarama. *Essays on Indian Writing in English.* Gulbarga : Journal of Indian Writing in English Publications, 1975.
The book contains several articles published earlier in different journals on various writers like Harindranath Chattopadhyaya, Manjeri Isvaran, and Venkataramani whose creative work has rarely been evaluated.
See 758, 2052, 2053, 3457, 3458, 3459, 3460, 3461, 8087.

285. ——. *Studies in Indian Fiction in English.* Gulbarga : Journal of Indian Writing in English Publications, 1987.
The book is an anthology of critical essays on Indian fiction in English by several critics. It contains 16 articles some paying attention to formal elements, some concentrating on the explication of a particular technique and others dealing with thematic concerns of individual works.
See 1751, 2151, 2783, 3090, 3509,4158, 4555, 4665, 5131, 5150, 5583, 6263, 6648, 7067, 7272, 7553.

286. Harrex, S. C. *The Modern Indian Novel in English.* Calcutta : Writers Workshop, 1977.

287. ——. *The Fire and the Offering : The English Language Novel of India 1935-1970.* Calcutta : Writers Workshop, 1977.
An exploratory and interpretative study of the English language novel of India between 1935-1970 in two

volumes. The first volume introduces the preliminary critical attitudes towards Indian English novel. The first chapter discusses the use of English by Indian writers while tracing the growth of Indian English fiction in terms of its scope and setting. The second chapter is entirely devoted to Mulk Raj Anand while the third one contains discussions of both themes and the writings of individual novelists — Khushwant Singh, Balachandra Rajan and Kamala Markandaya.

The second volume contains three chapters, one each on R.K. Narayan, Raja Rao, and G.V. Desani.

See 1657, 3083, 4461, 4580, 5416, 5417, 5420, 6266, 6424, 7924.

288. Harris, Michael. *Outsiders and Insiders : Perspectives of Third World Culture in British and Post-Colonial Fiction.* New York : Peter Lang, 1994.

Contains essays on Salman Rushdie, Raja Rao, K.S. Venkataramani, Anand and Narayan.

289. Harris, Wilson. *The Womb of Space : The Cross-cultural Imagination.* Westport : Greenwood, 1983.

Discusses the cross-cultural milieu in the works of several Commonwealth writers including Raja Rao.

See 6428.

290. Hemenway, S. *The Novel of India.* 2 Vols. Calcutta : Writers Workshop, 1972.

This is a two-volumed book making a contrastive survey of the two traditions "Anglo-Indian and Indo-Anglian". It consists of seven chapters of investigative analysis of the two traditions examining in each case the five problems namely language, audience, point of view, characterization and East-West theme thereby coming to a conclusion that Forster's *A Passage to India* is a classic among the Anglo-Indian novels and a touchstone. Similarly, among Indian English novels, Raja Rao's *The Serpent and the Rope* is seen as an equal achievement. The second volume is completely

devoted to Indian English fiction which contains four chapters. The author discusses Anand and Narayan as the pioneers of Indian English novel, while Bhabani Bhattacharya and Khushwant Singh as the popularizers. One chapter is devoted entirely to Raja Rao whom the author considers "the most original, philosophical, controversial and difficult novelist of India." The last chapter is 'Conclusion' which states that *A Passage to India* is a superior novel, but *The Serpent and the Rope* is its necessary complement and almost its equal as a novel of India.
See 1660, 2165, 4581, 5425, 6430, 7925.

291. *Indian Writers Meet.* Proc. of the Eighth All Indian P.E.N. Writers' Conference, Chandigarh, 1966. Bombay: P.E.N. All India Centre, 1968.
Presents relevant aspects of Indian literary scene. Contains an article on the writer and his material by Bhabani Bhattacharya.

292. Iyengar, K.R. Srinivasa. *Indo-Anglian Literature.* Bombay : International Book House, 1943.
One of the first books on Indian English literature, it gives a bird's eye-view of Indian-English literature written between 1880 and 1940. This short but comprehensive survey of Indian English literature is aimed at being an eye-opener to many educated men both in India as well as in other countries to realise that "there is a kind of literature known as Indian English Literature which will express the spirit of India in its true essence."

293. ——. *Literature and Authorship in India.* London : Allen and Unwin, 1943.
A very short book making a rapid survey of contemporary literary scene in India (between 1800-1942). Discusses some of the forces that have shaped the modern Indian literatures which include Indian English writing. Also suggests the future possibilities,

the problems and solutions for a healthy development of Indian literature.

294. ——. *The Indian Contribution to English Literature.* Bombay : Karnatak Publishing House, 1945.
Beginning with Raja Rammohan Roy the book covers a hundred years of poetry, drama and fiction.

295. ——. ed. *Indian Writers in Council.* First All India Writers Conference. Jaipur, 1945. Bombay : International Book House, 1947.

296. ——. *Study of Indian Writing in English.* Bombay : Popular Book Depot, 1959.

297. ——. *Indian Writing in English.* Bombay : Asia Publishing House, 1962. Rpt. in 1973 (Paperback), 1983, 1984.
The book, a comprehensive and authoritative cultural and literary history of Indian Writing in English, is a pioneering survey of Indian English Poetry, Fiction and Drama. While tracing the history of Indian English literature from Raja Rammohan Roy to the present day it tries to establish Indian English literature as a distinctive literature of India as well as one of the English literatures of the world.
Seven chapters are devoted to Indian-English fiction (16 to 22). While the 16th chapter deals with "The Novel : Themes, Backgrounds, Types," the other chapters are on individual writers — 'The Big Three', 'Women Novelists' and 'Bhattacharya and Malgonkar'. Chapter 22 makes a brief survey of the works of the minor novelists like Humayun Kabir, Sudhin Ghose, Anantanarayanan, G.V. Desani, Venu Chitale, K.A. Abbas, K.M. Munshi, Khushwant Singh, etc.
The third edition of this book has a 75-page post-script in which Sections V and VI deal with fiction written in seventies making an assessment of the same.
See 775, 1664, 2167, 2676, 3575, 4353, 5431, 6434.

298. ——. *Two Cheers for the Commonwealth.* Bombay : Asia Publishing House, 1969.
Contains speeches and writings of Prof. Iyengar on Indian English and Commonwealth literature.
See 5430.

299. ——, ed. *Indian Literature Since Independence : A Symposium.* New Delhi : Sahitya Akademi, 1973.
Contains summaries and comments by several critics upon literary trends in 20 languages during 25 years of Independence. Chapter 4 is on Indian English by Prema Nandakumar.

300. Jain, Jasbir. *Problems of Post-Colonial Literature and Other Essays.* Jaipur : Printwell Publications, 1991.
Contains two essays on Indian English fiction.
See 786, 7473.

301. ——, ed. *Women's Writing : The Text and Context.* Jaipur/New Delhi : Rawat Publications, 1996.
Focuses on the validity of women's writing and traces its contribution to the construction of a female self. Contains four essays on Nayantara Sahgal and one on Indian English fiction.
See 789, 7478, 7486, 7510, 7524.

302. ——. *Writers of the Indian Diaspora.* Jaipur/New Delhi : Rawat Publications. 1998.
See 563, 623, 3404, 4927, 4929, 4934, 4976, 6235, 7740, 8056.

303. Jain, Jasbir and Francine Krishna, eds. *Voices from India.* Jaipur : Printwell Publications, 1989.
An anthology of critical essays by several critics published as a *festschrift* to Prof. R.K. Kaul. Among several essays there is only one that is related to Indian English fiction : "Rosie and Daisy : Two Liberated Women in the Fiction of R.K. Narayan."
See 5307.

304. Jain, Jasbir and Amina Amin, eds. *Margins of Erasure : Purdah in the Subcontinental Novel in English.* New Delhi : Sterling Publishers, 1995.
The book, a collection of twenty essays by different critics, examines the nature and limitations of the system of "purdah" both in its physical (in the sense of a "veil" or "burqa") or metaphorical (in its wider connotation of seclusion, exclusion or segregation) referents which confer anonymity and erase selfhood, stifle self-expression and marginalize women by exploring the feminist perceptions and their socio-psychological implications in the novels of "native" as well as "diasporic" writers.
See 645, 720, 765, 789, 790, 834, 1465, 3065, 3151, 3436, 3439, 3450, 3536, 3615, 4336, 4457, 4909, 4910, 4912, 6983, 7185, 7559, 7881.

305. Jain, N.K., ed. *Women in Indo-Anglian Fiction : Tradition and Modernity.* Delhi : Manohar Publications, 1998.

306. Jha, Rama. *Gandhian Thought and Indo-Anglian Novelists.* Delhi : Chanakya Publications, 1983.
Shows how Gandhian thought acted as a catalytic agent in the growth of the Indian novel in English during the thirties and forties. While analysing the various tenets of Gandhian thought encompassing nearly all aspects of human life — social, spiritual and political — and how it stimulated the creative imagination of Indian novelists in English to shift their focus from romance to realism, the author tries to trace the relationship between Gandhian thought as embodied in Gandhian autobiographies and in the leading themes of the novels of Anand, Raja Rao, Narayan and Bhabani Bhattacharya and shows how Gandhi has provided the writers with a national context and a vision of society on the move towards political freedom and socio-political reconstruction.

The book contains eight chapters. The first three chapters present a typology of Gandhian thought and show how these are reflected in the fiction of the period. A detailed analysis of the impact of Gandhian thought on the four novelists — Anand, Narayan, Raja Rao and Bhattacharya — is undertaken in four separate chapters.
See 1670, 2170, 5443, 6438.

307. Joshi, Krishnanand N. and B. Shymala Rao. *Studies in Indo-Anglian Literature.* Bareilly : Prakash Book Depot, 1972.
A rapid survey of Indian English literary scene, along with a general assessment of four Indian novelists in English — Anand, Narayan, Raja Rao and Bhattacharya.

308. Jotwani, Motilal, ed. *Contemporary Literature and Society.* New Delhi : Heritage Publishers, 1979.
The book presents account of sixteen Indian national literatures as they have developed since Independence, throwing light on social, political, economic conditions in India today. "Indian English Literature" by Bhagwat Goyal is one among them.
See 749.

309. Juneja, Om P. *Post-Colonial Novel : Narratives of Colonial Consciousness.* Creative New Literatures Series 5. New Delhi : Creative Books, 1995.

310. Juneja, Om P. and Chandra Mohan, eds. *Ambivalence: Studies in Canadian Literature.* New Delhi: Allied Publishers, 1990.
Contains an article on Anita Desai.
See 2857.

311. Jussawala, Feroza F. *Family Quarrels: Towards a Criticism of Indian Writing in English.* New York Berne : Peter Lang, 1985.
A revised Ph.D. dissertation submitted to the Utah University, this book studies the relationship between

Indian literature in English and the critics of this literature, mainly from the point of view of socio-linguistics. Judges several Indian novels in English from a relativistic mode of criticism that relies more on situation.

312. Jussawala, Feroza and Reedway Dasenbrock, eds. *Interviews with Writers of the Post-Colonial World.* Jackson : Univeristy Press of Mississipi, 1992 (released 1993).

313. Kachru, Braj B., ed. *The Other Tongues : English Across Cultures.* Urbana (Chicago) : University of Illinois, 1982, 1992.
Contains essays on Indian English fiction in relation to style and language.
See 865, 1016, 1276, 1879, 5794, 6523.

314. Kalinnikova, Elena J. *Indian Literature in Brief.* Ghaziabad : Vimal Prakashan, 1982.
To provide a "perspective" to Indian English Literature this book deals with the works of twelve novelists from Venkataramani to Arun Joshi.

315. ——. *Indian Literature in English.* Moscow : Nauk Publishing House, 1974.

316. ——. *Indian English Literature : A Perspective.* Ghaziabad : Vimal Prakashan, 1982.
The present study is a generalized research of the creative works of the Indian English writers. It traces the origin and development of Indian literature in English and tries to introduce and describe its eminent poets and novelists and their best works to readers all over the world.
The book contains eight chapters. While the first chapter traces the origin and development of Indian English literature the third, fourth and the fifth are concerned with fiction. Starting from the formation of Indian novels in English the book traces its growth from

Venkataramani to Manohar Malgonkar, Anita Desai and others, laying emphasis on all the distinguished writers like Anand, Narayan and Raja Rao. It focuses on the characteristic features of Indian English literature, its versatility, variety and uniqueness.
See 1425, 1673, 2174, 2692, 4085, 4360, 4599, 5451, 6444, 7482, 8088.

317. Kapadia, Novy & A.G. Khan, ed. *The Parsis : Madyan to Sajan : An Appraisal of Ethnic Anxieties Reflected in Literature.* New Delhi : Creative Books, 1997.
An anthology containing critical articles on Bapsi Sidhwa, Firdaus Kangra, Rohinton Mistry and Others.

318. Karnani, Chetan. *Indian Writing in English.* New Delhi : Arnold Associates, 1995.

319. Kaul, R.K. and Jaidev, eds. *Social Awareness in Modern Indian Literature.* Shimla : Indian Institute of Advanced Study, 1993.
A collection of 17 papers presented at a national seminar on "Social Awareness in Modern Indian Literature" held at Indian Institute of Advanced Study, Shimla in 1991. The book is divided into three sections and the last section, "Literature : Indian Writing in English" contains four articles.
See 808, 1288, 1614, 4110, 6439.

320. Kaur, Iqbal. *Gender and Literature.* New Delhi : B.R. Publishing Corporation, 1992.
An anthology of essays dealing with different aspects of feminist and its application to different texts.
See 1197, 1619, 2468, 3520, 4714.

321. Kaushik, Asha. *Politics, Aesthetics and Culture: Indian Political Novel.* New Delhi : Manohar Publications, 1988.
The book, originally a dissertation submitted to Rajasthan University for Ph.D. in the Department of Political Science, proposes to present a politico-cultural

perspective of India as reflected in the political novels written by Indian English authors. Political fiction treated here as a recorded form of culture and aesthetic-political criticism is seen as relevant to political analysis as a mode of cultural interpretation.

The book containing six chapters undertakes to present an inter-disciplinary approach to the study of the Indian English novel. Defining the political novel the author provides its intellectual and cultural perspectives. Treating political fiction as historical self-discovery she traces the evolution of a tradition of the protest novel.

322. Kerr, David and R.K.Dhawan, eds. *Australian Literature and Indian Literature : Studies in Mutual Response.* New Delhi : Prestige Books, 1991.

The book is a republication of the issue of the journal, *Commonwealth Review,* Vol. 2, Nos. 1-2, 1990-1991, a special number on Australian and Indian literature. The book contains two sections. The first one contains articles on Australian literature written by Indian scholars and the second section critical essays on Indian English literature by Australian critics. The second section contains 12 essays. While the first one is an introduction to Indian English literature by David Kerr the other essays are on poetry as well as on fiction. The fiction writers that are dealt with are Narayan, Anita Desai, Salman Rushdie, Nayantara Sahgal, Ruth Prawer Jhabvala and G.V. Desani.

See 2848, 3107, 3644, 5422, 5697, 7079, 7140, 7506.

323. Kessler-Harris, Alice and William McBrien, eds. *Faith of a (Woman) Writer*. Westport CT : Greenwood, 1988.

Contains an essay on R.P. Jhabvala.

See 3549.

324. Khan, A.G. *Canadian Literature and Indian Literature : New Perspectives.* Creative New Literatures Series-01. New Delhi : Creative Books, 1995.

The book is a collection of essays on Indian Writing in English and on Canadian Literature written by the author as he responded and reacted "to provocation" of these literatures. The book examines selected works from the point of view of inter-textuality and from a sociological point of view. Out of fourteen essays five are on Indian fiction in English.
See 4208, 4867, 4937, 7846, 7867, 8024, 8057.

325. Khan, M.Q. and A.G. Khan. *Changing Faces of Women in Indian Writing in English.* New Delhi : Creative Books, 1995.

326. King, Bruce, ed. *Literature of the World in English.* London : Routledge and Kegan Paul, 1974.
Out of the several articles on different countries by different critics, there is one on "India" by B. Rajan which surveys Indian English literature. There is an elaborate discussion on fiction writers particularly Narayan, Raja Rao, Anand and others. Exemplifies the traits of the critical and polemical writings of the country.
See 1081.

327. ——. *The New English Literature — Cultural Nationalism in a Changing World.* London : St. Martin, Press, 1980.
Studies in general terms, the emergence of 'new' national literatures after the second world war. R.K. Narayan figures among the individual writers discussed separately.
See 3585, 5467.

328. ——, ed. *The Commonwealth Novel Since 1960.* London : Macmillan 1990.
A survey of contemporary English fiction by Commonwealth writers. Contains an article on the Indian English novel by Syd Harrex.

329. Kirpal, Viney. *The Third World Novel of Expatriation : A Study of Emigre Fiction by Indian, West African and Carribbean Writers.* New Delhi : Sterling Publishers, 1989.

In an overall comprehensive study of expatriation in the novels of the third world novelists writing in English, the author examines the impact of expatriation on the different facets of the fictional works of the third world migrant novelists. Among them are Rushdie, Raja Rao, Kamala Markandaya whose fiction is carefully studied to answer several pertinent questions regarding the themes they choose, the value systems they offer, the kind of characters they create and the effects of exile on their language and technique.

The book is in three parts. Part I deals with the impact of the colonialization on expatriation and defining expatriates sensibility and part II dealing with some of the major modes of experience and Part III with the use of language.

The book is a modified version of the doctoral dissertation submitted to the University of Poona.

330. ——, ed. *The New Indian Novel in English : A Study of the 1980s.* New Delhi : Allied Publishers, 1990.

An anthology consisting of twenty seven essays by several critics on different novelists of the 1980s. While these essays are detailed critical studies encompassing different aspects such as themes, techniques, character, language and sensibility of the Indian novel in English of the 1980s, they also attempt to make an evaluation and assessment of "the particular literary character" of the decade. They also aim at showing the uninhibited experimentation with techniques like allegory, symbol, fantasy as a mode of writing and themes which set the novels of 1980s apart from those of the previous decades and how they have contributed to establish Indian English novel as a separate genre.

The book covers a whole range of writers from Mulk Raj Anand to Amitav Ghosh. The first part deals with the old masters — Narayan and Anand — while the second part contains a major thrust on second generation novelists from Kamala Markandaya and Nayantara Sahgal to Amitav Ghosh and Upamanyu Chatterjee. The third part is devoted to the poetics of the new Indian novel in English concentrating mainly on the form, style and narrative techniques of the New Indian novel in English.

See 817, 1039, 1742, 2348, 2667, 2712, 2767, 2769, 2828, 3158, 3306, 3319, 3390, 4101, 4548, 5154, 5320, 6793, 7066, 7134, 7182, 7228, 7288, 7435, 7474, 7475, 7489, 7753, 7829, 7830.

331. ——, ed. *The Post-modern Indian English Novel : Interrogating the 1980s and 1990s.* Bombay : Allied Publishers, 1996.

A sequel to the earlier book, *The New Indian Novel in English : A Study of the 1980s,* is a collection of thirty five essays by leading specialists and critics dealing with the recent trends and developments in the Indian English novels written between 1980 and 1995. It is divided into four sections titled "Stories without Ends," "Minority Discourses", "Dislocations" and "Deconstructing Post-modernism" which cover a whole gamut of Indian English fiction seen from a post-modernist point of view.

See 644, 1148, 2336, 2345, 2371, 2453, 2529, 2657, 2772, 3066, 3168, 3245, 3300, 3410, 3417, 3420, 4157, 4204, 4215, 4330, 4846, 4873, 4943, 5013, 5051, 5141, 5225, 6238, 6291, 6292, 6429, 6792, 6834, 7085, 7136, 7733, 7759, 7979, 8033.

332. Kohli, Devindra. *Indian Writers at Work.* Delhi : B.R. Publishing Corporation, 1991.

Brings into a book form the interviews published in the journal, *The Indian Literary Review* 1978-79. Among the twelve writers interviewed R.K. Narayan, Mulk Raj Anand, K.A. Abbas, Nayantara Sahgal, Shiv K. Kumar are some.

333. Kohli, Suresh. *Aspects of Indian Literature : The Changing Pattern.* Delhi : Vikas Publishing House, 1975.
Contains essays on the general trends of Indian literature including Indian English writings.
See 561.

334. Krishnaswamy, Shanta. *Women in Indian Fiction in English 1950-1980 : Glimpses of Women in India.* New Delhi : Asia Publishing House, 1984.
The book attempts to place in a critical perspective the nature and treatment of the women in six major Indian English novelists : Raja Rao, Narayan, Bhabani Bhattacharya, Kamala Markandaya, Jhabvala and Anita Desai. It traces the shifts in the general literary sensibility of the period towards Indian woman in each author and throws light on the increasing sense of woman's awakening consciousness and her confrontation with male domination and the tradition-oriented society. It also tries to show how the Indian woman, despite the changes in the norms, and in the standards of judgement and economic and educational progress, is essentially Indian in sensibility and likely to remain so in the future.
See 2177, 2707, 3587, 4603, 5477, 6455.

335. Kumar, Gajendra. *Indo-Anglian Novel Criticism : Tradition and Achievment.* Patna: Novelty & Co, 1998.

336. Kumar, Satish. *A Survery of Indian English Novel.* Bareilly : Prakash Book Depot, 1996.

337. Kumar, A.V. Suresh. *Six Indian Novelists : Mulk Raj Anand, Raja Rao, R. K. Narayan, Balachandra Rajan, Kamala Markandaya, and Anita Desai.* New Delhi : Creative Books, 1996.

338. Kushwaha, M. *Glimpses of Indian Research in Indian Literature.* New Delhi : Sterling Publishers, 1984.
Contains abstracts of selected dissertations (doctoral) on British, American, Commonwealth literatures out of which two are on Indian writing in English.

339. Lal, Malashri. *The Law of the Threshold : Women Writers in Indian English.* Shimla : Indian Institute of Advanced Studies, 1995.
The book provides a feminist methodology for interpreting literary texts in Indian English, offering "the law of the threshold" of which "Lakshmanarekha" is an archetype. Argues that women's personal lives are often disguised in fiction as narratives of a depersonalised time and place. The six writers discussed in individual chapters are Toru Dutt, Sarojini Naidu, Rama Mehta, Jhabvala, Anita Desai and Bharati Mukherjee.
See 2713, 3254, 3590, 4908, 5013.

340. Lal, P. *The Concept of an Indian Literature.* Calcutta : Writers Workshop, 1968.
A general assessment of modern Indian literature including Indian English writing. It consists of six essays out of which one is on Indian English. These essays are based on Lal's argument that the essential difference between ancient and modern literatures is that "the former embodies myth, ...while the latter is entirely mythless."

341. Larson, Charles R. *The Novel in the Third World.* Washington : Inscape Publishers, 1976.
The book is an attempt to make a comparative study of the novels of the third world — Africa, India, the Carribean, and the novels of native American writers of the United States and Afro-American works and South Pacific — to show how culture has shaped the literary form. "The very 'form' of the novels from cultures within the third world has often been strongly

influenced by those cultures themselves resulting in something contrary to our European concept of the novel in the West." Calling these novels "situational novels" the author examines the similarities of attitudes and responses of these writers comparing their works with the novels from cultures within the third world. The author also traces the evolutionary pattern of the third world novel from "Collective unconscious" as represented in the Protest literature chronicling the lives of the oppressed and exploited people and their protest against the colonial power to the individual consciousness as exemplified in the essays such as "Revolt and Rebirth: Cultural Renewal (Raja Rao's *Kanthapura* and Kamala Markandaya's *Two Virgins)* and "The Singular Consciousness: R.K. Narayan's *Grateful to Life and Death."*
See 4610, 5487, 6464.

342. Lindfors, Bernth and Bala Kothandaraman, eds. *South Asian Responses to Chinua Achebe.* New Delhi : Prestige Books, 1993.
Includes articles comparing Achebe's fiction with the works of Narayan.
See 5373, 5679.

343. MacDermott, Doireann and Susan Ballyn, eds. *Passage to Somewhere Else.* Proc. of the Commonwealth Conference held in the University of Barcelona. Sep.-Oct. 1987. Barcelona : University of Barcelona, 1988.
Discusses the attitudes of the expatriate new world writers to their new environment and the way in which these attitudes influence their creative contribution. Contains articles on Kamala Markandaya and Khushwant Singh.
See 4613, 7918.

344. Maes-Jelinek, Hena, Kristen Hold Peterson and Anna Rutherford, eds. *A Shaping of Connections :*

Commonwealth Literature Studies Then and Now. Sidney (Australia) : Dangaroo Press, 1989.
The book is a *festschrift* in honour of Prof. Norman Jeffares. Traces the development of Commonwealth Studies since the Leeds Conference in 1964. There is a note on the history of Indian English literature: "Despite its very considerate achievements Indian English literature is fighting an uneven battle for its survival against other literatures in Indian languages."
See 993, 2068, 6999.

345. Magill, Frank N. *Critical Survey of Long Fiction.* Englewood Cliff, N.J. : Salem Press, 1983.

346. Mahle, H.S. *Indo-Anglian Fiction : Some Perceptions.* New Delhi : Jainsons Publications, 1985.
The book contains four chapters, out of which one each is on R.P. Jhabvala and Kamala Markandaya, whereas the remaining two chapters are on John Masters and Girish Karnad.
As the author himself mentions these are not intended to be scholarly research articles but interesting comments made by an experienced teacher and critical reader.
See 869.

347. Mahood, M.M. *The Colonial Encounter : A Reading of Six Novels.* London : Rex Collins, 1977.
Contains an essay on R.K. Narayan's *The Man-Eater of Malgudi.*
See 5495.

348. Malhotra, M.L. *Bridges of Literature.* Ajmer : Sunanda Publications, 1971.
Contains comments of general nature on several Indian English novelists and men of letters.
See 2720, 4365, 5498, 5499, 7496.

349. Malik, Yogendra K., ed. *Politics and the Novel in India.* New Delhi : Orient Longman, 1978.

The book discusses Indian political novels, old and new, in nine languages — English, Hindi, Punjabi, Marathi, Bengali, Telugu, Gujarati, Kannada and Urdu. Out of several essays Carlo Coppola's essay, "Politics and the Novel in India" gives a general introduction to the political novel while Naik's essay "The Indian English Political Novel" defines political novel and discusses the treatment of the political themes in Indian English fiction.

See 956.

350. Manuel, M. and Ayyappa Paniker, eds. *English in India.* Madras : Macmillan, 1978.

The book is a collection of essays and studies by eminent scholars both from India and abroad published as a *festschrift* to Prof. Samuel Mathai. It offers a variety of attitudes and approaches to the continuing theme of English in India. Apart from the first essay which is a tribute to Prof. Mathai all other essays are of general nature. They consist of three types : those on Indian Writing in English, those on the impact of English language on Indian languages and those on the teaching of English language.

See 956, 1101, 1277, 3635.

351. Mathur, O.P. *Modern Indian English Fiction.* Delhi : Abhinav Publications, 1993.

The book is a collection of critical essays presented by the author at various seminars and conferences and published earlier in various Indian and foreign journals and books.

See 880, 1698, 1699, 1700, 1701, 4089, 4093, 5155, 5501, 5502, 5503, 6475, 6476, 6477, 7499, 7500, 7935.

352. ——. *Indian Political Novel and Other Essays.* Allahabad: Kitab Mahal, 1995.

A brief survey of Indian English and Hindi Political fiction of the Post-Independence era to show how various writers treated the major themes such as partition, princely states, imposition of emergency, exploitation of the poor etc., with "varying depths of understanding and perception and authenticity of experience and feeling." Comments that "in spite of the differences in emphasis, perspective and range these writers (both Hindi and Indian English) show the same democratic and secular foundations.

See 881, 1506, 4090, 4094, 7114, 7115, 7936.

353. Maya, D. *Narrative Colonialism : Postcolonial Images of the British in Indian English Fiction.* Delhi : Prestige Books, 1997.

354. McCuthion, David. *Indian Writing in English : Critical Essays.* Calcutta : Writers Workshop, 1969.

The book contains some seminal essays on the status of Indian English fiction in the 1960s. The book, one of the earliest studies on Indian English fiction, consists of eleven essays out of which three are of general nature and three are on individual novels and novelists. It has a longish introduction which surveys the origin and growth of Indian English fiction. The essays are thought-provoking dealing with the problems such as the validity of the genre, the concept of Indianness, the creative use of English, the failure of critical standards in India and the question of audience.

See 884, 885, 886, 3280, 6269, 6478.

355. McGraw, W., ed. *Inventing Countries : Essays in Post-Colonial Literatures.* Wollongong : Wollongong Univ. Publications, 1987.

356. McLeod, A.L., ed. *The Commonwealth Pen : An Introduction to the Literature of the British Commonwealth.* Ithaca (New York) : Cornell University Press, 1961.

Contains an article on Indian English literature.

357. ——, ed. *Subjects Worthy Fame : Essays in Comonwealth Literature.* New Delhi : Sterling Publishers, 1989.
The book is a collection of critical essays presented as a *festschrift* to Prof. H.H. Annaiah Gowda. It contains fifteen essays which represent the spectrum of contemporary literary studies ranging from the detailed interpretations of particular works to the valuation of individual writers' achievement. Out of these essays two are related to Indian English fiction.
See 1607, 2633.

358. Meera Bai, K. *Women Voices : The Novels of Indian Women Writers.* New Delhi : Prestige Books, 1996.
A naive study of the women characters as presented in the most popular novels of select women writers of Indian English fiction. Dividing the women characters under different heads such as conformists and non-conformists; introvert and extrovert; characters created by women and men, etc., discusses the novels of Anita Desai, Shashi Deshpande, Jhabvala, Kamala Markandaya, Raji Narasimhan, Santha Rama Rau and Nayantara Sahgal.

359. Mehta, P.P. *Indo-Anglian Fiction : An Assessment.* Bareilly : Prakash Book Depot, 1968.
The book is an endeavour to present an interpretative history of Indian English fiction from the beginning to 1968. It offers a comprehensive critical survey and assessment of Indian English fiction starting from the formative influences that are responsible for its growth to its achievement in the present age.

360. Mehta, Ved. *John is Easy to Please : Encounters with the Written and the Spoken Word.* London : Secker and Warburg, 1971.
The book contains six articles out of which one — "The Train had just Arrived at Malgudi Station" is related to Indian English fiction. It traces the author's encounter with Narayan.

361. Melwani, Murali Das. *Critical Essays on Indo-Anglian Themes.* Calcutta : Writers Workshop, 1971.
Contains brief comments on the trends in different genres of Indian English literature mostly reprinted from newspapers.
See 898, 899, 2315.

362. ——. *Themes in Indo-Anglian Literature.* Bareilly : Prakash Book Depot. 1977.

363. Metteke, Edith, ed. *Tensions Between North and South : Studies in Modern Commonwealth Literature and Culture.* Proc. of the 8th Commonwealth Literature Conference, Berlin. 14-18 June 1985. Wurzburg : Konigshausen and Neumann, 1985.
Contains articles on R.K. Narayan and Kamala Markandaya.
See 4691, 5561.

364. Mishra, Ganeswar. *How Indian is the Indian Novel in English.* Bhubaneswar : Post-Graduate Department of English, Utkal University, 1990.
Studies the Indian English novel in the context of Indian social, religious and narrative traditions.
See 907, 2341, 4628, 5507, 5508, 6483, 6484.

365. Mohan, Ramesh, ed. *Indian Writing in English.* New Delhi : Orient Longman, 1978.
The book is a collection of twenty four papers presented at a seminar on Indian English held at the Central Institute of English, Hyderabad in July 1972. The papers, as the editor claims, embody "a quest for the identity of Indian English."
See 592, 738, 776, 913, 915, 929, 965, 1269, 4325, 5641, 6500, 7946.

366. Mokashi-Punekar, Shankar. *The Indo-Anglian Creed.* Calcutta : Writers Workshop, 1972.
The book contains four articles, the last one being the Indo-Anglian creed, which tries, rather sweepingly, to

find out the pitfalls that can be seen in Indian Writing in English. Though much of the essay is to answer the question, "Why do Indians write in English" it contains some pertinent remarks on the writings of earlier poets and later novelists.
See 917.

367. ——. *Theoretical and Practical Studies in Indo-English Literature.* Dharwar : Karnatak University Press, 1978.

368. Moore, Cornelia and A. Raymond Moody, eds. *Comparative Literature East and West : Traditions and Trends.* Honolulu : University of Hawaii Press, 1989.
The book is the first volume of a new series entitled "Literary Studies : East and West" published by the college of languages/linguistics and literature, University of Hawaii. With a view to awaken cultural awareness the book focuses on the identifications and commonalties and differences in topos and methodology, the changing values over time and the perception and portrayal of the self in different cultures. Contains an article : "Salman Rushdie's *Midnight's Children* : Models for Story Telling."
See 7194.

369. Mukherjee, Meenakshi. *The Twice Born Fiction.* New Delhi : Arnold Heinemann, 1971.
The book critically surveys Indian English novels written between 1930 and 1964 to assess its problems, achievements and further possibilities. Designating the Indian English novel as "twice born" being the product of two parent traditions (Indian and English) the author analyses and evaluates the novels of her choice against the socio-historical background and traces certain marked trends or tendencies in the themes and techniques of these novels. She finds that the East-West encounter, asceticism and renunciation, myths and legends, Indianness and Gandhism are some of the popular motifs in Indian English fiction.

The book consists of eight chapters. While the first chapter, "Preamble," is of an introductory nature the second chapter discusses in general terms the Indian literary scene and the place of Indian English fiction in it. Chapter 3 "The Making of the Nation" deals with the novels that are concerned with large public issues and national or social problems while chapters 4 and 5 are devoted to the discussions of the themes "East-West Encounter," "Renunciation as an Ideal" respectively. Chapters 6 and 7 — "Myth as Technique" and "The Problem of Style" — examine the various experiments of Indian English writers "in giving English a distinctively Indian tone and colouring without doing violence to its basic linguistic structure."

370. ——, ed. *Considerations.* Bombay : Allied Publishers, 1977.
This collection of critical essays, as the author claims, is "a selective presentation of the grounds on which some Indo-Anglian writers and writings may be studied." The aim of the book is to bring together "a variety of approaches" as well as "a diversity of assessments" on Indian English literature. Of the twelve essays seven are on fiction—on individual writers and specific texts.
See 1079, 1711, 3093, 3281, 5386, 5463, 6478, 6490, 7931.

371. Mund, Subhendee Kumar. *The Indian Novel in English : Its Birth and Development.* Bhubaneswar. Parchi Prakashan, 1997.

372. Murti, K.V. Suryanarayana. *Kohinoor in the Crown : Critical Studies in Indian-English Literature.* Delhi : Sterling Publishers, 1987.
An anthology of essays on varied aspects of poetry and fiction. Articles have appeared in various journals earlier. The book contains fifteen articles dealing with the works of major writers such as Anand, Narayan, Rushdie and Others.

See 947, 1714, 1717, 1718, 1719, 5520, 5521, 7138.

373. Nabar, Vrinda and Nilufer, E. Bharucha. *Post-colonial Perspectives on the Raj and Its Literature*. Bombay : Univ. of Bombay, 1994.

374. Nagarajan, M.S., N. Eakambaram and A. Natarajan, eds. *Essays in Criticism on Indian Literature in English.* New Delhi : S. Chand & Co., 1991.
An Anthology of critical essays on all the genres — drama, prose, fiction and poetry written by several critics and published as a *festschrift* to Prof. T. Prabhakar. The articles reassess Indian literary trends from a contemporary point of view.
The book contains 20 essays of which 12 are on fiction.
See 1800, 2134, 2635, 2834, 4126, 4400, 4563, 4667, 5549, 6530, 7534, 7768.

375. Nageswara Rao, G., ed. *Laurel Bough* (Essays presented in honour of Prof. M.V. Rama Sarma). Bombay : Blackie and Sons, 1983.
A *festschrift* to Prof. M.V. Rama Sarma, the book offers a variety of critical perspectives in varied fields of literature such as epic, drama, poetry, criticism, comparative literature and Indian writing in English. There is one essay on Raja Rao, in the section "Comparative Literature" : "Raja Rao's *The Serpent and the Rope* and Patrick White's *The Solid Mandala : A Comparative Appraisal*" and four essays on Indian English fiction in the section : "Indian Writing in English."
See 5532, 6595, 7698, 7706, 7709.

376. Nahal, Chaman. *The New Literatures in English.* New Delhi : Allied Publishers, 1985.
The book critically examines the literatures written in English in countries other than England (America, Africa, Australia, India etc.,). It runs on two basic

assumptions — (1) social and psychological realism of literatures as distinguished from that of English Literature and (2) the linguistic experimentation in these literatures. There are three chapters on Indian writing in English to show the inventiveness of Indian writers from Mulk Raj Anand onwards.

See 951, 952, 1720, 2184, 2739, 3605, 7507.

377. Naik, M.K., S.K. Desai and G.S. Amur, eds. *Critical Essays on Indian Writing in English*. Dharwar : Karnataka University, 1968. Revised and enlarged edition, 1972. Paperback 1977. Rpt. by Macmillan (Madras), 1979.

A collection of perceptive critical essays on Indian English fiction written by several critics and published as a *festschrift* to Prof. Menezes.

Out of twenty-nine essays on various genres, thirteen essays are on Indian fiction in English. Two essays: Raja Rao's "The Writer and the Word", Anand's "The Story of My Experiment with a White Lie" are by the novelists themselves revealing their attitudes and approaches towards creativity.

See 589, 661, 815, 941, 954, 1073, 1086, 1710, 3466, 4551, 5742, 6497, 6510, 7949.

378. Naik, M.K., ed. *Aspects of Indian Writing in English*. Madras : Macmillan, 1979.

The book contains a collection of critical essays on a wide spectrum of subjects related to Indian English literature (poetry, drama and fiction) by twentyfour Indian and Western scholars as a *festschrift* to Prof. K.R. Srinivasa Iyengar. It is characterised by a fine combination of authority, selectivity and critical judgement. Out of twentysix essays four essays are on Indian writing in English in general and seven on fiction.

See 590, 857, 1009, 1144, 1189, 2049, 2161, 3283, 3637, 5540, 6566.

379. ——. *A History of Indian English Literature.* New Delhi : Sahitya Akademi, 1982.
A critical survey of the whole field of Indian writing in English including prose writings and literary and art criticism from the beginning to the present day (1982). It contains some rigorous critical evaluations of major writers.

380. ——. *Dimensions of Indian-English Literature.* New Delhi : Sterling Publishers, 1983.
This book, designed as a critical conspectus of the entire range of Indian writing in English, contains sixteen published essays concerning poetry, drama, novel and prose. Some of the essays are of general nature while others are in depth studies of individual works.
See 956, 957, 3087, 5527.

381. ——, ed. *Perspectives on Indian English Fiction.* New Delhi : Abhinav Publications, 1985.
The book contains seventeen essays on the major Indian English fiction writers and their works by scholars who are established critics of the genre. As the editor points out there are three types of essays in this book — "general evaluation of the major novelists", "intensive textual studies of outstanding novels" and "considerations of schools such as women novelists". Anand, Narayan, Raja Rao, Sudhin Ghose, Bhabani Bhattacharya, Manohar Malgonkar, Rushdie, Kamala Markandaya and Anita Desai have been discussed in the first category, *Untouchable, The Guide, The Serpent and Rope, All About H.Hatterr, Midnight's Childern* find critical treatment in the second category. The third category is the most sketchy one. Besides an article on Indian English women novelists, an essay on an overview of Indian English novelists of the Post-Independence era and on the Indian English short story are included. The final essay on "The Achievement of

Indian fiction in English" by Naik is a quick survey of the entire field with a focus on the best attempts both at choosing the themes and fictional techniques.
See 957, 1066, 1185, 1252, 1652, 1749, 1853, 2150, 2743, 3086, 3284, 4348, 4594, 5315, 5607, 6435, 6597, 7215, 7548.

382. ——. *Studies in Indian English Literature.* New Delhi : Sterling Publishers, 1987.
The book, a collection of critical essays, is a sequel to *Dimensions of Indian English Literature* (1984). It covers all the major forms (Poetry, fiction and drama) of Indian English literature. Some of the essays are published earlier in Periodicals.
See 961, 3086, 3463, 6504, 7143.

383. Nair, Rama, B. Gopal Rao and I. Venkateswarulu, eds. *Framing Literatures : Critical Articles.* New Delhi : Sterling Publishers, 1994.
The book is a collection of critical essays presented as a *festschrift* to Prof. M. Sivaramkrishna. The anthology contains 30 odd essays divided into four sections — "Overview," "Indian writing in English," "British Literature," "American Literature" and "Impressions". As pointed out by the editors the major thrust of these essays is "an unconditional commitment to the humanizing and life enhancing dogma of aesthetics." A good number of articles view literature from post-colonial Indian perspective. The essays on Indian English fiction deal with Narayan's *Waiting for the Mahatma,* Arun Joshi's *The City and the River* and Bharati Mukherjee's *Wife.*
See 1036, 1216, 4105, 5012, 5535.

384. Nandan, Satendra, ed. *Language and Literature in Multicultural Contexts.* Proc. of the fifth triennial conference held by the Association for Commonwealth Literature and Language Studies at the University of

South Pacific in 1980. Swva, Fiji: University of South Pacific, 1983.
Out of the 60 papers presented in the conference, 32 articles have been selected for inclusion in this volume out of which 7 are on Indian English fiction.
See 692, 951, 1214, 2739, 3561, 5349, 5557.

385. Narain Iqbal and Luthur Lutze, eds. *Literature, Social-Consciousness and Polity.* New Delhi : Manohar, 1983.
A collection of papers presented at the VII European conference on Modern South Asian studies at Talberg (Sweden) in 1983. Examines the pattern of relationship among literature, social consciousness, and polity in the countries of South Asian region. Contains an essay on Anand.
See 1726.

386. Narasimhaiah, C.D. *The Writer's Gandhi.* Patiala : Punjab University, 1967.
Discusses three Indo-English novels — *Untouchable, Kanthapura* and *Waiting for the Mahatma* — as novels projecting Gandhian image.

387. ——, ed. *Fiction and the Reading Public in India.* Mysore : University of Mysore, 1967.
A collection of twentyfour essays dealing with novels in various Indian languages including one on Indian English novel presented at a seminar in the University of Mysore (Nov. 1965). The purpose of the book is to present Indian viewpoint and literary trends to the Western world.
See 631, 818, 1117, 1231, 3524, 6510, 6639, 8086.

388. ——, ed. *The Swan and the Eagle.* Shimla : Indian Institute of Advanced Study, 1969.
The book, one of the earliest aimed at "winning critical recognition to Indian writing in English" specifically deals with the writings of the three major novelists — Anand, Raja Rao and Narayan. The author finds in the

writing of these writers "an essentially Indian sensibility" which has arisen out of a happy conjugation of the Swan (The East) and the Eagle (the West), and the innovativeness in the Indian use of English.
The book consists of six chapters on varied subjects — poetry, prose and fiction. Out of which three are on fiction.
See 1727, 5541, 6513.

389. ——, ed. *Indian Literature of the Past Fifty Years 1917-1967*. Mysore : University of Mysore, 1970.
The collection of papers in this volume were originally presented as papers at the two seminars sponsored by the University of Mysore in its Golden Jubilee Year— the first on "How Major is Our Literature of the Past Fifty Years?" and the second on "Indian Writing in English," the latter containing 16 essays out of which ten are on fiction.
See 588, 856, 986, 1130, 1711, 2231, 2716, 3097, 3281, 4683, 5130, 5456, 6496, 7954.

390. ——. *Moving Frontiers of English Studies in India*. New Delhi : S.Chand & Co., 1977.
Contains articles on Indian English and Commonwealth literatures.

391. ——, ed. *Commonwealth Literature : Problems of Response*. Madras : Macmillan, 1981.
This volume is a product of a seminar on Commonwealth literature and contains eighteen articles on various aspects of a comparative nature on Commonwealth fiction. To that extent the title of the book is misleading. There are four essays on general theoretical topics, four on common themes that attracted the attention of the Commonwealth writers, two essays on individual works or writers and the remaining are of introductory nature. While C.D. Narasimhaiah's "Introduction" focuses on the problems of response from non-native writers and critics of

Commonwealth fiction there are also essays which reflect the personal creative appreciation of the genre of the novel, such as the one from Anand.

See 597, 709, 798, 870, 1027, 1034, 1700, 1784, 2788, 3096, 6366, 6468, 6565.

392. ——, ed. *Women in Fiction and Fiction by Women.* Mysore : Dhvanyaloka Publications, 1986.

The book is a republication of the special issue of the journal, *Literary Criterion,* Vol. 20. No. 4. 1985.

See : 714, 991, 1244, 2434, 6454, 6519.

393. ——. *Essays in Commonwealth Literature : Heirloom of Multiple Heritage.* Delhi : Pencraft International,1995.

The book is a collection of essays each of them written by Prof. C.D. Narasimhaiah in response to an occasion. These essays evaluate the various constituents of Commonwealth Literature, notably Indian, African, Australian, West Indian and Canadian and posit how these constituents have come to acquire the right of 'vision' and register 'the appreciation of difference' with one another.

The book consists of seventeen essays out of which two are of general nature focusing on the background and heritage of Commonwealth Literature. Only two are related to Indian English fiction.

See : 5541, 7148, 7762, 8030.

394. Narasimhaiah, C.D., and S. Nagarajan, eds. *Studies in Australian and Indian Literature.* International Seminar on Australian and Indian literature held at Delhi from 12 to 16 January 1970. New Delhi : Indian Council for Cultural Relations, 1971.

Out of fifteen essays there are two on Indian English fiction.

See 590, 6424.

395. ——, eds. *Awakened Conscience: Studies in Commonwealth Literture.* New Delhi : Sterling Publishers, 1978.

The book consists of forty papers presented at the Fourth Triennial Conference at Delhi in January 1977. Out of these essays there are only four on Indian English fiction.

See 928, 1268, 3082, 5606.

396. Narasimhaiah, C.D. and C. Srinath, eds. *Indian Literature in English : Contemporary Assessment.* Bangalore : Dhvanyaloka Publications, n.d.

The book is a republication of the special issue of *Literary Criterion* 12.2-3. (1976) on Indian Writing in English. It contains articles on drama, fiction and poetry.

See 940, 989, 3635, 4145, 4556, 4683, 6816.

397. Narasimhan, Raji. *Sensibility under Stress : Aspects of Indo-English Fiction.* New Delhi : Asha Janak Publications, 1972.

Explores the reasons for the blunting of sensibility among the Indian English writers after the golden age of Indian English (the age of Narayan, Raja Rao and Desani) and attributes this to two reasons : a certain brain-washing by Western precepts and the resultant creativity blunted because of an overpeddling of English. Drawing a line between spoilt and unspoilt sensibility among the Indian English writers, the author overviews the history of English writing in India in thirteen short chapters. The quiet affection that English has generated among Indians was shown in Narayan's *The English Teacher* but Narayan's is not Anglo-Philism as there is a greater stress on nationalistic sentiments. Desani and Raja Rao are the two other writers whose traumatic confrontation with the West yields fruitful results. With Anita Desai's and the other novelists' attempt to internalize the East-West conflict, "the rot sets in". In the next six chapters the author shows how rotten is this rot by throwing light on the lack of sensibility in the Indian writers in English both in content and form.

"The Mirage of Love", "The Crumpling of Style", and other chapters were testimony to this attitude. Finally a chapter on Forster's influence on the Indian English novelists compares the difference between Forster's attitude towards India and Indians and the self-assured objectivity of the Indian English writers. Chapter 13 is devoted to novels written in Indian languages and translated into English and argues that even they come under the category of Indian English fiction.

398. Narayan, Gomamthi. *The Sahibs and the Natives : A Study of Guilt and Pride in Anglo-Indian and Indo-Anglian Novels*. New Delhi : Chanakya Publications, 1986.

A comparative study of the novels written by both British writers on India and Indian writers in English dealing with the theme of Indo-British relationship during the last days of the Raj (1940) in India. Its main focus is on the theme of guilt, shame and pride. It compares the divergent perspectives of Sahibs and the natives regarding the politics of Indian liberation delineating the psychology of colonialism and the ambivalence inherent in the rule-ruled relationship.

The book is based on the thesis that the perceived sense of guilt and shame in Anglo-Indian fiction is the result of the recognition by the British novelists of the "perversions and repressions of the Empire" while for the Indian novelists, it is a result of "the nightmarish scenes of partition". It explores the literary strategies of symbolic expiation such as scapegoating, re-enactment of past scenes of guilt, open declarations and other subtle means and shows how they have been handled by the two groups of novelists. The fictional writings that have been considered for analysis are those of John Masters, Paul Scott, Leslie Gillespie, Gerald Hanley and Philip Woodruff (among the British novelists) and the works of Anand, Manohar Malgonkar, Chaman Nahal, Nayantara Sahgal,

Balachandra Rajan, Khushwant Singh, Raj Gill, Attia Hosain, R.K. Narayan, and Kamala Markandaya. The book is based on a research project conducted by the author in the years 1973-78 and parts of this book have been published in the *Journal of South Asian Literature, Literary Criterion and Panjab University Research Bulletin.*

399. Narendra Kumar, V.L.V.N, ed. *New Perspectives on Indian Writing.* New Delhi : Prestige Books, 1997.
See 761, 1077, 2806, 2860, 2864, 3267, 4136, 4148, 4216, 5628, 5645, 7439, 7767, 8036.

400. Nasimi, Reza Ahmed. *The Language of Mulk Raj Anand, Raja Rao and R.K. Narayan.* New Delhi : Capital Publishing House, 1989.
Finds that the three novelists — Anand, Raja Rao and Narayan — use language in a constrictive way as they are "born to the language" of their fictional representations. Argues that each one has mastered the foreign medium by different strategies. Within the limitations Narayan's *(The Guide)* use of language is unusually creative with regard to the spiritual setting whereas Anand's *(Untouchable)* social realism and Raja Rao's *(Kanthapura)* philosophical ponderence come from sharp confrontation with the medium. In all the three the language "is engaged in (an) aesthetic activity to come to grip with reality."
See 1729, 5550, 6520.

401. Nayak, P.M. and S.P. Swain, eds. *Feminism and Indian English Fiction.* Bareilly : Prakash Book Depot, 1996.
The book is an anthology of essays dealing with the issues of feminism as projected in the Indian novel in English. Out of twelve essays two are of general nature ("Feminism and Our Fiction", "Feminism and Indian English Fiction") and ten are on individual novelists.
See 562, 1067, 2524, 2728, 2740, 3131, 3186, 4336, 4714, 5651, 7463.

402. Nelson, Emmanuel S., ed. *Reworlding : The Literature of Indian Diaspora.* Westport. CT : Greenwood, 1992.
Analyses the diasporic experiences of several Indian authors writing in English with an introduction tracing the history of such literature. Contains five articles on Indian English novelists.
See 1240, 4519, 4950, 4989, 5063, 5221, 6373, 7091, 7155, 7772.

403. ——. *Writers of Indian Diaspora : A Bio-Bibliographical Critical Source Book.* West Port: Greenwood Press, 1993.

404. New, William H. *Among Worlds : An Introduction to Modern Commonwealth and South African Fiction.* Ontario (Canada) : Porcepic, 1975.
Gives a thematic overview of Modern Commonwealth and South African fiction touching major works and major writers. Chapter 7 "South Asia : Fastidious Anti-Thesis" 193-224), has short comments and illustrations from novels of many Indian novelists including R.K. Narâyan. Chapter 8 contains both primary and secondary sources (bibliography) of the writers studied in this volume.

405. Nicholson, Kai. *A Presentation of Social Problems in the Indo-Anglian Novel.* Bombay : Jaico Publications, 1972.
A doctoral dissertation. Studies the social problems (the problems of adjustment in a society undergoing a great deal of socio-political stress and strain) as presented in the post-Independence era of Anglo-Indian (Paul Scott, Forster) and Indian English fiction.

406. Nightingale, Peggy, ed. *A Sense of Place in the New Literatures in English.* St. Lucia : University of Queensland Press, 1996.
A collection of papers presented at Macquarie University conference. Discusses Ruth Prawer Jhabvala

and Raja Rao along with others like Naipaul, Athol Fugard, Patrick White, Margaret Atwood etc.
See 707, 3675, 5378, 6611.

407. Niven, Alastair, ed. *The Commonwealth Writer Overseas : Themes of Exile and Expatriation* Brurelles : Librairie Marcel Dedier, 1976.
A collection of talks and papers presented at the Commonwealth Literature and Language Studies (European Branch) at the University of Stirling in 1975. There is a selection of talks by writers on their experience of exile-expatriation among which those of Kamala Markandaya, Saros Cowasjee, Raja Rao and Uma Parameswaran have been included.
See 689, 1038, 6377.

408. Noble, Allen and Ashok Dutt. *India : Cultural Pattern and Process.* Boulder (Coloroda, U.S.A.) : West View Press, 1982.
Contains essays on Indian English fiction.
See 737, 1639, 2656, 4569.

409. Olinder, Britta, ed. *A Sense of Place : Essays in Post-Colonial Literatures.* Proc. of the Gothenburg University Congress of Commonwealth Language and Literature, Sep. 1982. Gothenburg : the Dept. of English, Univ. of Gothanburg, 1984.

410. Padma, T. *Issues and Images : Studies in Indian English Literature : A Miscellany.* Vishakapatnam : Vagdevi Publishers, 1994.
Contains eleven chapters out of which one is on Arun Joshi's *The Last Labyrinth* exploring Jungian analysis, character interpretation and the person-person dichotomy and another article on Bharati Mukherjee's expatriate sensibility *vis-a-vis* the phenomena of roots.

411. Pallan, Rajesh K. *Indian English Fiction : A Select Study.* Jalandhar : Krishna Brothers, 1992.

Discusses comprehensively the use of myth in selected novels of Narayan, Raja Rao and Anand throwing light on the vision of human life and the cultural ethos embedded in them.

412. Pandey, Sudhakar and R. Raj Rao, eds. *Image of India in the Indian Novel in English 1960-1985*. Bombay : Orient Longman, 1993.

The book is a collection of some selected papers presented at a national seminar on "The Image of India in the Indian Novel in English, 1960-1985 " held at the University of Poona in March 1986.

The book contains 13 articles on thirteen novels which are discussed chronologically according to their year of publication. The thirteen novels discussed here represent "a significant phase in the development of Indian Writing in English" and reflect the country's social, economic, political and cultural concerns during 1960 and 1985.

See 2434, 2703, 2737, 2838, 2901, 4070, 4363, 4703, 4905, 5376, 6538, 6616, 7115.

413. Pandeya, S.M., ed. *Essays on Modern Fiction*. New Delhi : Vikas Publishing House, 1983.

The book is a collection of critical essays which are published in journals or anthologies or presented at conferences. Out of the fourteen essays in the book three essays are on Indian fiction in English. By close textual analysis the author tries to study the relevance of the theme to cultural context of the present day offering insights into the contemporary human condition and the motives of human behaviour.

See 1427, 2187, 5366, 5570.

414. Pandey, Surya Nath. *Contemporary Indian Women Writers in English*. New Delhi: Atlantic Publishers, 1999.

415. Pandit, M. L. *New Commonwealth Writings : A Critical Response*. New Delhi : Prestige Books, 1996.

The book is a collection of critical essays and notes written over a period of thirtfive years. The essays are attempts at independent examination of the chosen authors (Indian, African and Canadian) among whom R.K. Narayan, Rushdie, Mistry find a place.
See 1030, 1031, 3451, 5026, 5027, 5572, 7171, 7172, 7173, 7174, 8032, 8058, 8059.

416. Paniker, Ayyappa. *Indian Literature in English.* Madras : Anuchitra Publications, 1989.

417. ——, ed. *Indian English Literature Since Independence (1940-1990).* New Delhi : Indian Association of English Studies, 1991.
Contains essays on Indian English fiction.
See 2511, 2804, 2879, 2880.

418. ——, ed. *Contemporary Indian Fiction in English.* Trivandrum : The Dept. of English (Universtiy of Kerala), 1986.
The book is the product of the proceedings of the National seminar held at the University of Kerala on the 80th birthday of Mulk Raj Anand. The book contains sixteen essays out of which two are on Indian fiction in English in general and seven are on individual works. An interesting factor of the book is the rich and moving personal tributes to Anand by Shiv K. Kumar and Kamla Das with K.R. Srinivasa Iyengar's inaugural address which provides a bird's eye view of the whole scene of Indian English fiction.
See 846, 1261, 1688, 1764, 1847, 4120, 4636, 6482.

419. Paolucci, Anne, ed. *Problems in National Identity and Social Consciousness and the Writer as a Social Critic.* Whitestone (New York) : Griffon House, 1980.
A collection of selected papers read at the 4th Annual NDEA seminar on Foreign Area Studies, Columbia University, Feb. 28-29, 1980. Contains an essay, "National Identity and Social Consciousness in Modern

Indian Literature" which includes references to Indian English fiction.
See 862.

420. Parameswaran, Uma. *A Study of the Representative Indo-English Novelists.* New Delhi : Vikas Publishing House, 1976.
A full-length critical study of the pattern and development of Indian English fiction from 19th century to the present day (up to 1976). While attempting at a representative survey of Indian English fiction the author touches upon the merits and limitations of Indian fiction in English. The author in her survey divides Indian English novelists into four categories : early writers, native talents, native-aliens and a fourth group which consists of writers whose work transcends chronological or nationalistic categorization. The book consists of five chapters. Apart from "Introduction" the other chapters are devoted to each group separately.
See 1037, 2054, 4645, 5575, 6242, 6270, 6535.

421. Parker, Michael, Roger Starkey, eds. *Postcolonial literatures : Achebe, Ngugi, Desai, Walcott.* London : Macmillan, 1995.
Deals with literary theories, especially since 1968, and the growth of post-colonial literatures in English.
See 2704, 2721, 2751.

422. Pathak, R.S., ed. *Indian Fiction in English : Problems and Promises.* New Delhi : Northern Book Centre, 1990.
The book consists of seventeen essays on several authors as well as on individual works by different critics. Some of the main problems such as the quest for an assertion of identity, the choice of a medium, the artistic problems making allowances to the heterogeneous nature of the audience, the innovative techniques, the traits and tribulations of the Indian novel

in English along with its promises have been discussed. See 1186, 1426, 1567, 1623, 2042, 2650, 2697, 3126, 3329, 3519, 4092, 4692, 5681, 6605, 6626, 7190, 7566, 7812.

423. ——, ed. *Quest for Identity in Indian English Writing*. 2 Vols. New Delhi : Bahri Publications, 1992.
The book is a two volumed one, the first part of which is devoted to Indian English fiction and the second to poetry. The first one is a republication of the special issue of the journal, *Language Forum,* vol. 18.1-2 (1992) on "Quest for Identity in Indian English fiction" edited by R.S Pathak. The book contains 18 essays written by several critics on individual works of different novelists with the main focus on identity crisis and frustration of its search and/or affirmation.
See 2042, 2353, 2492, 2727, 3127, 3175, 3327, 3328, 4149, 4152, 4217, 4534, 4972, 5046, 5751, 6437, 7192, 7447.

424. ——, ed. *Recent Indian Fiction.* New Delhi : Prestige Books, 1994.
The book is an anthology of essays comprising fifteen papers by scholars making an objective assessment of the Indian English novel of the 1980s and 1990s. Evaluates thematic preoccupations, fictional forms and narrative techniques of twelve major novelists — Amitav Ghosh, Vikram Seth, Allan Sealy, Upamanyu Chatterjee, Shashi Tharoor, Farrukh Dhondy, Rohinton Mistry, Shashi Deshpande, Bharati Mukherjee, Nina Sibal, Namita Gokhale and Amit Chaudhuri.
See 2354, 2375, 3147, 3244, 3326, 3329, 3392, 4940, 4941, 5054, 7735, 7756, 7848, 8018, 8038.

425. ——, ed. *Indianization of English Language and Literature.* New Delhi : Bahri Publications, 1994.
A republication of the special issue of the journal, *Language Forum* 20.1-2 (1994).

426. ——, ed. *Indian Fiction of Nineties.* New Delhi : Creative Books, 1997.

427. ——. *Modern Indian Novel in English.* New Delhi : Creative Books,1999.

428. Pathan, B.A. *Gandhian Myth in English Literature in India.* Jaipur : Aavishkar Publishers, 1987.
The book is a study of the image of Gandhi in Indian English fiction in terms of its dynamic growth of being a myth. The author who finds the Gandhian impact in two ways (the historical and the fictional Gandhis) shows how the mythical Gandhi is made more fascinating in fiction. The text, instead of following the traditional method of discussing individual novels in terms of the Gandian myth, treats the Gandhian history chronologically and tries to find how each phase of Gandhian life has been treated by several Indian fiction writers. Hence, the division of the book into four major chapters on the subject (Birth of a Nation, the Herioc Age, The Partitioned Heart, Emergence of New India) with an "Introduction" and a final chapter "Conclusions". There is also an interesting chapter on the influence of Gandhian myth on other forms of literature.

429. Patil, V.T and H.V. Patil. *Gandhism and Indian English Fiction.* Delhi : Devika Publications, 1997.

430. Patil, Z.N. *Style in Indian English Fiction : A Study in Politeness Strategies.* New Delhi : Prestige Books, 1994.
The book analyses some Indian novels in terms of the operation of the principles of textual and interpersonal pragmatics discussing both positive and negative aspects in politeness strategies. The novels chosen for evaluation are of Anand, Raja Rao, Narayan, Khushwant Singh, Malgonkar, Chaman Nahal, Ahmed Ali, Humayun Kabir, Salman Rushdie, Sasthi Brata, Rama Mehta, Kamala Markandaya and Nayantara Sahgal.

431. Philip, David Scott. *Perceiving India: Through the Works of Nirad C. Chaudhuri, R.K. Narayan and Ved Mehta.* New Delhi : Sterling Publishers, 1986.
A study of the normative history of modern Indian intellectual life through a close analysis of the writings of Nirad C. Chaudhuri, R.K. Narayan and Ved Mehta. It examines the psychological processes of acculturation to an alien civilization and sketches an evolutionary progression from loss to recovery of the self.
See 5589.

432. Poddar, A., ed. *Indian Literature.* Shimla : Indian Institute of Advanced Study, 1972.
See 5461.

433. Prabhakar, T., ed. *The Indian Novel in English : Evaluations.* New Delhi : Phoenix Publishing House, 1995.
The book is a collection of critical essays on major novelists and their significant work covering most important aspects of the development of the genre of the novel in Indian English literature. Though the editor claims that "some of these articles have been already published in literary journals," all of them are published earlier either in journals or in anthologies.
See 665, 956, 1106, 1259, 1583, 1641, 1749, 2187, 2199, 2584, 2820, 3077, 3086, 4048, 4104, 4328, 4338, 4371, 4607, 4675, 5330, 5632, 5730, 6353, 6433, 6552, 7490, 7542.

434. Pradhan, N.S., ed. *Major Indian Novels : An Evaluation.* Ghaziabad : Vimal Prakasan, 1987.
The book is a collection of 12 essays on major Indian English novels. The essays, arranged in the order of publication of the novels, demonstrate as well the changing face of Indian English fiction over a forty years span, as proletarian, didactic novels gave way to more introspective fiction.

The purpose of the book as stated in the "Introduction" is "to choose a representative work and to provide an in-depth discussion leading to an overview of the novelist...to give to graduate students better range and depth and to scholars fresh insights and perspectives." See 1491, 1616, 2229, 2711, 3646, 4100, 4376, 4592, 5166, 5608, 6596, 7927.

435. Prasad, Anil Kumar. *The Village in Indo-Anglian Fiction.* Patna : Novelty & Co, 1994.

436. Prasad, Hari Mohan, ed. *Response : Recent Revelations of Indian Fiction in English.* Bareilly : Prakash Book Depot, 1983.

The book attempts to study the meaning and subtlety of the art of Indian fiction in English and the truth of its identity. It consists of two sections, the first of which is a conceptual one explicating the various facets of the fictional art, while the second makes a general appraisal of individual novelists as well as an in-depth, analytical study of the representative works of fiction by different critics.

See 1264, 1845, 2189, 2420, 2472, 2811, 2855, 3089, 3637, 4058, 4381, 4652, 5528, 6226, 6277, 6526, 6816, 7933.

437. Prasad, Madhusudan, ed. *Indian English Novelists : An Anthology of Critical Essays.* New Delhi : Sterling Publishers, 1982.

This is an anthology containing fourteen essays on several novelists, particularly the neglected authors of the old generation such as Ahmed Ali, Balachandra Rajan, and a number of the then newly-emerging novelists like Arun Joshi, Bharati Mukherjee, Chaman Nahal, M.V. Rama Sarma, Michael Chacko Daniels, Raji Narasimhan, Sasthi Brata and Veena Paintal by different critics.

The aim of the book is to draw attention to the novelists who have much potentiality and power but yet

neglected due to the critics "petty partisan affiliation." It attempts to demonstrate how effectively those novelists have evinced "an intensely felt Indian sensibility and new consciousness offering remarkable interpretations of imperishable Indian values as well as highlighting our cultural heritage."
See 1487, 2080, 2314, 2328, 2415, 2431, 2677, 4115, 5055, 5155, 5236, 6226, 6276, 7707.

438. Prasad, R.C. and A.K. Sharma, eds. *Modern Studies and Other Essays.* New Delhi : Vikas Publishing House, 1987.
A *festschrift* presented in honour of R.K. Sinha. Contains three essays on Indian English fiction.
See 1068, 4358, 5153.

439. Prasad, V.V. Rajendra. *Five Indian Novelists.* New Delhi : Prestige Books, 1990.
Analyses how the central theme of the self, the family and the society, with all their varying perspectives form the core of thought in five contemporary novelists — Rajan, Raja Rao, Narayan, Arun Joshi, and Anita Desai. It also looks at the central theme from two significant strains in contemporary Indian thought : transcendental and humanistic. In the seven chapters discussed the central five deal with individual writers with an introductory chapters on the socio-cultural milieu of the Indian novel in English and a concluding chapter which finds unity of the thought process in all the five novelists in spite of their varying modes of presentation.
See 2798, 4117, 5599, 6271, 6553.

440. Press, John. *Commonwealth Literature :Unity and Diversity in a Common Culture.* London : Heinemann, 1965.
Contains essays by Narayan, Rajan and others.

441. Radcliff-Umstead, Douglas, ed. *Transformations : From Literature to Film.* Kent : Romance Langs. Dept., Kent State University, 1987.

Contains an article on Narayan's *The Guide.*
See 5675.

442. Radha. K., ed. *Feminism and Literature.* Proc. of a seminar on feminism and Literature held as a part of the Silver Jubliee Celebrations of the Institute of English, Kerala University, Trivandrum from 8th Jan to 10th Jan. 1987. Trivandrum : Univ. of Kerala, 1987.
The book is an attempt to explore the writings by women and about women and discusses the ways and means for the study of literature with special reference to feminism and the concerns of women in our time. It throws light on several complex problems of women, both social and psychological, such as a search for feminine identity and the quest for self-definition.
Out of the thirtytwo essays dealing with various aspects of feminist literature which range from the Western concept of feminist literature and its relevance to Indian ethos to the new feministic consciousness in Indian as well as Indian English literature (poetry, drama and fiction), seven are on Indian English fiction.
See 570, 842, 1084, 1184, 1232, 1767, 2057, 2152, 2741.

443. Radhakrishnan, N. *Indo-Anglian Fiction : Major Trends and Themes.* Madras : Emerald, 1984.
A very brief and sketchy note on the major themes of Indian English fiction starting from the works of earlier novelists like Bankim Chandra, Lal Bahri and well-known writers like Anand, Raja Rao, Narayan, etc. to the lesser-known writers — Raj Gill, Nergis Dalal, Murari and others.

444. ——. *Research and Criticism.* Annamalai : Research Scholar Association, 1975.
Contains two articles on Indian English fiction.
See 593, 1072.

445. Raghavacharyulu, D.V.K, ed. *The Two-Fold Voice.* Vijayawada : Navodaya Publishers, 1971.
The book is the product of a seminar on 'Indian Writing in English' held at Guntur from 18-20 December 1970. Its aim is "to present a cross-section of critical views and values that could help the student of Indian Writing in English to discover [his/her] own stimulus and response and implicate his critical sensibility." Most of the essays in this volume were written by students.
See 1791, 3631, 4381, 5483, 5738, 6575.

446. ——. *The Critical Response.* New Delhi : Macmillan, 1980.
A collection of critical essays on American, Commonwealth, Indian and British traditions in literature, most of which are presented at seminars. Reflects a wide range of interests and concerns typical of contemporary literary scholarship in India.
See 3096, 5606.

447. Raizada, Harish. *The Lotus and The Rose* (Indian Fiction in English 1850-1947). Aligarh : AMU Faculty of Arts, 1978.
The book is a critical survey of Indian fiction in English between 1850 and 1947. The book attempts to evaluate the artistic merits of individual writers and to assess their contribution against the background of the different political and social changes in the life of the country. After tracing the origin and development of Indian fiction in English in the first chapter, "the Beginnings," the author discusses the growth of Indian English novel in three different stages of the nation's struggle for independence : (1) Before the advent of Gandhi in Indian politics, "The Indo-Anglian Fiction in the Era of National Awakening and Uprising (1900-1918)," (2) "Indo-Anglian Fiction in the Gandhian Era (1919-1936)", (3) "Indo-Anglian Fiction in the Period of Political Turmoil (1937-1947)." The last chapter "Conclusion" provides a "total view" of the Indian English novel.

448. Rajan, P.K., ed. *The Growth of the Novel in India.* New Delhi : Abhinav Publishers, 1989.
A survey, by different critics, of the novel in twelve major Indian languages including Indian English during the period 1950-80. Dealing with the major trends and tendencies that characterize the growth of the novel in India the book explores the established traditions and the new directions that the novel is likely to take in future.

449. Rajan, P.K., ed. *Changing Traditions in Indian English Literature.* New Delhi : Creative Books, 1995.
"A collection of occasional essays written by scholars under different compulsions which reveal their personal responses and critical perceptions." Out of several essays devoted to poetry, drama and fiction five are on fiction.
See 1764, 2462, 4916, 6517, 6532, 8034.

450. Rajan, P.K., K.M. George, A. Jameela Begum and K. Radha, eds. *Commonwealth Literature : Themes and Techniques.* Delhi : Ajanta Publications, 1993.
The book, an anthology published in honour of Prof. Ayyappa Paniker, consists of seventeen essays by leading critics in Commonwealth literature particularly post-colonial literatures in English. Out of seventeen articles there are two articles related to Indian English. One on Narayan by Syd Harrex and the other on the elements of fantasy in Indian English fiction by Prema Nandakumar.
See 983, 5424.

451. Rajeshwar, M. *Indian Women Novelists and Psychoanalysis.* New Delhi : Atlantic Publishers, 1998

452. Rajeshwar, M. and P.M. Rao, eds. *Indian Fiction in English.* New Delhi : Atlantic Publishers, 1999.

453. Raj Rao, R. *Ten Indian Writers in Interview.* Calcutta : Writers Workshop, 1991.

454. Ram, Atma. *Essays on Indian English Literature.* Aurangabad : Parimala Prakashan, 1983.

The book is an anthology of diverse articles on several subjects on Indian English literature published in some journals or presented/accepted as papers at conference, very often sketchy. The essays cover the works of Anand, Raja Rao, Narayan, Bhabani Bhattacharya, Anita Desai and Jhabvala.

See 1772, 1776, 1780, 2192, 2811, 3617, 5237, 5617, 6560, 6562.

455. ——. *Interviews with Indo-English Writers.* Calcutta : Writers Workshop, 1983.

The book presents interviews of the author with novelists : Mulk Raj Anand, Nergis Dalal, Nayantara Sahgal, K.A. Abbas, Khushwant Singh and Arun Joshi.

456. ——. *Morality in Tess and Other Essays.* New Delhi : Mittal Publications, 1996.

The book, published in honour of Mulk Raj Anand, is a collection of essays written by Atma Ram some of which were published earlier in journals and newspapers. Out of seventeen articles four are on Indian English novelists — Mulk Raj Anand, Anita Desai, Shiv K. Kumar and Bhabani Bhattacharya.

See 1781, 2193, 2812, 2813, 4259.

457. ——. *Indian Poetry and Fiction in English.* Delhi : Bahri Publications, 1991.

A collection of essays by Dr. Atma Ram published over the years in various periodicals and magazines, containing essays on Anand, Raja Rao, Anita Desai, Romen Basu, Pratap Sharma, Nayantara Sahgal, etc. and two interviews, one with R.K. Singh and the other with R.K. Srivastava.

458. Ramakrishna, D. *Close Encounters with the Muse : Essays and Letters on Indian Writing in English.* Eluru (Andhra Pradesh) : Published by D.V. Krishna Kumar, Secunderabad : Vecon Printers 1986.

The book comprises of essays and letters revealing how the personal acquaintance of the author with some of the writers like Mulk Raj Anand and Nayantara Sahgal has helped him in appreciating their philosophy of life. The articles included in this volume are the reactions of the author as a literary enthusiast to the works of the contemporary Indian writers in English.
See 1096.

459. Ramamurti, K.S. *The Rise of the Indian Novel in English.* Madhurai : Madhurai University, 1971. Rpt. by Sterling Publishers, 1987.
The book traces the rise of the Indian novel in English to certain socio-economic changes in 19th century India. It seeks to establish the view that its emergence was but one of the manifestations of a pan-Indian creative surge which operated simultaneously in all the languages in India, including English. It also aims "to redeem the older novels from neglect and adverse criticism."
The book consists of nine chapters of which the first two chapters are informative on the background and the genesis of the Indian novel in English. The earlier chapters devote their attention to the earliest of the Indian English novelists like Lal Behari Day, Toru Dutt, Krupa Bai, Mrs. Ghosal, Madhavaiah and others. The later chapters discuss a cross section of themes found in the recent novelists such as the East-West encounter and recent history of India. On the whole the book shows "the variety and multiplicity of the thematic and ideational strands which have gone into the making of the novels."

460. Ramaswamy, S. *Explorations : Essays on Commonwealth Literature.* Banglore : M.C.C. Publicaitons, 1988.
Out of the several articles (the author refers them as "stray essays") on different genres of Commonwealth literature only two are on Indian fiction in English.
See 6275, 6567.

461. ——. *Commentaries on Commonwealth Fiction.* New Delhi : Prestige Books, 1994.
The book contains essays on some of the writers of Canada (Hugh Maclennan, Morley Callaghan), Australia (Patrick White, Henry Handal, Richardson), Newzealand (Katherine Mansfield), Africa (Woly Soyinka) and India (Raja Rao, Vikram Seth, B. Rajan, and Rohinton Mistry). Some of the essays are interdisciplinary and some others are writers from a specific cultural perspective or a definite Indological-philosophical point of view. The essays, as the author pronounced, are commentaries on Commonwealth literature written over a period of twentyfive years in a variety of contexts. Some of them were published in journals earlier.
See 1112, 4945, 6275, 6567, 7768.

462. Rangra, Ranavir. *Interviews with Indian Writers.* Delhi : B.R. Publishing Corporation, 1992.
Out of the thirtyfive interviews collected in the book one is on Raja Rao entitled "Beyond the Body and Mind" conducted by the author in New Delhi on 4th May 1985.

463. Rao, A.V. Krishna. *The Indo-Anglian Novel and the Changing Tradition.* Mysore : Rao & Raghavan, 1972.
The book, one of the earliest written on Indian writing in English contains a critical examination of the novels of contemporary novelists writing in English — Anand, Raja Rao, Narayan and Kamala Markandaya — with a view to explore the attitudes and responses of these novelists to tradition and change and to trace the divergent visions of Modern India's destiny. While examining their responses and reactions to the changing tradition the author investigates their common cultural impulsion and their divergent aesthetic motivations and the distinct ways in which these novelists have used the novel as a basic literary form. He also brings into focus the significant similarities and contrasts among

these novelists in style, content and purpose of their writing.

The book contains six chapters. The first one is "Introduction" in which the author traces the development of Indian English fiction and shows how it has not only been a product of change but has also become a major vehicle of the consciousness of change encompassing various evolutionary cycles of the modern Indian sensibility. He divides the novels into four categories : The novel of experience (M.R. Anand), the novel of sensibility (Kamal Markandaya), the novel of affirmation (R.K. Narayan), the novel of prophecy (Raja Rao) and discusses them in terms of the novelists' work.

See 1783, 4663, 5633, 6572.

464. Rao, E. Nageswara. *The Critical Pursuit.* New Delhi : Reliance Publishing House, 1994.

The book is a collection of twenty essays selected by the author from the critical articles written by him in the last four decades. Fifteen of them were published in journals in India and abroad. Some of them were presented in seminars and conferences. Out of these articles two are on Indian fiction in English.

See 1787, 4667.

465. Rao, A. Ramakrishna. *Comparative Perspectives on Indian Literature.* New Delhi : Prestige Books, 1992.

The book is a *festschrift* presented to R.A. Jayantha. The anthology of essays presents diverse critical approaches evolved either from the traditional Indian concepts or Western poetics to evaluate Indian literature including Indian English fiction.

See 1124, 6537, 6568.

466. Rao, A. Ramakrishna and M. Sivaramkrishna, eds. *When East Meets West : Indian Thought in Anglo-Indian and Indo-English Fiction.* New Delhi : Sterling Publishers, 1994.

The book is a collection of papers presented at a seminar on "the impact of philosophy on Anglo-Indian and Indian English fiction" at Osmania University in 1986. Evaluates the influence of Indian philosophy on the novelists and the artistic means with which they explored its intricacies and presented in fictional medium. The book contains eighteen articles out of which ten are on Indian English fiction.
See 680, 1124, 2034, 2035, 2644, 2892, 3084, 4128, 4668, 5714, 6272, 6463, 6652.

467. Rao, M. Subba. *Readings in Indo-Anglian Literature : Prospective and Retrospective.* 2 vols. Delhi : Kanishka Publications, 1995.
A two-volumed book devoted to Indian English Literature — Poetry, drama, fiction and prose. While the second volume consists of articles on poetry the first volume sub-titled "Tradition and Modernity in Indo-Anglian Literature" contains articles on other genres out of which six are on fiction.
See 1788, 1789, 1790, 5649, 6580, 7539.

468. Rao, T.V. Subba. *Indian Writing in English : Is there Any Worth in it?* Madhurai : Kodal Publishers, 1976.
An unfavourable comment on Indian English literature in general. Feels that "the ordering of experience and its powerful expression is not possible in a language which is not our own."

469. Rao, B. Shymala and Krishnanand Joshi. *Studies in Indo-Anglian Literature.* Bareilly : Prakash Book Depot, 1972.
See 307.

470. Rao, C.R. Visweswara, ed. *Indian Writing Today* (Essays in honour of Prof. L.S.R. Krishna Sastry). New Delhi : Indian Association for English Studies, 1996.
The book is an anthology of essays presented in honour of Prof. Krishna Sastry. It deals with various approaches ranging from psychoanalysis to stylistic analysis, from political allegory to women's question in

the works of contemporary writers (post-modern novelists) including Anand, Raja Rao and Narayan.
See 1088, 1211, 2579, 3162, 3173, 4402, 4688, 4721, 5563, 5770, 6643, 6938,7517, 7827.

471. Ratnam, A., ed. *Chiaroscuro : Critical Essays on Indian English Literature* Parbhani (Maharastra) : Dnyanopasak Prakashan, 1991.
The book is an anthology of critical essays written with a view to re-evaluate and reinterpret some of the works of Anand, Narayan and Desai and to highlight the achievement of the lesser known writers like Prema Nanda Kumar and Ranga Rao.
See 652, 1786, 2816, 5223, 5639, 5643, 6795.

472. Reddy, G. Aswathanarayan. *Indian Writing in English and Its Audience.* Bareilly : Prakash Book Depot, 1978.
The book sets itself the task of "mapping critical responses" to Indian-English literature in order to sort out the literary issues from the socio-political polemic which has been the bane of this field of criticism since the times of Macaulay.

473. Reddy, D.J.P.N., ed. *Literary Spectrum* (Essays in Homage to Prof. N. Krishna Rao). New Delhi : Arnold Associates, 1995.

474. Reddy, P. Bayapa. *Studies in Indian Writing in English.* New Delhi : Prestige Books, 1990.
The book is a collection of critical essays dealing with various aspects of Indian writing in English. While the major focus is on Indian drama in English it contains four essays on Indian fiction in English and an interview with Raja Rao.
See 4386, 4684, 7225, 7226.

475. Reddy, K. Venkata. *Major Indian Novelists.* New Delhi : Prestige Books, 1990.
The book is a collection of research papers on Anand, Raja Rao, Narayan, Bhabani Bhattacharya and Kamala

Markandaya contributed by the author to several journals and books. The book discusses the themes, structures, narrative techniques, symbols, literary values and styles of the individual works of these authors, answering some of the serious charges levelled against some crucial evaluations of the novels chosen for study.
See 1135, 1792, 1793, 1794, 2203, 2204, 4685, 4686, 5658, 5659, 6583.

476. ——. *Critical Studies in Commonwealth Literature.* New Delhi : Prestige Books, 1994.

477. Reddy, K. Venkata and P.B. Reddy, ed. *The Indian Novel with Social Purpose.* New Delhi : Atlantic Publishers, 1999.

478. Riemenschneider, D. *Der Modern English- Sprachige Roman Indiens* (The Modern Indian Novel in English). Darmstadt : Thesen Verlag, 1977.

479. ——. *Shiva Tanzt.* Das indische Kulturlesebuch, Zurich : Unionsverlag, 1986. Rpt. in 1987.
Contains essays or excerpts from essays on Indian Literature by Raja Rao, Salman Rushdie and Ka-Naa Subramanyam.

480. ——. *The History and Historiography of Commonwealth Literature.* Tubingen : Narr, 1981.
Contains an essay on Indian-English literature by G. N. Devy.

481. ——. *Studies in Indian Ficiton in English.* Dharwad : Karnatak University, 1983.
Contains essays on Anand and Indian women writers writing in English in the 1970's.

482. ——, ed. *Critical Approaches to The New Literatures in English.* Essen : Blaue Eule, 1989.
See 7275.

483. Ringbom, Haken and Matti Rissanen, eds. *Proc. from the Second Nordic Conference of English Studies.* Abo (Finland) : Abo Academi, 1984.
Out of several essays one is on Indian English fiction.
See 1022.

484. Rizvi, S.N.A., ed. *The Twofold Voice : Essays in Honour of Ramesh Mohan.* Salzburg : Inst fun Anglistic and Americanistik University, 1982.
The book, a *festschrift* presented to Prof. Ramesh Mohan, contains two parts, one devoted to language and style and the other to literature. Part II has seven articles of which one is on Anita Desai.
See 2709.

485. Ross, Robert L., ed. *International Literature in English : Essays on the Major Writers.* Chicago /London : St. James Press, 1991.
The book is a collection of critical essays on several authors across the globe written by different critics on their attitudes and approaches. Out of fiftynine essays nine are on Indian English novelists.
See 1564, 2714, 3564, 4595, 5014, 5446, 6901, 7455, 7855.

486. Rushdie, Salman and Elizabeth West, eds. *The Vintage Book of Indian Writing 1947-1997.* London : Random House, 1997.

487. Rutherford, Anna. *Commonwealth.* Ianmark : Aarhus University, 1971.
Contains the essay, "Contemporary Creative Prose Writing in English."
See 745.

488. ——, ed. *From Commonwealth to Post-colonial.* Coventry (Australia) : Dangaroo Press, 1992.
Consists of the papers presented at the Silver Jubilee conference of the Association for Commonwealth Literature and Language Studies (Australia) on

"Tranformations : Cross-Cultural Communities, New Forms and Functions of Commonwealth Literature", in 1989.
Out of several essays six are on Indian fiction in English.
See 830, 833, 864, 871, 3389, 4642, 5022, 7099, 7728.

489. Rutherford, Anna, Lars Jensen and Shirley Chew, eds. *Into the Nineties : Post-colonial Women's Writing*. Coventry (Australia) : Dangaroo Press, 1994.
A reprint of the special issue, *Kunapipi* 16.1 (1994). Features a good selection of creative pieces by Indian writers, prefaced by short sections entitled "Why I Write?" The contributors include Shashi Deshpande, Gita Hariharan, Sunetra Gupta, Bharati Mukherjee, etc.

490. Sampietro, Luigi, ed. *Declarations of Cultural Independence in the English Speaking World : A Symposium*. Milan: D'Imperio Editore Navara, 1989.
See 684, 6996.

491. Sanyal, Samares, C. *Indianness in Major Indo-English Novels*. Bareilly : Prakash Book Depot, 1984
A survey of Indian English Fiction (particularly by major novelists) its growth and its thematic preoccupations aimed at showing how an Indian novel in English has been from the beginning "more a product of national consciousness than mere imitation of Western model." The author analyses the problems of the Indian novelists in English in presenting the nuances of Indian life and in using English as a medium of expression and shows that in spite of the European influence on their style and technique their novels in English truly express Indian consciousness and they have succeeded in their experiments in giving English an Indian tone and colouring thus making Indian writing in English a part of a cultural and linguistic unity of India. The book consists of seven chapters. Starting with the origin and

development of Indian English the author analyses the works, their thematic and technical concerns and relate them to Indian literary tradition.

492. ——. *English Language in India : Indo-Anglian Prose Style.* Elms Court : Artar H.S. Stockwell, 1987.
Tracing the development of English studies in India the author tries to find out both the advantages and shortcomings of its use in Indian fiction in English in 19th and 20th centuries. He specially chooses Narayan's fiction to show its distinct quality of naturalness characterised by control and subtlety. There are also two short chapters on Raja Rao's and Anand's use of language and diction.

493. ——. *Indian Asceticism in R.K. Narayan and Other Indian English Novelists.* Bareilly : Prakash Book Depot, 199?

494. Sarma, G.P. *Nationalism in Indo-Anglian Fiction.* Delhi : Sterling Publishers, 1970, 2nd ed. 1990.
A critical survey of Indian fiction in English, its genesis, growth and motivation. Claiming its birth to be in 1838 and its motivation as the consciousness of political dependence and reforming zeal in pre-Independence India and the euphoric and satiric reaction to the state of affairs in the country after Independence, the author states that the Indian fiction in English is not a transplantation but indigenous to the national soil.
The book contains eight chapters. While the first chapter briefly surveys Indian nationalism — social, religious, cultural aspects of it, the last one discusses the impact of the peculiar Indian environment on English language, the process of naturalization undergone by the English and the skilful and effective use of it by Indian novelists. It is a doctoral dissertation published in the form of a book.

495. Sarma, G.V.L.N., ed. *Essays and Studies.* Machilipatnam (Andhra Pradesh) : Triveni Publishers, 1977.
This is a felicitation volume presented as *a festschrift* to Prof. Viswanatham. It contains 18 critical essays written by different critics out of which three are on Indian fiction in English.
See 1157, 3636, 7943.

496. Sarma, S.K. *Twentieth Century Indian Writing in English.* Guntur (Andhra Pradesh) : Andhra University, 1977.

497. Saxena, O.P. *Glimpses of Indo-English Fiction.* 3 vol. New Delhi : Jainson Publications, 1987.
The three-volumed anthology of essays on Indian English fiction is the most unsystematic anthology that has been published in the area. The "contents" page does not mention the names of the contributors and we have to look for their names in the "Introduction" which doesn't contain mentions of either all the essays or the essays of the critics. (A little bit of an exercise for the researcher too!).
Even in the contents the volumes are uneven. For example the first essays of the second volume are verbatim reproduction of the first eight essays of R.M. Varma's *Some Aspects of Indo-English Fiction.* If this venture is to bring together several articles haphazardly from different journals or books the editor doesn't even mention this in his so-called "Introduction." However, all these articles except those of which the authorship is not specific have individual entries.
See
Vol. I. 1054, 2476, 3632, 4058, 5324, 5337, 5722, 5733, 5763, 5765.
Vol. II. 869, 1249, 2235, 3662, 3663, 3664, 4617, 4732, 4733, 5325, 5461, 5730, 5764, 5766, 5767.
Vol. III. 1814, 3633, 4084, 4130, 4333, 5677, 5678, 6358.

498. Seshadri, Vijayalakshmi. *The New Woman in Indian English Women Writers Since the 1970s.* New Delhi : B.R. Publishing Corporation, 1995.

499. Sharma, Govind Narain, ed. *Literature and Commitment : A Commonwealth Perspective.* Proc. of the third Commonwealth-in-Canada Conference held in 1985. Toronto (Canada) : TSAR, 1988.
Contains an article on Salman Rushdie.
See 7026.

500. Sharma, Krishna Dayal. *Protest in Post-Independence Indian English Fiction.* Jaipur : Bohra Publications, 1995.
The book deals with the theme of protest — political (protest against the alien rule as well as protest against the internal misrule), social and familial in post-Independence Indian English fiction. Also discusses the various modes and techniques depicted in the selected novels of Indian English writers. The novelists selected are Abbas, Anand, Malgonkar, Nahal, Bhattacharya, Jhabvala, Anita Desai, Khushwant Singh, Nayantara Sahgal. Also a brief comparison is made with writers of colonial countries to highlight the racial segregation and struggle.

501. Sharma, K.K., ed. *Indo-English Literature : A Collection of Critical Essays.* Ghaziabad : Vimal Prakashan, 1977.
The present volume is an attempt to make a comprehensive and critical appraisal of some of the basic aspects of the mind and art of major Indian creative writers in English. It comprises twenty essays out of which two are reproductions of already published articles. While a larger part of the book is devoted to fiction, there are some general articles such as "In Defence of Indian Writing in English" and "Literature and Naitonal Character in Regard to Indo-English Literature." The prominent fiction writers that

are discussed here are Anand, Raja Rao, Bhattacharya and Anita Desai.
See 583, 955, 1202, 1600, 1650, 1680, 2214, 2717, 5403, 5789, 6425, 6554, 6560.

502. ——, ed. *Feminism and Literature*. Delhi : K.K. Publications, 1996.
Deals with historical perspective of feminist movement: the genesis of feminism and its futurity.
See 1173, 2522, 3190, 7450.

503. Sharma, K.K. and B.K. Johri. *The Partition in Indo-English Novels*. Ghaziabad : Vimal Prakasan, 1984.
A comprehensive appraisal of the theme of partition in Indian English novels, the book tries to bring out the patterns of reaction by Indian English novelists to the horror and tragedy of partition. While writers like R.K. Narayan, Attia Hosain, Balachandra Rajan treat the theme of partition as a side issue in their novels. Manohar Malgonkar and Khushwant Singh depict the atrocity and shameful deeds, brutal killing and inhuman acts of violence in their novels. Chaman Nahal's *Azadi* offers a psychological treatment of partition while the Sikh novelists — Raj Gill, H.S. Gill and K.S. Duggal — have delineated the theme artistically.
See 1174, 1175, 3453, 4391, 5163, 5692, 6278, 7951.

504. Sharma, Sudharshan. *The Influence of Gandhian Ideology on Indo-Anglian Fiction*. New Delhi : Soni Book Agency, 1982.
An inadequate critical work on Gandhi's influence on Indian English fiction. Traces the influence of Gandhian ideology in several Indian English novels which include the novels of major (Anand, Raja Rao and Narayan) and minor writers (Abbas, Nagarajan, Venkataramani, Attia Hosain, Padmini Sen Gupta and others). While the author finds the political and economic aspects of Gandhian ideology in Anand's novels, the moral virtues are traced in Narayan's novels. Regards Raja Rao's

Kanthapura as the quintessence of Gandhian philosophy.

505. Sharma, S.D. *Thematic Dichotomy of Writing in Indian English Indology and Culture.* Bareilly : Prakash Book Depot, 198?.

506. Shirwadkar, Meena. *Image of Woman in the Indo-Anglian Novel.* New Delhi : Sterling Publishers, 1979.

A study of the image of woman in Indian English fiction from the Sita — Pativrata image — the shadowy, suffering pathetic creature, to the emergence of the new woman with an awareness of individuality, thus tracing the pattern of evolution of the images of woman from romantic idealization to realistic portrayal. The book contains five chapters. While the introductory chapter gives a general background to the types of women found in literature both in the East and the West the other chapters discuss the image of Indian woman from the 'dark room' of traditional Indian household to the arena of modern political and social activity both from the point of view of Western and Indian Writers. The last chapter is a summing up of all the chapters bringing together the male/female conflicts inherent in cultural, social and literary traditions, images, myths and attitudes.

507. Singh, Avadhesh K., ed. *Contemporary Indian Fiction in English.* New Delhi : Creative Books, 1993.

The book is a collection of papers contributed to a national seminar on "Critical Appraisal of Post-Independence Indian Fiction in English" organised by the Department of English, Saurastra University, Rajkot in February, 1991.

The book consists of fifteen essays of which seven are of general nature dealing with major issues of Indian fiction in English such as the concept of Indian novel, fiction of the interface, new voices in Indian English novels of 80s, etc. The rest of the essays are concerned

with the study of the fictional form, narrative technique and the major thematic preoccupations of the individual writers.
See 697, 824, 896, 897, 906, 1190, 1203, 1250, 1429, 2327, 2851, 2897, 3150, 4142, 4699, 7120, 7281, 8037.

508. Singh, Kirpal, ed. *Through Different Eyes.* Calcutta : Writers Workshop, 1984.
The book is the reprint of the special issue of the *Journal of Indian Writing in English,* Vol. 8 Nos. 1-2 (1983) devoted to foreign responses to Indian writing in English. It is a collection of essays on modern Indian writing in English making an objective evaluation of the works and turning it into a meaningful discussion of its appreciation. There are fourteen articles on all genres: poetry, fiction and drama.
See 575, 1482, 2585, 2893, 3558, 4400, 4649, 4728, 6402, 7490.

509. ——, ed. *The Writer's Sense of the Past : Essays in South-East Asian and Australian Literature.* CSAL/Nus : Singapore University, 1987.
A collection of papers presented at the conference on South-East Asian and Australian literatures held in Singapore in 1984. Contains articles discussing the problems of writers from "plural" societies in constituting their cross-cultural parts from a variety of perspectives and theoretical propositions. Contains an article on R.K. Narayan.
See 5392.

510. Singh, R.A. and V.L.V.N.Narendra Kumar, ed. *Critical Studies on Indian Fiction in English.* New Delhi : Atlantic Publishers, 1999.

511. Singh, R.K., ed. *Indian English Writing 1981-1985 : Experiment with Impression.* New Delhi : Bahri Publications, 1987.

The book, a reprint of *Language Forum* 12.1-4 (1988), presents overview of the literary activities in Indian English during the period, 1981-1985. It contains articles by different critics who examine "Indianness" in Indian English literature. It also presents the diversity of themes and styles, of the forms and techniques, of the veracity of Indian English creativity. The book is mostly devoted to Indian English poetry. Out of the 12 essays two are on fiction.
See 727, 2487, 7114.

512. ——, ed. *Anger in Action : Explorations in Indian Writing in English.* New Delhi : Bahri Publications, 1997.

513. Singh, R.S. *Indian Novel in English.* New Delhi : Arnold Heinemann, 1977.
The book is a general survey of Indian English novel from its inception in the 1860s to 1971 highlighting the distinct features of its development through various stages — the growth from historical romance, social realism and psychological probing into individual personality. It combines literary history with criticism.
See 1200, 1201, 1839, 2223, 2856, 3649, 4144, 4395, 4702, 5708, 6621.

514. Singh, Ram Sewak and Charu Sheel Singh. *Spectrum History of Indian Literature in English.* New Delhi : Atlantic Publishers. 1999

515. Singh, Shailendra Dhari. *Novels on the Indian Mutiny.* New Delhi : Arnold Heinemann, 1973.

516. Singh, Surendra. *Princely Life in Indian English Writing.* New Delhi : Reliance Publishing House, 1995.
The book deals with the different facets of princely life as depicted in Indian English fiction with special reference to Anand, Malgonkar, Markandaya, Jhabvala and S.K. Ghosh.
The study is an attempt in the direction of understanding the life-style of the medieval kings, queens

and concubines who lived anachronistically well beyond the time of medievalism.

517. Singh, Sushila, ed. *Feminism and the Recent Fiction in English.* New Delhi : Prestige Books, 1991.

The book is a collection of papers presented in a seminar on feminism held in Nov. 1989 at the women's college of the Banaras Hindu University during its Diamond Jubilee Year. It reviews the key issues concerned with feminism and its application in the reading of recent fiction in English which includes Indian English, British, American, Black American and Canadian fiction.

The book contains 24 essays of which 5 essays discuss the concept and the ideology of feminism while others analyse the novels of individual authors from the feminist point of view. The Indian English novelists discussed in this book are Kamala Markandaya, Anita Desai, Shashi Deshpande, Nayantara Sahgal, Mulk Raj Anand and Veena Paintal.

See 781, 953, 1032, 1204, 1837, 2778, 3167, 3172, 4586, 4714, 6227, 7309, 7549.

518. Sinha, K.N., ed. *Indian Writing in English.* New Delhi : Heritage, 1979.

The book is an anthology of twenty three essays on different genres and authors of Indian English literature out of which a major part is devoted to fiction. The articles on fiction are of two types: auto-biographical and critical. While the autobiographical/biographical writings on Mulk Raj Anand and Raja Rao ("An Interview with Raja Rao") are of particular interest towards an understanding of these writers, the other critical articles throw light on different aspects of such novelists as Anand, Raja Rao, Jhabvala and Narayan. In addition there are five articles on Indian writing in English which deal with some general characteristics of this branch.

See 660. 894, 1069, 1217, 1844, 3639, 5548, 5598, 6552.

519. Sinha, R.N. and Sinha, R.K., ed. *The Indian Novel in English.* Ranchi : Ankil Publishers, 1987.
The critical essays on the Indian novel in English in this collection are intended to be "periodic records of assessment". Each one of the fourteen essays is either the study of a specific novel or the exploration of some theme in one or several novels of a particular author. Apart from one general essay — "The Theme of the Partition of India in Indian novel in English" – and two on comparative literature: "Henrich Boll's *The Lost Honor of Katharine Blum* and Salman Rushdie's *Shame:* Narrative Stance and Strategies", "Oral Tradition in *Kanthapura* and *Arrow of God,*" the other essays are on individual works and writers.
See : 668, 2475, 2801, 4061, 4223, 5750, 6617, 6624, 7116, 7172, 7211, 7511, 7909.

520. Smith Larry E., ed. *Discourse Across Cultures : Strategies in World of Englishes.* London : Princeton Hall, 1987.
Contains an article on Raja Rao.
See 6543.

521. Soc des Anglicistes de l'Enseignement Superieur, ed. *Actes du Congres d'Amiens, 1982.* Paris : Dider, 1987.
See 5556.

522. Spencer, Dorothy, M. *Indian Fiction in English.* Philadelphia : Univ of of Pennyslvania Press, 1960.
The book is actually an annotated bibliography but it contains a long introductory essay which discusses certain aspects of Indian English writing such as characterization (the image of the ideal woman, peasant sensibility, etc.) and the attitudes and values of the novelists.

523. Srinath, C.N. *The Literary Landscape : Essays on Indian Fiction and Poetry in English.* Delhi Mittal Publications. 1986.

The book is an anthology of essays on Indian English fiction and poetry, many of them published earlier in journals. Though the blurb claims that the present book is intended to throw light on less-known, ever-ignored novels from the past, the essays are mainly concerned with the more well-known novelists such as R.K. Narayan, G.V. Desani and Arun Joshi. What makes the book interesting is its dealing with some general aspects of Indian life as reflected in the Indian writing in English — such as the changing idea of the down-trodden, the treatment of the river Ganga and the native themes found in Indian English fiction. Even in these general articles thrust is given to well-known novelists and their novels.
See 1212, 1213, 1214, 1215, 1850, 2037, 3102, 4145, 4146, 4147, 5719.

524. Srivastava, A.K., ed. *Alien Voices : Perspectives on Commonwealth Literature.* Lucknow : Print House, 1981.
The book offers various reasons for the study of Commonwealth literature and discusses the problems of its evolution and its assessment. While suggesting different approaches for its critical appreciation the author suggests the "comparative method" as the most rewarding one. Out of twentyone essays on several authors by different critics, eight are on Indian English fiction.
See 568, 622, 889, 1064, 1075, 1171, 1470, 4088, 4530, 5624, 6564.

525. Srivastava, Ramesh. K. *Six Indian Novelists in English : Raja Rao, R.K. Narayan, Kamala Markandaya, Bhabhani Bhattacharya, Anita Desai and Arun Joshi.* Ghaziabad : Vimal Prakashan, 1987.
The book is an anthology of critical essays on the six major Indian novelists. Many of them were presented in conferences and seminars and published in literary

journals. The book evaluates several representative works of these novelists bringing out their literary values, symbols, structures, narrative techniques and styles without, at the same time, ignoring their drawbacks. The book contains six parts each one dealing with a particular novelist. The part devoted to Kamala Markandaya is the largest one comprising nine chapters. See 2226, 2228, 2229, 2865, 2867, 4150, 4704, 4705, 4707, 4708, 4709, 4710, 4711, 4712, 4713, 5722, 5723, 6634, 6635.

526. ——, ed. *Colonial Consciousness in Black American, African and Indian Fiction in English.* Jalandhar : ABS Publications, 1991.
The book is an anthology consisting of seventeen critical essays on the theme of colonial consciousness. Some of them were written for the presentation in the seminar on "colonial consciousness" organized by the Dept. of English, Guru Nanak University, Amritsar in March, 1989. While the first essay "Colonial Consciousness and Identity Crisis : The Case of Black American, Indian and African Novelists," serves as an introduction to the theme of colonialism, nine essays out of seventeen deal with the novels of Indian writers in English.
See 805, 1836, 2142, 2606, 4334, 4716, 6396, 7473, 7937, 7945, 7984,

527. ——, ed. *Symbolism in Indian Fiction in English.* Jalandhar : ABS Publication, 1997
See : 1669, 2191, 2225, 2868, 3091, 3143, 3313, 4053, 4355, 4704, 4721, 5053, 5609, 5632, 6401,7115,7479, 7758, 7985.

528. Srivatsava, Sharad. *The New Woman in Indian English Fiction.* New Delhi : Creative Books, 1996.

529. Steinvorth, Klaus. *The Indo-English Novel : The Impact of the West on Literature in a Developing Country.* Weisbaden : Franz Steineer, Verlag, 1975.

Defines the terms "Indo-English'' and "Anglo-India" and surveys the Indian English novel from Bankim Chandra Chatterjee and Toru Dutt to Anita Desai and Arun Joshi. The book is based on the assumption that the Indian English novel is not genuinely 'Indian' : it is 'Indian' only in so far as that description goes, it is "a pretext for the depiction of exotic details and extravagance of language".

The book is divided into four parts. While the "Introduction" speaks of the general trends of criticism, "The Background" discusses the literary situation in India. The other part, "The Study of the Novels with a View to Their Effect on Readers", tries to demonstrate that Indian writers have foreign audience in mind by listing 'direct' and 'indirect' references. The last one "The Problem of Language" deals with the linguistic experiments by the novelists. The author feels that "the language of the most Indian English writers show a tendency towards pompous rhetoric ... emotional extravaganza or stereotypal phrases."

The Book is based on the doctoral thesis submitted to the University of Hamburg in 1973, originally written in German.

530. Subba Rayudu, A.V. *Gandhian Ideology and Indian Novel.* New Delhi : Prestige Books, 1998.

531. Suneel, Seema. *Man-Woman Relationship in Indian English Fiction* (with a focus on Shashi Deshpande, Rajendra Awasthi and Syed Abdul Malik). New Delhi : Prestige Books, 1995.

Examines the treatment of man-woman relationship in Indian fiction in English with special reference to three contemporary novels — Deshpande's *The Dark Holds No Terror,* Syed Abdul Malik's *The Tale of Nomadic Soul* and Rajendra Awasthi's *The Creeping Shadows.*

See 1228, 3182, 3183.

532. Syal Pushpinder. *Structure and Style in Commonwealth Literature.* New Delhi : Vikas Publishing House, 1994.
The book analyses the language, structure, and style of literary works in English by writers belonging to Commonwealth countries. It focuses on the transformations, variations and innovations that have taken place in the English language in the hands of non-native writers. While evaluating the works of some Commonwealth writers such as Achebe, Soyinka, Rushdie, Anita Desai and others, the author furthers a discussion of links of the writers with the cultural context, implications of readership and explores further interpretative possibilities. Out of the seven articles two are on Indian English novelists.
See : 2878, 7291.

533. Trivedi, Harish. *Colonial Transactions : English Literature and India.* Manchester : Manchester University Press, 1993.

534. Trivedi, Harish and Meenakshi Mukherjee, eds. *Interrogating Post-Colonialism : Theory, Text and Context.* Shimla : Indian Institute of Advanced Study, 1996.
The book is a collection of essays presented at an international conference in 1994 organized by the Indian Association for Commonwealth Literature and Language Studies with, and at, the Indian Institute of Advanced Study, Shimla.
The nomenclature, nature, ideology, scope and applicability of post-colonialism are interrogated in their many aspects and from a wider variety of approaches by scholars from India, Australia, Canada and England. While the first ten essays deal with theoretical and general issues relating to post-colonialism, the other essays examine post-colonialism with specific reference to Indian texts and contexts. Out of twenty essays ten are on Indian writing in English — eight are on general issues and two are on individual authors.

See 630, 719, 792, 849, 911, 1062, 1242, 1263, 1450, 3301, 6903, 8015.

535. Tucker, Martin and John Ferres, eds. *Modern Commonwealth Literature.* New York: Frederick Ungar Publishers, 1977.

A references book covering 175 authors of which 20 are from India, including Raja Rao, Narayan and Khushwant Singh.

536. Uma, Alladi. *Women and Her Family : Indian and Afro-American — A Literary Perspective.* Delhi: Sterling Publishers, 1989.

The book, a Ph.D. dissertation, discusses the status and role of woman in Indian and African cultures offering sociological perspectives. In its six chapters the author discusses the role of woman in her various capacities — woman as wife, as mother, as daughter, and as grandmother.

In the introduction the historical background of the development of the image of the Afro-American and Indian woman is stressed. Though apparently an inconceivable comparative study the book logically argues the nature and struggle of the woman in the two cultures. They have adopted themselves to certain circumstances, gone through experiences and come out of them "strong yet vulnerable, hurt but dignified". For this purpose she chooses the Indian women writers — Anita Desai, Shashi Deshpande, Kamala Markandaya and Nayantara Sahgal.

537. Vakel, Hilla, ed. *Indian Writers at Chidambaram.* Bombay : All India P.E.N. Centre, 1957.

Papers presented at the All India Writers' Conference, Annamalainagar, 1954.

538. Vanden Driesen, Cynthia. *Centering the Margins: Perspectives on Literatures in English from India, Africa and Australia.* New Delhi : Prestige Books, 1995.

539. Varma, R.M. *Some Aspects of Indo-English Fiction.* New Delhi : Jaisons Publicaitons, 1984.
The book contains research papers on Narayan, Jhabvala, Kamala Markandaya and others — presented by the author at various conferences and seminars in India. It touches upon some significant aspects of these novelists — for example, the bicultural world of Kamala Markandaya, the spiritual path and the suffering humanity in Jhabvala's novels, the vision of evil in Narayan's *The Man Eater of Malgudi,* the Hindu ethos and the physical setting as prominent pointers in the novels of Narayan.
See 1249, 2235, 3662, 3663, 3664, 4732, 4733, 5763, 5764, 5765, 5766, 5767.

540. Venugopal, C.V. *The Indian Short Story in English.* Bareilly : Prakash Book Depot, 1976.
The book is a pioneering and comprehensive study of the Indian short story — its origin, development, achievement and promise. It analyses the varied themes and subjects dealt with in the Indian short story and the technical devices to show how the form of the short story has its roots in ancient Indian texts like *Panchatantra, Jataka Tales,* etc., and how, at the same time, it is influenced by the modern Western short story. Individual chapters are devoted to major writers like Manjari Isvaran, Anand, Raja Rao and Narayan which illustrate how the short story has achieved its maturity in the hands of these writers, while Jhabvala, K.A. Abbas, Khushwant Singh and others are treated as belonging to the minor group in the chapter entitled "Other Writers."

541. Verghese, C Paul. *Problems of the Indian Creative Writer in English.* Bombay : Somaiya Publications, 1971.
The book is a summary of some sections of the author's dissertation on the problems of Indian writers in English. However, the present work, in its book form,

doesn't focus on the 'problems' of the Indian English writer, but presents a chronological discussion of some individual writers of poetry and fiction along with a general survey of Indian drama in English. As far as Indian fiction is concerned there are four chapters (8-11) devoted to some general aspects of Indian fiction in English followed by a critical assessment of the three major novelists : Anand, Raja Rao and Narayan.

It is in the general section on fiction that he discusses some of the problems that confront the Indian fiction writer writing in English — the major problems discussed being the suitability and adaptability of using English as a medium, the creation of Indian consciousness and the consequent themes that ensue from it.

See 1870, 5776, 6651.

542. ——. *Essays on Indian Writing in English.* Delhi : N.V. Publications, 1975.

The book is a collection of critical writings on all genres — poetry, fiction and criticism in Indian English literature — published in journals and newspapers. The aim of the book is to highlight the significant uses of the educated Indian mind.

See 1259.

543. Verma, C.D. *The Exile Hero and the Reintegrating Vision in Indian English Fiction.* New Delhi : Sterling Publishers, 1991.

The book aims at a critical examination of the archetype of the exile hero in some Indian novels in English. The novels chosen are Raja Rao's *The Serpent and the Rope,* Balachandra Rajan's *The Dark Dancer* and *Too Long in the West,* Arun Joshi's *The Foreigner,* Anita Desai's *Bye-Bye Blackbird,* Kamala Markandaya's *Possession* and *The Nowhere Man* and Chaman Nahal's *Into Another Dawn.*

The book discusses the nature and destiny of the central characters exiled from their own culture and society — "the nowhere men". In an alien culture they initially experience rootlessness — belonging neither to the East nor to the West, their disillusionment which ushers them into a process of spiritual awakening and self realization.

The book consists of six chapters besides an introduction : (1) The 'Exiles' — Fictional and Non-fictional; (2) The Exile : An Existentialist Transformation; (3) Departure : Transition from Innocence to Experience; (4) Temptation : Lure of the West; (5) The Return of the Native : Interplay between Memory and Desire; (6) Edge of Being : A reintegrating Vision.

544. Vinson, James, ed. *20th Century Fiction.* Great Writers Library. London : Macmillan, 1983.

545. Walsh, William. *A Human Idiom : Literature and Humanity.* London : Chatto & Windus, 1964

Presents a study of literature as a humanity (as a source of understanding human nature). Cites the works of Narayan as one of the examples.

See 5789.

546. ——. *A Manifold Voice.* London : Chatto & Windus, 1970.

Studies some of the works written in English by non-native writers to show not only their significant and creative contribution to English literature but also the extraordinary capacity of English language in expressing the sensibilities as varied as the Australian, Canadian, Indian, etc. Among the writers studied, R.K. Narayan finds a place.

See 5788.

547. ——, ed. *Readings in Commonwealth Literature.* London : Oxford University Press, 1973.

One of the earliest anthologies of the subject, the collection evaluates the individual contribution of writers in the Commonwealth literature including India. With a preliminary introduction explaining the relevance of the present anthology the book contains six sections each allotted to the literature of one country in Commonwealth. Out of the seven entries under India five are on fiction.
See 698, 1265, 1733, 5355, 5784, 6513.

548. ——. *Commonwealth Literature.* London : Oxford University Press, 1973.
The book is one of the earliest studies on Commonwealth literature which offers a personal chart of writing in the English language outside the traditions of Britain and the United States, particularly those writings of Commonwealth countries — India, West Indies, New Zealand, Canada, Africa and Australia. The chapter devoted to India makes a historical survey of Indian English literature — genre-wise — dealing with prose, poetry and fiction. In the survey of fiction a large part is devoted to Narayan's fictional output and his achievement.

549. ——. *Indian Literature in English.* London : Longman, 1990.
Offers a survey of poets, novelists, autobiographers etc., from Roy to Rushdie concentrating on a selected few for a detailed account. Among the novelists Raja Rao, Anand and Narayan and some women novelists such as Anita Desai and Kamala Markandaya find a place in the individual appraisals.

550. Wandrekar, Kalpana. *The Ailing Aliens* (A Study of the Immigrant Psyche in Six Indian English Novels). Gulburga : JIWE Publications, 1996.
Basing her arguments on Erich Formm's theory of social psychology considers the traumatic effect on the

displaced one developing itself into "immigrant psyche" as a stage in human evolution. Studies six Indian novels (Anita Desai's *Bye Bye Blackbird,* Markandaya's *The Nowhere Man,* Jhabvala's *A Backward Place,* Rajan's *The Dark Dancer,* Bharati Mukherjee's *Wife* and Arun Joshi's *The Foreigner)* in this context to exemplify the stages of ailment.
See 2901, 3667, 4159, 4741, 5067, 6281.

551. Williams, Haydn Moore. *Studies in Modern Indian Fiction.* 2 Vols. Calcutta : Writers Workshop, 1973.
This two-volumed book is one of the first full-length studies which makes a critical examination of the novels written in English of some of the representative Indian writers — Anand, Raja Rao, Narayan, Desai and Khushwant Singh.
There are three chapters in each volume. While the first chapter traces the origins of Indian writing in English and the political, social and literary backgrounds that are responsible for its emergence, the other five chapters are devoted to individual writers and their works.
See 1880, 3105, 5797, 6661, 7956.

552. ——. *Indo-Anglian Literature 1800-1970 : A Survey.* New Delhi : Orient Longman, 1976.
A general survey of Indian English literature from 1800 to 1970. Though the book deals with all the genres — poetry, drama, fiction and non-fiction — a larger part is devoted to Indian fiction.

553. ——. *Galaxy of Indian Writings in English.* Delhi : Akshat Publishers, 1987.
The book is a collection of essays on Indian English works written after 1930 (except those of Toru Dutt and Ghose) published earlier in journals and books. The author calls it a "classic" period of Indian writing in English during which time Indian English writing has gained maturity and recognition as is the case with the

works of Jhabvala, Narayan, Raja Rao, Desani, Salman Rushdie and other.

See 1283, 1284, 3106, 3108, 3674, 3676, 3677, 4400, 4744, 5798, 5800, 5801, 5802, 6662.

554. Wong, Sau-ling Cynthia. *Reading Asian American Literature : From Necessity to Extravagance.* Princeton (WJ) : Princeton University Press, 1993.

Suggests that Bharati Mukherjee is perhaps the first Asian American writer to exhibit a full awareness of the global context of contemporary Asian immigration with tales set "against a background of intertwined, transitional economic activities and mass uprooting caused by proxy wars in the third world."

555. Wunderlich, Horst. *Zwischen Dharma und Nation Building : Untersuchungen Zur Prasentation de Identitats Problematik inden Romanen Von R.K. Narayan, Raja Rao und Mulk Raj Anand.* Reihe Siegen 81. Heidelberg : Winter, 1988.

556. *World Authors.*Ed. John Wakeman, New York : H.W. Wilson Co., 1975.

557. Xavier Alphonse, S. *Kanthapura to Malgudi* New Delhi : Prestige Books, 1998

558. Yaravintelimath, C.R., G.S. Balarama Gupta, C.V. Venugopal and Amritjit Singh, eds. *New Perspectives in Indian Literature in English.* New Delhi : Sterling Publishers, 1995.

The book is an anthology of essays, *a festschrift* presented in honour of Prof. M.K. Naik. Contains perceptive essays and studies critically evaluating Indian literature in English by various critics both from India and abroad. Out of twenty essays five are on fiction.

See 587, 778, 858, 1013, 1285, 1634, 1852, 4091, 6445.

559. Zach, Wolfgang, ed. *Literature(s) in English New Perspectives.* New York/Frankfurt, Berlin, Paris : Peter Lang, 1990.
Contains an essay on Rushdie.
See 7086.

560. Zaman, Niaz, Shawkat Hussain, Firdaus Azim, Kaiser Haq and Syed Manzoorul Islam, eds. *Other Englishes : Essays on Commonwealth Writing.* Dhaka : Dhaka University Press, 1991.
The book is a collection of papers presented at a seminar on Commonwealth literature organized by the department of English, Dhaka University. The essays deal with wide range of subjects covering literatures from Australia, Pakistan, India, Africa, Canada and the West Indies starting from "towards a definition of Commonwealth literature" to "various facets of Commonwealth literature." Out of fifteen essays there are three on Indian English fiction. While Jasbir Jain examines the role of women writers in focusing their attention on women's issues, Arup Rudra analyses the novel *The Judas Tree* by Sanjeeb Dutta as an experimental work. Sujit Kumar Dutta's article discusses the cross cultural encounters in the works of Chinua Achebe and Raja Rao.

D. GENERAL ARTICLES

561. Abbas, K.A. "Social Realism and Change." Kohli, Suresh 145-154. ref. : 333.
A brief survey of Indian literature which includes the works of Anand, Bhattacharya, Raja Rao and his own to illustrate the creative and revolutionary impact of social realism on Indian literature and Indian life.

562. Abraham, John E. "Feminism and Our Fiction" Nayak and Swain 20-27. ref. : 401.
Discusses the theory of feminism and its exploration by Indian English writers.

563. Abraham, P.A. "Crisis of Unbelonging in Some Expatriate Stories from the Canadian and Indian Context." Jain, *Writers of the Indian Diaspora* 50-62. ref. : 302.
Discusses Bharati Mukherjee's three short stories from the collection entitled "Darkness".

564. Abrioux, Cynthia. "National Identities in the New literatures in English" *Commonwealth Essays and Studies* 18.1 (1995).
Explores the historical myths present in New literatures citing Salman Rushdie's *Shame* as an example to show how they are helpful in constructing national identities and how they contribute to the permanent "deformation" and "reformation" of such concepts. Comments that though ironical, open-ended and ambivalent, they are all the same part of our on going process of national myth-making.

565. Advani, Rukun. "Novelists in Residence" *Seminar* 384, Aug., 1991:15-18.

566. ——. "Academics as Writers." *Indian Review of Books* 4.4 (1994).

567. Aithal, S. Krishnamurty and Rashmi Aithal. "East-West Encounter in Four Indo-English Novels." *ACLALS Bulletin* 6.1 (1982) : 1-6.
Studies the relationship between Europeans and Indian expatriates in Markandaya's *Some Inner Fury,* Raja Rao's *The Serpent and the Rope.*, Desai's *Bye-Bye Black Bird,* and Malgonkar's *Combat of Shadows.*

568. ——. "Indo-English Fictional Experiments with Inter-Racial and Inter-Cultural Relationship." Srivatsava, A.K., *Alien Voices* 84-100. ref. : 524.
Discusses the Indo-English encounter between the two racial and cultural groups, with special reference to Kamala Markandaya's *Some Inner Fury,* Raja Rao's *The Serpent and the Rope,* Malgonkar's *Combat of Shadows,* and Anita Desai's *Bye-Bye Black Bird.*

569. ——. "Two Indo-English Fictional Experiments with Inter-Cultural Relationships." *Journal of South Asian Literature* 17.1(1982) : 251-257.
A comparative study of the novels — Kamala Markandaya's *Some Inner Fury,* and Manohar Malgonkar's *Combat of Shadows* — to show the different approaches of these writers to the Indo-English encounter involving specifically sex, love and marriage and to illustrate the possibilities and problems in establishing intimate and meaningful relationships between these two racial and cultural groups.

570. ——. "Women Crossed in Love : The Treatment of Unrequited Love in Women's Literature." *Journal of South Asian Literature,* 23.1 (1988) : 115-118. Also in Radha 1-7. ref. : 442.
Studies the theme of unrequited love in the selected works of Indian women writers — Mannu Bhandari's *Encircling Arms,* Raji Narasimhan's *A Toast to Herself,* and Veena Shanteswar's *Cross Roads,* to determine if the theme is handled in any special way in these works.

571. Alam, Qaiser Zoha. "The Image in Indian Fiction in English: A Note on Indianness." *Creative Forum* 1.3 (1988) : 30-36. Rpt. in Alam, *Language* 27-32. ref.:181.
Examines the kind of imagery used in Indian fiction in English and its inherent Indianness and remarks that its highly evocative quality is due to its transliteration into English from Indian languages.

572. ——. "The Cliches and the Indo-English Fiction." *Triveni* 61.2 (1992) : 35-43. Rpt. as "When All's Said and Done : The Cliches and the Indo-English Fiction" in Alam, *Language* 52-60. ref. : 181.
Traces the use of cliches in Indian writing in English, particularly in the writings of Narayan, Arun Joshi, Kamala Markandaya and Anita Desai and comments that Indian writers sometimes do not exert themselves to find a novel or original phrase but prefer to use

some pre-fabricated or conventional, overused 'pat' expressions.

573. Albertazzi, Silvia. "Passages : The Indian Connections From Sara Jeannette Duncan to Rohinton Mistry." Bindella and Davis 57-68. ref. : 223.

574. Alcock, Peter. "Something Different : Problems of Cultural Relativism in Non-European Literature." *ACLALS Bulletin* 5th Sep. (1978) : 48-66.

Argues the necessity of Westerners "to undergo, imaginatively, a degree of 'de-colonisation' and some sympathetic "reaculturation" to understand the third world fiction. Examines three African and Indian-English novels — Soyinka's *The Interpreters,* Anand's *Untouchable,* and Narayan's *The Guide,* — under three categories — "simple non-comprehension" (Soyinka's *The Interpreters),* "serious miscomprehension" *(Untouchables),* and "varying degrees of inadequate understanding" *(The Guide)* and shows how they are steeped in African or Indian ethos and philosophy, myths and oracles.

575. ——. "Distancing the Maya of the West : Elementary European Necessities." Singh, Kirpal 254-269. ref. : 508.

A reproduction of the article "Something Different : Problems of Cultural Relativism in Non-European Literature" (item No. 536) with a slight modification. Instead of *The Interpreters,* the author discusses Anita Desai's *The Fire on the Mountain,* in the first category under "simple non-comprehension."

576. Alexander, Meena. "Outcaste Power : Ritual Displacement and Virile Maternity in Indian Writers." *Journal of Commonwealth Literature* 24.1 (1989) : 12-29.

577. Ali, Ahmed. "Some Reflections on the Novel." *Journal of Indian Writing in English* 17.1 (1989) : 1-11.

Traces the different trends in the novel especially in

the developing countries during the last hundred and odd years (since the industrial revolution) emphasizing the influence of social, political and cultural movements on the writings of the novel. Concludes that the modern tendency is towards alienation.

578. Ali, Tariq. "Fiction as History, History as Fiction." *Indo-British Review* II.2 (1985) : 72-78.
See 6655.

579. Alphonso-Karkala, J.B. "Indo-English Fiction." *Literature East and West* 8.1 (1964) : 6-14.
A paper presented in the conference on Commonwealth literature of the Modern Language Association in December, 1963. A general survey of contemporary Indian literature in all regional languages including Indian-English literature. Traces the historical development of Indian-English fiction during the British rule in India from 1858-1947.

580. ——. "Themes in Contemporary Indian Novels." Alphonso-Karkala, *Comparative World Literature* 12-22. ref. : 184.
Examines the theme of inter-personal relationship and the relationship of man with his environment in the works of the contemporary Indian novelists, categorizing the novels into 3 groups : those that re-express the past, those that mirror social criticism and those that examine the aesthetic sensibility of the soul.

581. ——. "Indian Literture in the 20th Century : Survey of Trends." *Encyclopaedia of World Literature in the 20th Century*. Ed. Leonard S. Klein. 2nd ed. Rev. New York: Fredrick Ungar Publishing Co., 1982. 2. E-K : 432 – 440.

582. ——. "Indo-English Literature : Probleme der Identitat und Abgrenzung englische, anglo-englische, indo-englische Literatur." *Grundlagen zur Literatur in Englischer Sprache* Band 4 : Indian ed. Dr. Gernard Stilz. Universtat

Stuttgart Munchen : Wilhelm Fink Verlag, 1982 : 47-49.

583. ——. "Literature and National Character in Regard to Indo-English Literature." Sharma, K.K., *Indo-English Literature* 259-275. ref. : 501.

Opines that Indian-English Literature is "mongrel bred," "unrooted ... colonial bicultural byproduct..."

584. ——. "Indo-English Fiction 1857–1947." *Indian Book Reporter* 3.6 (1967) : 1-7.

585. Amur, G.S. "Marraige as Symbolic Strategy of Cultural Encounter." *Journal of Literature and Aesthetics* 1.3(1981) : 5-14. Rpt. as "The Theme of Marraige as a Symbolic Strategy in *Seetha, Esmond in India* and *The Serpent and the Rope"* in Amur, *Forbidden Fruit.* ref. : 190.

Examines the pattern of attraction and withdrawal in the man-woman relationship in inter-racial and inter-cultural marriages and its presentation through romantic, realistic and metaphysical modes in the novels, *Sita, Esmond in India* and *The Serpent and the Rope* respectively.

586. ——. "Promise and Fulfilment." *Indian Literature* 28.6 (1985) : 47-54.

Argues that Indian-English writings of 1985, while showing much promise, produce no work of major status.

587. ——. "Nightingales in our Garden : an Appraisal of Muslim Novelists in English." Yaravintelimath *et al.* 154-262. ref. : 558.

Analyses some of the novels written by Muslim novelists (Humayun Kabir's *Men and Rivers,* Ahmed Ali's *Twilight in Delhi,* Attia Hosain's *Sunlight on a Broken Column* and K.A. Abbas's *Inquilab)* to show that though they illustrate some aspect or the other of

Islamic culture, none of them is too purely ethnic or sectarian, and all of them reveal a commitment to humanistic values of universal significance.

588. Anand, Mulk Raj. "Old Myths and New Myths : Recital Versus Novel." *Banasthali Patrika* 5.13 (1969) : 27-36. Rpt. in Narasimhaiah, *Indian Literature of the Past Fifty Years* 109-120. ref. : 389.
Discusses "novel" as an art form. Finds little change in the content, but a revolution in the technique — from the epic to the bardic and to the three dimensional recital.

589. ——. "The Story of My Experiment with a White Lie." *Indian Literature* 10.3 (1967) : 20-22. Rpt. in Naik, *et al., Critical Essays* 4-18. ref. : 377.
An analysis of the creative process behind the printed page.

590. ——. "Pigeon-Indian : Some Notes on Indian English Writing." *Journal of Karnataka University* (Humanities) 16 (1972) : 69-90. Rpt. in Naik, *Aspects* 24-44. ref. : 378. Also in Narasimhaiah and Nagarajan, *Studies* 228-248. ref. : 394.
Makes a case for a creative use of English language by Indians with force and conviction. Examines in detail Indian words and colloquialisms that have entered into English vocabulary to demonstrate the elasticity of English as a language that is growing all the time.

591. ——. "Tradition and Modernity in Literature." *Journal of South Asian Literature* 10.1 (1974) : 45-50.
Points out that the content of literature does not change as it deals with human relations; only the form changes.

592. ——. "The Changeling." *Journal of English Studies* (Warangal) 4.1 (1972) : 229-238. Rpt. in *World Literature Written in English* 15.1 (1976) : 111-120.

Also in Mohan 11-20. ref. : 365.
A discussion on the scope of Indian English literature.

593. ——. "The Rhythm of Indian Life on Indian English." Radhakrishnan, *Research and Criticism* 59-61. ref. : 444.
Considers Indian English as one of the Indian languages and the literature written through that medium as one interpreting Indian life.

594. ——. "Creative Process." *Littcrit* 6, 4.1 (1978) : 1-3.
Comments generally on the creative process of writers with special reference to his own development.

595. ——. "Roots and Flowers : Two Lectures on the Metamorphosis of Technique and Content in the Indo-English Novel." *Littcrit* 14, 8.1 (1982) : 47-60. Published as a Booklet. Dharwad : Karnatak University Press, 1972.
Analyses the metamorphosis of technique (European form of art) and Indian content in *Untouchable* and *Kanthapura* to show the emergence of the Indian English novel as a genre.

596. ——. "The Taste of the Pudding." *Literary Criterion* 17.2 (1982) : 100-111.
Discusses the viability of standard English for his creative writing *vis-a-vis* his own experimentation with standard English for his creative purposes.

597. ——. "Reflections on the Novel." Narasimhaiah, *Commonwealth Literature* 49-54. ref. : 391.
A scholarly survey of the genesis and growth of the novel taking into account both Eastern and Western sources.

598. ——. "Reflections of a Novelist : Some Notes on the Novel." *Journal of Literature and Aesthetics* 2. 2-3 (1982) : 132-136. Rpt. in *Statesman* 20 Feb. 1983 : 1-1. Also in Amur, *et al.*, *Indian Readings* 3-13 ref. : 192.

A modified version of the essay "Reflections on the Novel" (item 559).

599. ——. "The Relevance of Indian English Literature." *Criticism and Research* 7 (1984-85) : 172-180.
A lecture delivered under the auspices of the Department of English, Banaras Hindu University.
Argues that Indian English is "the echo of inside, of human experience, of nature." Hence its relevance to Indian creative writing.

600 ——. "The Changeling : Indian English Literature : Its Relevance." *Literary Half-Yearly* 30.1 (1981) : 26-37.
Consists of general comments on the place of Indian English literature in contemporary Indian literature. Looks at Indian-English literature as a changeling born under particular circumstances but being reared under entirely different conditions.

601. ——. "An Undeclared War." *Littcrit* 4,3.1 (1977) : 11-24.
Discusses the internecine war between the "Brown Sahibs" and the 'Babus' and considers it as the chief cause for the crisis in Indian letters.

602. ——. "Pigeon-Indian : A Note on the Emergence of Indian English Literature." *Journal of Indian Writing in English* 20, 1-2 (1992) : 1-3.
Gives reasons as to why there is an echo of mother tongue behind all Indian English creative writings. Calls Indian English "Pigeon Indian."

603. ——. "Novel form in Ocean Stories." *Journal of Indian Writing in English* 25.1-2 (1997).

604. Anand, Shahla. "Images of Indian Princes and Courtly Concubines in Four Contemporary Works." *South Asian Review* July 1979 : 27-35.

605. ——. "Is Indian Society Congenial to the Creation of a Classic? A Writer's View." *Literary Criterion* 51.2 (1980) : 56-61.

Emphasizes that only a critical insider with an imagination to treat universal problems of the destiny of man can possibly write a classic in India today. Talks about his personal experiences as a writer and throws light on the challenges a novelist has to face in contemporary India.

606. Anjaneyulu, D. "Fifty Years of Indian Writing in English." *Swaraj* 7 (1968): 223-238.

607. ——. "Across All Barriers." *Statesman* 9 May 1968 : 6.

608. ——. "Indian Writers in English." *Thought* 13 March 1971 : 13-16.

609. ——. "Indian Writing in English from K.S. Venkataramani to Kamala Markandaya. *"Triveni* 32.1 (1963) : 19-28.
A general survey of Indian English fiction. Traces the evolution of Indian fiction in English and its establishment as one among Indian literatures and its vital role in national integration. Finds that Raja Rao's *The Serpent and the Rope*" marks a step in groping for a stage in the evolution of, what might be called an Indian form (apart from the theme and content) in English fiction."

610. ——. ''Recent Trends in English Language and Literature." *Hindu* 25 Oct. 1983 : 25-1.

611. Arulandram, H.G.S. "Indo-Anglian as a part of Indian Literature." *Ken* 2 (1986) : 25-32.
Discusses the place of Indian writing in English among Indian literatures and its creative originality.

612. Ash, Ranjana Sidhata. "Indian Women's Writing in English." *Kunapipi* 16.1 (1994) : 614-617. Rpt. in Rutherford *et al*. 614-617. ref. : 489.
Offers a summary of recent developments in publishing. Notes some of the thematic concerns of Anita Desai and Nayantara Sahgal among others and draws particular

attention to the multilingual features of works by Desai, Rukmini Bhaya Nair, etc.

613. Asnani, Shyam M. "Cavalcade of Indo-English Fiction." *Thought* 8 June 1974.

614. ——. "Contribution of Women to Indo-English Novel." *Triveni* 44.2 (1975) : 45-22.

A general survey of Indian English fiction written by women — from Toru Dutt (1857) to Anita Desai to show how in the development of the Indian English novel, the women writers have achieved a remarkable imaginative self-sufficiency which merits recognition in spite of its relatively later manifestation and limitation.

615. ——. "The Theme of Partition : The Indo-English Novel." *Triveni* 48.1(1979) : 58-67. Rpt. in Asnani, *New Dimensions* 38-50. ref. : 198.

A critical analysis of the theme of partition, in the novels *Train to Pakistan, A Bend in the Ganges* and *Azadi.* Points out that each of these novels treats the theme of partition with "stark realism" and an "absolute fidelity to the truth" to produce a "trenchant exposition of one of the most appalling episodes in ... Indian history."

616. ——. "The Indian Princes : Their Portrayal in the Indo-English Novel." *Commonwealth Quarterly* 3.2 (1979) : 85-104. Rpt. in Asnani, *Critical Response* 62-78. ref. : 197.

Compares and contrasts the treatment of the subject of the Indian princes in Anand's *The Private Life of an Indian Prince* and Malgonkar's *The Princes* and shows, through an analysis of the novels, that while Anand presents, from a psychological angle, "the disordered life of a prince who is "a decadent libertine" enslaved by a nymphomaniac harlot," Malgonkar gives a realistic and dispassionate interpretation of a human situation, a balanced political chronicle of the tumultuous times of India's integration after Independence.

617. ——. "Towards a Closer Understanding of the Indo-English Novel." *Journal of South Asian Literature* 16.2 (1981): 153-159. Rpt. in Asnani, *New Dimensions* 1-10. ref. : 198.

Focuses attention on the basic questions related to the use of language, the dialogue, the reading audience and the modes of narration in Indian English novel.

618. ——. "The Socio-Political Scene of the 1930's : Its Impact on the Indo-English Novel." Asnani, *Critical Response* 1-10. ref. : 197.

Outlines the socio-political scene of 1930's and comments that this is the period in which the realistic novel with some purpose made its appearance.

619. ——. "New Morality in the Modern Indo-English Novel." *Language Forum* 7.1-4 (1981-82) : 30-50. Rpt. in Dhawan's *Explorations* 59-70. ref. : 253. Rpt. in Asnani, *New Dimensions* 51-62. ref. : 198. Rpt. in Dhawan, *Indian Women Novelists* Set I. Vol. I. 104-116. ref. : 257.

Studies the new morality in the context of man-woman relationship discernible in Anand's *The Old Woman and the Cow,* Anita Desai's *Cry, The Peacock, Voices in the City* and *Where Shall We Go This Summer?* and Nayantara Sahgal's *The Day in Shadow.* The central theme is the existential predicament of woman as an individual and the problem is projected through incompatible couples.

620. ——. "Indian English Novel in Retrospect." *Littcrit* 24 & 25, 13.1-2 (1987) : 60-74.

A critical survey of Indian English fiction to show the shift of focus, both in theme and technique in the novels of the last two decades from those of the novels written earlier.

621. ——. "Two Recent Indian English Novels." Asnani, *New Dimensions* 136-141. ref. : 198.
See 7810.

622. ——. "Quest for Identity theme in Three Commonwealth Novels." Srivastava, A.K., *Alien Voices* 128-136. ref. : 524.
Examines Achebe's *No longer at ease,* Naipaul's *A House of Mr. Biswas,* and Markandaya's *The Nowhere Man* to show how the theme of exile and the problem of identity have been treated by these novelists.

623. ——. "Identity Crisis of Indian Immigrants. A Study of Three Novels." Jain, *Writers of the Indian Diaspora* 73-81. ref. : 302.

624. Banerjee, N.N. ''Recent Indian Writing in English." *Contemporary Indian Literature* 4.1 (1964) : 12-13, 4.2 (1964) : 24-26, 4.3 (1964) : 11-12, 4.4 (1964) : 12-13.

625. ——. "Form and Content of the Contemporary Indian Novel." *Contemporary Indian Literature* 13.3 (1973) : 5-7.

626. Baral, K.C. "Reading the Mother : Psychoanalysis and Indian Novel Written in English." Bande, *Mothers and Mother-Figures* 9-25. ref. : 205.
Basing his arguments on Freudian and Lacanian models, studies the psychoanalytical theories of motherhood from the stance of psychoanalytic feminist criticism, post-structuralism and deconstruction to ascertain his own theory of motherhood. Offers a psychoanalytic reading of the mother image in Indian English novels in general and Mulk Raj Anand's *The Seven Ages of Man* and *Morning Face* in particular.

627 Barche, G.D. "Facets of Feminism in Indian English Fiction." *Commonwealth Review* 6.1 (1994-95) : 127-134. Rpt. in Dass, *Feminism and Literature* 127-134.

ref. : 244. Also in Dhawan, *Indian Women Novelists* Set III. Vol.1. 9-17. ref : 257.

Studies the novels, Shashi Deshpande's *Roots and Shadows,* Desai's *Cry, The Peocock* and Nimbikar's *Temporary Answers* to show how each couple in these novels projects different facets of the problems involved in man-woman relationship, particularly concerning the struggle for liberty, equality, compatibility and self-reliance.

628. Basu, Tapan. "Writing of (f) India : The Stephanian as Contemporary Indo-Anglian Novelist." *Stephanian* 103.1 (1995) : 51-58.

629. Batra, Shakti. "Impact of Gandhi on Indian Writing." *Indian Literature* 17.3 (1974) : 38-51.

630. Belliappa, K.C. "Three Post-Colonial Novelists : Chinua Achebe, Tharoor, Advani." Trivedi and Mukherjee 203-212. ref. : 534.

Discusses the questions raised regarding the problems confronting a writer in post-colonial societies throwing light on the role of the writer *vis-a-vis* his society, the mode of interrogation and the preoccupation of the writers with the existential reality of their societies. While Achebe interrogates the problems of his society and uses his past creatively and locates solutions in *Anthills of the Savannah,* Tharoor comes to terms with the problems of society in the present day India by resorting to the use of myth in *The Great Indian Novel* and Advani indulges in fantasy.

631. Belliappa, Meena. "East-West Encounter : Indian Women Writers of Fiction in English." *Literary Criterion* 7.3 (1966) : 18-27. Rpt. in Narasimhaiah, *Fiction and the Reading Public* 18-27. ref. : 387.

Shows how Kamala Markandaya, Santha Rama Rau and Jhabvala use the theme of East-West encounter to portray human situation — particularly the exploration of factors that hamper harmonious relations between diverse races and cultures.

632. ——. "Urban Consciousness in Indian Fiction in English." *Creative Forum* 8.1-2(1988) : 93-100.

633. Berry, Margaret. "Reflections on India." *Carroll Quarterly* 20 (1966) : 36-78.

634. ——. "India : A Double Key." *Journal of Indian Writing in English* 6.1 (1978) : 30-38.

Suggests Anand's *The Big Heart* and Jhabvala's *A Backward Place* as suitable books for foreign students to understand the ideals and attitudes of the people in India and their life and thought.

635. Bey, Hamida. "Dilemma of the Indian Novelist." *Quest* 1, Feb.-Mar. 1956 : 11.

636. ——. "A Look at Indo-Anglian Fiction." *Thought* 13 Dec. 1969 : 18-19.

637. ——."Novels of a Ruling Class." *Thought* 13 Sep. 1969 : 13-16.

638. ——. "Ideological Labels for Novelists." *Thought* 24 Jan. 1970 : 15-18.

639. ——. "Indo-Anglian Narcissist." *Thought* 5 Dec. 1970 : 13-15.

640. Bharathalakshmi, M.V. and S. Krishna Sarma. "The Brown British : A Study of Recent Immigrant Novels." *Literary Half-Yearly* 18.2 (1976) : 53-70.

Discusses the problems of Brown Immigrants in Britain in Dilip Hiro's *A Triangular View,* Reginald and Jamila Massey's *The Immigrants,* Timeri Murari's *The Marriage,* Anita Desai's *Bye-Bye Black Bird* and Kamala Markandaya's *The Nowhere Man,* and points out how each writer views this problem from a different perspective.

Finds each novel suggesting a possible solution for

harmonious relationship between Brown immigrants and the natives.

641. Bharucha, Nilufer E. "The City as Hero." *Literary Criterion* 28.3 (1993) : 46-49.
Examines some of the novels which have Bombay as their setting and shows the cosmopolitan and commercial nature of the city to make it the protagonist of the novels. The novels discussed are Rohinton Mistry's *Tales from Firozsha Baag, Such a Long Journey,* Firdaus Kanga's *Trying to Grow,* Boman Desai's *Memory of Elephant* and Anita Desai's *Baumgartner's Bombay.*

642. ——. "The Parsi voice in recent Indian English Fiction : An Assertion of Ethnic Identity." Bharucha and Sarang 73-88. ref. : 216.
Studies the novels and short stories of Bapsi Sidhwa, Farrukh Dhondy, Rohinton Mistry, Firdaus Kanga and Boman Desai to show how they voice the assertion of an ethnic Parsi identity and how an understanding, accepting one's own ethnicity helps to assimilate into a wider social, national context.

643. ——. "Reflections in Broken Mirrors : Diverse Diasporas in Recent Parsi Fiction." *Wasifiri* 21 (1995) : 32-35.

644. ——. "The Charting of Cultural Territory: Second Generation Post-colonial Indian English Fiction." Kirpal, *The Post-modern Indian English Novel.* 355-367. ref. : 331.
Examines the charting of cultural territory (as envisaged by post-colonial critics) which involves a repossession of history in its politicization an awareness of differences "of nation, explicity, religion and gender" with the highly diasporic of fiction of the second generation post-colonial Indian English novelists born after decolinization and who began publishing their works in the 1980s.

Includes a critique of such writers as Rushdie, Ghosh, Upamanyu Chatterjee, Rohinton Mistry and Vikram Seth.

645. ——. "From Behind a Fine Veil : A Feminist Reading of Three Parsi Novels." Jain & Amin, *Margins* 174-185. ref. : 304. Rpt in *Indian Literature* 175, Sep.-Oct : 1996 : 132-141
Examines the world view provided by the Parsi women in Boman Desai's *The Memory of Elephants,* Rohinton Mistry's *Such a Long Journey* and Bapsi Sidhwa's *Ice Candy Man* from behind the veil of patriarchy, marginality and helplessness.

646. ——. "From Commonwealth to Post-colonial Literature : Old Wine in New Bottles." *Journal of Indian Writing in English* 25.1-2 (1997) : 59-68.

647. ——. "Inhabiting Enclosures and Creating Spaces : The Worlds of Women in Indian Literature in English." *Ariel* 29.1 (1998) : 93-108.

648. Bhaskaran, M.P. "Indianness of Indo-Anglian Writers and Their Critics." *Statesman* 4 May 1968 : 8.

649. Bhat, Yashoda. "The Image of Women in Indo-Anglian Literature." Bhat and Rao 25-42. ref. : 217.
Describes the different images of women as depicted by the novelists of first generation (Anand, Raja Rao, Narayan) as well as the recent ones (Anita Desai, Rama Mehta, Shashi Deshpande, Veena Paintal, Christine Gomez, etc.)

650. Bhatnagar, O.P. "Indian Political Novel in English." *Nagpur University English Teacher's Journal* 1.7 (Jan. 1981) : 17-31.

651. Bhatnagar, K.C. "Realism in Modern Indo-English Fiction." Dwivedi, *Studies in Contemporary Indian Fiction in English* 36-40. ref. : 269.
Defines the nature of the realistic novel and examines the Indian English novelists' approach to it. This

includes a discussion of the attitudes of a number of novelists to realism.

652. ——. "Colonial Encounter in Indian Short Story in English." Ratnam 17-24. ref. : 471.

Finds colonial situation as presented in Indian English short story "comico-ludicrous" and comments that "the colonial encounter has provided equally rich theme and occasions for caricature in Anand, comedy in Malgonkar, metaphysical speculations in Raja Rao and humanism in Jhabvala...."

653. Bhattacharya, Bhabani. "Literature and Social Reality." *Aryan Path* 26.9 (Sep. 1955) : 392-395. Rpt. in Srivastava, R.K., *Perspectives on Bhabani Bhattacharya,* 1-6. ref. : 2120.

Contains Bhattacharya's views on the role of the artist in society.

654. ——. "The Hybrid Indo-Anglian Novel." *Indian P.E.N.* 21, Mar. 1955.

A rejoinder to Iqbal Singh's article in *The Illustrated Weekly of India,* "The Indo-Anglian Novel : Study of a Hybrid." Argues against Singh's condemnation of Indian writing in English that it needs protection and survival.

655. ——. "Indo-Anglian." Baktiyar 41-48. ref. : 203.

A paper read at the symposium on the novel in Modern India held during the 50th All India Writers' Conference at Bhubaneshwar in 1959. A general essay on Indian English fiction dealing with its basic assumptions such as whether English is a fitting medium for Indian conditions.

656. ——. "The State and the Writer." *Indian P.E.N.* 24, Jan. 1958 : 1-3.

Deploring the tendency of the state to exert its power over the writers, advises them to discharge their social responsibility.

657. Bhushan, B.D. "Untouchability in Indian Fiction." *Yearly Review* 4 (1990) : 81-91.
Traces the treatment of untouchability (Harijan upliftment) in Anand's *Untouchable,* Bhabani Bhattacharya's *He Who Rides the Tiger* and Raja Rao's *Kanthapura* along with other Indian novels written in regional languages.

658. Bhyrappa, S.L. "The Indian Novelist and the Problem of the Concept of Man." *Literary Criterion* 21.1-2 (1986) : 6-12.
Criticises the attitude of the Indian English novelists towards adopting the European novel form and the European concepts of man and stresses the need for understanding the Indian concept of man in explicating the deeper human problems and crises that they are typically Indian.

659. Bijapure, A.A. "Shades of Anger-Responses." *Language Forum* 21.1-2 (1995) : 96-100.
Traces the varied responses of the characters to the "anger-situations" and shows how they depend on the position, status or the development of the personality of the respondent and how Khushwant Singh uses the language (the language of abuse) accordingly.

660. Bose, Amalendu. "Indian Writing in English." Sinha, K.N. *Indian Writing in English* 63-71. ref. : 518.
Enumerating certain major issues regarding Indian English literature (such as its literary category, its tradition, the yardstick with which it can be measured, the language — medium and the writer's identity), comments that in discussing and evaluating an Indian English writer, "the principal question always will be the question of identity, the degree of his Indianness."

661. Brunton, T.D. "India in Fiction." Naik, *et al.*, *Critical Essays* 212-222. ref. : 377.

Brings into focus some generalities about the tradition of the novel in general and examines Indian tradition by analysing a few well-known works of Indian fiction. Expresses his disappointment that Raja Rao's novels do not answer to his (Raja Rao's) own definition of the novel. Remarks that many novels in English by Indians are valued not so much for their power as fiction as upon their content.

662. "Can English be a Creative Language for Indians?" *Adam : International Review-Passages from India* 355-60 (1971) : 26-35.

663. Chaddah, R.P. "Mahatma Gandhi in Indo-Anglian Fiction." *Nagpur Times* 29 Jan. 1973.

664. ——. "The Mahatma in Modern Indo-English Fiction." *Indian P.E.N.* 42, Nov.-Dec. 1978 : 1-5.

Traces the influence of Gandhi, his ideas and ideals and their treatment in modern Indian English fiction both in the works of pre-Independence as well as post-Independence novelists and shows that there is a considerable change in the attitude of people (as shown in the works) towards Gandhi and his ideologies in the post-Independence period.

665. ——. "The Partition in Indo-English Fiction." *Journal of Indian Writing in English* 5.2 (1977) : 52-58. Rpt. in Prabhakar 34-38. ref. : 433.

Examines the theme of partition in Khushwant Singh's *Train to Pakistan,* Rajan's *The Dark Dancer,* Malgonkar's *Distant Drums, A Bend in the Ganges,* Attia Hosain's *Sunlight on a Broken Column* and Nahal's *Azadi* to show that all these novelists have somehow manipulated their characters into such situations as to utilise them to voice their political affiliations and grievances (but not the genuinely felt experience of the tragedy) except the novel *Azadi* which is nearer to the ethos of this national upsurge.

666. Chakrabarty, Dipesh. "Post-coloniality and the Artifice of History : Who speaks for "Indian Past?" *The New Historicism Reader*. Ed. H. Arun Vesser. London/New York: Routledge, 1994.
Investigates the subalternity of the academic discourse of "Indian history," with brief references to Salman Rushdie and Nirad Chaudhuri.

667. Chakravorty, D.K. "The Theme of Matrimonial Divergence in Three Indian Novels in English." Chakravorty 49-55. ref. : 230.
Shows how the theme of matrimonial divergence has been treated in the novels, *Cry the Peacock* (Anita Desai), *This Time of Morning* (Nayantara Sahgal) and *The Coffer Dams* (Kamala Markandaya) in different ways by the three writers.

668. ——. "The Theme of Partition of India in Indian Novels in English." Chakravorty 77-87. ref. : 230. Also in Sinha and Sinha 43-55. ref. : 519.
Examines the theme of partition of India and the consequent violence and bloodshed in the novels, *Train to Pakistan* by Khushwant Singh, *Twice Born Twice Dead* by Kartar Singh Duggal and *A Bend in the Ganges* by Malgonkar to show that violence is the result of the evils of narrow, partisan thinking.

669. ——. "The Pursuit of Obscure Salvations : An Approach to Three Indian Novels in English." Chakravorty 69-76. ref. : 230.
Examines the nature and purpose of the pursuit of salvation through god-men as is described in select Indian novels in English (especially in Bhattacharya's *A Dream in Hawaii,* Markandaya's *Possession,* and Sasthi Brata's *The Sensous Guru).*

670. Chakraborty, Mohan. "Contemporary Writing by the Fair Sex in India." *Deccan Chronicle,* 29 May 1988 : 3.

671. Chandar, K.M. "What Ails Indian Writing in English." *Creative Forum* 9.1-2 (1996) : 111-116.

672. Chandra Mohan. "Post-Colonial Imagination in Modern Canadian and Indian Fiction in English." Begum 99-109. ref. : 210.
Considers regionalism and nativism as important aspects of post-colonial imagination both in Canada and India.

673. Chandra, Suresh. "Indian English : Its Chroniclers." Chandra 5-8. ref. : 231.
Argues that the English used by Indian writers is the Indian variety of English (which he calls Indolish) distinguishable from other varieties of English as it represents recognisable aspects of Indian speech habits and culture, citing examples both from Indian English writers and Anglo-Indian writers.

674. ——. "Existential Heroes, East and West." Chandra 34-47. ref. : 231.
Contrasting the existential attitudes of Gian (Malgonkar's *A Bend in the Ganges)* with those of Rathan Rathore (Arun Joshi's *The Foreigner)* shows how the former sets himself free and sees beyond what is material and earthly. Even Rojack (Norman Mailer's *The American Dream)* is no match to him.

675. ——. "Feministic Aspects of Recent Indian Fiction : A Commentary." Awasthi 74-82. ref. : 199.
Examines the portrayal of women in Mahip Singh's *Who Walks With Me,* Nagarkar's *Seven Sixes Are Forty Three,* and Shashi Deshpande's *That Long Silence.*

676. Chatterjee, Kalyan K. "Indian English : Problems of Identity." *Quest* 99, Jan-Feb. 1976 : 57-59. "Notes".
Discusses the question of the need for English in India.

677. Chatterjee, Raj. "Indo-Anglian Fiction." *Statesman* 5 Nov. 1972 : 13.6.

678. Chauda, Pravin Sinha. "The Future of the Novel in English." *Modern Review,* Jan.-Feb. 1985 : 19-23.

679. Chaudhary, Shreesh. "Indianness in Indian Writing in

English." *Journal of Indian Writing in English* 18.2 (1990) : 55-65.

Argues that the features noticed at the syntactic and lexical levels are only peripheral aspects of Indianism; the true nature of Indianness can be found only at the thematic level. Illustrates the same by citing examples from Raja Rao's *Kanthapura.*

680. Chellappan, K. "The Near and the Far in Anglo-Indian and Indo-Anglian Fiction." Rao, Ramakrishna and Sivaramkrishna 1-10 ref. : 466.

Discusses the quest for self in terms of the spiritual journey as portrayed in the novels of L.H. Myers (*The Near and the Far),* Forster (*A Passage to India),* Raja Rao (*The Serpent and the Rope*) bringing into focus the similarities and differences in its portrayal.

681. Chew, Shirley. "Fictions of Princely States and Empire." *Ariel,* 17.3 (1986) : 103-118.

Shows how Anand *(The Private Life of an Indian Prince),* Malgonkar *(The Princes),* and Jhabvala *(Heat and Dust),* had access to the past through the literary works about the empire, namely William Krington's *The Private Life of an Eastern King,* E.M. Forster's *The Hill of Devi* and *A Passage to India* respectively. Also points out the manner in which these novelists have appropriated the literature of empire and reworked it to suit their purposes.

682. Childs, Peter. "England and India in Post-Independence Fiction." *Revaluations* 2.2 (1996) : 1-14.

683. Choudhury, Indra Nath. "Indian Literature after Modernism." *Commonwealth Review* 5.1 (1993-94) : 17-23.

684. Constable, Philip. "1935 : A Declaration of Indian Cultural Independence." Sampietro 149-155. ref. : 490.

685. Coppala, Carlo. "Attitudes Towards Gandhi and Gandhian Ideology in Some Indo-Anglian and Western Novels." *South Asian Review,* 5.2 (1981) : 88-105.
Discusses the nature and extent of Gandhi's influence on Indian English writers such as Anand *(Untouchable),* Raja Rao *(Kanthapura),* Narayan *(Waiting for the Mahatma),* Bhattacharya *(Shadow From Ladakh),* Abbas *(Inquilab),* Markandaya *(Some Inner Fury),* as well as Western novelists like John Masters *(Bhawani Junction),* Donald R.Robinson *(The Raj),* Stanley Wolpert *(Nine Hours to Rama)* and Paul Scott *(The Raj Quartet).* Shows that their attitudes, though divergent and varied, are positive : While Indian creative writers do offer some criticism of Gandhi in their works, Western novelists tend to portray Gandhi in highly sympathetic terms though they find it necessary to place anti-Gandhian sentiments in the mouth of many characters.

686. Costa, Brian. "Look Backwards : 25 Years of Indo-Anglian Writing." *Thought,* 3 Sep. 1972 : 16-18.

687. Couta, Maria. "Indian Writing in English : Language of Literature." *Economic and Political Weekly* 24 July 1982 : 1186-88.

688. Cowasjee, Saros. "Indo-Anglian Fiction." *Guardian* (Manchester) 15 Aug. 1961.

689. ——. "The Indian Writer in Exile." Niven, *Commonwealth Writer Overseas* 53-61. ref. : 407. Also in Cowasjee *Studies* 32-50. ref. : 236.
Considering alienated writers as different from the writers in exile the author narrates his own problems as an alienated writer in writing the novel, *Good Bye to Elisa.*

690. ——. "Princes and Politics." *Literary Criterion* 8.4 (1969) : 10-18.
Studies the treatment of the princes and the politics of colonial India in the novels of Malgonkar and Anand.

691. ——. "The Princes in Indian Fiction ." *Kakatiya Journal of English Studies* 2.1(1977) : 48-70. Also in Cowasjee, *Studies* 11-31. ref. : 236.
Paper presented at the Commonwealth Literature conference at York University, Downview, Ontario, in April 1974. An extension of the earlier article "Princes and Politics". Contrasts Anand's *The Private Life of an Indian Prince,* and Malgonkar's *The Princes* with J.R. Ackeley's *Hindoo Holiday,* Forster's *The Hill of Devi,* etc.

692. ——. "The Partition in Indo-English Fiction." *Language Forum* 7.1-4 1981-1982) : 16-29. Rpt. in Dhawan, *Explorations* 15-30. ref. : 253. Also in Nandan 110-119. ref. : 384. Also Cowasjee, *Studies,* 79-95. ref. : 236.
Paper presented at the fifth Triennial Conference of the Association for Commonwealth Literature and Language Studies in Suva, Fiji in Jan. 1980. Analyses seven Indian English novels dealing with the theme of partition and finds them containing fictional and dramatic potential.

693. Cronin, Richard. "Sex in the Indian Novel" Cronin 147-160. ref. : 239.
Taking Kaye' *The Far Pavilions* and Jhabvala's *Heat and Dust* as examples, explores the nature of sexual relations as depicted by them and suggests that they are, at best, volatile and at worst, hysteric.

694. Dasenbrock, Reed Way. "Intelligibility and Meaningfulness Multicultural Literature in English." *PMLA* 102.1 Jan. 1987 : 10-19.
Discusses the terms "intelligibility" and "meaningfulness" in the context of multi-cultural works and analyses four multi-cultural narratives — R.K. Narayan's *The Painter of Signs,* Maxine Hong Kingston's *The Woman Warrior,* Rudolfo Anaya's *Bless Me Ultima* and Witi Ihimaera's *Tangi* — to show how they mirror the

misunderstandings and failures of intelligibility in multi-cultural situations they depict.

695. ——. "The Politics of Stylistic Experimentation : A Commonwealth Perspective." *Journal of Indian Writing in English* 12.2(1984) : 48-70.
Taking the Irish example, the writer examines stylistic experimentation of African and Indian writers in English both in anti-colonial and post-colonial situations and makes incisive remarks on the style of Raja Rao and Rushdie.

696. Dass, Veena Noble. "Feminism and Literature." *Commonwealth Review* 6.1 (1995) : 9-12. Rpt. in Dass, *Feminism and Literature* 9-12. ref. : 244.
Discusses feminist criticism particularly "perspective" criticism which serves the cause of liberation.

697. Dave, J.V. "Indian Fiction in English : A Brief Study in Basic Incongruity Between Its Writer and Readership." Singh, Avadesh 42-47. ref. : 507.
Discusses the features of "normal fiction" and the anomalous position of the Indian English fiction to show how "unnormal Indo-Anglian fiction is and why it still matters."

698. Davies, M. Bryn. "British and Indian Images of India." *Ariel* 1.4 (1970) : 48-55. Rpt. in Walsh, *Readings* 3-10. ref. : 547.
A review article. Reviews Allen J. Greenburger's *The British Image of India* and Anand's *The Private Life of an Indian Prince.* Discusses the image of India as projected by the novelists Kipling, Forster, Thomson, etc. as analysed by Greenburger in his book.

699. Dayal, B. "A Critical Survey of Short Story Writing in India." Dayal 1-24. ref. : 247.
Describes the trends in and tendencies of short story writing in India and explains how Indian English short story writers combine in themselves the traits of

modern story telling, psychological realism and social realism and the ancient Indian tradition of story telling.

700. ——. "Minor Indo-Anglian Short Story Writers : Kaleidoscopic View." Dayal 207-254. ref. : 247.
Discusses the stories of Raja Rao, Khushwant Singh, Jhabvala, Bhattacharya (though not strictly minor) Isvaran, Manoj Das, Nahal , Usha John and others.

701. De Souza, Eunice. "Poorly Served Discipline." *Times of India* 7 July 1974.

702. ——. "Tradition and Religion in Indian Fiction." *Eve's Weekly* 29 Dec. 1973 : 39-43.

703. ——. "Four Expatriate Writers." *Journal of the School of Languages* 4.2 (1976-77) : 54-60.
Compares and contrasts the four expatriate writers of the third World — Farruk Dhondy, Dom Moraes, Jean Rhys and Jhabvala — their situation as well as their attitudes and achievements to show "the more relevant ways of writing about the third world."

704. Desai, Anita. "The Timid Movement of a Wing." *Indian Literary Review* 1.4 (1978): 11-13. Rpt. as "The Indian Writers Problems." *ACLALS Bulletin* 4 Ser. 2 (1975) : 12-14. Rpt. in *Literary Criterion* 12.4 (1975) : 24-36. Also in *Language Forum* 7.1-4 (1981-82) : 223-226. Rpt. in Srivastava, R.K., *Perspectives on Anita Desai* 1-4 ref. : 2576 and in Dhawan, *Explorations* 223-226. ref. : 253. Also in Dhawan, *Indian Women Novelists* 7-10. ref. : 257.
Talks about her commitment to the English language and her views about creative writing. Desai feels that "writing is not an act of deliberation, reason and choice but a matter of instinct, silence and waiting ... It is a process that does indeed employ language but also transcends it."

705. ——. "Aspects of the Indo-Anglian Novel : Women Writers." *Quest* 65, Apr.-June 1970 : 39-43.

Discusses the paucity of literature written by Indian women. "With all the richness of material at hand, Indian women writers have stopped short — from a lack of imagination, courage, nerve or gusto — of the satirical edge, the ironic tone, the inspired criticism of the lyric response that alone might have brought their novels to life."

706. ——. "Contemporary English Literature in India." *Littcrit* 15, 8 : 2 (1982) : 65-68. Also in *Book Review* Jan.-Feb. 1982 : 160-62.
Considers English as a legitimate language of expression in India. Feels that Indian English has its own clientele and specialised functions and discusses the enthralling experiments with English by some of the novelists like Desani, Sudhin Ghose and Salman Rushdie and their impressive achievement.

707. ——. *"Feng Sui or Spirit of Place."* Nightingale 101-109. ref. : 406. Also in Olinder 101-109. ref. : 409.
Discussing 'regionalism' and categorizing regional writers into different groups, Desai explains how time and place make the framework of her novel, *Fire on the Mountain.* Using memory, dream and reverie as tools she narrates how she captured the spirit of place, which, she feels, requires not the power of observation so much as a burning intensity of vision.

708. ——. "Indian Fiction Today." *Daedalus* 118 (1989) : 207-231.
A short selection from the novels of Indian writers. "The young writers have set themselves free from inhibitions and have found confidence."

709. Desai, S.K. "The Theme of Childhood in Commonwealth Fiction." Narasimhaiah, *Commonwealth Literature* 38-48. ref. : 391.
Studies the theme of Childhood in the works of Indian, African and New Zealand writers with a view to

discovering the effect of cultural variables on literary creation.

710. ——. "Indian Writing in English : Trends and Possibilities." *Literary Criterion* 18.2 (1983) : 51-59.
Is concerned with critical responses of Western critics and the response of Indians to this literature.

711. ——. "Indian Writing in English : The Predicament of Marginality." *Indian Journal of English Studies* 26 (1987) : 29-38.
Argues that the marginality of Indian writing in English can be compensated by translating the literature of regional languages, by writing criticism of Indian literature — theoretical and textual and by studying comparative literature.

712. Devasia, S. D. "Indian Contribution to the World of Fiction." *Thought* 28 July 1973 : 17-18.

713. Devy, G.N. "The Indian English Novel 1980-90 : An Overview." Bharucha & Sarang 7-18. ref. : 216.
A general assessment of the contribution of the eighties to the field of the Indian English novel.

714. Dey, Esha. "Woman as Object : The Feminine Condition in a Decadent Patriarchy." *Literary Criterion* 20.4 (1985) : 9-18. Also in Narasimhaiah, *Women in Fiction and Fiction by Women : The Indian Scene* 9-19. ref. : 392.
Discusses the passive role of the woman in a decadent patriarchal society and cites Raja Rao's *The Serpent and the Rope* as its exemplification.

715. ——. "The Role of Motherhood in Expatriate Discourse." Bande, *Mothers and Mother Figures* 26-33. ref. : 205.
Exploring the archetypal mother in the Indian ethos, in expatriate fiction *(Heat and Dust)* and *The Serpent and the Rope)*, shows how in Jhabvala the role of motherhood "emerges clear and unambiguous" while in Raja Rao it is "subtle and complex".

716. Dhalla, Kamal H. "Indo-English Short Story Anthologies 1945-75." *Indian P.E.N.* 44, July-Aug. 1978 : 1-5.

A general survey of the Indian short story in English as separate genre and its growth and development over the past three decades (1945-1975). Out of eight anthologies the author appreciates Meenakshi Mukherjee's *Let's Go Home* as stylistically the most mature anthology.

717. ——. "The Indo-English Short Story." *ELT Forum Journal of English Studies* 1.4 (1978) : 36-42.

718. ——. "The Indo-English Short Story : Background and Beginning." *Indian Scholar* 1.2 (1979) : 123-130.

A cursory article on the genesis and form of the Indian short story in English.

719. Dhar, T.N. "History, Myth and the Post-colonial : The Indian Context." Trivedi and Mukherjee 141-152. ref. : 534.

720. Dharkar, Rani. "Marriage as Purdah: Fictional Rendering of Social Reality." Jain and Amin, *Margins* 49-59. ref. : 304.

Demonstrates through an analysis of the novels of Shashi Deshpande and Bharati Mukherjee, two disparate writers — one operating from within the Indian context and in a realistic mode of writing and the other writing from the centre of power and employing the post-modern idiom — how marriage works effectively as purdah preventing woman from selfhood and individuality cutting her off from the mainstream of life.

721. Dhawan, R.K. "The Artist as Historian : Three Contemporary Novelists." Dhawan, *Three Contemporary Novelists* 1–32. ref. : 255. Also in Dhawan, *Commonwealth Fiction* Vol. 3. 238-268. ref. : 256.

Discusses the relationship of art with history by examining the novels of Khushwant Singh, Chaman

Nahal and Salman Rushdie and shows how the historical events of Indian freedom struggle and partition are artistically represented by these three novelists from three different focal points.

722. ——. "Indian Literature Today : An Introduction." *Commonwealth Review* 5.1 (1993-94) : 9-16. Rpt. in Dhawan, *Indian Women Novelists.* Set I. Vol. I. 7-26. ref. : 257.

723. ——. Introduction. Dhawan, *Indian Women Novelists* Set I. Vol. I. 7-26. ref. : 257.
A general introduction to Indian woman Novelists in English from a feminist perspective.

724. Dhonge, R. C. "The Concept of Indianness in Indian Fiction in English ." *Bulletin of the Deccan College Research Institute* 44 (1985) : 65-70.
Examines "Indian sensibility" as expressed in Indian English fiction both from linguistic and thematic points of view and finds that the main intention is to acquaint the Western reader with Indian culture and habits.

725. Dissanayake, Wimal. "Towards a Decolonized English : South Asian Creativity in Fiction." *World Englishes* 4.2 (1985) : 233-242.

726. Dorion, Mark. "To Convey in a Language that is 'Not one's Own the Spirit That is One's Own': Understanding Non-Native Culture and Literature." *Journal of Indian Writing in English* 14.1(1986) : 33-49.
Feels that by studying Indian and African writers, Europeans (particularly teachers) can broaden their understanding of and feel for the cultural heritage of the international students from these countries. Contains sketchy references to Narayan and Raja Rao.

727. Dwivedi, A.N. "Indian English Literary Scene : A Critique." *Language Forum* 12.4 (1986) : 159-167. Rpt. in Singh,

R.K., *Indian English Writing : 1981-1985* 159-167. ref. : 511. Also in Dwivedi, *Indian Writing in English* Vol. 2. 159-167. ref. : 270.

A general review of the critical response to Indian English literature; often finds it laudatory.

728. ——. "Indian Fiction in English : Retrospect and Prospect." Dwivedi, *Studies in Contemporary Indian Fiction in English* 3-30. ref. : 269. Also in Dwivedi, *Indian Writing in English* vol.2 : 1-15. ref. : 270.

A general survey of Indian fiction in English written since 1865.

729. ——. "Contemporary Indian English Short Story : An Over View." Dwivedi, *Indian Writing in English* vol. 2 : 126-138. ref. : 270.

A note on the development and growth of Indian short story in English.

730. Ekambaram, E.T. "Some Aspects of Indian Response to Fiction in English." *Literary Criterion* 7.3 (1960) : 8-17.

A general essay dealing with the novelist's predicament in building up a reading public in India. Argues that the development of the general taste of the public and the need for discriminating readers are necessary concomitants for the future of the Indian novel.

731. Ezekiel, Nissim. "Cross-Cultural Encounter in Literature." *Indian P.E.N.* 43, Nov-Dec. 1977 : 4-8. Rpt. as "Two Readers and their Text'' in Amirthanaygam, *Asian and Western Writers in Dialogue* 137-142. ref. : 186.

Discusses the problems involved in judging a work of literature containing cross-cultural encounters. Looks at the problem from the point of view of two hypothetical readers of the two cultural contexts-with special reference to the cross-cultural responses to Jhabvala's *Heat and Dust*.

732. Fisher, Marlene and Robert Mcdowell. "On Language and Literature." *World Literature Written in English* 18 (Nov. 1970) : 27-32.

733. Fiske, Adele M. "Karma in Five Indian Novels." *Literature East and West* 10.1-2 (1966). 98-111.
Explicates the meaning of the *Karma* theory according to Hindu religion and examines Anand's *Coolie,* Premchand's *Godan,* Raja Rao's *Kanthapura* and Vyankatesh Madulkar's *The Village had on Walls* (a translation) and Kamala Markandaya's *Nector in a Sieve*—to show the absence of such a concept in them, functionally.

734. "Focus on Indian Women Writers in English." *Economic Times* 26 Jan. 1986 : 5.

735. Gabriel G. and M.C. Gabriel. "Indian Short Story : Struggle for a Genre." *Thought* 1968. 15-17.

736. Gandhi, Gopal. "The Pulse within." *Seminar* 384, Aug. 1991 : 26-29.

737. Gemmill, Janet P. "The City as Jungle in the Indo-English Novel." Noble and Dutt, 45-67. ref. : 408.
Discusses the traumatic and destructive elements in the experience of the modern man towards city life in India with special reference to Anand's *Coolie,* Kamala Markandaya's *A Handful of Rice* and Anita Desai's *Voices in the City.*

738. Gokak, V.K. "The Concept of Indianness with reference to Indian Writing in English." Mohan 21-25. ref. : 365.
Discusses the meaning of Indianness in terms of style and diction, theme and philosophy of the author — in short, the writer's intense awareness of his entire culture.

739. Gokhale, Namita. "Indian Writing : The transition." *Hindu-Folio* 3, Aug. 1997.

740. Gomez, Christine. "New Horizons : Exploring the Possibilities of Feminist Literary Criticism on Indian Writing in English." Dhawan, *Indian Women Novelists*, Set I. Vol. I. 84-103. ref. : 257.
Evaluates feminist literary criticism as practised in the West today and indicates some of the avenues open to feminist literary criticism on Indian writing in English.

741. Gondal, Yogesh Chandra. "India and the West in the Indian Novel : A Note." *Viswabharati Quarterly* 38.1-2 (1972) 93-111.
Describes the complex and varied relationship between India and the West as portrayed by several Indian novelists (Kamala Markandaya, Bhabani Bhattacharya, Arun Joshi and Raja Rao being some of these novelists).

742. Goonertne, Yasmine. "Village *Versus* City : Contrasts in Indian and Srilanka Literature." *Literary Criterion* 13.3 (1978) : 42-55.

743. Gowda, Anniah, H.H. "Humour : Indo-Anglian Literature." Ezekiel 140-147. ref. : 272.
Traces the element of humour in Indian-English fiction from Venkataramani to Kamala Markandaya and comments that except in the short stories of SVV (*Soap Bubbles* and *More Soap Bubbles*), and G.V. Desani's *All About H. Hatterr,* the humour present in Indian English fiction is quite different from that of the West : the difference being in the native perspective.

744. ——. "Contemporary Creative Writers in English in India" *Literary Half-Yearly* 10.1 (1969) : 17-39.
Based on a public lecture under the auspices of the University of Queensland, Brisbane in August, 1968.
A brief survey of Indian English poetry and fiction (Narayan, Raja Rao, Anand, Rajan and Malgonkar) and an assessment of the writers' achievements and shortcomings.

745. ——. "Contemporary Creative Prose Writing in India" Rutherford, *Commonwealth Literature* 192-195. ref. : 487.

A brief survey of Indian English fiction from Venkataramani to the minor writers of 1971. A large part of the essay is devoted to Narayan and Raja Rao. Feels that Indian English writers (though great in their own way) "have not caught fire from the immense energy of the emergent India."

746. ——. "The Current State of Indian Writing in English." *Literary Half-Yearly* 12.2 (1971) : 15-20.

Discusses the aim and purpose of Indian English literature and the ineffectual treatment of the great events of history in some of the Indian English novels.

747. ——. "The English of the Indians and the Africans in their fiction." *Literary Half-Yearly* 17.1 (1976) : 23–38.

Examines the use of English as a medium of expression in the creative writings of the Indians and the Africans. Finds the choice of English as both practical and aesthetic.

748. ——."The Value of Pluralism in Canadian and Indian Literatures in English." *Literary Half-Yearly* 35.2 (1994) : 45-59.

749. Goyal, Bhagwat S. "Indo-English." Jotwani 32-47. ref. : 308.

A brief survey of Indian English literature from 1947 to 1977 which includes fiction, poetry, plays as well as criticism. Feels that fiction "occupies the pride of place in Indo-English literature."

750. ——. "Contrasting Images of Indian Short Story." Goyal, *Culture and Commitment* 143-146. ref. : 281.

A review article. Examines briefly the two short story collections — *Five + One* by C.M. Naim and *The Storm and Other Stories* by Sharat Kumar to show how Naim's stories are "powerful and significant parables of our time" conceived and executed in a spirit of protest, whereas the stories of Sharat Kumar are "pale and insignificant."

751. ——. "The World of Women Novelists." *Hindustan Times* 13 Aug. 1978 : 3. Rpt. in Goyal, *Culture and Commitment* 139-142. ref. : 281.
A Short but critical note on the general trend of the women novelists in India and the indelible imprint of Indian sensibility and culture on their novels.

752. ——. "Indo-English Novel Since 1947." Goyal, *Culture and Commitment* 43-51. ref. : 281.
A brief survey of Indian English novels written between 1947-1976.

753. Gupta, G.S. Balarama. "Indian Writing in English : Is there any worth in it?" *Journal of South Asian Literature* 16.2 (1981) : 173-180.
Against the critics, particularly Subba Rao who questions the validity and viability of Indian writing in English in his book, *Indian Writing in English : Is there any worth in it?* in which he dismisses the entire body of literature produced by scores of gifted Indian writers, the author argues that it is unfair to condemn Indian writers in English whose significant contribution brought a prestigious position for Indian writing in English (particularly of the novelists) in Commonwealth literature.

754. ——. "Projecting Indian Literary Image." *Littcrit* 2, 2.1 (1976) : 33-36.
Plea for projecting the Indian literary image through efficient translations.

755. ——. "A Note on Indian Writing in English." *Contemporary Indian Literature* 12.3 (1972) : 37-38.

756. ——. "Difficulties Before the Indian Writers." *Contemporary Indian Literature* 22.1 (1973) : 52-53.

757. ——. "What is there in Indian Writing in English?" *Ocarina* (Madras), Nov.-Dec. 1973 : 11-12. Also in *Calcutta University News* 6.4 (1973).

758 ——. "Some Reflections on Indian Writing." *Journal of Indian Writing in English* 1.2 (1973) : 53-60. Rpt. in Gupta, *Essays* 1-9. ref. : 284.

Pinpoints some of the difficulties the research student of Indian writing in English is faced with and pleads for the recognition of the significance of Indian writing in English, particularly by the universities.

759. ——. "The short story writers : Self, Society and Emancipation." Dinesh, *Between Spaces* 147-159. ref. : 262.

Highlights the achievements and limitations of Indian English women short story writers with particular emphasis on Shashi Deshpande, Dina Mehta, Kamala Das, Anita Desai, Nergis Dalal, Bharati Mukherjee, Sunita Jain and Sadique Peerbhoy, Jai Nimbakar etc. and comments that these writers have shown "varying degrees of competence in handling the form of the short story and realizing verbal structures to suit the portrayal of complex human relationships, especially of the man-woman variety.

760. ——. "Indian English Women short story writers : An overview." *Vikram Journal of English Studies* Vol. 1 (1993) 38-39.

761. ——. "Promoting Indian English Literature." Narendra Kumar, *New Perspectives* 36-46. ref. : 399.

762. Gupta, Rameswar. "Indo-English Literature : Some Views." *Banasthali Patrika* 12 (1969) : 4-9.

Presents the views of the experts — P.N. Mathur, P.S. Sundaram, P.E. Dustoor, Khushwant Singh and that of the editor of Banasthali Patrika, Rameswar Gupta, on Indian English Literature.

763. ——. "The Indian Writer's Responsibility." *Journal of Indian Writing in English* 1.1 (1973) : 74-78.
Citing examples of Sri Aurobindo, Tagore, P. Lal, Narayan and others, the author points out to the Indian writers' responsibility to know India—its hoary wisdom, its myths, legends, its gods and goddesses to be true to himself and to have a basic knowledge in the essentials of life.

764. Gupta, Sanjukta. "Indian Women Novelists : In Other Words." *Imprint.* Oct. 1987: 53-58.

765. Gupta, Santosh. "The Politics of Seclusion : Women in Purdah." Jain and Amin, *Margins* 12-23. ref. : 304.
Provides a historical background to the social and political aspects of purdah. Also discusses some literary texts written by women belonging to different educational and social backgrounds presenting varying attitudes towards the purdah.

766. Guptara, Prabhu S. "The Predicament of the Indo-Anglian Fiction." *Indian P.E.N.* 42 Mar.-Apr. 1976 : 1-5.

767. ——. "Indian Fiction in English." *British Book News.* Mar. 1982 : 140-141.

768. Harrex, S.C. "Search for an Indian Form of Indo-English Fiction." *Littcrit* 14, 8.1 (1982): 1-6.
An overview of the writer's experiments in Indianizing the Western novel form with special reference to Anand, Narayan, Raja Rao and Desani.

769. ——. "India" King, *The Commonwealth Novel Since 1960.* ref. : 328.

Discusses to contribution of the three major Indian English writers the modern trends they represent.

770. ——. "Shakespeare : Almost an Indian of My India." *Literary Criterion* 29.4 (1994) : 1-14.
Traces the impact of Shakespeare on the new literatures in English beginning with the literary symbiosis which

is referred to as creative intertextuality. Examines in detail Raja Rao's *The Cat and Shakespeare* and Desani's *All About H. Hatterr* to show how "both transformed Shakespeare to suit their literary needs."

771. Harrison, Francis. "Literary Representation : Partiton in Indian and Pakistan Novels in English." *Indian Literature* 145, Sep.-Oct 1991 : 94-110.

772. Hiatt, Shennon T. "The Oral Tradition as a Nativization Technique in Three Novels." *Journal of Indian Writing in English* 14.1 (1986) : 10-20.
Pointing out the effective use of oral tradition as a technique of nativization, the author examines three novels — Raja Rao's *Kanthapura,* Amos Tutuola's *The Palm-Wine Drunkard* and Leslie Harmon Silko's *Ceremony.*

773. Iyengar, K.R.S. "The Impact of Gandhain Thought on our Writers-English." *Indian P.E.N.* 25.3 (Mar. 1959) : 65-69.
Traces the impact of Gandhian thought and values on Indian English fiction beginning with Venkataramani's *Murugan The Tiller* and *Kandan the Patriot* to the novels of Anand, Raja Rao, Venu Chitale and Anand Lall.

774. ——. "Contemporary Indian Short Story." *Indian Literature* 13.3 (1970) : 36-45.
A survey of the Indian short story in the regional language as well as in Indian English.

775. ——. "The Women Novelists." Iyengar, *Indian Writing in English,* 435-477. ref. : 297.
Critically surveys in brief Indian English fiction written by women from Toru Dutt to Nayantara Sahgal and Vimal Raina.

776. ——. "Indian Writing in English : Prospect and Retrospect." Mohan 1-10. ref. : 365.

Considers Indian English literature as Indian literature because of its quality of Indianness in the choice of subject, in the texture of thought, play of sentiment and language and states that its function is to derive from and to promote an all-India consciousness.

777. ——. "Towards an Indian Sensibility in Indo-Anglian Fiction." *Littcrit* 14. 8.1 (1982) : 42-46.
Defines the word "Sensibility" in the context of Indian English fiction and comments that "few Indo-Anglian novels succeed in communicating Indian sensibility to the same extent as Achebe, Okara, Soyinka, Ekwensi and Rubadiri seem to be able to convey African sensibility in their novels."

778. ——. "Indian Writing in English and Modern Indian Literature." Yaravintelimath, *et al.* 37-45. ref. : 558.

779. Jaganmohana Chari, A. "Indian Writing in English : A Materialist Interpretation." *Kakatiya Journal of English Studies* 11 (1991) : 1-7.

780. Jaggi, Satya Dev. "Indo-English Fiction : At a Seminar." *Thought* 3 June 1972 : 15-16.

781. Jai Dev. "Problematizing Feminism." Singh, Susila. 48-63. ref. : 517.
Contains random thoughts on feminism, especially in the Third World novel and finds several of the novels as stereotypes. Analyses Sahgal's *The Day in Shadow* and shows how difficult a task feminism has in our country, for most of the novels written by women in India "are anti-feminist, pro-male."

782. Jain, Jasbir. "Strangers in Enemy Territory : Expatriates and Exiles." *Littcrit* 7, 4.2 (1978) : 31-35.
Discusses the problems of the Indian immigrants as depicted in the novels of Kamala Markandaya *(The Nowhere Man)*, Anita Desai *(Bye-Bye Blackbird)*, Jamila and Reginald Massey *(The Immigrants)* and Dilip Hiro *(A Triangular View)* and says that "though religion and

culture and attitudes play their part, the main cause for the alienation resides in a political fact — the fact of the Empire ."

783. ——. "The Changing Image of Gandhi in Indo-English Fiction." *Indian Literature* July-Aug. 1979 182-190.
Citing the examples of Anand's *Untouchable,* Raja Rao's *Kanthapura,* Narayan's *Waiting for the Mahatma* and Bhattacharya's *So Many Hungers* and *Shadow from Ladakh,* draws attention to the two extremes of Gandhian image — as an avatar and as a hypocrite — and points out that the image stopped oscillating between the two extremes and the focus is now on Gandhi, the man.

784. ——. "The Political Novel and the Contemporary Scene in Indo-English Fiction." *Indian Book Chronicle* Mar. 1988 : 62-65.
Giving a working definition of the political novel discusses in general terms what goes into the making of a political novel and examines Nayantara Sahgal's *Rich Like Us* and *Plans For Departure* to show how they fit into that description : "Her (Nayantara Sahgal's) work along with some of the work of Manohar Malgonkar and K.A. Abbas constitutes the main stream of political fiction in contemporary Indian writing in English.

785. ——. "Moving Beyond Lingual Construction." *Anuvad* June 1988 : 66-73.

786. ——. "Gandhi and the Indian Novel in English." Jain, *Problems* 83-95. ref. : 300.
Considers the influence of Gandhi in terms of character in terms of form. Discuss how the complexities of Gandhi's character broke existing role models in real life situations and also non-consequential experimentation in the form of the Indian novel in English.

787. ——. "Contemporary Indian Fiction in English : New Directions." *Littcrit* 24 & 25, 13.1-2 (1987) : 44-48.
Examines the novels of the last decade —particularly Anita Desai's *In custody,* Nayantara Sahgal's *Plans for Departure, Rich Like Us,* Bharati Mukherjee's *Wife, Darkness,* Shashi Deshpande's *Roots and Shadows* — to show that the areas of experience and sensibility expressed through their writings are far more different and far more excellent than their counterparts in regional languages : "the areas of experience not available to the writer of regional languages, the highly individualized exploration of the human psyche, the split nature of the modern women even in ironic distance achieved thorough comedy are different in Indo-English fiction..."

788. ——. "Gender and Narrative Strategy." Dinesh, *Between Spaces* 29-40. ref. : 262.
Discusses the question of relationship between gender and narrative strategies.

789. ——."Erasing the Margins : Questioning Purdah." Jain and Amin, *Margins* 1-11. ref. : 304. Also in Jain, *Women's Writing* 243-255. ref. : 301.
Examines the nature and function of the practice of purdah mainly as a gender ideology tracing the positive and negative aspects of the enforcement of purdah and doing away with it, throwing light on the many versions of the custom both in the Hindu and the Muslim familial lives.

790. ——. "The Male presence in the 'purdah' Novel." Jain and Amin, *Margins* 216-230. ref. : 304.
Focusing on the power-structures inherent in male-female relationship, discusses the action-oriented functions of the male in selected Indian English novels which treat the purdah system and shows how "purdah imposes on women the psychology of prisoners, of victims and the subordinate while it turns the men into

gaolers and abettors in the process of this subordination." The novels discussed are Attia Hussain's *Sunlight Light on a Broken Column* and Bapai Sidhwa's *The Pakistani Bride.*

791. ——. "The Displacement of the Mother and Female Relatedness." Bande, *Mothers and Mother Figures* 51-61. ref. : 205.
See 2578.

792. ——. "Post-Colonial Realities : Women Writing History." Trivedi and Mukherjee 161-176. ref. : 534.
Examines post-colonialism with reference to women's writing.

793. ——. "The Many Faces of Tolerance." *Language Forum* 24.1-2 (1998) : 31-39.

794. ——. "The Plural Tradition : Indian English Fiction." Singh & Singh. 55-90. ref. : 514.

795. James, Jancy. "Female Reality Across Cultural Borders : A Comparative Approach of Alice Munro's Fiction and Indian English Fiction." Begum, 65-72. ref. : 210.
Traces the fulfilment of female reality as expressed in the works of Alice Munro, Anita Desai and others within the parameters that emerge from the corresponding system of cultural values.

796. Jamil, Maya. "Indian and Pakistani Writers of English Fiction." *University Studies* (Karachi) 1 (1964).

797. Jamkhandi, Sudhakar R. "The Spiritual Dimension : Christianity, the Church, the Missionary in Selected Indo-English Novels." Dhawan, *Commonwealth Fiction* Vol. 1 : 103-111. ref. : 256.
Evaluates the Indian literary artist's attitude towards Christianity, taking *The painter of signs, Clear Light Of Day, Untouchable* and *The Serpent and the Rope* as examples.

798. Jayaraman, T. "The Need for an Adequate Critical Method for Assessing Indian Fiction in English." Narasimhaiah. *Commonwealth Literature* 13-19. ref. : 391.
Points out the futility of judging Indian fiction in English with the critical criteria applicable to other Commonwealth literatures with European affinities and sensibilities and stresses the need for a different critical stance and vocabulary to judge Indian writing in English.

799. Jha, Akhileswar. "Intellectual Poverty of Indian Literature." *Times of India.* 4 Sep. 1977 : 8.

800. ——. "A Search for Excellence." *Hindustan Times* 29 Aug. 1982 : 4.

801. Jha, Mohan. "The Theme of Communalism in Indo-Anglian Novels." *Indian Journal of English Studies* ns 2, 21 (1981-82) : 117-130.
Discusses "the nature, degree and mode of communalism" in Indian English novel with special reference to Anand's *Death of a Hero,* Khushwanth Singh's *Train to Pakistan,* and Manohar Malgonkar's *A Bend in the Ganges* and *Distant Drums.*

802. Jha, Rama. "Impact of Gandhi on Indo-Anglian Novelists." *Economic Times* 12 Oct. 1983 : 5.

803. ——. "The Influence of Gandhian Thought on Indo-Anglian Novelists of Thirties and Forties." *Journal of South Asian Literature* 16.2. (1982) : 103-172 .
Traces the relationship between the Gandhian thought and the creative writing of Anand, Raja Rao, Narayan and shows how Gandhian thought had affected the choice of themes, the art of characterization, the making of the plot and even the use of language in the novels of the thirties.

804. Juneja, O.P. "Colonalism and the Novel." *Journal of the M.S. University* (Humanities) 29.1 (1980) : 33-40.

Comments critically on Larson's views on the third world novels and points out to the historical accident of colonization and the evolution of a new body of literature. Also refers to the peculiar use of English language by the novelists like Achebe and Soyinka to convey racial consciousness and biculturalism.

805. ——. "Colonial Consciousness and Identity Crisis : The Case of Black American, Indian and African Novelists." Srivastava R.K., *Colonial Consciousness* 1-22. ref. : 526.
Discuses the treatment of the theme of colonial consciousness in the novels of Black American, Indian and African novelists.

806. ——. "Fictional Strategies for Colonial Consciousness : An African Perspective." Gowda 187-203. ref. : 280.
Extending Larson's view of the third world novels as situational novels, treats the Indian and the African novels as "experimental" novels — finding new and daring fictional strategies in them — which may be "linguistic-formalistic" types.

807. ——. "Domesticated English : Symbiotic or Syncretic : The Language of African and Indian Fiction Novel." *ACLALS Bulletin*. 7th ser. 1986 : 20-28. Rpt. in Dass and Mohan 26-34. ref. : 241.
Discusses the use of English by two Commonwealth nations the Indian and African. Argues that in the case of Indian-English novelists the domesticating of English is "symbiotic", whereas with the Africans it is "syncretic". Concludes that "if the African novelists have enriched the English language with their rich oral tradition, the Indians have tried to bring it the flavour of their regional languages, though not always as successful as Africans."

808. ——. "Colonialism, Social Awareness and the Indian English Novel." Kaul and Jaidev 151-158. ref. : 319.

A brief survey of the Indian English novel from Bankim Chandra Chatterjee's *Rajmohan's Wife* to Shashi Tharoor's *The Great Indian Novel* to show that the Indian English novel is essentially "a situational novel" focusing on the life of community, the essential characteristic being hybridity, polyglossia, heterogeneity and social commitment.

809. Jussawalla, Feroza. "Beyond Indianness : The Stylistic Concerns of *Midnight's Children.*" *Journal of Indian Writing in English* 12.2 (1984) : 26-47.

Commenting on the stylistic innovations and linguistic experiments of some of the post-Independence Indian fiction writers and poets in English such as Rushdie, Markandaya, P. Lal and Arun Kolatkar, says that these writers who are carried away with the creation of "linguistic sculptures" can be classified as 'midnight's children' for in attempting to create an Indian novel or poem in an Indianized English they remain in "pre-midnight darkness of the emphasis on stylistic experimentation in the history of Indian literature in English."

810. ——. "Decolonizing the Decolonizers : Breaking the Colonial Habit of Mind." *North Dakota Qarterly* (Spl. issue on Race, Class and Gender) 55.3 (1987) : 175-189.

A comparative estimate of the responses of critical habits in Indian and African writings. Confirms that while in the Indians there is an unconscious acceptance of the colonial habit, in Africa it is largely countered, questioned and rejected.

811. ——. "Indian Long Fiction." *Critical Survey of Long Fiction* vol 5. 2214-2228.

812. ——. "Chiffon Saris : the Plight of South Asian Immigrants in The New World." *Massachusetts Review* 29.4 (1988) : 583-595.

"To attempt to shed an Indianess, our South-Asian essences, in order to become wholly mainstreamed in the majority culture of North America or the British Isles is perhaps altogether too artificial."

813. Kalinnikova, I.V. "On the National specificities of Indo-Anglian Writer in English : A Soviet Review." *Journal of the School of Languages* 5.1-2(1977-78) : 27-34. Rpt. in *Literary Half-Yearly* 21.2 (1980) : 1-11.
Argues that regional peculiarities determine the "specific" characteristics of several novelists — the specificity of being a Punjabi as in the case of Anand, a Bengali as in the case of Bhattacharya, and a Tamilian as in the case of Narayan, though all of them have a national poetic vision.

814. ——. "India in Indian writing in English and British writing." *Problems of Modern Indian Literature.* ed. Prabakar Machwe. Calcutta : Statistical Publishing Society, 1971. 177-190.

815. Kantak, V.Y. "The Language of Indian Fiction in English." Naik, *et al., Critical Essays* 223-235. ref. : 377.
Examines the language used by Narayan, Raja Rao and Rajan in their fiction *(The Guide, Kanthapura* and *The Dark Dancer)* to show the various degrees of achievement in articulating the sensations and feelings of Indian life in a foreign medium and the level reached in the process of naturalisation.

816. ——. "Indo-English Fiction and the New Morality." *Indian Literature* 21.5 (1978) : 39-45.
The only new morality that one finds in Indian fiction in English, according to Kantak, is the reassertion of inherited values. Enumerates similarities and dissimilarities among the major Indo-English novelists — Narayan, Raja Rao and Anand — in their approaches to new morality.

817. Kapadia, Novy. "Narrative Techniques in the New Indian Novel." Kirpal, *The New Indian Novel* 239-250. ref. : 330.

Discusses the nature and function of several technical innovations in the novels of the 80s, particularly in Salman Rushdie's uninhibited experiments in *Midnight's Children* and *Shame,* Nina Sibal's *Yatra* and Amitav Ghosh's *The Circle of Reason* to present new sensibilities, meanings and themes.

818. Karanth, K.S. "How Deep is Western Influence on Indian Writers on Fiction?" *Literary Criterion* 7.2 (1966) : 33-40. Also in Narasimhaiah, *Fiction and the Reading Public* 126-133. ref. : 387.
Traces the influence of Western fiction in moulding the Indian novelists and mentions the Indian writer's deficiencies and shortcomings to reach the level of Western writers.

819. Karnani, Chetan. "Renaissance in Indo-Anglian Literature." *Banasthali Patrika* 5.13 (1969) : 110-112.
Describes Indian renaissance as an effort to recreate the cultural life that existed in the West and traces its beginning in Michael Madhusudan Dutt, Bankim Chander Chatterjee who wrote his first novel in English and its culmination in Tagore. The author feels that contemporary writers have failed in carrying it further to higher levels of achievement.

820. Kaul, R.K. "The Problems of Speech in Indo-Anglian Writing." *Quest* 85, Nov.-dec. 1973 : 65-87.
Examines the language used in the conversations in some of the Indo-Anglian novels and analyses the problems that the novelists — Anand, Narayan, Raja Rao, Kamala Markandaya and Rajan — faced and the solutions they arrived at in presenting a convincing picture of nativity to the reader.

821. Kaur, Charanjit. "The Autobiographical Perspective." Bharucha and Sarang 47-58. ref. : 216.
Traces the autobiographical strain in Gurucharan Das's *A Fine Family,* Anand's *The Bubble,* Chatterjee's

English, August, and Firdaus Kanga's *Trying to Grow.* Shows how they reveal the author's search for identity, especially with regard to such aesthetic questions as "confessional mode", aesthetic distance, authenticity of poetic truth, personalised account of history, etc.

822. Kaushik, R.K. "English Fiction by Indians : Novel : A Retrospect." *Weekly Round Table* (India) 10 Dec. 1972: 29-38.

823. ——. "Socialist Realism and the Indian Novel in English." Coppala, 89-116. ref. : 235.
Finds that Indian novelists in English had followed more ardently Gandhian philosophy rather than the Marxian one in dealing with the realistic problems of the people.

824. Khan, A.G. "Has IWE Turned Delinquent !" Singh, Avadesh, *Contemporary Indian Fiction in English* 48-53. ref. : 507.
Criticizes the present state of Indian Writing in English for its many omissions and commissions, the example for the former being "this swarm of writers who can mock and ridicule anything precious to us."

825. ——. "Liberated or Libidinous : Women Writing in English." Dhawan, *Indian Women Novelists* Set III. Vol. 1. 33-38. ref. : 257.
An unfavorable criticism against women writing in English — particularly against the writings of Shobha De, Kamala Das, etc.

826. Kher, Prafulla C. "Indian Writing in English Today." *Malayalam Literary Survey* 16.2 (1993) : 7-23.
Argues that Indian Writing in English in the present day has acquired a distinctive identity having found proper articulation. Discusses the changing paradigms both in poetry and fiction illustrating the same through examples.

827. Khubchandini, Lachman M. "Polygenesis of English Heritage : Creative Experiments in Non-native English." Bharucha and Sarang 219-226. ref. : 216.

828. Khullar, Ajit. "On Indo-Anglian Writing." *Thought* 11 Jan. 1975.

829. Kimbahana, Raveendra S. "The Contemporary Indian English Novel : A Minority Report." *Critical Practice* 6.1 (1999) : 74-81.

830. King, Bruce. "The Commonwealth Writer in Exile." Rutherford, *From Commonwealth to Post-Colonial* 39-43. ref. : 488.

831. Kirkpatrick, Joanna. "Women in Indo-English Literature : The Question of Individuation." *Journal of South Asian Literature* 12.3-4 (1977) : 121-129.
Investigates the issue of autonomy and self-chosen identity of women in modern Indian English literature — especially in Markandaya's *Two Virgins, Nectar in a Sieve,* and Narayan's *The Dark Room.*

832. Kirpal, Viney. "The Third World Fiction." Dhawan, *Commomwealth Fiction* Vol. 3. 210-225. ref. : 256. Rpt. in Dhawan, *et al.*, *Recent Commonwealth Literature* Vol. 2. 11-25. ref. : 260.
Argues that the third world fiction, particularly the African, the West Indian and in a varying degree, Indian fiction in English, is a reconstruction in fictional terms of de-colonization and the depiction of the national identity and achievement. Also discusses the use of language and technique in the third world fiction and the reader's response to it.

833. ——. "Has the Indian Novel Been Understood?" Rutherford, *From Commonwealth to Postcolonial* 303-315. ref. : 488.
Questions the reliability of Eurocentric readings which treat the Indian novel in English simply as a derivative form and argues that a methodical survey of the

narrative structure of Indian English fiction, especially the episodic and digressional elements, shows the influence of indigenous oral narratives, the Sanskrit classical tradition, and the popular folk tradition.

834. ——. "Purdah in Indian English Writing." Jain and Amin, *Margins* 24-32. ref. : 304.
Examines the use of purdah in Salman Rushdie's *Shame,* Gurucharan Das's *A Fine Family,* and Nayantara Sahgal's *Mistaken Identity* to show how each one depicts a new aspect of the purdah throwing light on its perniciousness and condemning it as a sign of backwardness, conservativeness and orthodoxy. Also comments that "the depiction becomes more complex with novels written in the last decade or so where a distinctly feminist perspective makes the portrayal of purdah a political one.

835. ——. "Post-modern Strategies in the Indian English Novel." *Litticrit* 22-2 (1996) : 21-33.

836. Kohli, Devinder. "Indian English : A Kichri of Words." *Times Literary Supplement* 1 Dec. 1989 : 1332.

837. Kohli, Suresh. "Indo-English Literature : Good Harvest Bright Prospects." *Soviet India* 20 Aug. 1970 : 17–18.

838. ——. "Indian Writing in English." *Weekend Review* 22 Aug. 1967 : 31-32.

839. ——. "The Indian Women Novelists in English." *Times Weekly* (New Delhi) 8 Nov. 1970 : 13.

840. ——. "Indian Writing in English Today." *Thought* 8 May 1971 : 17-20. 15 May 1971 : 18-19.

841. ——. "Mahatma Gandhi : Indian English Fiction." *Patriot* (Mag.) 12 Sept. 1982 : 4.

842. Kothandaraman, Bala. "Betwixt the Devi and the Devil : The Feminist Dilemma in Indian Fiction in English." Radha, 1-13. ref. : 442.

A critique of the several feminist theories and their approaches to creative writing with special reference to some of the recent Indian English women fiction writers — from the earlier writers such as Markandaya and Anita Desai to Raji Narasimhan and Bharati Mukherjee.

843. Krishnamurthi, M.G. "Indian Writing in English : Some Critical Problems." *Humanist Review* 1.4 (1969) : 435-452.
A plea for a serious and disinterested attention towards Indian fiction in English with a conscious understanding of the special problems they encounter (the problem of audience, the problem of idiom and the problem of communicating particular nuances of a sensibility through a second language an Indian writer in English faces).

844. Kudchedkar, Shirin L. "The Second Coming : Novels of Partition." Bharucha and Sarang 59-72. ref. : 216.
Examines the socio-political issues, particularly the theme of partition presented in the novels written during 1980s and 90s –– Bapsi Sidhwa's *Ice Candy Man, The Pakistani Bride,* Gurucharan Das's *A Fine Family,* Bhishma Sahni's *Tamas* relating political atrocities to human nature — the concept of honour and masculinity as well as the view of women and sexuality.

845. Kumar, Shiv K. "Some Indian Writers of English Fiction." Gokak. ref. : 277.

846. ——. "Some Reflections on Modern Indian Novel in English." Paniker, *Contemporary Indian Fiction in English* 117-121. ref. : 418.
Discusses how modern Indian novel in English had acquired a new dimension both in the domain of content and structure.

847. ——. "Indo-Anglian Novelists." *Hemisphere* Aug. 1974 : 26-29.

848. ——. "Women in Modern Indian Fiction." *Hindustan Times,* 9 Dec. 1990. IV.

849. Kumar, T. Vijay. "Post-Colonialism or Post-colonialism: Relocating the Hyphen. Trivedi and Mukherjee 195-202. ref. : 534.

850. Kushwaha, M.S. "A Neglected Area of Indo-Anglian Writing." *Journal of Indian Writing in English* 6.1 (1978) : 23-27.

A plea for the recognition of English translations from native Indian languages as an important field of literary activity in the area of Indian Writing in English.

851. Lal, Malashri. "Indian Women Novelists : Notes Towards Feminism." George and Goodman, 297-316. ref. : 276.

852. Lal, P. "Literary Tradition-6 : Indian Writing in English." *Illustrated Weekly of India* 25 Oct. 1964.

853. ——. "Indian Writing in English." *Harvard Educational Review* 34.2 (1964) : 316-319.

854. ——. "English and English Writing in India." *Conspectus* 2.2 (1966) : 37-47.

855. ——. "Indian Writing in English Since Independence." *Illustrated Weekly of India* 29 Jan. 1967 : 32-34.

856 ——. "Contemporary Indian Fiction in English : Its Background and 'Tone'." Narasimhaiah, *Indian Literature Of the Past Fifty Years* 26-35. ref. : 389.

Discusses 'the tone' and 'the texture' of Post-Independence Indian Fiction in English and feels that the task of Indian writer lies in discovering a suitable "idiom" to transform creatively the bewilderingly rich material that is in front of him.

857. ——. "Myth and the Indian Writer in English." Naik, *Aspects* 15-18. ref. : 378.

Criticizes modern Indian literature, which includes Indian writing in English, as being deficient in projecting the complete view of man because of the writer's ignorance of the Indian myth. Stresses the need of studying and absorbing myth-values and structures of one's own land to become a good writer.

858. ——. "Second Thought on English in India." Yaravintellimath, *et al.* 15-17. ref. : 558.

859. Lal, P. and Suresh Kohli. "Indian Writing in English : Two Views." *Indian and Foreign Review* 15 Feb. 1971 : 16-18.

860. Le Roy, David J. "Evil as Portrayed in Five Indian Novels." *Thought* 12 May 1962.

861. Leard, Abha Prakash. "Indian Women's Fiction and the Post-Colonial Critic." *Literary Half-Yearly* 39.1(1998) : 88-97.

862. Lewis, Robin Jared. "National Identity and Social Consciousness in Modern-Indian Literature." Paolucci 38-42. ref. : 419.

863. Linda, Hutcheon. "The Politics of Post-modernism: Parody and History." *Culture Critique* 5 (1986-87) 179-207.

864. Lokuge, Chandani, "The Cross Cultural Experience of a Pioneer Indian Woman Writer of English Fiction." Rutherford, *From Commonwealth to Postcolonial* 102-16. ref. : 488.

865. Lowry, Ann. "Style and Range in New English Literatures." Kachru 283-293. ref. : 313.
See 1276.

866. M.K.V. "Indian Writers in English." *Times of India* 27 Oct. 1968 : 8. Rpt. in *Times of India* (Delhi Edition) 2 Dec. 1968 : 9.

867. Machwe, P. "Prominent Women Writers in Indian Literature after Independence." *Journal of South Asian Literature* 12.3-4 (1977) : 145-150.

A Sweeping survey of the writings of women writers in Indian languages which include Indian English writers as well.

868. Madan, Mohini V. "The Genre of Neo-Socio-Political Novel." *Indian Literature*, Sep.-Oct, 1996 : 124-131.

869. Mahle, H. H. "East-West Passage." Saxena, *Glimpses* Vol. 2. 295-304. ref. : 497. Also in Mahale 99-110. ref. : 346.

See 4617.

870. Mahapatra, Jayanta. "Recent Commonwealth Fiction : Writing from Three Different Cultures." Narasimhaiah, *Commonwealth Literature* 30-38. ref. : 391.

Finds that Witi Ihimara's *Tangi* and *Whanau,* Obi B. Egbuna's *Daughter of the Sun* and *Emperor of the Sun,* and Narayan's novels, though rooted in three different cultures, are based on a ground of realism and have become more meaningful to the reader on account of a conservative moral potency than the rush and purposelessness of post-modernistic literatures, especially from the United States and West European countries.

871. Malak, Amin. "From Margin to Majority : Minority Discourse and the 'Third World' Fiction Writers in Canada." Rutherford, *From Commonwealth to Post-colonial* 44-52 ref. : 488.

Examines select writers of Caribbean and South Asian origin including Bharati Mukherjee and Rohinton Mistry. Discusses Mistry's ironic method in his short story "Squatter" from his collection of short stories *Tales of Firozsha Baag.*

872. Malhotra, M.L. "Recent Indo-Anglian Fiction : Continuity and Change." *Banasthali Patrika* 9.21 (1976) : 20-30.

A brief survey of Indian English fiction particularly that of Bhabani Bhattacharya, Nayantara Sahgal, Anita Desai and Arun Joshi. Against the charge that Indian English fiction is far too inert and lacks movement or animation, the author points out to the shifting trends in emphasis and attitudes.

873. Malik, Keshav. "The Indian Writer's Problems." *ACLALS Bulletin* 4th Ser. 2 (1975).

874. Markandaya, Kamala. "Why do we write in English?" *Adam International Review* 36 (1971) : 42-43.

875. Mandy, C.R. "Some Indian Authors in Candid Retrospect." *Miscellany* 8, Sep.-Oct. 1961 : 17-20.
Records the author's personal contact with and impressions of some of the Indian writers in English. Remarks that his experiences with these writers made him feel that they lack, on the whole, the warm heartedness of the artists "although they are not really disagreeable or difficult in the temperamental, ageing soprano manner."

876. Mann, Haven Sachdeva. "Cracking India : Minority Women Writers and the Contentious Margins of Indian National Discourse." *Journal of Commonwealth Literature* 29.2 (1994) : 71-94.
Regarding Bapsi Sidhwa, Nina Sibal, Namjoshi, Kamala Das as "marginally constituted by the hegemonic culture," analyses their novels to show the ways in which their narratives 'crack' the unified Indian nationalist discursive tradition to establish the complexity of the modern Indian nation-state. Comments that their novels "not only underscore their contestations of the dominant patriarchal national discourse but also to articulate heterogeneity and plurality operative within sub-continental woman's resistance."

877. ———. "U.S. Multiculturalism Post-Colonialism and Indo-Anglian Literature: Some Issues of Critical Pedagogy and Theory." *Journal of the Midwest Modern Language Association* (Iowa city) 27.1 (1994) : 94-108.

878. Marath, S. Menon. "Three Indian Novelists." *Life and Letters* Dec. 1948 : 187-192.

879. Mathai, Samuel. "Indian Writing in English." *Indian P.E.N.* 38 Sep. 1972 : 215-218.
Guest Editorial.

880. Mathur, O.P. "The Indian Protagonist and the Western Experience." Dhawan, *Commonwealth Fiction* Vol. 1. 70-120. ref : 246. Rpt. in Mathur, *Modern Indian English Fiction* 1-29. ref. : 351.
Finds three types in the Western-influenced protagonists in Indian English novels — namely those in whom the Western experience has been in its very process of its absorption; those that show the results of the Western experience after their return and those in whom "the whole panorama of their experience and its results has been unrolled."

881. ——. "Post-Independence Indo-Political Novel : Pointer for a Comparative Study." Mathur, *Indian Political Novel* 1-66. ref. : 352.
A brief survey of Indian English and Hindi literatures dealing with post-independence political fiction to show how various writers treated the themes concerning the political happenings in India.

882. Mazumdar, S. "Indian Writing in English : An Identity Search." *Patriot* 9 Mar. 1986 : 4.

883. ——. "Indo-Angilan Writing and Gandhiji." *Link* 20 Nov. 1983 : 39-40.

884. McCutchion, David. "Introduction to Indian Writing in English." *Miscellany* 29, July-Aug. 1968 : 5-18. Rpt. in McCutchion 5-18. ref. : 354.
Discusses the reasons for the emergence of Indian writing in English and the consequent diverse creative expression of writers. Looks literature as an outcome of social phenomena.

885. ——. "Indo-Anglian Nostalgia." *Miscellany* 29, July-Aug. 1968 : 64-66. Rpt in McCutchion 83-85. ref. : 354.

Finds nostalgia as a favourite mode of the Indian novel in English since Independence and discusses Attia Hosain's *Sunlight on a Broken Column* as a sentiment.

886. ——. "Indian Writing in English." *Miscellany* 29, July-Aug. 1968 : 19-38. Rpt in McCutchion 19-39. ref.:354.
An essay on the historical development of Indian Writing in English from 1865 to date (1969). Evaluates the contribution of several early writers and critics of the genre.

887. ——. "Can English be a Creative Language for Indians?" *Adam International Review* 36 (1971) 26-35.
Tracing the growth and development of Indian English finds Narayan and Sudhin Ghose as "satisfying Indian novelists."

888. ——. "The Indian Novel in English." *Studies in the Novel* 4.2 (1972) : 304-320. Rpt. in *Jadhavpur Journal of Comparative Literature* 2(1973) : 1-20.
Addresses himself to several important general and specific questions regarding Indian novelists writing in English *viz.*, (i) to whom does the novelist write and for what purpose ? (ii) is it possible to write authentic realistic novels in English about a milieu where the medium of expression is another language, and (iii) the exploration in English of the novelists own spiritual dilemma.

889. ——. "Quest for Identity : Theme in Three Commonwealth Novels." Srivastava A.K., *Alien Voices* 128-136. ref. : 524.
Examines Achebe's *No Longer at Ease,* Naipaul's *A House for Mr. Biswas* and Markandaya's *The Nowhere Man* to show how the theme of exile and the problem of identity have been treated by these novelists.

890. Meera Bai, K. "Tradition and Modernity : The Portrayal of Women by Women Writers." Dhawan, *Indian Women Novelists* Set I. Vol. 1. 35-46. ref. : 257.

Traces the conflict between tradition and modernity in terms of women characters and shows how they are presented differently by different novelists. "If traditional women who still retain their individuality make their appearance in the novels of Kamala Markanadaya, women who face challenges in their quest for self-fulfilment are seen in Nayantara Sahgal's novels. Likewise women who opt for modernity for convenience and not out of conviction are presented by Jhabvala."

891. ——. "Identity Crisis : The Problem of the Cultural Transplant." Dhawan, *Indian Women Novelists* Set I. Vol. I : 117-128. ref. : 257.

Discusses the phenomenon of the juxtaposition between the East and the West and the reluctant cultural alienation and the loss of identity faced both by the expatriates and immigrants as seen in the novels of Kamala Markandaya, Jhabvala, Anita Desai and Nayantara Sahgal.

892. ——. "Feminism as an Extension of Existentialism: Women in Indian English Fiction." *Commonwealth Review* 6.1 (1994-95) : 135-140. Rpt. in Dhawan, *Indian Women Novelists* Set II. Vol.1. 26-32. ref. : 257. Also in Dass, *Feminism and Literature* 135-140. ref. : 244.

Examines the portrayal of women characters in certain Indian English novels (of Anita Desai, Nayantara Sahgal, Raji Narasimhan's *Forever Free,* and Narayan's *The Dark Room)* and comments that "these hypersensitive and highly individualistic women amply illustrate that more or less feminism can be viewed as an extension of existentialism."

893. ——. "The Theme of East-West Encounter : The Expatriate Writer's Personal Dilemma." Dhawan, *Indian Women Novelists* Set III. Vol. 3. 9-14. ref. : 257.

Citing the examples of Kamala Markandaya *(Possession, The Nowhere Man)* and Jhabvala *(Esmond in India, A*

Backward Place and *A New Dominion)* evolves a proposition that "the theme of East-West encounter ... may almost be taken as some kind of vicarious re-enactment of the personal dilemma of the expatriate writers themselves, with all the accompanying trauma, disillusionment and disappointment."

894. Mehrotra, Raja Ram. "Indian English : Some Myths and Misconceptions." Sinha, K.N., *Indian Writing in English* 195-205. ref. : 518.

Draws attention to some of the popular notions and misconceptions about the linguistic aspects of Indian English. Remarks that "the English used in India cannot but take the mould from the contextual spectrum of its speakers — their life style, their thought ways, the very ethos that they breathe."

895. ——. "The Language of Indian Writing in English : Some Socio-Linguistic Evidences." *Journal of South Asian Literature* 2.2 (1987) : 103-116.

Enumerates several stylistic and socio-linguistic evidences to establish the Indian Character of the Indian English fiction writers (He also includes Jhabvala in this category), especially the use of Indian words, collocations, non-economy of words and phrases, use of rhetorical and ornamental languages, etc.

896. Mehta, Digish. "Fiction of the Interface : Kipling or Rushdie?" Singh, Avadesh. 28-32. ref. : 507.

Taking Suresh Joshi's Gujarati short story in its English translation as an example, proposes criteria for distinguishing English Indian fiction and Indian English fiction — the main distinction lying in "the act of imagining India." While Kipling belongs to the former, Rushdie belongs to the latter category.

897. Mehta, Purnima. "The Feminine Image in the Indo-Anglian Novel of the Post-Independence Era." Singh, Avadesh 143-147. ref. : 507.

Discuses briefly the changing perspective of the concept of womanhood as it emerges from the works of Raja Rao, Rajan, Anita Desai, Arun Joshi and others from "a revivalist tendency to glorify the ancient heritage" to a reformist approach "to be judged by an equitable standard."

898. Melwani, Murali Das. "Gentle Voice of Indo-Anglian Literature." *Thought* 28 Aug. 1971 : 15-17. Rpt. in Melwani, *Critical Essays* 36-41. ref. : 361.
Calls Ruskin Bond as the "gentle voice of Indo-Anglian literature." Finds in his work (short stories) affinities with that of Kipling and other Anglo-Indian writers and remarks that he is the link between British writers on India of the 19th Century and the present day Indian English writers.

899. ——. "Failing of Indo-Anglian Novelists and Their Critics." *Statesman* 28 Dec. 1978 : 8. Rpt in Melwani, *Critical Essays* 19-23 ref. : 361.

900. ——. "In Defence of Pulp Literature." *Quest* 100, Mar.-Apr. 1976. 63-65.
Describes the growth of "a lower level of literature," which he calls 'pulp literature', especially in Indian fiction in English. Attributes this growth to the extension of the readership beyond the upper and the upper middle classes which provide them an escape from their hum-drum lives.

901. ——. "Experimental Story in English." *Thought* 15 May 1971 : 14-15.

902. ——. "Indo-Anglian Neglect of the Short Story." Melwani, *Critical Essays* 12-18. ref. : 361.

903. Merchant, Minaz. "A Comment on 'Indian Writing'." *Free Press* (Mag.) 8 Nov. 1987 : 15.

904. Merchant, Naina. "An Overview of Indian English Writing." *Free Press* (Mag.) 8 Nov. 1987 : 15.

905. Mishra, A.L. "Problems of Indo-Anglian Literature." *University of Rajasthan Studies in English* 4(1969) : 63-66.

906. Mishra, D.S. "New Voices in Indian English Novels of 80s." Singh, Avadesh 33-36. ref. : 507.
Describes Nayantara Sahgal, Shiv K. Kumar and Firdaus Kanga as some arresting new voices of the 80s, for their primary concern is to express their voices overtly and artistically "to develop a better understanding of contemporary situations."

907. Mishra, Ganeswar. "The Hindu Tradition and the Novelist's Worldview." Mishra 68-136. ref. : 345.
Traces the Hindu background of the Indian English novel to suggest how much of the Hindu tradition, particularly the literary and the artistic, survived in its worldview, motive and characterization. Examines Narayan's *The Man-Eater* and Raja Rao's *Kanthapura,* with reference to Hindu religious texts like the *Bhagvat Gita* and the *Vishnu Purana* to show that their worldviews are Hindu and Puranic.

908. ——. "The Indian Novel : A New Literary Genre." *Journal of Literary Studies* 15.2 (1990) : 1-14.
Discusses the various changing trends in Indian novel in English.

909. Mishra, Pankaj. "Expatriate Writers : Much Ado About Nothing." *Indian Review of Books* July-Aug. 1995 : 2-8. "In Focus."

910. Mishra, Vijay. "The Dialectic of 'Maya' and the Principle of Narrative Structure in Indian Literature." *ACLALS Bulletin,* 5th Ser. 2 (1979) : 47-60.
Exploring the ramifications of the relationship between literature and the historical matrix in Indian literature, from the point of view of Marxian aesthetics, explains how this relationship the 'text' and the 'Real' can be evidenced from three texts belonging to three distinct

periods of Indian literary and philosophical tradition — Sankara's *Commnetary on Vedanth,* Tulasidas's *Ramacharita Manas* and Narayan's *The Guide.*

911. ——. "Diaspora's Migrancy Border : The Familiar Temporariness." Paper presented at the IACLALS conference on "Interrogating post-colonialism." organised by IACLALS and Indian Institute of Advanced Study 3 to 5 Oct. 1994 at Shimla. Published under the title "New Lamps for Old : Diaspora's Migrancy Border" in Trivedi and Mukherjee 67-88. ref. : 534.

912. Mohan, Devinder. "The Differential and Integral in Indian Writing in English." *New Quest* 49, Jan-Feb. 1985 : 37-41.
Discusses the double task of the Indian writer in English exploring cultural forms through an alien medium : "He faces differential of his unmasked-self and discovers identity. He also visualizes an integral self, although in "glass-darkly", and is quite aware of the loss."

913. Mohan, Ramesh. "Some Aspects of Style and Language in Indian English Fiction." Mohan, 192-202. ref. : 365.
Hits upon certain popular misconceptions regarding the nature and validity of Indian English and says "that Indian English has been the product of an evolutionary, creative process, obviously influenced by Indian languages and not of a derivative one."

914. ——. "The Rapunzel Syndrome in Indo-English Fiction." *Indian Journal of English Studies* 30 (1992-93) : 25-33.
Studies the portrayal of woman in Indian English Fiction — particularly Anita Desai's *Cry, The Peacock,* Shobha De's *Socialite Evenings,* Raji Narasimhan's *For Ever Free* and Nayantara Sahgal's *The Day in Shadow* and finds that "the Indian English fiction in its treatment of women exhibits what can be called "the Rapunzel syndrome" (the fairy tale motif).

915. Mokashi-Punekar, Shanker. "Indian Writing in English : A Statement of Some Stylistic Issues." Mohan, 140-147. ref. : 365.
Examines some of the stylistic issues in the novels of Bhabani Bhattacharya, Anita Desai, Rajan and others and illustrates a generalised pattern of literary phenomenon, particularly the absence of an in-depth knowledge of the Indian life and the behavioural patterns.

916. ——. "Indian Fiction : Problems of Periodization." *Littcrit* 5, 3.2 (1977) : 1-4.
Suggests that in periodization theory there are two simultaneous perspectives *viz.*, the dominant thought currents prevailing at a given time and the literary vogues dominant in England or America and makes a passing reference to Anand's *Untouchable* as an example.

917. ——. "The Indo-Anglian Creed." Mokashi-Punekar 29-72. ref. : 366.
Makes a spirited defense of Indian English writers and concludes that the creative writer in India has a vital role to play in the growth of Indian culture.

918. Moraes, Dom. "Indian Literature in English." *Indo-International Centre Quarterly* 3.2 (1976) : 143–156.

919. Motiwalla, Mumtaz. "The Indian Writers Today." *Indian P.E.N.* 20 Oct. 1954 : 15.
Defends Indian English writing and P.E.N.'s concern for it elaborately quoting from Bhabani Bhattacharya's article "Indo-Anglian Writing : An Author's Protest."

920. Mukherjee, Dhurjati. "Indo-Anglian Writers : Anand and Bhattacharya." *Society and Commerce* 2.2 (1973) : 104-105.

921. Mukherjee, Meenakshi. "Awareness of Audience in Indo-Anglian Fiction." *Quest* 62, Jan.-Mar. 1967 : 37–40.
Describes such tendencies of Indian English writers as an overemphasis of overcultural items and rituals, and

pleads that the Indian writer in English should concentrate on *what* has to be written rather than on *for whom* it is being written.

922. ——. "Style in Indo-Anglian Fiction." *Indian Writing Today* 4.1 (1970) : 6-13.
Analyses the linguistic and stylistic experiments in some major Indian English writers (Raja Rao, Bhabani Bhattacharya, and Anand to name a few) to show "a particular reality" through their novels.

923. ——. "Four Indo-Anglian Novelists." *Miscellany* 39, June 1970. 27-33.
A brief study of four Indo-Anglian Novels — Santha Rama Rau's *Remember the House,* Kamala Markandaya's *Some Inner Fury,* Anita Desai's *Cry, the Peocock* and Attia Hosain's *Sunlight on a Broken Column* to show the general characteristics of the Indian English novels — the presentation of personal narrative against the background of modern Indian history, the conflict of values between the family and the individual, an awareness for the social changes. Considers these novels as competent experiments.

924. ——. "English in the Indian Literary Landscape." *Indian and Foreign Review* Aug. 1972 : 11-12.
Comments on the contribution of Indian writers in English in enriching contemporary Indian literature.

925. ——. "English Fiction by Indians : New Directions." *Weekly Round Table* (India) 10 Dec. 1972 : 29-38.

926. ——. "Landmarks in Post-Independence — Indo-Anglian Literature." *Indian P.E.N.* 39.4 (1973) : 9-14.
A brief survey of the works of fiction, poetry and drama written after Independence (1947-1972). Traces certain trends and tendencies of the Post-Independence period, particularly the shift of emphasis from the public issues to the personal concerns of the individual by giving the examples of *Bye-Bye Black Bird* (Anita

Desai), *The Foreigner* (Arun Joshi), *The Serpent and the Rope* (Raja Rao), and *The Man-Eater* (Narayan).

927. ——. "Literature of Exile." *ACLALS Bulletin,* 4th Ser. 2 (1974) : 27-32.

928. ——. "Inside the Outsider." Narasimhaiah *et al., Awakened Conscience* 86-91. ref. : 395.
Studies the inter-cultural relationships found in several Indian fiction writers in English and shows how their exposure to outside culture influences their writings.

929. ——. "The Language of the Indo-Anglian Novelists." Mohan, 150-156. ref. : 365.
Discusses the problems the creative writer encounters in using English as the medium. Offers an illuminating commentary on the diction, syntax and imagery in the context of 'unique' situations in which contemporary Indian novelists find themselves. Justifies the Indian-English novelists' experiments with language saying that these experiments are neither intended to create an Indian English nor to reveal the quintessence of Indian sensibility but to suit his or her own individual needs. Anand, Raja Rao, Narayan and Sudhin Ghose render the essence of a regional reality through English while Kamala Markandaya, Anita Desai, Sahgal and Malgonkar use English as any cultured native speaker of that language.

930. ——. "Over-Kill : The State of Research in Indo-Anglian Fiction." *Journal of Literary Studies* 2.2 (1979) : 1–9.
Comments on the mediocre quality of research in the field of Indo-Anglian fiction and warns that "unless we control our generous bountiful impulses there is a danger that Indo-Anglian writing will eventually be killed with professional kindness."

931. ——. "Indo-English : A Natural Part." *Indian Literature.* Nov.-Dec. 1980 : 102-112.

A brief survey of the literary landscape of Indian-English writings of 1979.

932. ——. "Who is an Indian Writer." *Indian Express,* 22 Aug. 1982 : 1.

933. ——. "Towards Liberation : Four Recent Novels from India." *Westerly* 29.2 (1983) : 66-72.

A general survey of recent Indian English novels — Anita Desai's *Clear Light of Day,* Shashi Deshpande's *The Dark Holds No Terror,* Raji Narasimhan's *Forever Free* and Shouri Daniels's *The Salt Doll* — to show the change of focus in the fictional matrix from the unrealistic portrayal of homogenized Indian culture as practised by the earlier novelists (like Narayan and Raja Rao) to the heterogeneous reality — the tensions arising out of diverse cultures within India — as seen in the novels of Anita Desai, Shashi Deshpande, Shouri Daniel and Raji Narasimhan.

934. ——. "The Exile of the Mind." Bennet and Miller 7-14. ref. : 213.

Categorizes different kinds of exile and makes succinct remarks about the "experience of exile in literature" with reference to India. While the first part of the essay discusses the literature of exile — the obsessive concern of the Indian writers of exile with roots, nostalgia and finally mythicization of the lost country — the second part is devoted to the "exile of the mind" and refers to those who have internalized an alien epistemic model.

935. ——. "Text, Pretext and Context." *Link* 16 Mar. 1986 : 28-36. Paper presented in a seminar on "Indian Literature in English and English Translations" under the auspices of the Sahitya Akademi, New Delhi on 24-28 Feb. 1984.

936. ——. "The New Writers : Short Fiction to the Fore" *Indian Review of Books* 2.1 (1992) : 24.

937. ——. "The Anxiety of Indianness : Our Novels in English." *Economic and Political Weekly* 27 Nov. 1993 : 2607–2611.

938. ——. "Women Creative Writers in Indian English Literature." Dinesh, *Between Spaces* 9-19. ref. : 262.
A keynote address of the national seminar on "Women Creative Writers."

939. Mukherjee, Sujit. "The Indo-Anglian Novelist as Best-Seller." *Literature East and West* 1-2 (1969) : 83-93. Rpt. in *Quest* 65, Apr.-June 1970 : 34-43.
Speculates on the aspects that should be contained in Indian English novels to sell well.

940. ——. "Indo-English Literature in the Classroom." *Literary Criterion* 12.2-3. (1976) : 215-219. Narasimhaiah and Srinath, *Indian Literature in English* 215-219. ref.: 396.
Outlines a modest proposal in favour of using Indian English Writing as an occasional experimental alternative to British/American texts for learning English in a classroom.

941. ——. "Indo-English Literature — An essay in Definition." Naik *et al.*, *Critical Essays* 19-30. ref. : 377.
Differentiates between Indo-Anglian and Indo-English, the former referring to "the original literary creation in the English language by Indians" and the latter to "translations into English from literature in Indian languages."

942. ——. "India's Entry into English Fiction." *Quest* 48, Aug. 1965 : 51-55.

943. Mund, Subhendu. "Towards a Synthesis : the Theme of Reform in the Indian Novel in English of Nineteenth Century." *Ravenshaw Journal of English Studies* 3.2 (1993) : 71-82.
A brief survey of 19th Century Indian English fiction and the treatment of the theme of reform in the

changing milieu of the society : "Indian novelists while exposing the evils of their society, sought a studied synthesis through reform and liberalism. The ideal of reform and the spirit of inquiry stemmed out of this very synthesis."

944. ——. "Colonial Dilemma : A Study of Cultural Collision and Assimilation in The Early Indian English Fiction." *Ravenshaw Journal of English Studies* 8.1(1998) : 101-105.

945. Murali, S. "Indigenousness and the Indian Writer in English." *Journal of Indian Writing in English* 21.2 (1993) : 1-10.
Finds that Indian Writing in English "has passed through a variety of phases — colonial, post-colonial and one of creative decolonizing." It has "for the most part in its evolutionary process, revealed the unconscious pulsations of the Indian psyche, in a remarkable degree of cohesiveness and integrity."

946. Murthy, K.S.R. "The Indian Women Novelists Writing in English." *Littcrit* 6, 4.1 (1978) : 33-42.
An analytical survey of the fiction in English written by Indian women from Toru Dutt to Anita Desai. The writer finds in the fiction of the recent writers like Santha Rama Rau and Anita Desai the same qualities, tendencies and predilections seen in the earlier writers such as Mrs. Goshal.

947. Murthy, K.V.S. "The Concepts of Heroism in Indo-Angian Literature." *Aryan Path* 44.6 (1973) : 247-254. Rpt. in Murti 1-10. ref. : 372.
Relates the traditional Indian literary conception of the hero to the treatment of heroism by recent Indian writers. *viz.*, the idealistic hero of Anand, the comic persons of Narayan and the metaphysical hero of Raja Rao.

948. Nabar Vrinda. "The Tale of the Teller" *Seminar* 384, Aug, 1991 : 19-22.

949. Nagarajan, K. "The Development of the Novel in India." *Arts and Letters* 23.1 (1949) : 44.

950. Nahal, Chaman. "Writing a Historical Novel." Dhawan, *Three Contemporary Novelists* 39-47. ref. : 255.
Presents his views on historical fiction, especially as to how history becomes a new myth or metaphor to dramatize actual events in fictional terms and the problems he encountered in writing such historical novels as *Azadi* and *The Crown and the Loincloth.*

951. ——. "The Second Generation of Indian English Novelists." Nandan 264-327. ref. : 384. Rpt. in Nahal 88-111. ref. : 376.
Traces the development of the Indian novel in English by the second generation novelists (Bhabani Bhattacharya, Anita Desai, Nayantara Sahgal, Raji Narsimhan, Uma Vasudevan, Manohar Malgonkar, and others) and finds their novels superior to "the nowhere novels" of the first generation (Raja Rao, Narayan and later novels of Anand) "as their major concerns are related to specific humanism, individual happiness, morality freed from the shackles of metaphysics, synthesis not merely of ethnic strains but also that of the East and the West and their free and more confident use of English language."

952. ——. "Indian Political Novels." Nahal 134-152. ref. : 376.
Works out a definition of the political novel and examines some of the works of Anand, Bhabani Bhattacharya, and Nayantara Sahgal to show how the basic framework of these novels is political.

953. ——. "Feminism in Indian English Fiction." Dhawan, *Indian Women Novelists* Set I. Vol. I. 27-34. ref. : 257. Rpt. as "Feminism in English Fiction : Forms and Variations," in Singh, Sushila. 14-21. ref. : 517.

Defines feminism as a mode of existence in which the woman is free from the dependence syndrome and cites the novels of Bhabani Bhattacharya, Nayantara Sahgal, Uma Vasudev, Rama Mehta, as presenting "the replacement models" in the place of the orthodox ones. Considers *The Day in Shadow* of Nayantara Sahgal and the *The Song of Anasuya* of Uma Vasudev as good feminist novels.

954. Naik, M.K. "Gandhiji and Indian Writing in English." *Banasthali Patrika* 9.15 (1970) : 55-66. Rpt. in Naik *et al.*, *Critical Essays* 370-381. ref. : 377.
Evaluates Gandhi as an Indian writer in English as well as his impact on Indian writings in English.

955. ——. "In Defence of Indian Writing in English." *Journal of Karnataka University* (Humanities) 18 (1974) : iii-vii. Rpt. in Sharma, K.K., *Indo-English Literature* 1-8. ref. : 501.
Examines the charges made against Indian Writing in English and maintains that the steady interest this genre has aroused in English speaking countries shows that it has merits other than those of sheer novelty and exoticism. Argues that Indian Writing in English has a steady footing in the literary landscape.

956. ——. "The Political Novel in Indian Writing in English." *ACLALS Bulletin* 4th Ser. 2 (1975) : 33-42. Also in Naik, *Dimensions* 116-131 ref : 380. Rpt. in Manuel and Paniker 16-29. ref. : 350. Also in *Asian Studies* 6 (1975) : 6-15. Rpt. in Malik 6-15. ref. : 349. Also in Prabhakar 19-33. ref. : 433.
A perceptive essay on the genre of Indian English political novel. Defines it as a piece of fiction devoted to a presentation of political ideas or the fiction in which action, character and setting are all firmly grounded in politics and surveys the major Indian-English political novels.

957. ——. "The Achievement of Indian English Fiction." *Journal of Karnatak University* (Humanities) 26 (1982) : 30-42. Rpt. in Naik, *Dimensions* 99-115. ref. : 380. Also in Naik, *Perspectives* 235-253. ref. : 381.
A historical survey of Indian English fiction — its themes and techniques, its growth and development — to determine its achievement.

958. ——. "Post-Independence Indo-English Fiction." *Littcrit* 14, 8.1 (1982) : 7-12. Rpt. in Dhawan, *Commonwealth Fiction* Vol. 1. 62-69. ref. : 256.
Traces the development of Indian English fiction after Independence with its characteristic themes, preferences and trends.

959. ——. "Indian English Literature." *Radical Humanist* Jan. 1983 : 29-31.

960. ——. "Dove-Tailing Two Worlds." *Indian Literature* Sep.-Oct. 1987 : 27-32.
See 7226.

961 ——. "Towards an Aesthetic of Indian English Literature." Naik, *Studies* 158-174. ref. : 382.
Demonstrates the validity of Indian aesthetic approaches in evaluating modern Indian novels in English.

962. ——. "Once More unto the Breach : In Defence of Indian Writing in English Yet Again." *Journal of Indian Writing in English* 25.1-2(1997) 1-8.

963. Nalapat, Madhav. "Indo-Anglian." *Century* 17 Feb. 1968 : 12.

964. Nambiar, D.C. "Indian Women Novelists : Writing in English." *Journal of School of Languages* 2.1 (1974) : 75-84.
Considers Indian women novelists in English as second generation novelists whose work deals mainly with Indian consciousness and everyday reality from a feminist point of view

965. ——. "Stylistic Studies in Indian Writing in English — A Suggested Framework." Mohan, 157 - 172. ref.: 365. Talks about some of the stylistic devices used by Indian fiction writers in English which include malapropisms, mixed metaphors, the shift of registers, native-regional words and idioms translated into English, their tendency to compounding, etc.

966. Nandakumar, Prema. "English Writing by Indians : Another Rich Year." *Indian Literature* 3.1 (1959-60) : 52 - 55. A general survey of Indian Writing in English, produced in 1959-60.

967. ——. "The Achievement of the Indo-Anglian Novelist." *Literary Criterion* 5.1 (1961) : 152-165. Extols the achievement of Indian English novelists, particularly those who had written novels between 1958-61 by examining some of them like Nagarajan's *Chronicles of Kedaram,* Bhabani Bhattacharya's *A Goddess Named Gold, He Who Rides the Tiger,* Rajan's *The Dark Dancer,* Raja Rao's *The Serpent and the Rope.* Finds *The Serpent and the Rope* as verily a novel in thousands written 'beautifully' in an 'alien' language and as such is an achievement. Feels that the Indian English novelist can hold his own in the "tolerant republic of English letters."

968. ——. "A Review of Current Indian Writing — Indian Writing in English." *Indian Literature* 7.2 (1964) : 45-51.

969. ——. "Indian Writing in 1964 : English (Annual Review)." *Indian Literature* 8.2 (1965) : 51-59.

970. ——. "English : A Piquant Effect. Annual Review." *Indian Literature* 9.4 (1966) : 25-33.

971. ——. "English : Lyricists Lead. Annual Review." *Indian Literature* 10.4 (1967) : 9-19.

972. ——. "English Writing by Indians : Another Rich Year." *Indian Literature* 11.4 (1968) : 19-32.
A survey of Indian Writing in English of the year 1967.

973. ——. "Indian Writing in English : A Growingly Significant Literature." *Indian Literature* 2.4 (1969) : 39-49.
A Yearly review of Indian Writing in English.

974. ——. "Indian Writing in English : Three Cheers." *Indian Literature* 13.4 (1970) : 27-41.
Annual review of Indian Writing in English.

975. ——. "Indian Writing in English : How Major?" *Indian Literature* 14.4 (1971) : 56-69.
A general survey of Indian writings in English produced in 1970s and their achievement. Comments that "there was a definite downward trend in the publication of readable Indian English fiction.

976. ——. "Indian Writing in English: 1971." *Indian Literature* 15.4 (1972) : 25-34.
A review of Indian writing in English in the year 1971. Finds Nayantara Sahgal's *The Day in Shadow* as the most satisfying work.

977. ——. "Indian Writing in English : 1972-73." *Indian Literature* 17.4 (Oct.-Dec. 1974) : 77-87.
"Cumulative harvest" of Indian Writing in English of 1972-73. Feels that Kamala Markandaya and Timeri Murari deserve more than a passing mention.

978. ——. "Indian Writing in English." Iyengar, *Indian Literature Since Independence* 42-70. ref. : 299.
A brief survey of Indian writing in English including fiction.

979. ——. "Indian Writing in English." *Indian Literature* 20.4 (1977) : 95-108.
A review of Indian Writing in English produced in 1976.

980. ——. "Indian Writing in English." *Indian Literature* 21.6 (Nov.-Dec. 1978) : 134-153. Yearly review.

981. ——. "Indian Novels in English : Adventures 1938 –1988." *Littcrit* 24 & 25, 13.1–2 (1987) : 22–31.
Discusses a few attempts of Raja Rao, G.V. Desani, Ranga Rao *(Fowl Filcher),* Nina Sibal *(Yatra),* S.P. Mani *(In Person)* at structures novelty. Finds that the innovations and experiments mark a bright future for the Indian English novel.

982. ——. "A Unifying Force that Flames as Creative Fire : Writing in English 1988." *Indian Literature* 134, Nov.-Dec. 1989 : 36-48.

983. ——. "The Elements of Fantasy in Indian English Fiction." Rajan, *et al., Commonwealth Literature* ref.: 450.
Considers Rushdie's *Midnight's Children,* Ranga Rao's *Fowl Filcher,* Sibil's *Yatra,* Tharoor's *The Great Indian Novel* and Alean Sealy's *Trotter Nama* and *Hero* as fantasy fiction and shows how these writers superimpose mythopoeic fantasy on present reality and transmute our every day life as an adventure into other realms of consciousness.

984. Narasimhaiah, C.D. "Indian Writing in English." *India* (1962) : 159-68.
Annual Review.

985. ——. "Why the Animus." *Literary Criterion* 7.2 (1966) : 1-10.
Feels that Rajan's critical outbursts against *The Literary Criterion* (the journal) is implicitly against Indian writers who had received major attention in the journal as "prejudiced" and "meaningless".

986. ——. "How Major Is Our Literature of the Past Fifty Years?" *Literary Criterion* 7.4 (1967) : 80-89. Rpt. in Narasimhaiah, *Indian Literature of the Past Fifty Years* ref. : 389.

987. ——. "Indian Writing in English : An Introduction." *Journal of Commonwealth Literature* 5 (July, 1968) : 3-15.

An assessment of the nature of the achievement of Indian English writings both in poetry and fiction.

988. ——. "Indian Writing in English : An Area of Promise." *Journal of Commonwealth Literature* 9.1 (1974) : 35 – 49.
Against Naipaul's comment that the novel in India is not concerned with the condition of men, a response to the here and now, the author argues and offers through the works of Raja Rao, an area of promise for the Commonwealth reader.

989. ——. "Indian Writing in English : Reply to Dom Moraes." *Literary Criterion* 12.2-3.(1976) : 6-15. Narasimhaiah and Srinath, *Indian Literature in English* 6-15. Ref. : 396
Comments on Dom Moraes who calls himself a 'proper critic' and brings into focus his faulty judgements on Toru Dutt, Nissim Ezekiel, Anand and Raja Rao.

990. ——. "Literature in the Global Village : An Enquiry into the Problems of Response." Amrithanayagam. *Asian and Western Writers* 79-82. ref. : 186.
Argues that for a contemporary novelist either from Asia or the West his experiences in an environment of the metropolis with its problems of overcrowding crime, pollution and modern technology are more important than the forces of traditional cultures. Considers Narayan's *The Vendor of Sweets* and Raja Rao's *The Serpent and the Rope* as examples of the phenomenon.

991. ——. "Women in Fiction and Fiction by Women : An Introductory Talk." *Literary Criterion* 20.4 (1985) : 1-8. Rpt. in Narasimhaiah, *Women in Fiction* 1-18. ref.: 392. Also published in Narasimhaiah, *Function of Criticism in India.* Mysore : Central Institute of Indian Languages, 1986. 245-257.
A general note on feminist writings and their treatment of women. Makes a reference to Raja Rao's treatment of women in *The Serpent and the Rope* and

"Javani", the short story and comments that "hardly anyone else, women writers included, has created more interesting women than Raja Rao."

992. ——. "The Rise of the Indian Novel : An Introductory Talk." *Literary Criterion* 21.1-2 (1986) : 1-5. Rpt. in Narasimhaiah, *Function of Criticism in India.* Mysore : Central Institute of Indian Languages, 1986 : 169-176.
Argues against the accusation that Indian novel is a mimicry of the West, quoting novelists like Narayan, Raja Rao and Arun Joshi whose fictional milieu is rooted in timeless India.

993. ——. "Commonwealth Literature : Problems of Response." Maes-Jelink, *et al.* 192-202. ref. : 344.
Makes general comments about some critical responses to literatures of non-native nations. Objects to the "intelligent Indian critic's ostentatious failure" to bring to his study of Indian English fiction either his profound awareness of India or "the sophistication he has applied to Shakespeare, Eliot and Laurence." Also makes critical comments on some Indian novels in English including Raja Rao's *Kanthapura* and Naranyan's *The Guide.*

994. ——. "Gift of Exile." Benett and Miller 57-68. ref. : 213.
Tracing the history of the exile theme from *The Ramayana* days, deals with some of the exile novels in Indian English writing. Discusses how in all these, as in Nehru's autobiography and in Kippling's *Kim,* exile becomes a motif for a metaphysical search.

995. ——. "The Cross-cultural Dimensions of English in religion, Politics and Literature." *Journal of Indian Writing in English* 25.1-2(1997).9-25.

996. Narasimhan, Raji. "Sophistication in Indo-English Writing." *Hindustan Times* 15 Dec. 1973 : 5. Also in *Overseas Hindustan Times,* June 1974, 5.

997. ——. "Indo-English : Criticism without Criteria." *Indian Horizons* 24.1 (1975); 45-71.
Argues that "the language aspect in Indo-English writing is the last important in the search for its overall calibre."

998. ——. "How Indian Are You?" *Humanities Review* 2.3-4 (1980) : 53-58.
Correspondence between Brij Raj Singh and Raji Narasimhan.

999. ——. "Indian English : New Depths, New Dimensions." *Indian Literature* Nov.-Dec. 1981 : 24-33.
A survey of Indian English literature — fiction, poetry and translations, published in 1980-81. Considers this period as a fruitful one particularly because English writing has taken to new dimensions and illustrates this point analysing Anita Desai's *Clear Light of Day,* Arun Joshi's *The Last Labyrinth,* Malathi Rao's *Passion Fruit,* etc. Remarks that there is a genuine aesthetic sense in these novels.

1000. "Indo-English : The Inclusive Voice." *Indian Literature* Sep.-Oct. 1982 : 158-169
A brief survey of Indian English fiction of 1978.

1001. ——. "Indian English : Breaking Fresh Ground." *Indian Literature* Nov.-Dec. 1982 : 14-24.
A brief review of the novels (published in 1981) — Y.P. Dhawan's *Journey through Hell*, Salman Rushdie's *Midnight's Children,* Chaman Nahal's *The Crown and the Lion Cloth* etc.

1002. ——. "Lack Lustre and Unexciting." *Indian Literature* Nov.-Dec. 1984 : 49.
A survey of Indian English literary scene in 1983. Comments that except one sensational work — Salman Rushdie's *Shame* — most of the works published in 1983 are lack lustre and unexciting as they add nothing new to English writing. Discusses some of the papers delivered at the Indo-English seminar conducted in

Britain in 1983 and published as a book entitled *The Eye of the Beholder.*

1003. ——. "Unshackling Brain Language : Recent Indian English Short Story Collections." *Indian Literature* July-Aug. 1987 : 129-134.

Examines the stories of Sadique Peerbhoy, Mira Balasubramanian and P.M. Nityanandan and climactic points of human predicaments, "speaking in tongueless, universal cadence."

1004. Narayan, Gomathi. "Indo-Anglian Novels on the Partition of India : Strategies in Expiation." *Panjab University Research Bulletin* (Arts) 8.1-2 (1977) : 35-47.

Studies Malgonkar's *A Bend in the Ganges,* Rajan's *The Dark Dancer,* Attia Hosain's *Sunlight on a Broken Column,* Khushwant Singh's *Train to Pakistan,* Raj Gill's *The Rape* and Nahal's *Azadi* — from the point of view of the guilt and shame expressed in them for the atrocities of partition. Discusses the nightmarish schemes of violence in these novels as Indian writers' effort to achieve literary expiation.

1005. ——. "British Fathers and Indian Sons : Guilt and Pride for the Indian Freedom Movement in the Post-Independence Indian Novel in English." *Journal of South Asian Literature* 17.1 (1982) : 207-224.

An extension of the article "Indo-Anglian Novel on the Partition of India : Strategies in Expiation" with more examples. Citing relevant examples, shows that Indians portrayed in the novels with pre-Independent India as their locale showed a greater sense of pride for their Indianness than those that are found in the novels with partition as their background.

1006. ——. "Shiva-Natraj as a Symbol of Paradox in Indo-English and English Novels." *Journal of South-Asian Literature* 21.12 (1986) : 208-216.

While Malgonkar *(A Bend in the Ganges)* emphasizes the contradictory elements in the dancing figure, Rajan and Narayan *(The Dark Dancer* and *Mr.Sampath)* explore the mediation or trans-dual aspects, Scott *(Raj Quartet)* has exploited both the contradictory and the mediatory possibilities.

1007. Narayan, R.K. "The Fiction Writer in India : His Tradition and His Problems." *Atlantic Monthly* Oct. 1953 : 119-120.
Discusses the literary tradition of India and the problems of the writer writing in English.

1008. ——. "Gods, Demons and Modern Times." *Literary Criterion* 10.3 (1972) : 47-54.
A talk given by Narayan in Autumn 1972 at Columbia University, New York. Reveals Narayan's attitude towards Indian myths and legends.
Feels that it is inevitable for the writer to see the world and its affairs through the concepts of myths and legends and see their relevance even in modern times. Argues that the motives and methods remain unchanged whether we are watching the events of the epic age or of modern times.

1009. ——. "English in India : The Process of Transmutation." *Times of India,* 2 Dec. 1964. Rpt. in Naik, *Aspects* 19-23. ref. : 378. Also in Press, John, *Commonwealth Literature.* ref. : 440.
Analyses the flexibility of English language as used by Indians.

1010. Narayan, Shymala A. "Indian English Novel : Steady Growth." *Littricit* 9, 5.2 (1979) : 20 - 27.
A general survey of Indian English fiction since 1930s : "The vitality of the genre is shown by the wide variety of novels — social novels (Anand, Bhattacharya, Abbas) Philosophical-metaphysical novels (Raja Rao), Psychological Studies (Anita Desai), entertainment pure and simple (Malgonkar) novels of tourist pre-occupation (Markandaya and Jhabvala)."

1011. ——. "Experimental Novel and Traditional Novel and Traditional Indian Story Telling : A Note on Some Indian English Novelists." *Journal of Literature and Aesthetics* 2.2-3. (1982) : 42-48.

Relates the experimental novel to the traditional Indian story telling, citing the examples of Bana's *Kadambari,* Dandin's *Dasakumaracharitra* and analyses the experimental features in the novels of G.V. Desani, Raja Rao, Sudhin Ghose and M. Ananthanarayanan.

1012. ——. "Criticism : An Assessment." *Littcrit* 14, 8.1 (1982) : 20-24.

Documents the critical writings on Indo-English fiction.

1013. ——. "Voyage as Motif in Indian English Fiction." Yaravintelimath *et al.* 127-136. ref. : 558.

Discusses the diverse uses of the motif of voyage resulting in exploring the physical, psychological, symbolic and philosophical aspects of life in Indian English fiction. The novels discussed here include Anantanarayan's *The Silver Pilgrimage,* Bharati Mukherjee's *Wife,* Boman Desai's *Memory of Elephants,* Amitav Ghosh's *In an Antique Land,* Anurag Mathur's *Inscrutable Americans,* Indira Ganesan's *The Journey,* Nina Sibal's *Yatra,* etc.

1014. Nayak, P.M. and S.P. Swain. "Cultural Change and the Quest for Identity : A Study in Indian English Fiction." *Quest* (Ranchi) 7.1-2(1993) : 11-19.

While making a survey of Indian English fiction briefly the authors point out to the cultural change and welter of values emanating from the writers' Indo-European duality and ambivalence resulting in rootlessness and perpetual quest for identity.

1015. Nelson, Cecil. "Syntactic Creativity and Intelligibility." *Journal of Indian Writing in English* 12.2 (1984) 1-14.

A linguistic interpretation of the interaction of the English mono-lingual reader with a bilingual-bicultural text such as Raja Rao's *Kanthapura*. Raises the issues of stylistic innovation and communicability.

1016. ——. "My Language, Your Culture, Whose Communicative Competence?" *World Englishes* 4.21 (1985) : 243-250. Also in Kachru, Other Tongues : English Across Cultures, 1992 : 327-339. ref. : 313.

1017. ——. "New Englishes, New Discourses : New Speech Acts." *World Englishes* 10.3 (1991) : 317-323.

1018. Nemade, Balachandra. "Against Writing in English : an Indian Point of View." *New Quest* 49, Jan.-Feb. 1985 : 31-36.

Describes Indian English writer as "Hindu Caliban" and states that Indian Writing in English is "the extension of Western literary culture." Cites Chaudhari's *An Autobiography of an Unknown Indian,* Narayan's *The Guide* and Kolatkar's *Jejuri* as Examples.

1019. Niven, Alastair. "An Introduction to Indian Fiction in English." *Review of National Literature* 10 (1979) : 44-58.

Surveys the achievement of Indian fiction in English beginning with Bankim Chandra's *Rajmohan's Wife.* Provides critical insights into the works of the major writers. Niven concludes that the Indian novel in English has reached "an uncertain point where a combination of academic conversation in universities (both in India and elsewhere) and a revitalization of indigenous fiction in mother tongues seriously threatens to "dispose it" but its "tough surviving personality" will not allow itself to be displaced.

1020. ——. "Losing Colour under Another Sky? British Perceptions of Indo-Anglian Literature." *Indo-British Review* 11.1 (1984) : 118-131.

Contains some general comments on select Indian fiction writers like Narayan, Raja Rao, etc. from the point of view of British critics.

1021. ——. "Notes on Indian Literature." *Orient Review* 3 (Jan. 1957) : 25-41.

1022. Olinder, Britta. "The Price of Independence : The Partition of India in Some Indo-English Novels." Ringbom and Rissanen 591-600. ref. : 483.

1023. Padhye, Prabhakar and Sadanand Bhatkal. "Indian English (editorial)." *Indian Writing Today* 3.2 (1969) : 3–6.

1024. ——. "Indian Writing in English (editorial)." *Indian Writing Today* 11.4.1 (1970) : 3-6.

1025. ——. "Indian Writing in English (editorial)." *Indian Writing Today* 5.1 (1971) : 63-66.

1026. Pallan, Rajesh K. "Impact of Mahatma Gandhi on Indian English Fiction." *Indian Book Chronicle* June 1998 : 9-10.

1027. Pandeya, S.M. "In the International Style Immerse : A Note on the Shape of Commonwealth Fiction." Narasimhaiah, *Commonwealth Literature* 20-29. ref. : 391.

In a general, sweeping note on the style used in Commonwealth fiction, suggests that some Indian English fiction writers like Narayan, Raja Rao, K.A. Abbas and Bhabani Bhattacharya make use of "free indirect styles of modern realism in varying degrees."

1028. Pandia, M.N. "Indo-Anglian Fiction Since Independence." *Triveni* 27.3 (1956) : 204-212.

A brief survey of Indian English fiction written between 1947-1956 and its progress and achievement.

1029. ——. "Indo-Anglian Novel : Bridge to Global Understanding." *Hindu* 20 Sep. 1970 : 1.

1030. ——. Pandit, M.L. "Some Expatriate Indian Writers in English: an Introduction." Pandit 11-16. ref. : 415.

A brief survey of Indian English literature with a focus on expatriate writers.

1031. ——. "Fiction Across Worlds: Some Writers of Indian Origin in Canada." Pandit 87-92. ref. : 415.
Discusses the various ways in which the immigrant writers of Indian origin in Canada (Bharati Mukherjee, Nazmeer Sidiq and Rohinton Mistry) convert their experience into fiction.

1032. Pandya, Sudha. "Feminist Critical Theory : A Search for a New Paradigms." Dhawan, *Indian Women Novelists* Set I. Vol. I. 73-83. ref. : 257. Also in Singh, Sushila, 37-47. ref. : 517.
Traces the evolution and development of feminist criticism.

1033. Pane, Ira. "Literature by the Baby-log." *Seminar* 384, Aug 1991 : 37-39.

1034. Paniker, Ayyappa K. "Man and God in Indian and African Fiction : A Study based on *Kanthapura, Arrow of God and Mookajji's Visions.*" Narasimhaiah, *Commonwealth Literature* 107-116. ref. : 391.
Considering Raja Rao, Achebe and Karanth as religious novelists investigates the ways in which these three novelists in their respective works come to terms with the subject of man's perennial fascination with the operation of the divine in nature, in the individual human being and in the day-to-day social interactions of mankind.

1035. ——. "Colonialism, Post-Colonialism and Decolonization : An Approach to the Comparative Study of Canadian and Indian Fiction." Begum 110-117. ref. : 210.
A comparison with the major trends related to colonialism, post-colonialism and decolonization in Canadian and Indian fiction in English.

1036. ——. "The Post-colonial Experience in Indian Literature." Nair *et al.* 36-46 ref. : 383.

Discusses the colonial hangover on Indian post-colonial perceptions.

1037. Parameswaran, Uma. "Native Aliens and Expatriates." Parameswaran, *A Study of Representative Indo-English Novelists* 85-140. ref. : 420.
Dividing the South Indian novelists in English into three groups — the early writers, the native-talents and the native-aliens — shows that the last category of writers differ from the others in their being 'uni-lingual' which determines their choice of the subjects, as well as their stylistic variations. Contains a detailed discussion of the novels of B. Rajan and Kamala Markandaya besides some passing remarks on the fiction of Nayantara Sahgal.

1038. ——. "What Price Expatriation?" Niven, *The Commonwealth Writers Overseas* 42-52. ref. : 407.
Discusses the problems expatriation imposes on creative writing, citing examples from Indian English fiction and suggests some critical criteria in evaluating expatriate fiction.

1039. Paranjape, Makarand R. "Inside and Outside the Whale : Politics and the New Indian English Novel." Kirpal, *The New Indian Novel* 213-226. ref. : 330.
Works out a definition of political novel and uses Rushdie's *Shame* and Pratap Sharma's *Days of the Turban* as two distinct examples of the same, represented here by two concepts — Orwell's "Inside Whale" (political quietism) and Rushdie's "Outside Whale" (political activism).

1040. ——. "Distinguishing Themselves : New fiction by Expatriate Indian Women." *World Literature Today* 65.1 (1991) : 72-74.
Reviews five novels (Padma Perara's *Birth Day Death Day,* Suniti Namjoshi's *The Conversations of Cow,* Ravinder Randhawa's *A Wicked Old Woman,* Leena

Dhingra's *Amritvela* and Agnes Sam's *Jesus is Indian and Other Stories.*

1041. ——. "Caste of Indian English Novel." *Economic and Political Weekly* 5 Oct. 1991 : 2298-2301.

1042. ——. "Politics of Misreading." *Economic and Political Weekly* 25 Dec. 1991 : 3022.

1043. ——. "The Ideology of Form : Notes on the Third World Novels." *Journal of Commonwealth Literature* 26.1 (1991) : 19-32.

1044. ——. "Indian Fiction in English — a Good Time To Be a Writer." But ... *Indian Review of Books* 2.1 (1992) : 21-22.

1045. ——. "Tradition, Modernity and Post-modernity/Region, Nation and Internation : Challenges in Theory." *Littcrit* 40, 21.1 (1995) : 5-22.

1046. ——. "Indo-Anglian and Anglo-Indian Ideology, Politics and Cross Cultural Representation." *New Quest* 111, May-June 1995 : 133-142.

1047. ——. "Common Myths and Misconceptions about Indian English Literature." *New Quest* 129, May-June 1998. 134-141

1048. ——. "Post-Independence Indian English Literature — Towards New Literary History." *Economic and Political Weekly* 2 May 1998 : 1049-1056.

1049. Parasuram, Laxmi. "Feminine Fiction in India." *Commonwealth Quarterly* 3.9 (1978) : 73-80.
Discusses the distinctive qualities of women's fiction and shows how they are based on personal and autobiographical elements related to femininity and feminine condition.

1050. Parry, Graham. "Indian Fiction and Criticism." *Journal of Commonwealth Literature* 13.1 (1978) : 76-81.

1051. Parthasarathy, R., Anita Desai and Kesav Malik. "The Indian Writer's Problem." *Literary Criterion* 11.4 (1975): 26-36.
Discusses the use of language, particularly the language of the interior, by Indian writers. It implies "the language of their (the characters) thoughts, their interior selves, the image, the symbol, the myth, the feat of associating them, of relating them, of constructing with them."

1052. Pathak, R. S. "The Indo-English Novelist's Quest for Identity." *Language Forum* 7.1-4. (1982) : 1-15. Rpt. in Dhawan, *Explorations* 1-14. ref. : 253.
Examines the issue of 'alienation' implicit in the writer's milieu and shows how this quest merges into a search for the self which is crucial to his relationship with society and the world.

1053. ——. "What Ails the Indian Writer in English?" *Journal of Literature and Aesthetics* 3.1 (1983) : 29-42.
Finds "...uprootedness and alienation from the common stream of life as the elements of Indian writer's ailment, their excessive Westernization as the cause and effect of their rootlessnes and their inability to draw on an indigenous frame of references."

1054. ——. "Alienated Protagonist in the Indo-English Fiction." Saxena, *Glimpses* Vol. 1. 68-98. ref. : 497.
Traces the treatment of the theme of alienation in its various forms — social, philosophical and psychological — either as a basic theme or a recurrent motif in Indian English novels from pre-Independence era to the present day.

1055. ——. "Indianization of English Language and Literature." *Language Forum* 19.2 (1993) : 1-21.
Discusses the process of Indianization in Indian English Literature and the experiments with the language made by writers like Desai, Rushdie, Namitaa Gokhale, Shobha De and others.

1056. Pathan, B.A. "Partition in Indian English." *Journal of Karnatak University (Humanities)* 29 (1985) : 26-33.
Discusses the nature of the tragedy of partition as depicted in the novels — *Train to Pakistan, A Bend in the Ganges, Azadi, Distant Drums, The Dark Dancer, Sunlight on a Broken Column* to show the divergent approaches to the same theme.

1057. Patil, Z.N. "The Use of Aggravating Language in Indian English Novels." *Indian Journal of English Studies* 28 (1987) : 20.
Studies the 'aggravating' language used by the writers of Indian English fiction in terms of socio-pragmatics of Indian English and its social uses pointing out the rationality operative behind it.

1058. ——. "Expression of Politeness in Indian English Novels." *Indian Linguistics* 57.1-4 (1996) : 141-152.

1059. Perry, John Oliver. "Political Issues and Critical Definition for Indian-English Writing." *World Literature Written in English* 28.2 (1988) : 363-367.
Posits a relationship between contemporary politics and critical issues dealt with in creative writing and argues that Indian writers in English must be judged by their response to their 'unique political situation'.

1060. Peters, John D. "Some American Reflections on Indian Literature in English." *Journal of Indian Writing in English* 14.2 (1986) : 1-9.
See 5588.

1061. Prasad, G.J.V. "Really Imagined." *Seminar* 384, Aug. 1991 : 23-25.

1062. ——. "Reply-paid Post-colonialism : The Language of Indian English Fiction." Trivedi and Mukherjee 187-194. ref. : 534.

1063. Prasad, Hari Mohan. "Tension in Togetherness : An Explication of Biculturalism in Indo-English Fiction." *Chandrabhaga* 4(1980) : 28-38.

An explication of tensions issuing from biculturalism and its metamorphosis in terms of tradition and modernity in Indian English fiction.

1064. ——. "Theme of Exile in Indo-English Novel." Srivastava, A. K., *Alien Voices* 210-216. ref. : 534.
Discusses the experience of exile and the problems of alienation and biculturalism as leading to psychological trauma in the fictional characters in Santha Rama Rau's *Remember the House,* Nayantara Sahgal's *A Time to be Happy,* Rajan's *The Dark Dancer,* Kamala Markandaya's *The Nowhere Man,* Anita Desai's *Bye-Bye Blackbird* and Raja Rao's *The Serpent and The Rope.*

1065. ——. "Dimensions of Realism in Indo-English Fiction." *Indian Journal of English Studies* ns 2. 21 (1981-28) : 131-140.
Analyses the concept of realism as found in Indian fiction in English and states that it encompasses the whole gamut of idealistic and Marxist socialism and psychological realism.

1066. Prasad, Madhusudan. "Some Post-Independence Indian English Novelists : an Overview." Naik, *Perspectives* 213-224. ref. : 381.
Brief survey of the contribution of some Indian English novelists, the minor writers like Khushwant Singh, B. Rajan, Menon Marath, Gidwani, Shahane, etc.

1067. Prasad, S.N. "Feminism and Indian English Fiction." Nayak and Swain 28-36 ref. : 401.
A general comment on feminism citing examples from the novels of Raja Rao, Bhabani Bhattacharya, Narayan. Feels that "woman need not waste away her womanliness for nurturing feminist movement. Ultimately every woman is more precious than the movement known as feminism."

1068. Prasad, S. Sheileshwar. "Man-Woman Relationship in Post-Independence Indo-Anglian Novel." Prasad and Sharma 284-290. ref. : 438.

1069. Prasad, Umeshwar. "Indo-Anglian Criticism : Problems and Positions." Sinha, K.N., *Indian Writing in English* 206-212. ref. : 518.
Deplores the lack of proper critical tools to evaluate Indian English literature, especially fiction. Offers a methodology based on some essential questions in this direction.

1070. Puri, Meenakshi. "Trends in Indian Fiction." *Thought* 16 June 1973 : 19-20.

1071. Radha, K. "Fugitives from Self and the City in Margret Atwood's *Surfacing* and Some Indian Novels in English." Begum 21-32. ref. : 210.
Traces the attempts of escape and withdrawal from the City by the protagonists in the novels — Atwood's *Surfacing,* Anita Desai's *Where Shall We Go This Summer?, Fire on the Mountain* And Arun Joshi's *The Strange Case of Billy Biswas* seeking refuge in mountains and islands which are symbolic of primitive reality, consequent to disillusionment and disappointment.

1072. Radhakrishna, N. "The Image of Gandhi in Indo-Anglian Novels." Radhakrishna, *Research and Criticism* 62-75. ref. : 444.
A brief survey of Gandhian fiction (Narayan's *Waiting for the Mahatma* and *The Vendor of Sweets,* Nagarajan's *Chronicles of Kedaram,* Anand's *Untouchable* and *The Sword and the Sickle,* Raja Rao's *Kanthapura,* Venkataramani's *Kandan the Patriot,* Bhattacharya's *Shadow from Ladakh,* and Anand Lall's *The House of Adampur)* to show how varied is the treatment of Gandhi as a symbol, a myth, an idea etc.

1073. Raghavacharyulu, D.V.K. "The Task Ahead — the Problem of Literary History for Indian Writing in English." Naik, *et al., Critical Essays* 31-38. ref. : 377.

Suggests some criteria for a historical evaluation of Indian writing in English.

1074. Rai, Alok. "Black Skin, Black Masks." Bharucha and Sarang 89-104. ref. : 216.
Focuses on Salman Rushdie's *The Satanic Verses* which is no longer the name of a book; it has become "the index of a seismic cultural shock, one that has opened up fissures and fault-lines, exposed weaknesses, revealed connections."

1075. Raizada, Harish. "Impact of Mahatma Gandhi on Indo-English Fiction." Srivatsava, A.K., *Alien Voices* 136-146. ref. : 524.
Traces the theme of the national movement in Indian fiction in English to show how it has given a very comprehensive and vivid account of the personality of Gandhi.

1076. Raj, Dominic M. "Some Thematic Experiments in Indo-Anglian Fiction." *Journal of Literature and Aesthetics* 2.2-3 (1982) : 36-1.
A discussion of the experiments in the choice of themes of some Indian English novelists and their commitment to social change and the ensuing problems. Prefers Anand's novels of commitment to Raja Rao's novels of "Aryan sensibility."

1077. Rajagopalachari, M and K.Sampath. "Fictional Treatment of the Decline and Fall of the Indian Prince : A Note on Selected Novels." Narendra Kumar, V.L.V.N. *New Perspectives* 36-46. ref. : 399.

1078. Rajan, B. "The Indian Virtue." *Journal of Commonwealth Literature* 1 (1965) : 79-85.
Maintains that the expression of "inwardness and Indianness" is a function of the writer's ability to proclaim the deeper life of his vision.

1079. ——. "Identity and Nationality." Mukherjee, *Considerations* 1-4. ref. : 370.

Discusses the most dominant areas of interaction between literature and social life and offers a reliable framework of critical values that can judge not only the creative writing but can also throw light on the historical and geographical situation.

1080. ——. "Writing in English." *Illustrated Weekly of India* 26 May 1963.

1081. ——. "India." King, *Literature of the World in English* 79-97. ref. : 326.
Focuses on the range of literary possibilities open to the Indian writers in English to use English as their creative medium and the issues involved in it. Discusses at length the novels of Raja Rao, Anand, Narayan and Kamala Markandaya.

1082. Rajan, C.K. "The Use of English in Indo-Anglian Fiction." *Journal of Literature and Aesthetics* 2.2 (1982) : 94-101.
Discusses the use of English in Indian English fiction and the difficulties it imposes on its practitioners.

1083. Rajan, P.K. "Patterns of Cultural Orientation in the Approach to Indian Reality." *Littcrit* 15, 8.2 (1982) : 29-43.
Attempts to examine the interesting currents and cross-currents of similarities and variations discernible in the approach to Indian reality in the writings of Naipaul *(An Area of Darkness),* Forster *(A Passage to India),* Anand *(The Big Heart)* and Nirad Chaudari *(The Continent of Circe).*

1084. ——. "Three Heroines — Indulekha, Sita and Gauri : A Study in Feminine Consciousness." *Indian Literature* May-June 1987 : 109-118. Rpt. as "Indulekha, Sita and Gauri : Towards a New Feminist Consciousness" in Radha 1-10. ref. : 442.
A comparative estimate of three literary works — Chander Menon's *Induleka* (1989), Kumaran Asan's

Chinthavistayaya Sita ('Sita Lost in Thought') and Anand's *Gauri* (1960) written over a period of seven decades. Discusses not only how the three heroines embody in different ways the expanding frontiers of feminine consciousness in the process of discovering their identity, but also the different means through which they become conscious of it.

1085. ——. "Indian English Literature : Does It Have a Tradition?" *New Quest* 109, Jan.-Feb. 1995 : 33-38, 65.

1086. Raja Rao. "The Writer and the Word." *Literary Criterion* 7.1 (1965-67) : 76-78. Also in Amur, *Colonial Consciousness* 1-3. ref. : 193. Naik, *Critical Essays* 1-3. ref. : 377.
A talk given in a seminar at Mysore in 1965. Investigates the nature and function of the word and its significance to the writer and the reader.

1087. Rajeshwar, M. "The Inner World of Indian Women : Neurotic Characters of Indian Women Novelists." *Commonwealth Review* 6.1 (1994-95) : 141-145. Rpt. in Dhawan, *Indian Women Novelists* Set III. Vol. 1. 49-54. ref. : 257. Also in Dass, *Feminism and Literature* 41-45. ref. : 244.
Studies the neurotic characters and their problems and solutions in *Cry, The Peacock, Where Shall We Go This Summer?* (Anita Desai), *That Long Silence* (Deshpande), *Wife* (Bharati Mukherjee), *Get Ready for Battle* (Ruth Prawer Jhabvala, *A Silence of Desire* (Kamala Markandaya), *The Day in Shadow* (Nayantara Sahgal) and categorizes them into three distinct groups — some moving from neurosis to psychosis, others arriving at a compromise and yet another group, compulsive idealists basing their arguments on Freud's theory contained in his *Civilization and Its Discontent.*

1088. ——. "Psycho-Analysis and Indian Writing in English: Promises and Possibilities." Rao, Visweswara 22-38. ref. : 470.

Suggests that the use of psychoanalysis, particularly psychoanalytical character study, will benefit the creative and critical writings.

1089. Rajiva, Stanley, R. "Contemporary Indian Writing in English." *Quest* 60, Jan.-Mar. 1969 : 72-75.
A general response to the positive and negative values in Indian writing in English in the early days of its emergence.

1090. Rakashat, Puri. "Indo-English Writing and the Critic." *Hindustan Times* 29 Nov. 1976 : 7..

1091. Ram, Atma. "Indians are Slow to Recognize Talent in their Midst." *Tribune* 26 June 1977.

1092. ——. "A Writer's Revolt." *Tribune* 8 Dec. 1985 : 14.

1093. Ram, Atma and Usha Bande. "Many Faces of Tolerance : A View from Four Short Stories." *Language Forum* 24.1-2 (1998) : 99-107.

1094. Ramachandran, C.N. " 'Groping for Space' : Tentative comments on a few Recent Indian Novels in English." *Journal of Indian Writing in English* 25.1-2 (1997) : 48-57.

1095. Ramakrishna, C. "Indian Writing in English and the Concept of Covert Culture." *Journal of English Studies* (Warangal) 4.2 (1972) : 281-288.
Defines the idea of "covert culture" following the explanation by Bernad Bowron, Leo Marks and Arnold Ross *(American Quarterly,* Vol. 9, No. 40) that it refers to traits of culture generally not acknowledged by those who have them. Applies this concept to Indian writers in English including Khushwant Singh and Arun Joshi.

1096. Ramakrishna, D. "Acadamics and Yogis : Reflection on the Recent Indian English Fiction." *Journal of Indian Writing in English* 7.2 (1979) : 89-76. Also in Ramakrishna ref. : 458.

A review article on Bhabani Bhattacharya's *A Dream in Hawai* and Shiv K. Kumar's *The Bone's Prayer.* Presents the academic and spiritual quests of the protagonists in the light of contemporary situations.

1097. ——. "Multiculturality and Indian (English) Literature." *Kakatiya Journal of English Studies* 11 (1991) : 22–30.

1098. Ramakrishna, E.V. "The Politics of Language and the Language of Politics." *Littcrit* 16.2 (1990) : 55-69. Rpt. in Bharucha and Sarang 19-32. ref. : 216. See 2814.

1099. Ramamurti, K. S. "The Puranic Tradition and Modern Indo-Anglian Fiction." *Indian Writing Today* 4.1(1970) : 42-46.
Traces the puranic Tradition of story telling and the deeper implications of the impact of that tradition on the themes and techniques used by contemporary writers, particularly Raja Rao, Narayan and Bhabani Bhattacharya.

1100. ——. "The Indo-Anglian Novel in the Course of English Literature." *Onlooker* (Littcrit) 1.1 (1975) : 18-23.
While answering some of the common objections to Indian English novels being prescribed for study in a course of English literature, the writer points out how a study of Indian English literature, "can be aesthetically stimulating and intellectually satisfying." Discusses themes and techniques and the pan-Indian nature of the Indian English fiction.

1101 ——. "The Rise of the Novel in India and the Rise of English Novel." *Vagartha* 19 (1977) : 1-9. Rpt. in Manuel and Paniker 108-116. ref. : 350.
A fairly comprehensive document on the beginnings of the Indian novel in English.

1102. ——. "The Indian Women Novelists writing in English." *Littcrit* 6, 4.1 (1978) : 33-42.

An analytical survey of the fiction in English written by Indian women writers from Toru Dutt to Anita Desai. The writer says that the earlier writers such as Toru Dutt, Mrs. Ghosal, Miss Sorabjee, etc., showed in their writings qualities, tendencies and predilections which continue to manifest themselves in the writings of the more recent writers like Santha Rama Rau, Anita Desai and others.

1103. ——. "Bankim Chandra and the Indian Novel in English." *Journal of Indian Writing in English* 6.2 (1978) : 37-45.

Discusses Bankim Chandra's *Rajamohan's Wife* and shows how, despite its faults, is a realistic portrayal of the life of the times. Considers Bankim Chandra as a true pioneer of the Indian novel, of the Indian novel in English in particular.

1104. ——. "Ambivalence in Attitudes to Colonisation in the Pioneers of the Indian Novel in English." Gowda 107-120. ref. : 280.

Traces the treatment of colonial encounter in the early Indian English novels (the novels written in the last quarter of 19th century and the first quarter of 20th century) such as Lal Bahari Day's *Govinda Samanta,* Madhaviah's *Lieutenant Panju* and *Clarinda,* S.M. Mitra's *Hindupore* and S.K. Ghosh's *The Prince of Destiny* and shows the ambivalent attitude of Indians to the colonial encounter as reflected in these novels. Finds the attitude of these writers non-committal.

1105. ——. "On Teaching Indo-Anglian Novel." *Journal of Indian Writing in English* 7.2 (1979) : 61-70.

An abridged version of a paper presented at the seminar on teaching of English literature held on 23.2.1979 at the Autonomous Post-graduate Centre, Tiruchirapalli. It is based mostly on teaching the novel *The Guide* to the students. A fuller discussion is contained in his dissertation, "Indo-English Novels as Textbooks in

Indian Universities" submitted to the Central Institute of English and Foreign Languages, 1972. Suggests some new approaches on 'teaching' the novel.

1106. ——. "Does Indian Novel in English Have a Future?" *Cygnus* 2.1 (1980) : 9-18. Rpt. in Prabhakar 12-18 ref. : 433.

A survey of the Indian novel written in English since 1864 conducted with a view "to understand the reality of the situation and visualize the possibilities of development or growth which the future might hold for this important branch of literature." Discusses the uniqueness, innovativeness and distinctiveness of the novels of Raja Rao, Narayan and others.

1107. ——. "Patterns of Distinctiveness in the Language of Commonwealth Fiction — A Comparative Study of the Language of Achebe, Naipaul, Narayan and Nagarajan." *Literary Half Yearly* 22.2 (1981) : 85-100.

A brief consideration of some of the stylistic peculiarities, particularly the ironic dimension of the style in the writings of Achebe, Naipul, Narayan and Nagarajan which make their work distinctive.

1108. ——. "Indian Novels in English and English Translation of Indian Novels : A Comparative Note." *Jadhavpur Journal of Comparative Literature* 23 (1985) : 49-62.

Studies the two categories of the Indian novels in English — Indian novels in English and English translations of Indian novels in juxtaposition and argues that the English renderings of the Indian novels, at least the best among them are second creations showing merits and characteristics similar to those of Indian novels originally written in English.

1109. ——. "East-West Understanding as Reflected in British Writing on India and Indian Writing in English." *Jadhavpur Journal of Comparative Literature* 20-21 (1982-83) : 59-70.

Examines the East-West theme — particularly the interactions between the East and the West at purely human level — in the novels on Indian written by Britishers (Kipling, Forster, John Master and others) and in the Indian-English novels of S.K. Ghosh *(The Prince of Destiny)*, Raja Rao *(Kanthapura)* and S.M. Mitra *(Hindupore)*, to show the difference in their treatment.

1110. ——. "Gods and Men in Commonwealth Short Story." Dhawan, *Commonwealth Fiction* Vol 3.121-131. ref. : 256.

While enumerating two kinds of short stories which treat the relationships of God and men (one type in which human beings interact with superhuman beings, and the second bringing out a metaphysical concern for human life), finds the latter kind more dominantly found in modern Indian short story writers in English.

1111. Ramaswamy, N.S. "Old and New Books." *Sunday Standard* 25 July 1976 : 8.

1112. Ramaswamy, S. "Humour in Commonwealth Short Story." Ramaswamy, *Commentaries* 13-22. ref. : 461.

Discusses the element of humour present in Commonwealth short story which includes Indian English short story.

1113. Rao, Chalapathi M. "The Indo-Anglian". *Illustrated Weekly of India* 24 May 1963.

1114. Rao, A.V. Krishna. "The Gandhian Legend in Indo-English Fiction." *Triveni* 31.4 (1963) : 59-64.

Compares the treatment of Gandhi in the novels of Raja Rao, Anand, Narayan, Nagarajan and others. Finds *Kanthapura* as a masterly exposition of the Gandhian phase of Indian national movement as well as the myth making, hero-worshipping tradition of India and feels that the image of Gandhi as a prototype of the sthalapurana of *Kanthapura* to the status of a 'jagat purana'.

1115. ——. "Feminine Sensibility in Indo-Anglian Fiction." *Triveni* 35.4 (1967) : 51-58.
Finds a new creative release of the feminine sensibility in the Indian-English women novelists.

1116. Rao, M. Madhusudana. "Is Indian Writing in English a Genre or Necessity?" *Triveni* 58.1 (1989) : 34-37.
Examines the significance and position of the Indian writing in English in its four literary forms — poetry, fiction, drama and prose and questions the validity of it as a genre.

1117. Rao, M. Rama. "The Short Story in Modern Indian Literature." Narasimhaiah, *Fiction and the Reading Public* 213-228. ref. : 387.
Comments generally on the short story form. The stories of Narayan, Anand and Venkataramani are included in the survey.

1118. Rao, Ravishankar. "Indian and African Fiction : Point of Convergence : Indianness as a Political or Critical Issue for Indian Literature." *New Quest* 62, Mar.-Apr. 1987 : 85-90.
Several common factors in Indian and African fiction in recent years, discussed from the point of view of the theories of comparative literature.

1119. Rao, K. P. "Indian English Literature of Yesterday and Today : A Brief Survey of Poetry, Drama, Fiction, Biography and Criticism." *All India Weekly Literary Annual* 5.12 (1946) : 85-87.

1120. Rao, K.S. Narayana. "The Indian Novel in English : Problems and Perspectives." *Papers Read in the 28th International Congress of Orientalists : Abstract of Papers*. South Asia (Canberra, 1971) : 53-54. Rpt. in Davis A.R. 102-118. ref. : 245.

1121. ——. "The Indian Novel in English : A Search for Identity." *Studies in the Novel* 4.2 (1972) : 296-303.

This essay is a slightly revised version of the paper read at the sixteenth annual convention of the National Council of Teachers of English on 27th November 1970 at Atlanta, Georgia. Finds that the Indian novel in English still lingers on "tentativeness" and is in the process of self-definition — in search of its identity with regard to its subject matter, form and technique and its possible readership.

1122. ——. "The Untranslated Translation and Aesthetic Consequences : Indian Fiction in English." *Southern Review* (Adelaide) 8.3 (1975) : 189-204.

1123. ——. "The Teaching of Indian Literature in the USA : Problems and Perspectives." *Proc. of the Seventh Congress of the International Comparative Literature Association.* Stuttgart : Kunt and Wissen-Enrich Bieber, 1979 : 713-718.

1124. Rao, A. Ramakrishna. "Images of Guru in the Indian Novel : A Comparative Study." Rao A, Ramakrishna 39-44. ref. : 465. Rpt. in Rao and Sivaramkrishna 182-187. ref. : 466.

Examines the nature and function of the guru in some Indian English Novels, including Ruth Prawer Jhabvala's *A New Dominion.*

1125. Rao, B. Shymala. "Indo-Anglian Prose and Fiction." *Century* 15 Aug. 1970 : 19-20, 23.

1126. ——. "A Bird's Eye View of Indo-Anglian Prose and Fiction." *Triveni* 40.4 (1972) : 61-66.

1127. ——. "Women Writers in Indo-Anglian Fiction." *Century* 20 Jan. 1972 : 25-34.

1128. Rao, B. Shymala and Krishnanand Joshi. "Indo-Anglian Literature : A Brief Survey ." Joshi and Rao 1-8. ref. : 307.

A brief introduction to the authors and their major works — Toru Dutt, Sarojini Naidu, Tagore, Aurobindo,

Anand, Raja Rao, Narayan and others. Talks about their use of English as a creative medium and the various styles they adopted.

1129. Rao, C. Vimala. "The Achievement of the Indian Women Novelists." *Literary Criterion* 12.2-3 (1976) : 219–224. Rpt. in Narasimhaiah, *Indian Literature of the Past Fifty Years* 213-224. ref. : 389.
An assessment of the achievement of Indian women novelists — Kamal Markandaya, Santha Rama Rau, Nayantara Sahgal, Ruth Prawer Jhabvala and Anita Desai. A brief study of their novels to show that the important recurrent theme is "an exploration of their identity and study of their arrival at a self-awareness" and to present India in all her multifaceted character.

1130. Rao, Urmila. "The Post-Independence Indian Novel." *Indian P.E.N.* 37. Oct. 1971 : 268-270.
A report on the seminar on "The Post-Independence Indian Novel" held by the P.E.N.'s All India Centre on August 26, 1971.

1131. Rau, Santha Rama. "New Voices from India." *American Association of University Women's Journal* Oct. 1964 : 2-6.

1132. ——. "India as Portrayed in Novels — A True Image?" *Indian Publishers and Book Sellers* 11.3 (Mar. 1961) : 188-189, 207, 203 and 204. Rpt. as "Songs of India Badly Out of Tune." in *New York Times Book Review* 31 July 1960 : 1, 24.

Discusses the way India is represented in the Western novels (the novels of Forster, Kipling and Masters) in comparison to the Indian ones.

1133. Raveendran, P.P. "Nationalism, Colonialism and Indian English Literature." *Indian Literature* 175, Sep.-Oct. 1976 : 151-159.

1134. Ray, Robert J. "A Look at Recent Indian Novels in English." *Books Abroad* 37, (1963) : 286-288.

1135. Reddy, K. Venkata. "Towards Indian English." *Triveni* 52.2 (1983) : 51-54. Rpt. in Reddy, Venkata, *Major Indian Novelists* 97-102. ref. : 475.

Discusses broadly the linguistic devices used by Indian creative writers in English (Anand, Raja Rao and Narayan) and shows how they have succeeded in giving English language a peculiar Indian tone, colour and resonance, thereby foregoing the medium, "Indian English".

1136. ——. "From English Literature to Literature in English : An Indian Perspective." *Critical Studies* 189-195. ref. : 476.

1137. Reddy, John. "Courtesy and Conflict : The Strange Character of the Briton in India and Pakistan English Fictions." *Ariel* 29.1(1998) 67-68.

1138. Riemenschneider, Dieter. "Indian Women Writing in English : The Short Story." *World Literature Written in English* 25.1 (1985) : 312-318. Rpt. in *The Story Must Be Told* ed. Peter Stummer. Wurzburg : Konigshansen and Neumann, 1986 : 171-178.

Paper presented at a seminar on Commonwealth Literature at Munich, West Germany, 1984.

Discusses the thematic and ideological preoccupations of the modern Indian short story by women. Feels that the way the stories are told and given linguistic and formal shape reflect the efforts of the female mind in India to redefine women in the context of the tremendous economic, social and, to some extent, intellectual changes.

1139. ——. "Indische Kultur Zwischen : Tradition und Moderne." *Forschung Frankfurt* No. 1/2 (1988) : 2-10.

Survey of some recent developments in Indian English literary trends.

1140. ——. "Tagores Lyrik erlangte welturf erst durch Ubersetzung Die Rezeption indischer Literatur." *Borsenblatt* No. 68 (26 Aug. 1968) : 2215-2218.
Briefly surveys the reception of Indian English literature, especially in Germany.

1141. ——. "Trends in der indischen Literatur." *Der Uberblick* 21.1 (1985) 58-61.
Short survey of the recent developments in Indian English literary trends.

1142. ——. "Die indo-Englishche Literatur." *Literaturen in Englischer Sprache.* ed. Heinz Kosock Und Herst Prien Brintz. Bon : Bouvier, 1977 : 219-238.
Survey of the development of Indian English literature from the beginning to 1977.

1143. ——. "Critical Studies of Indo-English Literature." *Kritikon Litterarum* 3.1 (1974) : 61-66.

1144. ——. "British Characters in Indo-Anglian Fiction." Naik, *Aspects* 137-149. ref. : 378.
Categorizes the British characters portrayed by Indian English fiction writers into two mahor categories — those that belong to the colonial period and those of the post-Independence era, generally it is the dichotomy of cultures and their claim on the individual that was at the centre of the majority of the novels.

1145. ——. "The Indo-English Novel." *Indian Literature.* Sep-Oct. 1983 : 27-39. Rpt. in Dhawan, *Commonwealth Fiction* Vol. I. 49-61. ref. : 256.
A sweeping generalization of the thematic concerns of some Indian-English novelists between 1930-1960. Develops certain formal characteristics of Indian English novels based on a selected few, followed by an assessment of the major novelists including certain "sparse comments" on the linguistic patterns found in the novels.

1146. ——. "Marginalizing the centre — centering the periphery: The Reception of Indian Literature in English" *Littcrit* 40, 21-1 (1995) : 52-76.

1147. Ross, Robert L. "The Emerging Myth : Partition in the Indian and Pakistanian Novel." *ACLALS Bulletin* 7th Ser. 4 (1986) : 63-39.
Finds that there are two distinct strands of approach to the theme of partition — one is the realistic mode and the other more symbolic. Suggests, especially on the basis of some recent novels (of Rushdie and Sidhwa) that a new and more fertile approach — the mythical one — is in the offing.

1148. Roy, Anjali. "Post-modernism Goes Native : Decentering Narrative in Recent Indian Fiction." Kirpal, *Postmodern Indian English Novel* 383-399. ref. : 331.
Instead of echoing Western post-modern trends demonstrates how "Indian fiction in English has taken a "regressive turn by seeking literary antecedents in traditional narrative forms while accepting, at the same time, that the decentering impulse that enables this counter discourse might itself be a post-modernist phenomenon."

1149. Roy, David J. Le. "Evil Portrayal in Indian Novels." *Thought* 12 May 1962.

1150. Roy, Sunita. "Paradoxes of Patriarchy : Feminist Motifs." Dhawan, *Indian Women Novelists* Set. I. Vol. 1. 47-57. ref. : 257. Rpt. in Dinesh, *Between Spaces* 20-38. ref. : 262.
Makes a distinction between feminist literature and feminist motifs and discusses Kamal Das's works in terms of language and rhetoric.

1151. Rushdie, Salman. "The Empire Writes Back with a Vengeance." *Times* 3 July 1982.

1152. Rustomji, Roshni. "Expatriates, Immigrants and Literature : Three South Asian Women Writers." *Massachusetts Review* 29.4 (1988-89) : 655-665.
Treatment of the life of the immigrants and expatriates as depicted in the works of the three Indian women writers of fiction — Santha Rama Rau, Kamal Markandaya and Bharati Mukherjee.

1153. Sambandan, D. G. "Indo-English Writing." *Modern Review* 140.2 (1976) : 76-79.

1154. Sarma, G. P. "The Language of Indo-Anglian Fiction." *Vagartha* 7, (1974) : 22-31.
A note on Indian English that expresses the Indianness of any thinking, speaking and arguing. Deals with the experimentation by novelists like Anand and Raja Rao with English language for serious artistic purposes.

1155. Sarma, S. K. "Indo-Anglian Critical Scene : Towards a Perspective" *Rajasthan Journal of English Studies* 11 (1980) : 30-34.
Discusses the critical attitudes current in Indian English Literature.

1156. Sastry, L. S. R. Krishna. "Gandhi and Gandhism in Indo-Anglian Fiction." *Triveni* 38.3 (1969) : 74-84.
Traces the influence of Gandhian ideology and personality on Indian English fiction with particular reference to K.S. Venkataramani's *Murugan the Tiller* and *Kandan the Patriot,* Anands's *Untouchable* and *The Sword and the Sickle* and Raja Rao's *Kanthapura.*

1157. ——. "East-West Encounter in Indo-Anglian Fiction." Sarma, G.V.L.N., 102-113. ref. : 495.
A critical survey of the East-West theme in Indian English fiction from A. Madhaviah to Kamala Markandaya and Arun Joshi to show the consistent viewpoint of all writers that "East is East and West is West."

1158. ——. "The East-West Theme in the Indo-Anglian Novel." *Indian Journal of English Studies* 26 (1987) : 62-67.
Examines some of the Indian English novels—Jhabvala's *A Backward Place, Esmond in India* and some short stories, Markandaya's *Possession,* Raja Rao's *The Serpent and the Rope,* Rajan's *Too Long in the West* and Arun Joshi's *The Foreigner,* that deal with the East-West theme and trans-cultural exploration to affirm That the predominant note is one of protest.

1159. Satchidanandan, K. "On Indian Writing in English." *Indian Literature* 167 (1995) : 5-8.

1160. Satyanarayan, K. "Politics of (Self) Representation : A Case of a "debrahminised" Brahmin." *Economic and Political Weekly* 23 Nov. 1991 : 2716.
A comment on Paranjape's article "Caste of the Indian English Novel."
See 832.

1161. Saxena, Alka "Feminism: Time to Stop Suffering in Silence." Dhawan, *Indian Women Novelists* Set III. Vol. I. 18-25. ref. : 257.
A note on feminism and feminist writers and their objectives. Shows how fiction educates women to fight against the injustice done to them.

1162. Seshadri-Crooks, Kalpana. "At the Margins of Post-Colonial Studies." *Ariel* 26.3 (1995): 47-71.

1163. Seshadrinathan, N. "Indian Traditions and Contemporary Writers." *Unilit.* (India) 21.1 (1982) : 12-16.

1164. Shahane, Roshan "On the Periphery of the City." Bharucha and Sarang 33-46. ref. : 216.
Discusses the question of identity of the minority group in Mistry's *Tales from Firoz Sha Baag* (communal minority — The Parsis), Desai's *Baumgartner's Bombay* (racial minority — Jewish race) Deshpande's *That Long Silence* (the gender minority) and Firdous Kanga's *Trying to Grow* (the minority of physically handicapped)

and shows how these novelists selecting characters and situation which are often peripheral could "successfully project the life of men and women, who, with their littleness, might-otherwise have been lost in the very multiplicity of this big city (Bombay)."

1165. Shahane, V. A. "Indo-Anglian Fiction and the Question of Form." *Journal of Indian Writing in English* 2.22 (1974) : 33-36.
Quoting Raja Rao's idea of form as "metaphysical comedy" and Meenakshi Mukherjee's insistence on the mythical form, Shahane states that "a truly great Indo-Anglian novel, which will be an aesthetic embodiment of the form, is yet to be born."

1166. ——. "Some Aspects of the Indian English Writers' Creative Use of English." *Literary Criterion* 17.1(1982) : 75-88.
Discusses the experiments in the use of English language by Raja Rao, Anand, Desani, Bhattacharya and others and points out the deviations from the accepted norms of English usage in lexical, syntactical and structural aspects of their language as specimens of creative English.

1167. ——. "Criticism of Indo-English Writings : Achievements and Failure." *Littcrit* 14, 8.1 (1982) : 13-19.
Attempts to evaluate the criticism published on Indian English writings — its achievements and failures.

1168. ——. "Modern Experimental Novel in English : Some Aspects." *Journal of Literature and Aesthetics* 2.2-3 (1982) 49-56.
Examines the nature, quality and range experimentation of the Indian novelists in English with special reference to G.V. Desani's *All About H. Hatterr,* Raja Rao's *Kanthapura, The Serpent and the Rope* and *The Cat and Shakespeare,* and Salman Rushdie's *Midnight's Children.*

1169. ——. "Indo-English Literature in the English : Prospectus and Possibilities." *Criticism and Research* 6 (1983-84) : 143-149.
Discusses the prospectus of the novel as a genre in world literature.

1170. ——. "Search for Critical Perspectives on Indian Writing in English." *Journal of South Asian Literature* 20.1 (1985) : 205-219.
Argues in favour of the need for evolving an acceptable framework of principles of literary criticism for the task of evaluating the significance of Indian creative writing.

1171. ——. "Indo-English Literature : Its Major Concerns and Its Academic Rationale." Srivatsava, A.K., *Alien Voices* 9-30. ref. : 524.
Discusses the aims and objectives of Indian English creative literature and the criteria for its judgement as well as critical approaches towards Indo-English writing.

1172. Sharma, K. K. "The 1947 Upheaval and the Indian-English Novel." *Language Forum* 7.1-4. (1981-82) : 30-50. Rpt. in Dhawan, *Explorations* 30-50. ref. : 253.
Evaluates Khushwant Singh's *Train to Pakistan,* Malgonkar's *A Bend in the Ganges*, Rajan's *The Dark Dancer,* Attia Hosain's *Sunlight on a Broken Column,* Raj Gill's *The Rape* and Chaman Nahal's *Azadi* from the point of view of their common theme — partition. Finds *Azadi* as the best novel written on this theme.

1173. ——. "Feminism : Some Observations." Sharma, K.K., *Feminism and Literature* ref. : 502.
Discusses the historical perspective of feminist movement.

1174. Sharma, K. K. and B. K. Johri. "The Partition as a Side Issue in Indian English Novels : R.K. Narayan's *Waiting for the Mahatma,* Balachandra Rajan's *The Dark Dancer* and Attia Hosain's *Sunlight on a Broken Column.*" Sharma and Johri, 1-32. ref. : 503.

Traces the treatment of the theme of partition in Indian English novels. In the novels of Raja Rao, Narayan, Attia Hosain though partition is a side issue it has lent thematic strength and beauty to them.

1175. ——. "Recent Sikh Novelists on the Partition : Raj Gill's *The Rape* H.S. Gill's *Ashes and Petals,* Kartar Singh Duggal's *Twice Born Twice Dead.*" Sharma and Johri, 120-155. ref. : 503.

Treatment of the theme of partition.

1176. Sharma, Lalit M. "Assertion and After : Tentative Notes in the Indian English Novel." *Literary Voice* 3 (1996) : 5-13.

1177. Sharma, R.C. "Contemporary Indo-Anglian Fiction." *Triveni* 47.3 (1978) : 70-75.

A brief review of Indian English novels such as Anand's *Untouchable,* Narayan's *Waiting for the Mahatma, The Vendor of Sweets,* Raja Rao's *Kanthapura,* and Kamal Markandaya's *Nectar in a Sieve* to show how they project the new social vision of independent India.

1178. Sharma, Sudarshan. "Working Class and the Indian English Novelists." *Link* 28 Aug. 1983 : 36-40.

1179. ——. "Gandhi's Concept of Brahmacharya as expounded by Indian English Novelists." *Link* 6 Nov. 1983 : 39-40.

1180. Sharpe, Patricia. "The Challenge to the Indian Writer Today." *Quest* 59, Oct-Dec. 1968 : 31-39.

1181. Sharrad, Paul. "Considerations of the Post-colonial Studies in connection with India." *Littcrit* 40, 21.1 (1995) : 47-71.

1182. Shepherd, Ron. "Suffering in Indo-English Fiction." Dhawan, *Explorations* 51-58. ref. : 253.
Shows how a selected group of Indian English novelists treats human suffering as their major theme. Discusses Raja Rao's *Kanthapura,* Anand's *Untouchable,* Narayan's *The Guide,* and Khuhswant Singh's *Train to Pakistan.*

1183. Shirwadkar, K. R. "Third World Consciousness : Faith and Frustration." Amur et al. *Indian Readings* 44-51. ref. : 192.
Examines the thematic concerns in the works of Achebe, Soyinka, Naipul, Anand, Raja Rao and others to show how the end of colonialism and the consequential illusions and disillusions had been a traumatic experience for the sensibility and the consciousness of the Third World. Comments on the pessimism of the African novelists which he contrasts with the basic optimism of the Indian novelists.

1184. Shirwadkar, Meena. "Image of Woman in Indo-English Novels." Radha 1-8. ref. : 442.
Discusses the variations of the images of women in Indian English fiction, ranging from the traditional woman as a worshipper of man to the new image of the woman struggling against the oppressive social norms of the male-dominated society.

1185. ——. "Indian English Women Novelists." Naik, *Perspectives* 200-212 ref. : 381.
In her discussion of the contribution of the women novelists throws light on the early novels of Anita Desai, Nayantara Sahgal, Uma Vasudev, Vimala Raina and others.

1186. Shukla, R.C. "Indian Fiction in English : Some Problems." Pathak, *Indian Fiction in English* 15-24. ref. : 422.
Focuses on the several problems that confront the Indian English novelist today, without providing a possible answer to anyone of them.

1187. Shukla, S. B. "Indianness of Indian Fiction in English." Dwivedi, *Studies Contemporary Indian Fiction* 74-81. ref. : 269.
Observes some false notes in the 'Indianness' of Indian English fiction particularly in the novels of Kamala Markanadaya, Anita Desai, Malgonkar, Arun Joshi, K.A. Abbas, Bhabani Bhattacharya and says that "Indian fiction in English must be not only Indian but genuinely Indian if it has to survive in India as well as abroad."

1188. Shukla, H. L. and Asha Khare. "Gender and Politeness Codes in Indian Fiction." *Language Forum* 19.1-2 (1993) : 145-150. Rpt. in Pathak, *Indianization of English* 145-150. ref. : 425
Analyses the relationship between gender and politeness codes in Indian English novels both in linguistic and non-linguistic domains and investigates the degree of variation in the use of politeness codes by the male and female characters in them.

1189. Singh, Amritjit. "Contemporary Indo-English Literature : An Approach." Naik, *Aspects* 1-14. ref. : 378.
Makes an exhaustive study of the subject and analyses the problems that beset Indian writers in English.

1190. Singh Avadesh K. "Indian English Fiction : A View from the Balcony." Singh, Avadesh, 9-21. ref. : 507.
A brief survey of Indian fiction in English of the 1980s.

1191. ——. "Un/out Doing Prospero — A Study of the Language of Anger in Indian English Novel." *Language Forum* 21.1-2 (1995) : 46-56.
Provides an insight into the rebel spirit of some of the recent Indian Novelists (Upamanyu Chaterjee, Rohinton Mistry, Firdaus Kanga, Peerbhoy Pannawalla) who articulate their "discourse of dissatisfaction" against the increasing oppression of the mind, body and soul in varying contexts.

1192. ——. "The Sense of Community in the Parsi Novels." *Literary Criterion* 31.3 (1996) : 28-38.
Examines the novels written by some Parsi writers *Such a Long Journey* (Mistry), *The Fire Worshippers* (Perin Bharucha), *Trying to Grow* (Firdaus Kanga) and *Bombay Duck* (Farruk Dhondy) to show how their work exhibit the consciousness of their community in such a way that the community emerges as a protagonist. Comments that these novels form a group centralizing the Parsi community in one way or another while remaining at the same time conscious of individual, national and transnational issues.

1193. Singh, Brij Raj. "Looking for a Classic in Indian English Writing." *Humanisties Review* 2.1 (1980) : 15-21.
Defines what a classic is and describes its essential characteristics and tries to explore Indian fiction in English, particularly that of Raja Rao, Anand and Narayan to find a novel in the status of a classic like *War and Peace* or *The Divine Comedy.* Finds Narayan's fiction somewhere near the status of a classic and *Azadi* as a more genuine landmark in our quest for the classic as it projects a new, better world which is basic to a classic.

1194. Singh, Iqbal. "The Indo-Anglian Novel : A Study of a Hybrid." *Illustrated Weekly of India.* Mar. 1955.

1195. Singh, Khushwant. "Some observations on Indian Novel in English." Dwivedi, *Studies in Contemporary Indian Fiction* 31-35. ref. : 269. Rpt. from *Khushwant Singh's Views of India.* Ed. Rahul Singh. Bombay : IBH Publishing Co., 1974 : 270-275.
Contains general comments on the Indian novel in English, its aim and readership. Finds that the pre-Independence writers — Raja Rao, Anand and others — were committed to the theme of Independence, and the post-Independence writers like Santha Rama Rau, Nayantara Sahgal, Bhabani Bhattacharya and others —

are absorbed in providing information on different aspects of India.

1196. ——. "Indo-English Literature : Some Views." *Banasthli Patrika* 4.12 (1969) : 7.
Feels that 'literature' is too pretentious a word to describe a small bundle of books written by Indians in English. Deplores the absence of a feel of the English language in many Indian writings written in English.

1197. Singh, Manjit Inder. "Imagination and the 'Other' : Post-Modern Feminist Poetics and Indo-Anglian Fiction." Awasthi 1-17. ref. : 199. Rpt. in Kaur 85-102. ref. : 320.
Carefully traces the gynocritical, political, ethnocentric or sociological-cultural motifs as seen in a set of novels written by Indian women fiction writers in English.

1198. Singh, Narasingh. "Nativization of English in India." *Language Forum* 19.2 (1993) : 70 -74. Rpt. in Pathak, *Indianization of English* 70-74. ref. : 425.
A brief note on the means and methods of nativization of English (the use of native expressions and words in English structures) in endowing it with a national identity.

1199. Singh, R.K. "Intolerance : The Psychic List for Solutions in Recent Indian English Fiction." *Language Forum* 24.1-2 (1998) : 13-30.

1200. Singh, R.S. "Indo-English Fiction : A Retrospective Introduction." Singh, R.S., *Indian Novel in English* 7–37. ref. : 513.
Traces the origin and growth of Indian English fiction from Bankim Chandra Chatterjee to the present day (1977) analysing their themes.

1201. ——. "Fictional Techniques." Singh, R.S., *Indian Novel in English* 179-203. ref. : 513.
Surveys Indian English fiction with a view to examine

the diverse techniques, stylistic variations and experimental tendencies of Indian English writers.

1202. ——. "Facets of Consciousness in Recent Indo-English Novel." Sharma, K.K., *Indo-English Literature* 231-242. ref. : 501.
Discusses the major themes in the novels that appeared between 1968-1976, especially those of Arun Joshi, Kamala Markandaya, Anita Desai, Raja Rao and Chaman Nahal.

1203. ——. "Indian Fiction in English." Singh, Avadesh 22-27. ref. : 507.
Enumerates briefly the changing trends of Indian Fiction in English from pre-Independence period to the present times and finds "that the possibility of growth of the Indo-English fiction in unlimited."

1204. Singh, Sushila. "Recent Trends in Feminist Thought : *Tour de Horizon.*" Dhawan, *Indian Women Novelists* Set I. Vol. I. 58-72. ref. : 257. Also in Singh, Sushila 22-36. ref. : 517.
Discusses the critical theories of feminist thought current in the present day world and shows how these are present in select women writers in the area of Indian English fiction.

1205. Singh, Veera . "India's Contribution to English Literature." *Rajasthan Pathrika* 13 Aug. 1989 : 111.

1206. Sircar, Arjya. "The Crisis in Indo-Anglian Fiction : The Linguistic Aspect." *Commonwealth Quarterly* 5.20 (1981) : 2-16.
A theoretical discussion of the linguistic aspects of the English language as a medium of expression for creative writing by Indians. Finds English language as ineffective to give expression to Indian ethos and social milieu — its manners, customs, spoken and unspoken attitudes, its mental and moral and innermost cravings.

1207. ——. "The Struggle with an Alien Tongue : The Glory and the Grief." *Language Forum* 19.2(1993) : 64-69. Rpt. in Pathak, *Indianization of English* 64-69. ref. : 425.
Stating that "English will Indianize itself in its own way, in its own time and according to its own compulsions" the author comments on "The unhybridization of English" by Anand, Raja Rao, and Bhattacharya and criticises the apologetic tone and the self-conscious efforts of Anita Desai, Kamala Markandaya, Manohar Malgonkar and others using English as their creative medium. Appreciates Upamanu Chaterjee, Gurucharan Das, Shashi Tharoor and others saying that their English is not too different from standard English in its essentials, even though in tone, cadence and choice of diction there is a distinct Indianness."

1208. Sivadasan, C.P. "Two Proletarian Novels." *Indian Literature,* May-June 1987 : 199-124.
Traces the similarities in Anand's *Untouchable* and Thakazhi's *Thottiyude Kakan* ('The Scavenger's son) and remarks that the novelists turn away from the stylized romantic themes to dwell on the humiliation of the outcast whose life is "inseparably bound with dirt and excrement."

1209. Sivaramkrishna, M. "The Paradox of the Twice-Born Fiction and the Question of Form." *Journal of Literary Studies* 2.2 (1979) : 133-149.
Analyses the implications of the paradox that emanates from the essential authenticity of sensibility which co-exists with a curious absence of any indigenousness of form.

1210. ——. "Recent Indian English Fiction." Dass and Dhawan, *Fiction of the Nineties* 21-28. ref. : 243.

1211. ——. "Some Indic Views of Texts." Rao, C. Visweswara 15-21. ref. : 470.

Discusses Indian poetics (*gunas, purusharthas etc.)* and their application in Indian texts.

1212. Srinath, C.N. "The Grandeur of Landscape in Indian Fiction in English." Srinath, 117-126. ref. : 523.
A brief discussion of the treatment of nature and its meaningful role in Indian fiction in English with particular reference to Raja Rao's *Kanthapura* and *The Serpent and the Rope,* G.V. Desani's *All About H. Hatterr,* R.K. Narayan's Malgudi Novels and Arun Joshi's *The Strange Case of Billy Biswas.* Finds that "the measure of the writer's achievement is in proportion to his communion not only with the landscape around but within too."

1213. ——. "Native Roots and Novel Foliage : An Understanding of the Achievement of Indian Fiction in English." *Literary Criterion* 21.1-2 (1986) : 69-85. Rpt. in Srinath 98-116. ref. : 523.
A paper read at a seminar on "The Rise of the Indian Novel in English" held at Dhvanyaloka, Mysore in 1984. Traces the achievement of Indian Fiction in English citing the examples of *Comrade Kirillov, the Cat and Shakespeare, All About H.Hatter, The Silver Pilgrimage, The Apprentice* and *Swami and Friends.* Shows how these novels are essentially Indian.

1214. ——. "Paraih at Cross-Roads : Image as Symbol of Regeneration in English." Nandan 307-316. ref. : 384. Rpt. in Srinath 70-84. ref. : 523.
A paper read in the International Conference held at Fiji, 1980. Examines how the image of the pariah is portrayed in some of the Indian novels such as *Untouchable, Kanthapura* and *The Cat and Shakespeare,* as a symbol of regeneration to show "how the pressures of such a situation have a telling influence on both language and literature."

1215. ——. "The River and the Audience : Treatment of the

Ganga by Western and Indian Writers." Srinath, 85-97. ref. : 523.

A paper read at Dhvanyloka at a seminar on "Western Response to India" in 1981. Examines the treatment of the river Ganga by an Indian historian Nehru, by novelists Raja Rao and Desani, by foreign travel writers (Mark Twain and Naipaul) and also Forster and Thoreau.

1216. Sriraman, T. "Indian Englishes." Nair *et al.* 18-23. ref. : 383.

1217. Srivatsava, Kamata Charan. "Indian Writing in English : Some Reflections." Sinha, K.N., *Indian Writing in English* 72-76. ref. : 518.

Traces the genesis , history and the choice of English as the medium of Indian English Literature. Pleads for the right critical attention and argues that Indians write in English not for recognition but due to creative compulsions.

1218. Subramanyam, Ka Na. "Why Did Pioneer Fictionists Write in English." *Deccan Chronicle* 7 Aug. 1988.

1219. ——. "English Fiction by Indians : A Case for Indian English." *Weekly Road Table* (India) 10 Dec. 1972 : 29-38.

1220. ——. "Indian Novelists and New Morality." *Hindustan Times* 30 Oct, 1977 : 1.

1221. ——. "Ten Great Novels of India : *The Generations.*" *Mirror* Mar. 1983 : 21-26.

1222. ——. "Ten Great Novels of India : *The Whispering Earth.*" *Mirror* Mar. 1983 : 18-22.

1223. ——. "What Indian Literature Lacks." *Statesman* 18 Dec. 1988 : 5.

1224. Sundaram, P.S. "Indo-Anglian Literature." *Eve's Weekly* 13 Aug. 1978 : 68-69.

1225. ——. "Single and Double Vision : Anand, Raja Rao and Narayan." *Rajasthan University Studies in English* 7 (1974) : 68-78.

1226. Sunderajan, Rajeswari. "The Feminist Plot and the Nationalist Allegory : Home and World in Two Indian Women Novelists in English." *Modern Fiction Studies* 39.1 (1993) : 91-92.
See 3181.

1227. Sundaram, Sudha. "Partition in Historical Fiction." *Literary Criterion* 28.3 (1993) : 23-39.
Calling some of the historical novels that dealt with partition as partition novels, shows how they "are triggered off by a specific historical event only to transcend it and assert the universality of man." The novels discussed are Khushwant Singh's *Train to Pakistan,* Malgonkar's *A Bend in the Ganges,* Bapsi Sidhwa's *Ice Candy Man,* and Guru Charan Das's *A Fine Family.*

1228. Sunil, Seema. "The Theme of Man — Woman Relationship in Contemporary Indian Fiction." Sunil 7-9. ref. 531.
Examines the treatment of the theme of the man-woman relationship in some of the contemporary Indian English novels. The novels discussed are Sahgal's *Storm in Chandigarh,* Shobha De's *Socialite Evenings,* Bharati Mukherjee's *Wife* and R.W. Desai's *Fraility Thy Name is (Wo) man.*

1229. Takahshi, Akira. "Indian-English Literature : Why and How in English." *Journal of Indian and Buddhist Studies* (Japan), 35.1 (1986) : 497-501.
Discusses the larger thematic and artistic concerns of the Indian English novels of the 1980s. Examines some of the novels of (Shashi Tharoor's *The Great Indian Novel,* Khushwant Singh's *Delhi,* Firdaus Kanga's *Trying to Grow,* Anita Desai's *Baumgartner's Bombay,* etc.) to show how these novelists tackle with confidence

new themes and experiment with new techniques. Self-referentiality, exploration of ethnic origins, new linguistic devices are some of these new themes and techniques.

1230. Taneja, G. R. "Indian Fiction Today." *Yearly Review* 4 (1990) : 92-101.

A brief survey of Indian fiction in English written in 1980s.

1231. Taranath, Rajeev. "A Note on the Problem of Simplification." Narasimhaiah, *Fiction and the Reading Public* 205-212. ref. : 387.

1232. Tharu, Susie. "Women's Writing in India: Questions for a New Literary History." Radha 1-10. ref. : 442.

An attempt to document the tradition of women's writing in late nineteenth and early twentieth century India and to suggest some dimensions along which we might understand and appreciate the women's commitments and their urgencies.

1233. ——. "Savithri's Pedigree : Victorian Racism and the Image of Woman in Indo-Anglian Literature." *Women in Culture and Ideology*. Ed. Suresh Vaid & Kumkum Sangari. New Delhi : Kali, 1986.

1234. Theime, John. "V.S. Naipul and the Hindu Killer." *Journal of Indian Writing in English* 9.2 (1981) : 20-86.

Finds Naipul's readings of Narayan extremely stimulating.

1235. Theising, I. P. "Indo-Anglian Fiction." *Quest* 53, Apr.-June 1967 104-105.

Comments on Meenakshi Mukherjee's article on "Awareness of Audience in Indo-Anglian Fiction." Feels that "the investigation of the awareness of audience in Indo-Anglian Fiction means to go into the real author-reader relationship which is an important objective for a sociology of literature."

1236. Thomas, T.K. "The Hindu Ethos — A Novelist's Perspective." *Religion and Society* 20.4 (Dec. 1973): 54-71.

1237. Thorpe, Micheal. "Some English Reactions to Indian English." *Literary Half-Yearly* 22.1 (1981) : 94-100.
Discusses briefly the state of Indian English and its general and literary uses in conversation and journalism. Finds that the native writers could not get over the use of a "wooden and stilted phrasing" whereas the language used by others exposed to the West either for studying or to stay abroad is `natural'.

1238. ——. "Making History : Fiction, History and Indian Mutiny." *World Literature Written in English* 26.1 (1986) : 179-187.
Makes a comparative reading of the Western (Farell's *The Seige of Krishnapur,* etc.) and Indian (Malgonkar's *The Devils Wind)* novels that treated the 1857 Mutiny to show that its treatment in literature is by far more humane ('a true vision of history with human dimensions') than the historical documents on the Raj.

1239. Tiffin, Helen. "Commonwealth Literature and Comparative Methodology : Post-Colonial Framework." *World Literature Written in English* 23.1 (1984) : 26-30.

1240. Trapping, Craig. "South Asians/North American New Dwellings and the Past." Nelson, *Reworlding* 33-49. ref. : 402.
Discusses the writings of some post-colonial immigrant fiction writers belonging to the 'Fifth World' (the world of the economically and politically displaced immigrants of the 20th C, transposed into alien context) from the point of view of the diversity of creative expression in the background of multiculturalism. The authors discussed include Rohinton Mistry, Bharati Mukherjee, Suniti Namjoshi, Vikram Seth and Sara Suleri.

1241. Tripathy, J.P. "Contemporary Indo-English Fiction : A Study in Religious Sensibility." *Studies in Contemporary Literature* (Allahabad) 2(1997) : 35-44.

1242. Trivedi, Harish. "India and Post-colonial Discourse." Trivedi and Mukherjee 231-248. ref. : 534.

1243. Tyrner, A. G. "Indo-Anglian Literature and the Indian Elite." *Cornell Journal of Social Relations* 1.1 (1966) : 25-32.

1244. Uma, Alladi. "To Accept or Rebel." *Literary Criterion* 20.4(1985) : 79-90. Also in Narasimhaiah, *Women in Fiction* 79-90. ref. : 392.

Traces the changing trends in the status of woman as portrayed in the fiction of Indian women novelists in English (Rukmani in Markandaya's *Nectar in a Sieve,* Sita in Anita Desai's *Where Shall We Go This Summer?* Shree in Raji Narasimhan's *For Ever Free,* Rashmi in Nayantara Sahgal's *The Time to be Happy* and of some Afro-American women writers from being self-effacing and self-sacrificing to being a rebel and self-assertive.

1245. Vaid, Krishna Baldev. "The Modern Indian Novel : Some Basic Questions." *Literary Criticism : European and Indian Traditions.* Ed. C.D. Narasmhaiah. Mysore : University of Mysore Publications, 1966.

Finds in the conclusive part of the essay, that Indian novels in English is superficial, intended to "sell" India to the foreign reader.

1246. Vaidyanathan, Rama. "Nissim Ezekiel on Indo–Anglian Fiction." *Journal of Literature and Aesthetics* 2.2-3 (1982) : 17-19.

An interview. Contains Nissim Ezekiel's views on Indian English novel, the future of Indian English literature, his own search for a new breakthrough in poetry, even his political attitudes.

1247. Valentine, Tamara M. "Cross-Sex Conversation in Indian English Fiction." *World Englishes* 4.3 (1985) : 319-332.

1248. Vandor, Elst M. "Les Romancier Indo-Angleus Sont-ils des mutants." *Commonwealth* (France) 2 (1976) : 63-69.

1249. Varma, R. M. "The Breakdown of Village Community in Indo-Anglian Fiction." Varma 14-31. ref. : 539. Also in Saxena, *Glimpses* Vol. 2. 174-191. ref. : 497.
A study of two novels — Bhattacharya's *Shadow from Ladakh* and Markandaya's *Nectar in a Sieve* to show how "industrialization is itself a strong dissolvent of the obsolete rigidities of an old social structure."

1250. Ved, Naresh. "Towards a Concept of Indian Novel." Singh, Avadesh 37-41. ref. : 507.
Builds up the concept of Indian novel as a novel depicting Indian life, land, people and its milieu.

1251. Venkateswarulu, I. "Gandhi and the Indo-English Novel : A Study in Influence." Amur, *Indian Readings* 52.58. ref. : 192.
Examines the theory of Gandhian non-conformism and its fictional treatment in the novels of Narayan *(Waiting for Mahatma, The Vendor of Sweets),* Raja Rao *(Kanthapura)* Anand *(Untouchable),* Bhattacharya *(Shadow from Ladakh)* and Malgonkar (*A Bend in the Ganges*).

1252. Venugopal, C. V. "The Indian Short Story in English : A Survey." *Banasthali Patrika* 4.12 (1969) : 98-104. Rpt in Naik, *Perspectives* 225-234. ref. : 381.
Traces the growth and development of Indian short story in English and finds Tagore, Anand and Narayan as the best practitioners of the art.

1253. ——. "Images of the West in Indian Writing in English." *Journal of Karnatak University* (Humanities) 25 (1973) : 127-132.

1254. ——. "Technique in the Indian Short Story in English." *Journal of Karnatak University* (Humanities) 18 (1974) : 115-125.

An assessment of the Indian short story in English as a genre.

1255. ——. "Freedom Movement and the Indian English Short Story : A Note on Three Representative Stories." *Journal of Karnatak university* (Humanities) 30 (1986) : 24-28.

Draws attention to three highly significant facets of the impact of the national freedom struggle (the Spirit of freedom, the spirit of love and the spirit of sacrifice), citing the examples of Raja Rao's 'Narasinga'. 'Isvaran's Between Two Flags', and Nagarajan's 'Non-Co-operation'.

1256. ——. "Between Two Flags : A Study of Three Indian English Short Stories on the Colonial Theme." *Journal of Karnatak University* (Humanities) 28 (1984) : 20-24.

Studies Manjeri Isvaran's "Between Two Flags". Anand's "The Lady Rana" and Saros Cowasjee's "Another Train to Pakistan" as pointers to a variety of imaginative approaches to the colonial theme.

1257. Venugopal, C.V. and M.G. Hegde. "Indian Women Short Story Writers in English : A Critical Study." Dhawan, *Indian Women Novelists* Set I. Vol. I. 204-227. ref. : 257.

A critical survey of Indian short stories written by women writers to study the growth and achievement of the genre. While enumerating the strong points and limitations of women as short story writers the author points out the possible causes for not taking the short story by women writers seriously. Finds Jhabvala, Raji Narasimhan, Bharati Mukherjee, Sujatha Balasubramanyam, Shashi Deshpande and others as some excellent writers showing promising future.

1258. Verghese, Paul. "The Problems of the Indian Novelists in English." *Bansthali Patrika* 4.12 (1969) : 83-97.

Discusses the problems of the Indian novelist in English with regard to his use of English in dealing with Indian themes and projecting an Indian image.

1259. ——. "Indian English and Man in Indo-Anglian Fiction." *Indian Literature* 13.1 (1970) : 6-25. Also in Verghese, *Essays* ref. : 542. Also in Prabhakar 7-11. ref. : 433.

Discusses the nature and concept of Indian English and the adaptation of it by the Indian creative writers in English, especially the novelists, and shows how the Indian social, cultural and linguistic set-up has affected the features of the English language. Feels that the Indianness of Indian English consists in its cultural overtones and undertones and not in a legalization of the 'ignorant' misuse of English.

Examines the image of man in Indian English fiction, particularly in the novels of Anand, Raja Rao, Narayan, Bhattacharya, Kamala Markandaya, Arun Joshi and Anita Desai and finds that most of the novels (except Anita Desai's and Arun Joshi's) present an integrated view of man's identity, his place in the society and the social values within which he works out his destiny but not man's relation with himself and with God, thus defining the nature of man and his place in the universe.

1260. ——. "Indian Writing in English." *Indian Book Industry* 8.6 (Sept. 1973) : 18-20.

1261. ——. "Indian Fiction in English : Its Future." Paniker, *Contemporary Indian Fiction in English* 111-116. ref. : 418.

Raises some questions regarding the future of Indian fiction in English, especially that of seriousness and consistency in the novelists' vision of life and the distinctiveness of style and says that a disinterested criticism of this fiction as literature is very much needed to develop healthy trends and tendencies in the genre and to ensure its future.

1262. Verma, Rajiva. "The Indian Novel in English — Some Recent Titles." *Yearly Review* 1 (1987) : 100.
A brief survey of Indian English novel written between 1983-1987. Finds new talent — Amitav Ghosh, Vikram Seth, Namita Gokhale, Jayashree Chatterjee, V.A. Shahane — and the continuity of the creative activity by the established writers in the field of Indian English fiction. Finds that in matters of style and technique the Indian novel in English has acquired great sophistication.

1263. Vijayasree, C. "The Politics and Poetics of Expatriation : The Indian Version(s)." Trivedi and Mukherjee 221-230. ref. : 534.

1264. Vyas, B.O. "Novelists till Nineteen Fifties: Denizen of Eternity." Prasad, H.M., *Response* 233-306. ref. : 436.
Traces some of the eternal values found in the major novels of the matters of Indian English fiction and finds in them the simplicity and naturalness of form and technique.

1265. Walsh, William. "Nataraj and the Packet of Saffron : The Indian Novel in English." *Encounter* Oct. 1964 : 78. Rpt. in Walsh, *Readings* 50-57. ref: 547.
A general survey of Indian novel in English up to 1960 and a brief note on the contribution of the big three — Anand, Raja Rao and Narayan — to the genre.

1266. ——. "The Indian Novelists." *Times of India* 12 Oct. 1964.

1267. ——. "Modern Indian Writing in English." *Indian and Foreign Review* 15 Nov. 1972 : 17-19.

1268. ——. "The Indian Sensibility in English." Narasimhaiah, *Awakened Conscience* ref. : 395.
Discusses generally certain major forces which expressed Indian sensibility through literature. Includes early writers like Ramamohan Roy and Vivekananda and later writers like Nirad Chaudhari, Narayan, Anand, and Nissim Ezekiel and A.K. Ramanujan to prove his point.

1269. ——. "The Big Three." Mohan, 26-36. ref. : 365.
Offers an analysis of the work of the three major novelists — Anand, Raja Rao and Narayan, writing in 1930s and says that they gave a definite direction to the Indian novel in English. Discusses the dominant traits of all the three.

1270. ——. "India and the Novel." *The New Pelican Guide to English Literature : The Present.* Ed. Boris Ford. Middlesex (England) : Pelican Books, 1983.

1271. Wankhada, M. N. "India as Reflected in Post-Independence Indo-Anglian Novel." *Lok Rajya* 1 Feb. 1974 : 47-49.

1272. Wasi, Jehanara. "Short Story Dominates Indian Scene." *Economic Times,* 17 July 1986.

1273. ——. "Indian Women Writers." *Economic Times.* 23 Nov. 1986 : 4.

1274. Wattal, Ameeta Mullo. "Feminism in Commonwealth Literature : A Difference of View." *Commonwealth Review* 6.1 (1995) : 13-20. Rpt. in Dass, *Feminism and Literature* 13-20. ref. : 244.

1275. Weir, Ann Lowry. "Western Women in South Asian Fiction." *South Asian Review* July 1979 : 10-17.

1276. ——. "Style and Range in New English Literatures." Kachru 283-293. ref. : 313.
Stray comments on the stylistic variations found in Anand's *Untouchable,* Naipaul's *The Mystic Masseur* and *A House of Mr. Biswas.*

1277. Wendt, Allan. "Babu to Sahib, Contemporary Indian Literature." *South Atlantic Quarterly* (1964) : 166-188. Rpt. in Manuel and Paniker, 94-107. ref. : 350.
Traces the growth of Indian English from Babu (the pidgin English forced on civil servants of the British) to Sahibs (those rich who have become so thoroughly imbued with the forms and Western attitudes) and demonstrates that Raja Rao is an example for both :

"Raja Rao seems to be a babu who has not sufficiently mastered his medium in *Kanthapura...*" and becomes a sahib in writing *The Serpent and the Rope,* where he presents "European setting, character..."

1278. ——. "Indian Fiction for Indians : A Study of the Short Fiction in the *Illustrated Weekly of India.*" *Literature East and West* 10.1-2 (1966) : 40-47.
This article is based upon an examination of about 72 issues of the *Illustrated Weekly of India* covering 18 months during 1962-1963. Have chosen seven stories for a brief comment on the scope and variety of short fiction.

1279. "What is Wrong with Indianness (English Fiction)?" *Statesman* 11 Nov. 1972 : 6 : 14.

1280. White, Robin. "Fiction in India." *Reporter* 14 Feb. 1963 : 59.

1281. ——. "Fiction in India." *Current Events* 10.8 (1964) : 41-45

1282. Williams, Haydn Moore. "English Written in Free India 1947-67 : *Twentieth Century Literature* 16.1 (1970) : 3-15.
A general survey of English writing in India during 1947-67, with an emphasis on Indian fiction in English. Contains some interesting comments on Narayan, Raja Rao and Jhabvala.

1283. ——. "Indian Literature in English : Colonial and Post-Colonial Social Change and Indian Inwardness." Williams, *Galaxy* 1-11. ref. : 553.
Traces the growth and development of Indian literature in English from the period of Raja Ram Mohan Roy to 1960s. Examines the novels written both in pre-Independence and post-Independence periods and illustrates how the inwardness of freedom struggle is articulated differently by the novelists like Raja Rao, Narayan, Markandaya, Anita Desai and others.

1284. ——. "Kinds of Comedy in Indian Fiction in English : R.K. Narayan, R. Prawer Jhabvala, Govind Desani." Williams, *Galaxy* 26-8. ref. : 553. Also in Dwivedi, *Studies in Contemporary Indian Fiction in English* 61-73. ref. : 269.
Discusses the relative merits of the treatment of the different types of comic mode by Narayan *(The Man-Eater of Malgudi* and *The Sweet Vendor)*, R.P. Jhabvala *(The Householder)* and G.V. Desani *(All About H. Hatterr)*.

1285. ——. "The Writer as Exile in Indian Writing in English." Yaravintelimath *et al.* 25-36. ref. : 558.
A brief note on the literature of ex-colonial writers.

1286. Williams, Mark. "The Novel as National Epic." King, *The Commonwealth Novel Since 1960.* ref : 328.
Offers a comparative study of the fiction of Wilson Harris, Salman Rushdie and Ken Hulme. Considers Rushdie pre-eminently a post-modernist writer whose India is "teamingly..... manifold, multitudinously shapeless".

1287. Wood, John R. "Colonialism and Post-Colonialism in Canada and India : A Comparative Approach." Begum X-XV. ref. : 210.
An inaugural address at the seminar on "Post-Colonialism in Canadian and Indian English Literature." Makes a perceptive assessment of Indian and Canadian literatures during the pre-colonial, colonial and post-colonial phases whose similarities he finds startling and dissimilarities instructive.

1288. Yadav, Kumkum. "Gandhian Influence on Indo–English Novelists." Kaul & Jaidev 167-176. ref. : 319.
Discusses the portrayal of Gandhi in Indian English fiction and the possibility of several themes that Gandhi offers to the Indian writer.

1289. Yadav, R. S. "Indo-English Writing and the Indian Myth." *Hindustan Times* 29 July 1972 : 5.

1290. Yadugiri, M. A. "Content Structure in Three Indian Short Stories." *Language Forum* 7.1-4 (1981-82) : 71-79. Dhawan, *Explorations* 71-79. ref. : 253.
Analyses three short stories - Narayan's "Lawley Road", Annad's "A Pair of Mustachios", and Raja Rao's 'Javani' from the point of view of Tomashevskij ideal of 'motifs' in the content structure of fiction.

1291. Yaseen, Mohd. "Aesthetics of the Indo-Anglian Political Novel." Dinesh and Joshi 75-88. ref. : 263.
Discusses the aesthetics of political novel distinguishing between propagandist political novels and novels with political undertones in Indian English fiction. Comments that "despite the limitations our Indian English novelists have succeeded in putting us on the international wavelengths and perhaps, the world is more enlightened today about the Indian political milieu than ever before."

C. DISSERTATIONS

1292. Afzal-Khan Fawzia. "Genre and Ideology in the Novels of Four Contemporary Indo-Anglian Novelists — R.K. Narayan, Anita Desai, Kamala Markandaya and Salman Rushdie." Tufts U, 1986. DA XLVII-1328. Published under the title *Cultural Imperialism and the Indo-English Novel : Genre and Ideology in the Novels of R.K. Narayan, Anita Desai, Kamla Markandaya and Salman Rushdie.* University Park, Pennsylvania State University Press, 1993.

1293. Alphonso-Karkala, John. "Indo-English Literature in the 19th Century." Columbia U, 1964. Mysore : University of Mysore, 1970.

1294. Amir Ali, Shamim. "A Stylistic Analysis of Indo–Anglian Fiction." Ravi shankar U, 1980.

1295. Angappan, V. R. "Shaping of History into Art : A Study of the Indian Princes in the Indian English Novels." Madras U, 1988.

1296. Arumugam, Chitra. "The Family Saga (with reference to the novels of Salman Rushdie, Boman Desai, Nina Sibal, Alan Sealy), Diss. (M. Phil). Jawaharlal Nehru U (Delhi).

1297. Badal, Rakesh Kumar. "Critical Survey of Indo–Anglian Novel with Special Emphasis on the Post-Independence Period." Awadesh Pratap Singh U, 1972.

1298. Badve, V. "Narrative Techniques in Indian Fiction in English with Particular Reference to the Novels of Mulk Raj Anand, Manohar Malgonkar, R.K. Narayan and Raja Rao." Shivaji U, 1979.

1299. Bald, Suresh R. "Indian Novelists 1919-1947 : A Study in Political Consciousness." Harvard U, 1968.

1300. Banerjee, Uma. "Indian English Women Novelists with Special Reference to Kamala Markandaya, Nayantara Sahgal, Santha Rama Rau and Anita Desai." Aligarh Muslim U, 1986.

1301. Belliappa, Meena. "Indian Women Writers of Fiction in English : A Study of Post-Independence Writing." Mysore U, 1968.

1302. Bhagat Aparna. "Indo-Anglian Writing with Special Reference to R.K. Narayan, Kamala Markandaya and R. Prawer Jhabvala and Its Significance for Higher Education in India." Diss (M.Phil.) London U, 1975.

1303. Bhalla, K. H. "A Critical Appraisal of the Indo-English Short Story 1945-75." Bombay U, 1980.

1304. Bhatnagar, Manmohan. "Political Consciousness in Indo-Anglian Fiction : A Study of Bhabani Bhattacharya, Manohar Malgonkar and Nayantara Sahgal." Maharshi Dayanand U (Rohtak, India), 1980. New Delhi : Bahri Publications, 1991.

1305. Bhatnagar, Om Prakash. "Indian Political Novel in English : A Study" U of Nagpur, 1991.

1306. Bhatt, P. N. "A Thematic Study of the Novels of R.K. Narayan, Mulk Raj Anand, Manohar Malgonkar." Saurashtra U, 1978.

1307. Bhatt, S. L. "Indianness in the Novels of Indo-Anglian Women Writing." Bombay U, 1982.

1308. Bisht, Priya Vrat. "The Feminine Principles in Modern Indian English Novel : An Interdisciplinary Approach." Himachal Pradesh U, 1987.

1309. Biyani, Om Prakash. "Socio-Literary Study of the Indo-English Short Story 1934-60." Nagpur U, 1986.

1310. Chakravarthi, V.V. "The Indian Short Story in English : A Critical Study." Karnatak U, 1983.

1311. Chakrapani, Y.S. "Man-Woman Relationships in Indian English Fiction of R.K. Narayan, Raja Rao, Kamala Markandaya and Anita Desai." Karnatak U, 1991.

1312. Chandar, K.M. "Colonialism and Literature : A Study of Some Indian and African Novelists in Their Social Context." Mysore U, 1980.

1313. Chandra, Vinita. "Constructing National Identities : Indo-Anglian Fiction." Rutgers U (New Brunswick), 1996. DA 1 May 1977, 57 : 1, 47-48.

1314. Chatterjee, Chandra. "World Within : A Study of Novels in English by Indian Women 1956-1980." IIT (Delhi), 1983.

1315. Chatterjee, D. "Image of Gandhi in the Indo-Anglian Novel." Lancaster U, 1977.

1316. Chattopadhya, Krishna. "A Study of the Calcutta Short Story." Calcutta U, 1980.

1317. Chaturvedi, M.B. "Impact of Indian Freedom Struggle on Indo-Anglian Fiction" Agra U, 1989.

1318. Dayal, Barameswar. "Critical Study of the Themes and Techniques of the Indo-Anglain Short Story Writers with Special Reference to Mulk Raj Anand, R.K. Narayan and K.A. Abbas." Magadh U, 1984. Ranchi: Jubilee Prakashan, 1985.

1319. Derret, M. E. "The Novel in India." Diss. (M.A). U of London, 1963. Published under the title, *The Modern Indian Novel in English : A Comparative Approach.* Brussels : University Libre de Bruxolles, 1966.

1320. Deverajan, Padmini. "Critical Analysis of Select Indian Novels in English in Terms of Indian Aesthetics." Annamalai U, 1990.

1321. Dhalla, K.H. "A Critical Appraisal of the Indo-English Short Story 1945-75." U of Bombay, 1980.

1322. Geetha, T.N. "Indian Women Short Story Writers in English : A Study." Gulbarga U, 1989.

1323. Gondal, Yogesh Chandra. "Tradition and Social Change in the Indian Novel in English." U of Delhi, 1983.

1324. Gupta, Rashmi. "Development of Feminine Sensibility in Indo-Anglian Fiction with special Reference to Kamala Markandaya, Nayantara Sahgal, Ruth Prawer Jhabvala, Anita Desai." Rajasthan U, 1981.

1325. Guzman, Richard Ramirez. "Bande Mataram : Nationalism, Personality and Literary style in four Third World Writers." U of Virginia, 1977. DA 38.7 (1978) : 4180A.

1326. Harbans Lal. "Treatment of Gandhi in Indo-Anglian Novel 1967-1977." Punjab U, 1981.

1327. Harris Michael T. "Outsiders and Insiders : Perspectives of Third world Culture in British and Post-Colonial Fiction." Indiana U, 1986, DAI 47(8) 87F 3033A.

1328. Harrex, S.C. "A Study of Indian Novelists Writing in English from 1930 to the Present (1968)." U of Tasmania (Harbart), 1969.

1329. Hubal, Teresa Dawn. " 'India, The New Myth-Collective Fiction' : the Construction of History in British and Indian Fiction about India's Independence Movement." U of Western Ontaria, 1991. DA53 (1993) : 3895-6A.

1330. Janaki Devi, P. "East-West Encounter in the Indo-Anglian Literature : A Selected Study of Raja Rao, R.K. Narayan, Kamala Markandaya." Andhra U, 19?.

1331. Jaya, N. S. "Character and Characterization in Indian Fiction in English with Special Reference to R.K. Narayan." U of Madras, 1988.

1332. Jeyaraju, M. A. "Indo-Anglain Historical Fiction : Critical Assessment." U of Madurai, 1990.

1333. Jha, Rama. "The Impact of Gandhian Thought on Indo-Anglian Novelists." U of Delhi, 1982. Published under the title *Gandhian Thought and Indo-Anglian Novelists.* Delhi : Chanakya Publications, 1983.

1334. Jitendra Nath. "The Impact of Gandhism on Indo–Anglian Fiction." Bihar U, 1971.

1335. Johri, Brijkant. "The Theme of Partition in Indian English and Hindi Novels." Meerut U, 1984.

1336. Joshi, Mukta. "Social Problems in Post-Independence Indo-Anglian Fiction with Particular Reference to Women Writers." Avadh U, 1983.

1337. Jussawalla, Feroza. "Family Quarrels : Towards a Criticism of Indian Writing in English." U of Utah, 1983. Jackson (U.S.A) : University Press of Mississipi, 1992. Released in 1993.

1338. Kanthimathinathan, I. S. "The Five Historical Novels in English and Tamil : A Comparative Study." Madurai U, 1989.

1339. Kapru, Anju. "The Rise of the Indian Novel in English." U of Texas (Austin), 1992.

1340. Katamble, Vaman Dudepa. "Rural Novel in Indian Writing in English 1920–1970." Shivaji U, 1977.

1341. Kaur, Paranjit. "Indo-English Women Novelists." Kurukshetra U, 19?

1342. Kaushik, Asha . "Political Criticism in Post-Independence Indo-Anglian Novel." Rajasthan U, 1986. New Delhi : Manohar Publications, 1988.

1343. Khurana, Kanwal Kumar "Treatment of Marital Discard in Indian Novel in English." Kurukshetra U, 1991.

1344. Kirpal, Vineypal Kaur. "The Impact of Expatriation on Colonial Fiction : Two Examples." Poona U, 1982.

1345. Kumari Kamlesh. "Hinduism in the Indo-English Novel 1947-1977." Punjab U, 1985.

1346. Kumari Ramesh. "Impact of Gandhian Thought in Indo-Anglian Novelists of 1930s and 40s. Delhi U, 1983.

1347. Mahashabde, A. M. "Theme of Disintegration in Indo-Anglian Fiction." Vikram U, 1988.

1348. Malkarn, Kusum. "English Fiction by Indian Writers : A Study in Meaning and Method." Banares Hindu U, 19?

1349. Manapure, Sudhakar Krishna Rao. "Humanism in Indo-English Novels 1925-1955." Nagpur U, 1979.

1350. Meerabai, K. "Women as Presented by Women Writers of Indo-Anglian Fiction with Particular Reference to Kamala Markandaya, Anita Desai, Nayantara Sahgal and R.P. Jhabvala." Venkateshwara U, 1988.

1351. Mehdi, Adul. "Novels about the Partition of India : A Study of Selected Novels in Urdu and English." Diss. (M.Phil). Jawaharlal Nehru U, 1988.

1352. Mehta, Mohanlal. "Portrayal of Rural India in Indo-English Novel" Gurunanak U, 1991.

1353. Minocherhomji, Roshan Nadirsha. "Indian Writers of Fiction in English." U of Bombay, 1945.

1354. Mishra, Ganeswar. "Indian Novel in Egnlish : Content, Form and Language." Kent U, 1978.

1355. Mitra, Indrani. "Colonialism, Nationalism and the Cultural Construction of Woman : Ideological Tensions in the works of Three Indo-English Women Writers." Kent State U, 1992.

1356. Mose, D.R. "The Novels on Indian Partition." Diss (M.Phil.). Shivaji U, 19?.

1357. Mukherjee, Meenakshi. "Indo-Anglian Fiction 1930-1964 : Themes and Techniques." Poona U, 1969. Published under the title *Twice Born Fiction : Themes and Techniques of the Indian Novel in English*. New Delhi : Arnold Heinemann, 1971.

1358. Mukherjee, Mukta. "The Use of Myth in Indo-Anglian Fiction." Punjab U, 1983.

1359. Muralidas. "Indian Short Story in English." U of Gauhati, 1976.

1360. Nambiar, K. Chandrashekaran. "Women Writers of Indian English Fiction : A Study of Novel and Style 1947-67." Osmania U, 1973.

1361. Narayanan, G. M. "Tryst with Destiny : Guilt and Shame in Anglo-Indian and Indo-Anglian Novels." IIT (Delhi), 1979.

1362. Oberoi, Narender Kumar. "Sociology of Indo-Anglian Novel with Special Reference to the Novels of Mulk Raj Anand, R.K. Narayan, Raja Rao." Punjab U, 1980.

1363. Padmini, Nithil. "Indian Women Novelists." U of Madras, 1973.

1364. Pandia, Mahendra Navansuklal. "The Indo-Anglian Novel as a Social Document." U of Bombay, 1950.

1365. Pandya, Bhogilal G. "Characteristics of Indo–Anglian Fiction after Independence." Gujarat U, 1984.

1366. Parasher, S. V. "Certain Aspects of Function of Form of Indian English : A Socio-linguistic Study." Central Institute of English & foreign Languages, 1980.

1367. Parikh, Bharati A. "Female Sensibility in Indo-Anglian and Black American Women Novelists." M.S. U of Baroda, 1991.

1368. Parry, B. "The Image of India : Some Literary Expressions of the British Experiences in India." U of Birmingham, 1966-67.

1369. Pathak, Ilaban. "A Study of the Indo-English Women Novelists." Gujarat U, 1980.

1370. Pathan, B. A. "Gandhian Myth in Indian Novels in English." Karnatak U, 1985. Jaipur : Aavishkar Publishers, 1987.

1371. Patil, Z. N. "Style in Indian Fiction in English : A Study in Politeness Strategies." U of Poona, 1988. New Delhi: Prestige Books, 1994.

1372. Perera, Senath Walter. "If Served They Be God, the Conjunction Cannot Be Hurtful : A Comparative Approach to Protest Fiction in India, Kenya and the West Indies." U of New Brunswick, 1971, DA 52 (1991) : 1319.

1373. Perkins, Susan Harvard. "Reflections of Modern Culture in Indo-Anglian Literature : Illustrations from Novels of R.K. Narayan and Mulk Raj Anand." U of California, 1957.

1374. Pillai, N. Radhakrishna. "The Dominant Themes in Indo-Anglian Fiction." Annamalai U, 1979.

1375. Pradhan, Shanta. "Modern Elements in Indian English Fiction with Special Reference to Raja Rao, Anita Desai, and Arun Joshi." Gauhati U, 1990.

1376. Prasad, V. V. N. Rajendra. "Self, Family and Society in the Novels of Rajan, Raja Rao, R.K. Narayan, Arun Joshi and Anita Desai. " U of Krishnadevaraya, 1986. New Delhi : Prestige Books, 1988.

1377. Pushpakumari, V. "Feminism in the Novels of Indian English Women Novelists." Karnatak U, 1987.

1378. Rahman, K. "Race Relations in English Fiction between 1919 and 1939." Birmingham U, 1962/63.

1379. Raizada, H. C. "Treatment of Political Theme in Indian English Fiction 1900-80 : A Critical Study." Diss (D.Litt). Aligarh Muslim U, 1990

1380. Rajappa, K. "Indian Writer of Fiction in English (R.K. Narayan)." Mysore U, 1973.

1381. Rajeshwar M. "The Inner World of Indian Women Novelists in English : A Study of the Theme of Neurosis." Kakatiya U, 1991.

1382. Ramakrishna Murthy, V. "Real and Imagined Worlds: Society and Politics in Indo-English Novels 1935-1975." Osmania U, 1986.

1383. Ramamurti K. S. "Indo-English Novels as text books in Indian Universities." Central Institute of English and Foreign Language, 1972.

1384. ——. "The Rise of the Indian Novel in English." Madurai Kamaraj U, 1974. New Delhi : Sterling 1987.

1385. Rao, A.V. Krishna. "The Indo-Anglian Novel and the Changing Traditions : A Study of the Novels of Mr. Anand, Kamala Markandaya, R.K. Narayan and Raja Rao." Mysore U, 1964. Mysore : Rao & Raghavan, 1972.

1386. Rao, A. V. K. "Tradition and Change in Indian Fiction in English." Nagarjuna U, 19?.

1387. Rao, M. Madhusudan. "The Existentialist Strain in Contemporary Indo-English Fiction." Osmania U, 1986.

1388. Ray, Sangeetha. "The Construction of the Indian Woman: Feminism, Nationalism and Imperialism in British and Indian Literatures from 1850-1920." U of Washington, 1991. DA52 (1991), 1754A.

1389. Reddy, G. A "Indian Writers in English and Its Audience : Responses to Indian Writing in English in India and Abroad." Diss (M.A), Mysore U, 1975. Bareilly : Prakash Book Depot, 1978.

1390. Riemenschneider, Dieter. "Der moderne english sprachige Roman Indiens. (The Modern Indian Novel in English)." Johann Wolfgang Goethe-Universtat, 1974, Darmstadt : Thesen Verlag, 1974.

1391. Sagar, V. J. "Social Themes in the Works of Some Women Novelists in English, American and Indo-Anglian Literature." Karnatak U, 19?

1392. Sahayam, John. "Indo-Anglian Writers." U of Madurai Kamaraj, 1986.

1393. Sambamurthy, V. Indira. "The Use of Myth in Indo-Anglian Fiction with Special Reference to R.K. Naryan, Raja Rao and Sudhin Ghose." Osmania U, 1984.

1394. Sanyal, Samares. "Indian Heritage and Indo-Anglian Fiction : A Critical Assessment of the Representative Indian Themes in Some Major Indo-Anglian Novels." Calcutta U, 1981. Published under the title *Indianness in Major Indo-English Novels*. Bareilly : Prakash Book Depot, 1984.

1395. Sarma, Gobinda P. "Nationalism in Indo-Anglian Fiction : A Study of Indian Nationlism as Reflected in It." Gauhati U, 1974. New Delhi : Sterling, 1978, 1990.

1396. Sarma S. Thyagaraja. "Fusion of Techniques and Vision in Indo-Anglian Fiction." U of Madras, 1987.

1397. Satendra Raghuraj Singh. "City and the Indian Novel." Delhi U, 1990.

1398. Satyanarayana. "Indian Fiction in English." Karnatak U, 19?

1399. Satyanarayana, N. "New Morality in Indian English Fiction with Special Reference to Anand, Narayan and Arun Joshi." Kakatiya U (Warangal), 1987.

1400. Sharma, Alpana. "Indian Nationalism and Indo–Anglian Literature : A Critical Revaluation of Writing Race into the English Language." U of Pittsburgh, 1990. DA 51 (1991) 3749A.

1401. Sharma, K. "The Contribution of Women Novelists to Indo-Anglian fiction." Saurashtra U, 19?.

1402. Sharma, Sudershan. "Influence of Gandhian Ideology on Indo-Anglian Fiction." Saurashtra U, 1981. New Delhi : Soni Book Agency, 1982.

1403. Sheperd, Ronald. "Aspects of Identity in the Indo-English Novel : A Study of Three Novelists — Raja Rao, R.K. Narayan and Mulk Raj Anand." Adelaedu U, 1974.

1404. Shirwadkar, K.R. "Indian Novel in English and Social Change: A Thematic Study." Marathwada U, 1986.

1405. Shirdwadkar, Meena K. "The Image of Women in Indo-Anglian Fiction." Marathwada U, 1977. New Delhi : Sterling Publishers, 1979.

1406. Sikri, Adarsh. "Quest for Identity in Indo-Anglian Novel." Guru Nanak U, 1991.

1407. Sikri, Bindu. "Use of Defence Mechanism in Indo-Anglian Fiction." Gurunanak U, 1991.

1408. Singh, Jagdev. "Partition in Human Feelings." Punjab U, 19?

1409. Subbarayudu, G. K. "The City and the Novel : A Study of English Fiction of Some Commonwealth Countries." Diss (M.Phil). Hyderabad U, 1980.

1410. Suresh Kumar A. V. "Non-Indian Characters : Anglo-American and European in the Novels of Mulk Raj Anand, Raja Rao, R.K. Narayan, B. Rajan, Markandaya and Anita Desai." Osmania U, 1990.

1411. Swain, Prafulla Chandra. "Image of the Post-Independence India in Indo-Anglian Fiction." Utkal U, 1985.

1412. Tyraner-Stastny, Alice Gabrielle. "Indo-Anglian Literature and the Colonila Elite : Studies of Projections, Rationlizations, Distortions and Reflections of Colonial Indian Elite through and Analysis of the Themes, Portraits, and Style of Selected Indo-Anglian Novels." Cornell U, 1969.

1413. Uma, Alladi. "Woman and Her Family : Indian and Afro-American : A Literary Perspective." State University of New York (Buffalo), 1983. Delhi : Sterling, 1989.

1414. Valsala Kumari M. The Indian Short Story in English : Themes and Techniques." U of Kerala, 1989.

1415. Vasantha, V. A. "A Survey of South Indian Novelists," Madhurai U, 1977.

1416. Venugopal, C. V. "The Indian Short Story in English : A Survey." Karnatak U, 1969. Bareilly : Prakash Book Depot, 1976.

1417. Verghese, C. Paul. "Problems of the Indian Creative Writers in English." Poona U, 1968. Bombay : Somiya Publishers, 1971.

1418. Vishwanatha Rao, Cheemakooti. "Indian Fiction in English Since 1947." Karnatak U, 1977.

1419. Wandrakar, Kalpana Sudhir. "A Social Psychological Perspective on the Immigrant Characters." Poona U, 1991.

1420. Wilkinson, G. N. "Modern Indian Novel in English Since Independence : A Study." Sussex U, 1970.

PART II
INDIVIDUAL AUTHORS

Individual Novelists

KHWAJA AHMAD ABBAS

A. Primary Sources

I. Novels

Tomorrow is ours : The Novel of the India of Today. Bombay : Popular Book Depot, 1943. Rpt. as *Divided Heart.* New Delhi : Paradise Publications, 1968.

Defeat for Death : A Story without Names. Baroda : Padmaja Publications,1944.

Inquilab : A Novel of Indian Revolution. Bombay : Jaico Publications, 1955; New Delhi : India Paperbacks, 1977.

Ajanta. Bombay : Jaico Publications, 1962.

When Night Falls. Delhi : Hind Pocket Books, 1968.

Mera Nam Joker. Delhi : Hind Pocket Books, 1970.

Maria. Delhi : Hind Pocket Books, 1971. New Delhi : Orient Paperbacks, n.d.

Bobby. New Delhi : Sterling Publishers, 1973.

Boy Meets Girl. Delhi : Sterling Publishers, 1973.

That Woman. New Delhi : Orient Paperbacks, 1973.

Distant Dream. New Delhi : Sterling Publishers, 1975.

Barrister-at-Law. New Delhi : Orient Paperbacks, 1977.

The Walls of Glass. New Delhi : Himalaya Books, 1977

A Day Like Another Day. Delhi : Vikas Publishing House, 1977.

The Naxalites. Delhi : Lok Publications, 1979.

The World is My Village. Delhi : Ajanta Publications, 1983,1984.

Bombay, My Bombay : The Love Story of the City. Delhi : Ajanta Publications, 1987.

II. Short Story Collections

Not All Lies. Delhi : Raj Kamal Publications, 1945.

Rice and Other Stories. Bombay : Kutub Publications, 1947.

Blood and Stones and other Stories. Bombay : Hind Kitabs, 1947.

Cages of Freedom and other Stories. Bombay : Hind Kitabs, 1952.

One Thousand Nights on a Bed of Stones and other Stories. Delhi: Jaico Publications, 1957.

The Black Sun and other Stories. Bombay : Jaico Publications, 1963.

The Most Beautiful Woman in the World (short stories). New Delhi : Paradise Publications, 1968.

Four Friends (short stories). New Delhi : Arnold Heinemann, 1977.

Men and Women (Specially Selected long and Short Stories). New Delhi : N.V. Publications, 1977.

The Gun and Other Stories. New Delhi : Arnold Heinemann, 1985.

The Thirteenth Victim. Delhi : Amar Prakashan, 1986.

III. Non-Fiction

I Write as I Feel (Selections from Bombay Chronicle). Bombay : Hind Kitabs, 1948.

I Am Not an Island : An Experiment in Autobiography. New Delhi : Vikas Publications, 1977.

"Art, Literature and the People." *Blitz* 5 Oct. 1974.

"My Literary Credo." *Indian Literature* Sept.-Oct. 1979 : 24-28.

"Had They Turned Professional Writers." *Patriot* (Mag) 19 May 1985 : 1.

B. Secondary Sources : Critical Works

I. Books

1421. Chandalia, Hemendra Singh. *Ethos of Khwaja Ahmad Abbas : A Study in Social Realism*. Jaipur Bohra Prakashan, 1996.

1422. Hasib, Ahmed. *The Novels of Khwaja Ahmad Abbas : A Study of His Art and Vision.* Delhi : Seema Publications, 1987.
The book is a comprehensive evaluation of the diverse trends discernible in the life and works of the novelist. It makes a detailed examination of the novels of Abbas with a view "to determining whether or not the integrity of the novelist as a literary artist has been affected by his commitment to a social ideology." It also traces the exact form which his social vision takes and the diverse influences that have gone into the making of the novelist.

II. Research Articles

1423. Dayal, B. "K.A. Abbas : A True Humanist." Dayal 163-204, ref. : 247.
Examines the humanistic values as expressed in the short stories of Abbas and finds him as a social critic and a true humanist on par with Mulk Raj Anand.

1424. Guptara Prabhu, "Abbas", *Contemporary Novelists* 5 ed. 1-3. ref. : 234.

1425. Kalinnikova, Elena J. "The Son of India : K.A. Abbas." Kalinnikova, *Indian English Literature : A Perspective* 111-112. ref. : 316.
Discusses the novels and short stories of K.A. Abbas and evaluates his achievements as anti-fascist and anti-imperialist.

1426. Kumar, Sunil. "K.A. Abbas's *The Naxalites* : An Unusual Story of Unusual people." Pathak, *Indian Fiction* 79-84. ref. : 422.

Traces the genesis of the naxalite movement to the great Bengal famine of 1943 and explores the minds of the characters at the subconscious level showing the morbid nature of their thinking and their concept of revolution. Though "it is an unusual story of unusual people," it successfully portrays reality.

1427. Pandeya, Shiva M. "K.A. Abbas : Inquilab." Pandeya 252-392. ref. : 413.
Discusses the novel in the light of the Indian theory of *rasasutra* appropriating the elements of *bhava, vibhava* and *anubhava,* which are woven into the form of an ironic comedy.

1428. Raj Rao, R. "Caste, Culture and Civilization : *Prajapathi* and *The World is My Village." Language Forum* 11.1-4 (1985-86) : 116-127. Rpt. in Dhawan, *Comparative Literature* 116-127. ref. : 254.
See 7814.

1429. Sinha, R.N. "The Two Windows of K.A. Abbas : A Note on His Short Story." Singh, Avadesh 135-142. ref. : 507.
Highlights some of the distinguishing aspects humanism, social consciousness etc.) of Abbas as a short story writer.

1430. Singh, Santa Serbjeet. "Khwaja Abbas *vs*. Babucracy." *Economic Times* 14 Sept. 1980 : 5

1431. Yaravintelimath, C.B. "*Inquilab* : An Autobiographical Novel." *Journal of Karnatak University* (Humanities) 31 (1987) : 9-18.
Compares *Inquilab* with Abbas's autobiography, *I Am Not an Island,* to show how the facts of the author's life have been blended into the general history of the freedom struggle and integrated into the fabric of the novel.

III. Reviews

1432. Jai Dev. Rev. of *Bombay My Bombay : The Love Story of the City*. *Indian Book Chronicle* Sept.-Oct. 1986 : 213-215.

1433. Jain, S.P. "The False But Impregnable Walls." Rev. of *The Walls of Glass*. *Indian Literary Review* May 1978 : 50.

1434. Joshi, Chandra. Rev. of *The Naxalites*. *Hindustan Times* 1 July 1979 : iv.

1435. Khullar, Keya. Rev. of *Thirteenth Victim*. *Statesman* 6 Dec. 1987 : xii.

1436. Mand, Pankaj Kumar. Rev. of *Barrister-at-Law*. *Hindustan Times* 22 Oct. 1978: iv.

1437. Raj Rao, R. Rev. of *The World is My Village*. *Illustrated Weekly of India* 3 June 1984 : 70.

1438. Rev. of *The Walls of Glass*. *Times of India* (mag.) 11 Jan. 1977 : 10.

1439. Rev. of *The World is My Village*. *Tribune* 11 Aug. 1984 : 4.

1440. Rev. of *Inquilab*. *Times of India* (Mag.) 19 June 1977 : 10.

1441. Rev. of *Bombay My Bombay*. *Patriot* 28 June 1987 : 4.

1442. Sarkar, Satyandra Nath. Rev. of *The Naxalites*. *India Today* 16 Aug. 1979 : 97, 99.

1443. Wasi, Jehanara. Rev. of *Bombay My Bombay : The Love Story of the City*. *Indian Horizons* 36.1-2 (1987) : 50-57.

IV. Dissertations

1444. Dayal, Barameshwar. "Critical study of the themes and techniques of the Indo-Anglian short story writers with special reference to Mulk Raj Anand, R.K. Narayan, and K.A. Abbas." Magadh U (Bodh Gaya), 1983. Ranchi : Jubliee Prakashan, 1985.

1445. Hasib, Ahmed. "Khwaja Ahmed Abbas : A Study of His Novels." Banaras U, 1983.

1446. Tiwari, Anil. "Thematic and Structural Concerns in the Novels and Stories of K. A. Abbas." Dr. H.S. Gour U, 19?.

1447. Waquiddin, S. "Social Concern in the Novels of K.A. Abbas." Kashi Vidyapith, 19?.

SOHAILA ABDULLAH

The Mad Woman of Jogan. New Delhi : Harper Collins. 1998.

S.A. ABDULLAH

The White Terror of the Khybar. London : S.W. Partige, 1934.

AMRITA ABRAHAM

The Last Necklace and other Stories. Bombay : Ratnabharati, 1974.

R. ACHARYA

Adventures of Little Devil. Bombay : Ratnabharati, n.d.

The Brave Little Bear. Bombay : Ratnabharati, n.d.

The Adventures of Pilla the Pup. Bombay : India Book House, n.d.

SHANTA ACHARYA

Not This, Not That. Delhi : Rupa & Co, 1994.

UMRAO JAN ADA

The Courtesan of Lucknow. Delhi : Hind Pocket Books, n.d.

VIVEK ADARKAR

A. Primary Sources

We Could Be Happy Together (short stories). New York : Asia Publishing House, 1972.

B. Secondary Sources

I. Review

1448. Nebel, Joyce. Rev. of *We Could Be Happy Together. World Literature Written in English* 14.2 (1975) : 426.

1449. Rev. of *We Could Be Happy Together. Indian P.E.N.* Feb.-Mar. 1974:7. Notes.

VEENA ADIGE

The Meeting and other Stories. Calcutta : Writers Workshop, 1985.

SAMUEL PONDIPEDDI ADINARAYAN

A Day at Their Races : A Collection of Twenty Short Stories, Madras : Higgin Bothams, 1970.

Valour Enshirned. New Delhi : Orient Longmans, 1971.

The Hit and the Sword. Madras : Christian Literary Society, 1986.

Where Do I Come In ? : A Novel. Annamalai : Annamalai University Publications, 1989.

RUKUN ADVANI

A. Primary Sources

First Fictions : Introduction II. London : Faber, 1992.

Beethoven Among the Cows. New Delhi : Ravi Dayal, 1994.

Short Stories. Bombay : Sterling Publishers, 1994.

B. Secondary Sources : Critical Capital Works

1450. Belliappa, K.C. "The Post-Colonial Novelists : Achebe, Tharoor, Advani." Trivedi and Mukherjee 203-212. ref. : 534.
See 630.

1451. Rao, K. Damodar. "Possible Stories and Multiple Endings : Rukun Advani's *Beethoven Among the Cows* as a open-ended Narrative." *Kakatiya Journal of English Studies* 15 (1995) : 67-79.

SAID DEHLVI AHMAD

Fear of Hell. Delhi : Dini Book Depot, 1972.

A.S. AHMED

I Understood : A Novel . New Delhi : Arnold Heinemann, 1985.

HUMERA AHMED

Checkmate and Other Stories. Calcutta : Writers Workshop, 1995.

M.R. AHMED

Zindagi. Lahore : Madina Press, n.d.

Q. KAZI AHMED

Random Short Stories. Calcutta : Khyber House, 1951.

ANITA PANJWANI AHUJA

Flames of Fervour. New Delhi: Har Anand Publication 1996

INDRANI AIKATH-GYaLISEN

A. Primary Sources

I. Novella and Stories

Daughters of the House. New Delhi : Penguin Books, 1991.

A Novella and three stories.

Crane Morning/Gwener Firingee. New Delhi : Penguin (India) Books, 1993

II. Non-Fiction

"The Writer's Predicament" *Indian Review of Books* Sep.-Oct. 1993. 35-36.

BHAKULAKUNDA R. RAJAM AIYAR

A. Primary Sources

I. Novels

True Greatness Or *Vasudeva Sastri,* London : Allen & Unwin, 1925. Published serially in *Prabudha Bharati* from

1896-1898. Republished in the author's collected works under the Title *The Rambles of the Vedanta*. Madras : Thomson 1905. Calcutta : G.P. Lee, 1946.

II. Short Stories

Miscellaneous Stories. Madras : Prabudha Bharati Publications, 1896-98.

B. Secondary Sources : Critical Works

I. Research Articles

1452. Parameswaran, Uma. "Rajam Aiyar's *Vasudeva Sastry*." *Literary Endeavour* 6 : 2-4 (1984-85) : 55-67.
Critically evaluates the novel and comments that the novel, *Vasudeva Sastry*, has an insubstantial story line, archaic and abrupt language and crudely manipulated characters. Considers it as a worthy work of missionary literature.

1453. Viswanathan, S. "Rajam Iyer's *Vasudeva Sastry* or *True Greatness :* Apologue or Religious Novel." *Journal of Indian Writing in English* 2.1 (1974) : 47-53.
Considers Rajam Iyer a pioneer of Indian fiction in English. Discusses the novel's merits and demerits and finds the novel more an 'apologue' rather than a religious novel on account of the domination of the vedantic deliberations — the sermons and the parables.

R.P. AIYAR

In The Crime Light. Bombay : India Book House, 1967.

H.R. AIYER

Sringara Manjari : *The Courtesan Who Inflamed Love*. Bombay : Jaico Publications, 1961.

P. PADMANABHA AIYER

Indian Tales. Srirangam : Srivani Vilas Press, 1924.

AJEET COUR

Dead End and Other Stories. New Delhi : Sterling Publishers, 1997.

PARESH P. AJMERA

Talking Computers. Calcutta : Writers Workshop, 1993.

AHMED MOHIDEEN AKHTAR

The Heart Turns In (Poems, Essays, Stories and Stray Thoughts). Madras : Published by the Author, 1974.

The Blood Red Bangles. Madras: P.K. Books, 1976

The Monument. Tiruchirapalli : Gita Press, 1977.

They Lived for Love. Madras : I.A., Saleem, 1984.

AKILON

Flower of Gold. New Delhi : Sterling Publishers, 1978.

MEENA ALEXANDER

A. Primary Sources

I. Novels

Nampally Road. San Francisco : Mercury House, 1991. Bombay : Disha Books, 1991.

Manhattan Music. San Francisco : Mercury House, 1997.

II. Short Stories

ed. *Truth Tales : Contemporary Stories by Women Writers of India.* New York : Feminist Press, 1990.
Contains one English Story, "Midnight Soldiers," by Vishwapriya Iyengar.

III. Non-Fiction

Fault Lines : A Memoir. New Delhi : Penguin Books, 1993.

IV. Interviews

Govindaswamy, R. Raja. "In Conversation: an Interview with Meena Alexander." *Kavya Bharati* 7 (1995) : 91-100.

Mohanty, Sachidananda. "Stitching It Together : An Interview with Meena Alexander." *Literature Alive* 4.3 and 5.1 (1992): 24-31.

B. Secondary Sources : Critical Works

I. Research Articles

1454. Dutt, P. Karnani. A Reader's Odyssey into Meena Alexander's *Nampally Road."* Dhawan, *Indian Women Novelists* Set III. Vol. 3. 222-228. ref. : 257.
Examines the novel in terms of its theme, locale and the use of Indian words.

1455. Kumar, Manjusree S. "Journey Through Time : Meena Alexander's *Fault Lines."* Dhawan, *Indian Women Novelists* Set III. Vol. 3. 208-221. ref. : 257.

II. Reviews

1456. Hashmi, Alamgir. Rev. of *Truth Tales. World Literature Today* 66.1 (1992) : 206-207.

1457. Perry, John Oliver. Rev. of *Nampally Road. World Literature Today* 65.2 (1991) : 364–365

1458. Rao, Sushiela N. Rev. of *Manhattan Music. World Literature Today* 72.2 (1998) : 456-457.

AAMIR ALI

A. Primary Sources

I. Novels

Conflict. Bombay : National Information and Publication, 1947.

Via Geneva. Bombay : Pearl Publicaton, 1967.

Assignment in Kashmir. Delhi : Hind Pocket Books, 1973.

B. Secondary Sources

I. Reviews

1459. Mayadas, Lina. "Coming of the Age." Rev. of *Assignment in Kashmir. Quest* 85, Nov.-Dec. 1977 : 90-91.

AHMED ALI

A. Primary Sources

I. Novels

Twilight in Delhi. London : Hogarth Press, 1941. London/New York/Bombay : Oxford University Press, 1966, 1984. Delhi : Sterling Paperbacks, 1973. Delhi : Oxford Unversity Press, 1991. New Delhi : New Direction, 1994.

Ocean of Night. London : Peter Owen, 1964. Delhi : Hind Pocket Books, 1992. Serialized in 1964 in *The Illustrated Weekly of India.*

Of Rats and Diplomats : A Novel. Hyderabad : Sangam Books, 1985. New Delhi : Orient Longman, 1985. Karachi : Akrash Publishing, 1986.

II. Short Stories

The Prison House. Karachi : Akrash Publishing, 1985.

III. Non-Fiction

"The Raison D'etre of *Twilight in Delhi." Journal of Indian Writing in English* 23.1-2 (1995) : 137-147.

IV. Inverviews

Coppola, Carlo. "Ahmed Ali in Conversation." *Journal of South Asian Literature* 28.2 (1993). Rpt. in *Journal of Indian Writing in English* 23.1-2 (1995) : 63-79.

Farrukhi, Asif Aslam. "An Interview with Ahmed Ali." *Journal of Indian Writing in English.* 23.1-2 (1995) : 92-97.

Jha, Rama. "Meeting Ahmed Ali in Chicago" *Patriot* 29 Jan. 1984. Rpt. in *Journal of Indian Writing in English* 23.1-2 (1995) : 86-91.

Rasheed, N.M. "The Progressive Writer's Movement in Its Historical Perspective." *Journal of South Asian Literature* 13 (1977/78) : 91- 97.
Comments and reactions to an interview with Ahmed Ali.

Shamsie, Muneeza. "Memories of Another Day." An Interview. *Newstime* Aug. 1990. Rpt. in *Journal of Indian Writing in English* 23.1-2 (1995) : 80-85.

B. Secondary Sources : Capital Works

I. Special Issues

1460. *Journal of South Asian Literature* 28.2 (1993).

1461. *Journal of Indian Writing in English* 23.1-2 (1995).

II. Research Articles

1462. Anand, Mulk Raj. "Letter on Ahmed Ali." *Journal of Indian Writing in English* 23.1-2 (1995) : 49-52.

1463. Anderson, David D. "Ahmed Ali and *Twilight in Delhi.*" *Mahfil* 7.1-2 (1971) : 81-86. Rpt. as "Ahmed Ali and the Growth of a Pakistani Literary Tradition" in *World Literature Written in English* 14 (1975) : 436-449. Also in *Journal of Indian Writing in English* 23.1-2 (1995) : 111-118.
Discusses the genesis of the novel *Twilight in Delhi* and its urdu translation and the seminal role of *Twilight in Delhi* in developing Pakistani literary tradition.

1464. Askari, Muhammad Hasan. "A Novel by Ahmed Ali." *Makhzan* (Lahore) May 1949. Rpt in *Journal of Indian Writing in English* 23.1-2(1995) : 98-110.

1465. Begum, Jameela. "Reconstructing Personal History : The Purdah in *Twilight in Delhi* and *Sunlight on a Broken Column.*" Jain and Amin, *Margins* 206-215. ref. : 304.
Considers the novels as recreation of personal and political history of the 'marginal group', the Muslim community. Argues that the joys, sorrows and experiences of the unsung women characters give us "an insightful account of the lives of Muslim women smoothered within the great walls of pretentious heritage."

1466. Brander, Laurence. "The Novels of Ahmed Ali." *Journal of Commonwealth Literature* 3 (1967) : 76-86.
Considers *Twilight in Delhi* and *Ocean of Night* as most remarkable in presenting a view of the rich splendid world of the Muslims.

1467. "Ahmed Ali." *Contemporary Novelists.* 5th ed. 21-23. ref. : 234.

1468. Coppola, Carlo. "The Short Stories of Ahmed Ali." *Studies in the Urdu Ghazal and Prose Fiction.* Ed. Muhammed Umar Memon. Madison : Centre for South Asian Studies, University of Wisconsin, 1979. 211-242.

1469. ——. "Ahmed Ali : Bridges and Links, East and West." *Journal of Indian Writing in English* 23.1-2 (1995) : 13-18.

1470. Gowda, Annaiah H. "Ahmed Ali's *Twilight in Delhi* and Achebe's *Things Fall Apart.*" *Literary Half-Yearly* 21.1 (1980) : 11-18. Rpt. in *Language Forum* 11. 1-4 (1985-1986) : 171-179. Also in Dhawan, *Comparative Literature* 171-179. ref. : 254. Also in Srivastava, A.K. *Alien Voices* 53-60. ref. : 524.
Compares and contrasts the two novels, *Twilight in Delhi* and *Things Fall Apart* to draw affinities and to show how these two novelists "handle societies whose milieu was fast disappearing under the impact of the British rule and the narrative incidents are carefully located in time."

1471. Hashmi, Alamgir. "The Novelists Rejuvenation : Ahmed Ali and His Novels" *Nation* (Lahore) 22 Jan. 1988 : 7.

1472. ——. "English Version of Ahmed Ali's Short Stories" *Nation* (Lahore) 29 July, 1988 : 7.

1473. ——. "Ahmed Ali : The Transition to a Post-Colonial Mode." *World Literature Written in English* 29.2 (1989) : 148-152. Rpt. in *Journal of Modern Literature* 17.1 (1990) : 177-182.

A brief note on Ali's recent novel *Of Rats and Diplomats.*

1474. ——. "Ahmed Ali" *Journal of Indian Writing in English* 23.1-2(1995) : 8-12.

1475. Ikramullah, Begum Shaista Suhrawardy. "Ahmed Ali : A Tribute." *Journal of Indian Writing in English* 23.1-2 (1995) : 35-38.

1476. Jackson, Carlton. "Ahmed Ali." *Journal of Indian Writing in English* 23.1-2 (1995) : 47-48.

1477. Jeyaraju, M.A. and D. Mirathula. "Nostalgic Nocturne : Ahmed Ali's *Ocean of Night* as a Period Novel." *Journal of Indian Writing In English* 27.1 (1999) : 32-43.

1478. King, Bruce. "From Twilight to Midnight : Muslim Novels of India and Pakistan." *The World of Muslim Imagination.* ed. Alamgir Hashmi. Islamabad : Gulmohar Press, 1986. 243-259.

1479. Kumar, Anita S. "*Twilight in Delhi* : A Study in Lyricism." *Indian Literature* 29.2 (1976) : 25-38.

Considers *Twilight in Delhi* as a poetic novel and Ahmed Ali as a lyrical novelist by examining the peculiar quality of lyrical phonemes deployed in the novel and suggests that the novel possesses "a fragile sublimity... a piquancy and sustained beauty not possible outside simple present tense forms."

1480. Memon, Muhammad Umar and Orooj Ahmed Ali. "Curriculum Vitae of Ahmed Ali." *Journal of Indian Writing in English* 23.1-2(1995) : 1-7.

1481. Muraz, Commander Ghaffar Ahmed. "Professor Ahmed Ali." *Journal of Indian Writing in English* 23.1-2 (1995) : 61-62.

1482. Niven, Alistar. "The Historical Imagination in the Novels of Ahmed Ali." *Journal of Indian Writing in English*

8. 1-2 (1980) : 1-13. Also in Singh Kirpal *Through Different Eyes* 1-13. ref. : 508.
Ahmed Ali's urban novels depict several levels of experience associating religious wisdom with a historic vision. Both novels *(Twilight in Delhi and Ocean of Night),* located in Delhi and Lucknow respectively, describe a culturally well-endowed past and "big creatures against barbaric modernism". Also traces influence of T.S. Eliot's metaphysical thought on Ali.

1483. Prasad, Ch. A. Rajendra. "The Saga of City and Man : A Study of Ahmed Ali's *Twilight in Delhi." Journal of Indian Writing in English* 23.1-2 (1995) : 125-131.
Shows how Ahmed Ali by infusing many layers of meaning and perception metamorphosised the novel from a study of a city (Delhi as an embodiment of whole culture) and a man (Mr. Nihal, the protagonist, as a representative Indian Muslim of the pre-independent India) into the sagacious study of city and man.

1484. Quraishi, Mazhar Mumtaz. "Professor Ahmed Ali as I Saw Him." *Journal of Indian Writing in English* 23.1-2 (1995) : 27-29.

1485. R.V.S. "The Delhi of Ahmed Ali." *Journal of Indian Writing in English* 23.1-2 (1995) : 30-38.

1486. Rahman, Tariq. "Remembering Ahmed Ali." *Journal of Indian Writing in English* 23.1-2 (1995) : 53-55.

1487. Raizada, Harish. "Ahmed Ali." Prasad, Madhusudan *Indian English Novelists* 1-22. ref. : 437.
Discusses the impact of Ahmed Ali's literary credo on his novels to assess his achievement as a novelist of realistic fiction.

1488. Shamsie, Muneeza. "Twilight in Karachi." *Journal of Indian Writing in English* 23.1-2 (1995) : 27-29.

1489. Singh, K. Natwar. "Face of a Friend." *Journal of Indian Writing in English* 23.1-2 (1995) : 32-34.

1490. Stilz, Gerhard. "Live in Fragments, No Longer : A Conciliatory Analysis of Ahmed Ali's *Twilight in Delhi.*" *Journal of Indian Writing in English* 16.2 (1988) : 69-88.
Points out the qualities and weaknesses, achievements and insufficiencies arising from the novelist's existential ambivalence.

1491. Trivedi, Harish. "Ahmed Ali's *Twilight in Delhi.*" Pradhan 41-73 ref. : 434.
Discusses Ali's brilliant evocation in *Twilight in Delhi* of the sense of transience of Muslim-Indian culture and old Moghul Delhi. Also examines the artistic integrity and imaginative truth embedded in the novel and declares that it is "no less a political novel than a poetic one, in its profound and integral engagement with the forces of society and history and communal and national destiny."

1492. Wort, Richard. "Dawn in Lucknow." *Journal of Indian Writing in English* 23.1-2 (1995) : 39-40.

1493. Zaman, Mukhtar. "Professor Ahmed Ali : The Rebel that was." *Journal of Indian Writing in English* 23.1-2 (1995) : 19-26.

1494. Zeno (Safdar Mir). "Cultural Notes: A Writer Committed to Progressivism," *Dawn* (Karachi) 13.

1495. ——. "Professor Ahmed Ali and the Progressive Writer's Movement." *Journal of Indian Writing in English* 23.1-2 (1995) : 119-124.

III. Reviews

1496. "Caught." Rev. of *Ocean of Night. Times Literary Supplement.* 25 June 1964 : 557.

1497. Dondhi, Reeta. Rev. of *Twilight in Delhi. Democratic World.* 20 Dec. 1973: 17.

1498. Futehally, Laeeq. Rev. of *Twilight in Delhi. Quest* 52, Jan.-Mar. 1967.

1499. Hashmi, Alamgir. Rev. of *The Prison House. World Literature Today* 61.1 (1987) : 158.

1500. ——. Rev. of *Of Rats and Diplomats. World Literature Today* 61.4 : 678-679.

1501. Rao, Vimala. Rev. of *Twilight in Delhi. Literary Criterion* 8.1 (1967) : 93-95.

1502. "Tales of Indians." Rev. of *Twilight in Delhi. Times Literary Supplement.* 7 Dec. 1940 : 619.

SYED RASHADATH ALI

A Noble Friend : Stories for Children. Calcutta : P. Lal, 1987.

Barbie's Wonderful Holiday. Bombay : Lalvani, 1972. Bombay : Subash Publishers, 1977.

Thank You Jane Austen : A Novel for Teenagers. New Delhi : Hemkunt Press, 1973.

For the Love of a Begum. Hyderabad : Privately Published, 1989.

LOUIS ALMEIDA

Good-Bye Goa. Panaji : Casa J.D. Fernandes, 1973.

JOHN B. ALPHONSO KARKALA

Passions of The Nightless Night. Delhi : Hind Pocket Books, 1974.

Joys of Jayanagar. Mysore : Privately Published, 1985.

STEPHEN ALTAR

A. Primary Sources

I. Novels

Neglected Lives. London : Andre Deutsch, 1979.

The Gold Child. London : Andre Deutsch, 1987.

Renuka. London : Andre Deutsch, 1988.

II. Short Stories

Great Indian Hunting Stories. New Delhi : Penguin Books, 1988.

B. Secondary Sources

I. Reviews

1503. Advani, Rukun. "Alters Fiction Flows Subtly." Rev. of *Renuka. India Today* 15 Dec. 1989 : 195.

1504. Singh, Nihal. Rev. of *Neglected Lives. Statesmen* 9 Sept. 1979 : I

STEPHEN ALTER AND WIMAL DASSANAYAKE (eds)

Penguin Books of Short Stories. New Delhi : Penguin Books, 1989.

VIOLET ALVA

Blood for Love : True Murder Stories. N.P: n.p., n.d.

EULALIA ALVAREA

Short Stories. Bombay : By the Author, 1965.

SYED AMANUDDIN

Passager to the Himalayan. Calcutta : Prayer Books, 1979.

AMRINDER

A. Primary Sources

Lajo. New Delhi : Sharma Publishers, 1990.

B. Secondary Sources : Critical Works

I. Research Articles

1505. Lahiri, Tapati. "Victims of Fundamentalism in Amrinder's *Lajo* and Taslima Nasrin's *Lajja*." Bande, *Victim Consciousness* 141-148. ref. : 206.

1506. Mathur, O.P. "Amrinder's *Lajo* and Khushwant Singh's *Delhi :* Sikhs in A Crisis of Identity." Mathur, *Indian Political Novel* 115-123. ref. : 352.
Focuses on the changing flux of the emotional reaction between the Sikhs and Hindus due to disturbing external events and shows how the two writers portray the

tragedies of the Sikh lives led to their rudely shaken identity.

J.S. ANAND

Tresspassers (A Novel set in Modern Punjab). Calcutta : Writers Workshop, 1995.

Confession of a Corpse and Other Stories. Calcutta : Writers Workshop, 1989.

MULK RAJ ANAND

A. Primary Sources

I. Novels

Untouchable (with an introduction by E.M. Forster). London : Laurence and Wishart, 1935. London : Bodley Head, 1970. Toronto : Copp Clark, 1970. Harmondsworth. Penguin Books, 1986. Bombay : Kutub-Popular, 1950. Delhi, Hind Pocket Books, 1970.

Coolie. London : Laurence and Wishart, 1936. New York : Liberty Press. 1952. Bombay : Current Book House, 1953. London : The Bodley Head, 1972. Toronto : Copp Clark, 1972. Delhi : Hind Pocket Books, 1973. New Delhi: My Fair Paperbacks, 1981. New Delhi : Penguin Books, 1993.

Two Leaves and a Bud. London : Laurence and Wishart, 1937. Bombay : Kutub-Popular, 1946. New York : Liberty Press, 1954. Delhi : Orient Paperbacks, n.d. New Delhi : My Fair Paperbacks, 1981.

Lament on the Death of a Master of Arts. Lucknow: Naya Sansar, 1938. Delhi : Hind Pocket Books, 1967.

The Village. London : Jonathan Cape, 1939. Bombay : Kutub-Popular, 1960. Delhi : Orient Paperbacks, n.d.

Across the Black Waters. London : Jonathan Cape, 1940. Bombay : Kutub-Popular, 1955. Delhi : Vision Books, 1940. New Delhi : Orient Paperbacks, 1980.

The Sword and the Sickle. London : Jonathan Cape, 1942. Bombay : Kutub-Popular, 1955. New Delhi : Arnold Heinemann, 1984.

The Big Heart. London : Hutchinson,1945. Madras: Subbaiah Chetty, 1947. Bombay : Kutub-Popular, n.d. New Delhi : Arnold Heinemann, 1980.

Seven Summers : The Story of an Indian Childhood. London : Hutchinson, 1951. Bombay : Kutub-Popular, 1960. New Delhi : Orient Paperbacks, 1970, Arnold Heinemann, 1986.

Private Life of an Indian Prince. London : Hutchinson, 1953. Toronto : Copp Clark, 1970. Delhi : Hind Pocket Books, 1972.

The Old Woman and the Cow. Bombay : Kutub-Popular, 1960. republished as *Gauri.* Delhi : Arnold Heinemann, 1960, 1981. Delhi : Hind Pocket Books, 1976.

The Road. Bombay : Kutub-Popular, 1961. New Delhi, Sterling Publishers, 1974, 1987.

Death of a Hero : Epitaph for Maqbool Sherwan. Bombay : Kutub- Popular, 1963. Delhi : Orient Paperbacks, n.d. New Delhi : Arnold Heinemann,1985.

Morning Face. Bombay : Kutub-Popular, 1968. Delhi : Arnold Heinemann, 1976.

Confession of a Lover. New Delhi : Arnold Heinemann, 1976.

The Bubble. New Delhi : Arnold Heinemann, 1984.

Little Plays of Mahatma Gandhi (a novel in dramatic dialogues). New Delhi : Arnold Hienemann, 1992.

Nine Moods of Bharata. New Delhi : Arnold Associates. 1998.

II. Short Story Collections

The Lost Child and Other Stories. London : J.A. Allen, 1934.

The Barber's Trade Union and Other Stories. London : Jonathan Cape, 1944. New Delhi : Arnold Heinemann, 1944. Delhi : Orient May Fair Paperbacks, 1977.

The Tractor and the Corn Goddess and Other Stories. Bombay : Thacker and Company, 1947.

Reflection on the Golden Bed and other Stories. Bombay : Current Book House, 1954. New Delhi : Arnold Publishers, 1989.

Selected Stories. Moscow : Foreign Languages Publishing House, 1954. 1955.

The Power of Darkness and Other Stories. Bombay : Jaico Publishers, 1959.

Lajwanti and Other Stories. Bombay : Jaico Publishers, 1966.

Between Tears and Laughter. New Delhi : Sterling Publishers, 1973. 1991.

Folk Tales of Punjab. New Delhi : Sterling Publishers, 1974. *Selected Short Stories.* ed. M.K. Naik. New Delhi : Arnold Heinemann, 1977.

The Lost Child and Two Lyrical Stories. New Delhi : Abhinav Publications, 1995.

Anand, Mulk Raj and Iqbal Singh, eds. *Indian Short Stories.* London : The New Indian Publishing House, 1946.

Anand, Mulk Raj and S. Babu Rao. *Panorama : An Anthology of Modern Indian Short Stories.* New Delhi : Sterling Publishers, 1986.

For Children

Indian Fairy Tales (Retold). Bombay : Kutub-Popular, 1946. Rpt. 1966.

The Story of Man. Amritsar : Sikh Publishing House, 1952.

ed. *The Story of the Indian Post Offices.* New Delhi : Post and Telegraph Department, 1954.

More Indian Fairy Tales (Retold). Bombay : Kutub-Popular, 1958.

Aesop's Fables (Retold). Bombay : Dhawante-Popular, 1960.

The Story of Chacha Nehru. Bombay : Rajpal & Sons, 1965.

A Day in the Life of Mohenjo-Dara. New Delhi : Children's Book Trust, 1968.

III. Non-Fiction

(Select articles and books mostly related to critical & creative writings).

"Toward a New Indian Literature." *Left Review* 2.12 (1936).

Letter to the Editor on *Two Leaves and a Bud. Spectator* 5685 (1937).

Letter to the Editor on *Two Leaves and a Bud. Spectator* 5697 (1937).

"English Novels of the Twentieth Century on India." *Asiatic Review* 39.139 (1943).

"I Believe in Man." *In Search of Faith.* ed. Ernest W. Martin. London : Lindsay Drummond, 1943.

"Where is the English Novel?" *Our Time* 3.6 (1943).

"Novelists in Exile." *Our Time* 4 (1945).

Apology of Heroism. Bombav : Kutub-Popular, 1946. Delhi : May Fair Paperbacks, 1975.

Introduction to *Rice and Other Stories* by K.A. Abbas. Bombay : Kutub-Popular, 1947.

The King Emperor's English. Bombay : Hind Kitabs, 1948.

"A Writer's Confession of His Faith." *Bharat Jyoti,* 27 Apr. 1952.

The Story of Man. Amritsar : Sikh Publishing House, 1952.

"The Continuity of Tradition." *Marg* 9.1 (1955).

"The Emergence of the Hero in the Modern Indian Novel." *Illustrated Weekly of India* 9 Dec. 1956 : 42-49.

"Trends in the Novel." *Cultural Forum* Nov. 1961. Tagore Number.

"New Bearing in Indian Literature." *Literary Review* 4.4 (1961). Anand was the guest editor of this issue.

"Is Indian Literature Sufficiently Indian ?" *United Asia* 13.6 (1961).

"The Writer at Bay." *Seminar* May, 1961.

"International Literary Seminar." *Cultural Forum* 4.3 (1962).

"The Writer's Role in National Integration : A Discussion." *Indian Literature* 5.1 (1962).

"Creative Writing in the Present Crisis." *Indian Literature* 6.1 (1963).

"The Concept of an Asian Mind." *Contemporary Indian Literature* 4 (1964).

"Shaw Talks to Shakespeare." *Cultural Forum* 6.3 (1964).

Letter to E.M. Forster. *E.M. Forster : A Tribute.* ed. K. Natwar Singh. New York : Harcourt, Brace & World, 1964.

"East-West Dialogue." *Indian Writers in Conference.* Ed. Nissim Ezekiel. Bombay : P.E.N. All India Centre, 1964.

"What Shakespeare Means to Me ?" *Contemporary Indian Literature* 5, 6-7 (1965).

"How I Became a Writer ?" *Contemporary Indian Literature* 5.11-12(1965). Rpt. in *Mirror* May 1977.

"A Note on Modern Indian Fiction." *Indian Literature* 8.1 (1965). 44-57.

"Is Universal Criticism Possible ?" *Literary Criterion* 7.1(1965): 68-75. Rpt. in *Literary Criticism : European and Indian Traditions.* Ed. C.D. Narasimhaiah. Mysore : University of Mysore Press, 1966.

"The Role of Creative Writers and Artists in the Developing Countries of Afro-Asia." *Afro-Asia and World Affairs* 3.1(1966) : 18-21.

"Modernism in Indian and Soviet Literature." *Amity* 4.1(1966) : 44-47.

"The Krishna Theme in Indian Art : The Best of Lovers." *Cultural Forum* 9.1-2 (1967-1968).

"The Sources of Creative Writing." *Indian Literature* 7 (Sep. 1967).

"The Story of My Experiment with a White Lie." *Indian Literature* 10.3 (July-Sep., 1967) : 28-43. Rpt. in Naik, *et al. Critical Essays* Madras : Macmillan, 1979. 4-18.

"At What Price, My Brother." *Indian Literature* 1.1 (1967) : 52-60.

"Folk Tradition as an Aid to Modern Expression." *Indo-Asian Culture* 17.3 (1968) : 3-6.

"The Task Before the Writer." *Indian Culture* 6.1 (1963) : 70-77.

"The Question of Modernity." *Modernity and Contemporary Indian Literature.* Simla : Indian Institute of Advanced Study, 1968.

"Writer's Role in Modern Society." *Contemporary Indian Literature* 9.1 (Jan. 1969).

"Profile of E.M. Forster." *Literary Half-Yearly* 10.2 (1969).

"Old Myths and New Myths — Recital *versus* Novel." *Banasthali Patrika* 5.13 (1969) : 27-36. Rpt. in Narasimhaiah, *Indian Literature of the Past Fifty Years.* Mysore : University of Mysore Publication, 1970. 109-120.

"What Good is Literature For?" *Banasthali Patrika* 5.14 (1970). 81-83.

"About the Lost Child and Other Allegories." *Indian Literature* 13.1 (1970) : 28.

"Pigeon-Indian : Some Notes on Indian English Writing." *Studies in Australian and Indian Literature.* Eds. Narasimhaiah and Nagarajan. New Delhi : Indian Council of Cultural Relations, 1971, 228-248. *Journal of Karnatak University* (Humanities), 1972 : 69-90. Also in *World Literature Written in English* 21.2 (1982) : 325-336.

"The Changling-An Indo-Anglian Novelist's Credo." *Indian and Foreign Review* 9.23 (1972).

Roots and Flowers : Two Lectures on the Metamorphosis of Technique and Content in the Indian Novel. Dharwad : Karnatak University Press, 1972.

Author to Critic : The Letters of Mulk Raj Anand to Saros Cowasjee. Ed. Saros Cowasjee, Calcutta : Writers Workshop, 1973.

"Trends in the Modern Indian Novel." *Journal of Indian Writing in English* 1.1 (1973) : 1-6.

"The Rhythms of Indian Life — On Indian English." *Research and Criticism.* Ed. Radhakrishnan. Annamalai : Research Scholar Association 1975. 59-61.

"The Changling." *World Literature Written in English.* 15.1(1976) : 110-120. Also in *Journal of English Studies* (Warangal) 4.1 (1972) : 229-238.

The Humanism of M.K. Gandhi. Bombay : Tata Press, n.d.

"On the Use of Epithets, Swear Words, Curses and Imprecations." *Littcrit* 3, 2.2 (1976) : 1-5.

"Literature's Revolutionary Message." *Youth Times* Oct. 28, Nov. 10, 1977.

"The Meaning of Words." *Mirror* Sep.1977.

"An Undeclared War (The Internecine war between Brown Sahibs and Babus). *Littcrit* 4, 3.1 (1978). 11-24.

"Why I Write?" *Indo-English Literature.* Ed. K.K. Sharma. Ghaziabad : Vimal Prakashan, 1977. 9-22. Rpt. in *Kakatiya Journal of English Studies* 2.1 (1977) : 244-255. Also in Sharma, K.K. *Perspectives on Mulk Raj Anand.* Ghaziabad : Vimal Prakashan, 1978. 1-6.

"Creative Process." *Littcrit* 6, 4.1 (1978) : 1-3.

"My Childhood." *Indian Literary Review* 1.1 (1978) : 37-40.

"The Continuity of Myths, Symbols and Images." *Marg* 32.1 (1978) : 5-8.

"Pigeon-Irish and Pigeon-Indian." *Commonwealth Quarterly* 3.10 (1979) :

"Reflections of a Novelist." *Tribune* 5 May 1979.

"Reflections of a Novelist : Some Notes on the Novel." *Journal of Literature and Aesthetics* 2.2-3 (1982) : 132-136.

"Images and Words." *Illustrated Weekly of India* 8 June 1980.

"Old Myth and New Myth." *Marg* 33.4 (1980) : 40A.

"Narcissism or Solidarity." *Osmania Journal of English Studies* 1983 : 19-26.

Conversations in Bloomsbury. New Delhi : Arnold Heinemann, 1981.

"The First and Last Impact of E.M Forster : Some Reminiscences." *Approaches to E.M. Forster : A Centenary Volume.* Ed. V.A. Shahane, New Delhi : Arnold Heinemann, 1981.

"Content and Form in *Untouchable* and *Kanthapura.*" *Littcrit* 14, 8.1 (1982) : 47-60.

"As I Walk Along Gorky Street." *Tribune* 22 Nov. 1987.

"Compulsion for Creativity." *Tribune* 8 May 1988.

"Intellectual Statesman." *Tribune* 3 Jan. 1988.

"Destination Man : Nehru's Vision of New Order." *Tribune* 12 Nov. 1989.

"The Sources of Protest in My Novels." *Literary Criterion* 18.4 (1983) : 1-12.

Afterword. *Response : Recent Revelations.* Ed. Hari Mohan Prasad. Bareilly : Prakash Book Depot, 1983. 307-335.

"The Relevance of Indian-English Literature." *Criticism and Research* 7 (1984-85) : 172-180.

"English is a valid Literary Medium." *Times of India* 26 May 1990 : 8.

"Many Obstacles to Free Media." *Times of India* 10 Jan. 1990 : 7.1-6.

"Is Indian English Literature *Deshi* or *Videshi?*" *Indian Book Chronicle* June 1990 : 15-16.

"Pigeon-Indian : A Note on the Emergence of Indian English Literature." *Journal of Indian Writing in English* 20.1-2 (1992) : 1-3.

"R. Tagore : The founder of the Indian Novel." *Viswabharati Qarterly* 2.1-4 (1991-1992).

"Rhythm Is What Is Common to All Heightened Expression." *Literary Criterion* 28.4 (1993) : 81-87.

"Mulk Raj Anand Remembers." *Indian Literature* 36.2 (1993) 176-86.

Old Myth and New Myth : Letters from Mulk Raj Anand to K.V.S. Murti. Calcutta : Writers Workshop, 1992.

IV. Interviews

Bald, Suresh Renjen. Interview (personal). 24 July 1971.

Chatterjee. A Very Personal View. *Youth Times* 5 Apr. 1974 : 22.

Eskay. Interview with Mulk Raj Anand. *Patriot* 28 May 1982 : 2.

Fisher, Marlene. "A Day with Mulk Raj Anand." *Illustrated Weekly of India* 12 Aug. 1973 : 44-45.

——. Interview with Mulk Raj Anand. *World Literature Written in English* 13.1P (1974) : 109-122.

Jafri, Sultana. "Mulk Raj Anand : Remove the Threat of War." Interview. *Soviet Land* Dec. 1985 : 30.

Khandala. "Conversation with Mulk Raj Anand" (Tape), 19 May 1973.

Lalji, Mishra. Interview with Mulk Raj Anand. *Creative Forum* 2.2. 1989.

Mathur, O.P. "Anand on Society and Literature." Excerpts from an Interview with Mulk Raj Anand. *Mulk Raj Anand : A Home Appraisal.* Ed. Atma Ram. Hoshiarpur : Charravak Publications, 1988. 162-176. Rpt. in Mathur, *Modern Indian English Fiction.* Delhi : Abhinav Publications, 1993. 192-202.

Nahal, Chaman. "Speak up for the Down and out." Interview with Mulk Raj Anand. *Hindustan Times* 24 Dec. 1995 : 13.

Rajan, P.K. "A Decadent Society Needs Renewal." *Hindu* 11 Dec. 1983 : 22.

——. "A Dialogue with Mulk Raj Anand." Rajan, *Studies in Mulk Raj Anand.* Delhi Abhinav Publications, 1986.

Ram, Atma. Interview with Mulk Raj Anand. Ram, *Interviews With Indian English Writers.* Calcutta : Writers Workshop, 1983. 9-20.

Ratan, Jai. "Meeting with Mulk Raj Anand." *Miscellany* 8, Sep.-Oct. 1961.

Sahgal, Pavan. "Experiment with an Alien Tongue." Interview. *Times Weekly* 13 May 1973, 15.

Samatharaj, Dipak. "A Conversation with Mulk Raj Anand." *Chandrabhaga* 9 & 10 (1983) : 113-123.

Sethi, Vijaya Mohan. "Short Stories of Mulk Raj Anand." Interview. *Punjab Journal of English Studies* 3 (1988) : 73-80. Also in Sethi *Mulk Raj Anand. The Short Story Writer.* New Delhi : Ashish Publishing House, 1990. 17-27.

Singh, Sushila. "The Lost Child at 80s." Interview with Mulk Raj Anand. *Times of India* 8 Dec. 1985.

Verma, K.D. "An Interview with Mulk Raj Anand." *South Asian Review* 15.12 (July, 1991) : 31-38.

B. Secondary Sources : Criticial Works

I. Bibliographies

1507. "Bibliography of the Novels and Stories by Mulk Raj Anand in various languages." *Contemporary Indian Literature* V. 1965.

1508. Cowasjee, Saros. "Select Bibliography." *So Many Freedoms.* Delhi : Oxford University Press, 1977. 191-200.

1509. Packham, G. *Mulk Raj Anand: A Checklist.* Mysore: Literary Press, 1978.

1510. Paul, Premila. "Bibliography." *The Novels of Mulk Raj Anand. A Thematic Study.* New Delhi : Sterling Publishers, 1983. 164-180.

1511. Ram, Atma, ed. "Select Bibliography." *Mulk Raj Anand: A Home Appraisal.* Hoshiarpur: Chaarvak Publications, 1988 : 231-253.

1512. Seth, Vijayanand. "Select Bibliography." *Mulk Raj Anand : The Short Story Writer.* New Delhi : Ashish Publishing House, 1990. 92-97.

1513. Sharma, K. K. Comp. "Select Bibliography." *Perspectives on Mulk Raj Anand*. Ghaziabad (Delhi) : Vimal Prakashan, 1978 : 181-186.

II. Special Issues

1514. *Contemporary Indian Literature* 5.11-12 (1965). Special Issue on Mulk Raj Anand. Nov.-Dec. 1965.

1515. *Kakatiya Journal of English Studies* 2.1 (1977). Special Number on Mulk Raj Anand.

III. Books

1516. Abidi, S.Z.H. *Mulk Raj Anand's Untouchable : A Critical Study*. Bareilly : Prakash Book Depot, 1972.
A guide intended to help the students.

1517. ——. *Mulk Raj Anand's Coolie: A Critical Study*. Bareilly: Prakash Book Depot, 1976.

An analysis of the various aspects of the Novel written for the students.

1518. Agnihotri, G.N. *Indian Life and Problems in the Novels of Mulk Raj Anand, Raja Rao and R.K. Narayan*. Meerut : Shalabh Book House, 1984.
See 179

1519. Anjaneyulu, T. *Critical Study of the Selected Novels of Mulk Raj Anand, Manohar Malgonkar and Kushwant Singh*. New Delhi. Atlantic Publishers. 1997.

1520. Berry, Margaret. *Mulk Raj Anand : The Man and the Novelist*. Amsterdam : Oriental Press, 1971.
The work endeavors to trace Anand's faith as a man and writer and to relate that faith to his creative work. The author shows that Anand's concerns move from the social order to the economic and then to the political ultimately integrating all of them into what she calls "Bhakti Yoga". The basis of such a faith was seen in Anand's Indian heritage, long experience in the West and his unquestionable dedication to humanity. Suggests

that Anand's emphasis on social change has driven him to several alternatives and ultimately settled down to the humanistic ethic, which, in terms of Indian sensibility, may be called "Bhakti Yoga".

1521. Cowasjee, Saros. *Author to Critic : The Letters of M.R. Anand to Saros Cowasjee.* Calcutta : Writers Workshop, 1973.

The book is a collection of letters written by the novelist to the author during 1965 to 1971. The letters offer an expiation upon Anand's humanistic attitude to life which is the central concern of his work.

1522. ——. *Coolie : An Assessment.* New Delhi : Oxford University Press, 1976.

A perceptive critical study of the novel. Treats the novel as Anand's most representative achievement.

1523. ——. *So Many Freedoms.* New Delhi : Oxford University Press, 1977.

A comprehensive study of Anand's life and works, the former being given more importance for it is Anand's life and his times which have had multiple influences on his creative work. Though tries to be objective in its assessment of Anand's fiction, the burden of the book is to argue that Anand's historical, 'documentary' novels have achieved an artistic excellence, the culmination of which is found in *The Private Life of an Indian Prince.*

1524. Dhar, T.N. *History-Fiction Interface : M.R. Anand, Nayantara Sahgal, Salman Rushdie, Shashi Taroor and O.V. Vijayan.* New Delhi : Prestige Books, 1999

1525. Dhawan, R.K., ed. *The Novels of Mulk Raj Anand.* New Delhi : Prestige Books, 1992.

The book is an anthology of critical essays by different critics on several aspects of Anand's aritistic achievement as a novelist as well as a short story writer. While elucidating and interpreting Anand's fictional works, the book also makes an assessment of his contribution to Indian English fiction.

See 1563, 1575, 1579, 1595, 1598, 1602, 1616, 1617, 1630, 1632, 1633, 1656, 1666, 1685, 1690, 1706, 1721, 1745, 1749, 1765, 1768, 1798, 1802, 1808,1809, 1829, 1830, 1831, 1832, 1833, 1855, 1863.

1526. Fisher, Marlene. *The Wisdom of the Heart : A Study of the Works of Mulk Raj Anand.* New Delhi : Sterling Publishers, 1985.

A full length study of Mulk Raj Anand both as a man and a writer. A greater part of the book is devoted to biographical details offering new and interesting facts about Anand's life and insights into his concept of humanism which is his primary source of inspiration. Discussing at length how Anand's personal experiences and struggles are integrated into his works and how they are responsible for the making of the novelist, the author states the purpose of the book is "to introduce Mulk Raj Anand to audience and potential readers of his works to whom he is unknown or little known."

1527. Gautam, G.L. *Mulk Raj Anand's Critique of Religious Fundamentalism : A Critical Assessment of His Novels.* Delhi : Kanti Publishers, 1996.

Traces religious obscurantism in contemporary India and shows how Anand rejects it throughout his literary career. Out of the seven chapters the first and the last alone discuss Anand's responses to religious fundamentalism whereas in the other five chapters social and religious forces that determined the lives of the common people find a discursive description.

1528. George, C.J. *Mulk Raj Anand : His Art and His Concerns.* New Delhi : Atlantic Publishers, 1994.

1529. Gupta, G. S. Balarama. *Mulk Raj Anand : A Study of His Fiction in Human Perspective.* Bareilly : Prakash Book Depot, 1974.

An analytical survey of Anand's fiction with a view to interpret Anand's humanistic vision of life in terms of comprehensive historical humanism.

1530. Khan, S.A. *The Novel of Commitment : Mulk Raj Anand.* New Delhi : Atlantic Publishers. 1999.

1531. Lindsay, Jack. *The Elephant and the Lotus*. Bombay : Kutub-Populars, 1965.
A monograph which makes a critical evaluation of Anand as a novelist and short story writer. It also serves as an introduction to the study of the author.

1532. ——. *Mulk Raj Anand : A Critical Essay.* Bombay: Hind Kitabs, 1948.

1533. Murti, K.V.S. *The Sword and the Sickle : A Study of Mulk Raj Anand's Novels*. Mysore : Geetha Book House Publishers, 1983.
Considers Anand as the originator of the art of writing fiction in India about Indians in an Indian way. Analyses Anand's novels to show him as a novelist and a myth-maker, drawing, at many stages, from his auto-biographical experiences. Finds Anand Dickensian in his social concerns. Calls his humanism "an ideal one of the brand of Tolstoy."

1534. ——. *Old Myth and New Myth : Letters from Mulk Raj Anand to K.V.S. Murti.* Calcutta : Writers Workshop, 1992.

1535. Naik, M.K. *Mulk Raj Anand.* New Delhi : Arnold Heinemann, 1973.
An in-depth analysis of the entire corpus of Anand's fiction (including the short stories) to show that his work is a characteristic product of the modern Indian ethos and his major theme is the confrontation between tradition and modernity. Feels "that the measure of his artistic success is the extent to which he comprehends the nature of both tradition and modernity and that of the confrontation." Naik finds that sometimes Anand's

vision is distorted resulting in "pleading, overwriting and sentimentality." The book takes the course of a usual full-length study of the author and his works. Drawn in ten short chapters it traces the development of this prolific novelist and short story writer from his earlier creative phase up to 1972, all the while keeping a track of Anand's understanding of the humanistic spirit in man and the impending dangers it confronts.

In his final assessment of Anand as a creative writer, Naik focuses both on his shortcomings as a writer and his achievements. "In spite of his doctrinaire convictions" says Naik, "his humanitarian compassion ... gives an unmistakable ring of sincerity" to his writings.

1536. Nasini, Reza Ahmed. *Language of Mulk Raj Anand, Raja Rao and R.K. Narayan.* New Delhi : Capital Publishing House, 1989.

See 400.

1537. Niven, Alastair. *The Yoke of Pity : A Study in the Fictional Writing of Mulk Raj Anand.* New Delhi : Arnold Heinemann, 1978.

The book is a perceptive study of Anand's major fiction in the light of the remark "Can a great literature be didactic?" Considering Anand as a major 20th century novelist, the author tries to show, through the analysis and evaluation of his work, that the central energy and tension of Anand lies in the blend of his "intellectual desire for objectivity and the emotional urge for commitment." The aim of the book is to make a fresh study of Anand's novels to show that they belong primarily to art as they are the products of imagination and sensibility and to prove that Anand has not sacrificed his art to ideology. Drawing attention to the social, economical and political movements that influenced Anand and stimulated his creative genius

Niven concludes that "Anand is the first Indian novelist to present the realities of modern India."

1538. Paul, Premila. *The Novels of Mulk Raj Anand : A Thematic Study*. New Delhi : Sterling Publishers, 1983.
Starting with a premise that "the distinction of Anand as a writer lies in his themes — both in their choice and in their treatment," the author sees several political, economic, social and cultural factors that make up the large bulk of Anand's fiction. She chooses to trace the treatment of the caste system, the class system, religion, education and the status of woman as treated by Anand and feels that an understanding of these will hold the key to Anand's creative mind.

1539. Prasad, Shaileswar Sati. *Insulated and The Injured* (on Mulk Raj Anand). Patna : Janaki Prakashan, 1997.

1540. Rajan, P.K. *Studies in Mulk Raj Anand*. Delhi : Abhinav Publications, 1986.
The book is a collection of essays on Anand's fiction in which the author seeks to discover the essential form of his works evolving out of the content-form interaction within the text. Presents a comprehensive vision of Anand's art.
See 1759, 1760, 1761, 1762, 1763, 1765, 1766.

1541. ——. *Mulk Raj Anand : A Revaluation*. New Delhi : Arnold Associates, 1994.
Argues that "there is an inherent pattern of dualism in Anand's humanist view of life" and studies the use of theme, form and dialect in Anand's novels "to understand the precise nature of ambivalence and its function in the work of art."

1542. Ram, Atma, ed. *Mulk Raj Anand : A Home Appraisal*. Hoshiarpur : Charvak Publications, 1988.
The present book seeks to provide some critical and source material on Anand "so as to suggest new perspectives on his works". Mostly biographical-critical

in their nature the eleven essays deal with the major themes in the individual novels from *Untouchable* to *The Bubble.* The most interesting aspect of the book is a longish chronology of Mulk Raj Anand's life and achievement. There is an introduction by the editor on the works by and on Anand.

See 1562, 1566, 1569, 1577, 1613, 1615, 1662, 1743, 1752, 1778, 1826, 1874.

1543. Ramamurthy, S. *The Novels of Charles Dcikens and Mulk Raj Anand.* Trichy : By the Author, 1994.

A comparative study of the novels of Charles Dickens and Anand to show the psychological affinity between the two writers which is evidenced in the treatment of the moral crisis of their respective contemporary social milieu.

1544. Riemenschneider, Dieter. *An Ideal Man in Mulk Raj Anand's Novels.* Bombay : Kutub-Populars, 1967.

1545. Sethi, Vijay Mohan. *Mulk Raj Anand : The Short Story Writer.* New Delhi : Ashish Publishing House, 1990.

The book is a study of Anand's shorter fiction in terms of its philosophical content and innovative technique. It consists of twelve essays out of which six essays are published in several magazines and newspapers. It covers the entire range of Anand's shorter fiction beginning with that written during Anand's formative years and its relation to his later work and his innovative techniques both in structure and language. It also contains the chapters on "A Lesson in Compassion," Presenting Anand's Credo — and an interview on his short stories.

See 1815, 1816, 1817, 1818.

1546. Sharma, K.K., ed. *Perspectives on Mulk Raj Anand.* Ghaziabad : Vimal Prakashan, 1978.

The book, comprising twelve new and four already published articles, presents "a comprehensive and objective assessment of almost all the basic aspects of the thematic and technical sides of Anand's fiction." These articles seek to examine Anand's fiction from more than one critical stance: immesurable formative influence on Anand, his fictional credo, *Karma* or aesthetic symphony, his theory of the novel, characterization, etc. Besides an interesting "Introduction", there is a valuable reprint of the author's own confessional essay, "Why I write?"

See 1600, 1650, 1653, 1658, 1680, 1698, 1725, 1730, 1740, 1756, 1773, 1803, 1822, 1827, 1828, 1876.

1547. Sharma, Ambuj Kumar. *The Theme of Exploitation in the Novels of Mulk Raj Anand.* New Delhi : Deep & Deep Publications, 1990.

The book analyses the theme of exploitation in Anand's novels from different angles — social, economic, political, emotive and aesthetic as well as techniques of its presentation. An effort has been made in the sixth and seventh chapters to trace the ingredients of extra-religious exploitation. Anand's vision of exploitation has been shown as tinged with Gandhian, humanistic and Marxian concepts.

1548. Singh, Vaidyanath. *Social Realism in the Fiction of Dickens and Mulk Raj Anand.* New Delhi : Commonwealth Publishers, 1997.

1549. Sinha, K.N. *Mulk Raj Anand.* New York : Twayne Publications, 1972.

The book, published in the Twayne World Author series, is one of the earliest evaluations of Anand's achievement as a novelist. It emphasises both the prophetic and passionate characteristics of his fiction, progressively detectable in his development as a novelist. Tracing Anand's commitment to humanism and the influences that caused it. Sinha discusses the development of Anand's growth as a fiction writer from his earlier novels *(Untouchable, Coolie)* to his later novels, the novels of passion (the trilogy, *The Big*

Heart, The Private Life of an Indian Prince). It also contains a critique of Anand's short stories. Assessing Anand's virtues and limitations as a novelist the author finally concludes that Anand is "primarily a novelist of the passionate moment" who "imposes a moral order on the non-order of experience.

IV. Research Articles

1550. Agnihotri, G. N. "Mulk Raj Anand — His Progressive Prole-tarianism" Agnihotri 61-82. ref. : 179.
A general assessment of Anand as a novelist. Discusses Anand's novels as problem novels dealing with various kinds of economical and social exploitations and some topical political questions.

1551. Alcock, Peter. "Some Thing Different : Problems of Cultural Relativism in Non-European Literature." *ACLALS Bulletin* 5th ser 1 (1978)) : 48-66. See 574.
Discusses Mulk Raj Anand's *Untouchable.*

1552. Amur, G.S. "Individual Consciousness and Social Reality in Mulk Raj Anand's *Untouchable* and Shivatam Karanth's *Choma's Drum.*" Amur, *Essays* 117-129. ref. : 191. Also in Amur, *Forbidden Fruit* . ref. : 190. Compares and contrasts the treatment of the theme of untouchability in Anand's *Untouchable* and Karanth's *Choma's Drum* and shows how it is merged with the personal theme of the alienation of the hero, exhibiting his psychological conflict and inner consciousness "Theirs is a kind of consciousness which in the case of Anand, is more intellectualized while Karanth made it romantically subjective."

1553. "Anand" *World Authors — 1950-1970.* 50-53. ref. : 520.

1554. Arora, V.N. "Mulk Raj Anand's Claim to Fame." *English Association Journal* (1965) : 26-30.

1555. Asnani, Shyam M. "Untouchability and Mulk Raj Anand's

Untouchable." Banasthali Patrika 6.16 (1971) : 31-36.
Discusses the term "Untouchability" both in the Hindu religious context as well as in its social context and analyses the novel to show Anand's own definition of it. Says that, though the novel attacks social snobbery and prejudices, it is not "a dissertation on socio-ethical problem" but a pointer towards "the intolerance and egoistic feelings" which "are at the root of our social and personal troubles."

1556. ——. "Socio-Political Concerns in the Novels of Mulk Raj Anand." *Triveni* 45.1 (1976) : 38-50.
A study of the exploitation of foreign imperialism as well as casteism and superstition and religious dogma in the first trilogy *(Untouchable, Coolie* and *Two Leaves and a Bud)*. While considering the novels as "illuminating documents of human interest" the author focuses on Anand's faith in the 'elemental goodness of man' and 'power of love'.

1557. ——. "The Theme of East-West Encounter in the Novels of Mulk Raj Anand." *Littcrit* 7, 4.2 (1978) : 11-19.
Treatment of East-West dichotomy in *Untouchable. Two Leaves and a Bud, Coolie* and *The Big Heart.* Comments that Anand's portrayal of English characters are not artistically satisfying and Anand's art suffers on account of his propagandist point of view.

1558. ——. "A Critique of Mulk Raj Anand's Literary Creed." *Commonwealth Quarterly* 4.15 (1988) : 64-85. Rpt. in Asnani *New Dimensions* 116-131. (1988) : ref. : 198.
Argues against the detractors (Margaret Berry, K.K. Sharma, Saros Cowasjee, D. Ramakrishna) who find gradual evolution in Anand's concept of the novel and establishes that Anand's literary perspective has undergone no significant change and that he has given as much regard to the style and the technique of the novel as to the functions of a novelist.

1559. ——. "Form and Technique in Mulk Raj Anand's Novels." *Indian Scholar* 2.2 (1980) : 89-103.
An evaluation of Anand as a novelist who is "a veritable artist in a language which is not his own." Also brings into focus the salient features of Anand's art — his humanistic point of view, his comprehensive grasp of life, realism, technique of characterization and his experiments with language.

1560. ——. "The Indian Princes : Their Portrayal in the Indo-English Novel." *Commonwealth Quarterly* 3.2 (1979), 85-104 Rpt. in Asnani, *Critical Response* 62-78. ref. : 197.
See 616.

1561. ——. "Social Protest in Mulk Raj Anand." Asnani, *Critical Response,* 10-24. ref. : 197.
Studies Anand's first three novels — *Untouchable, Coolie* and *Two Leaves and a Bud* to show that there are three distinct levels perceivable in his protest novels — protest against the tyranny of the caste-system, *(Untouchable),* protest against the inhuman treatment of the capitalist class, *(Coolie)* and protest against the colonial exploitation *(Two Leaves and a Bud).*

1562. ——. "Mulk Raj Anand and the Bloomsbury Elite Group". Ram, *Mulk Raj Anand : A Home Appraisal* 149-161. ref. : 1542.
Traces the earlier influences of the Bloomsbury group on Mulk Raj Anand's personality. Also enumerates five real tests in order to evaluate the novelist — these are mainly drawn from the stalwarts of the group.

1563. ——. "New Morality in the Modern Indo-English Novel, A Study of Mulk Raj Anand, Anita Desai and Nayantara Sahgal." *Language Forum* 9.1-4 (1981-82) : 30-50. Rpt. in Dhawan, *The Novels of Mulk Raj Anand* 39-49. ref. : 1525. Also in Dhawan, *Indian Women Novelists* Set I. Vol. I. 104-116. ref.: 257. Rpt in Dhawan, *Explorations*

30-50. ref. : 253. Also in Asnani, *New Dimensions* 51-61. ref. : 198.
See 619.

1564. ——, "Mulk Raj Anand : Of Crushed Humanity." Ross 75-87. ref. : 485.

1565. Aston, N.M. "Mulk Raj Anand's *Death of a Hero* : A Study." *Commonwealth Review* 5.2 (1993-94) : 101-106. Rpt. in Dhawan, *Indian Literature Today.* ref. : 258.
A critical evaluation of the novel.

1566. Awasthi, Kamal N. "*The Sword and the Sickle* : A Study in Heroic Consciousness." Ram, *Mulk Raj Anand : A Home Appraisal* 111-126. ref. : 1542.
Studies the novel as "a work focusing heroic consciousness of the suppressed India." Traces the growth of the protagonist's consciousness from orphanhood to heroism and shows how a realisation of his self leads him "to marshal forces of brotherhood to strike at the citadel of suppression and injustice."

1567. Bais, H.S.S. "An Endless Search : A Psycho-Analytical Study of Anant in Mulk Raj Anand's *The Big Heart.*" Pathak, *Indian Fiction in English* 38-46. ref. : 422.
Examines the motif of 'search' in terms of the character, Ananta. While at the surface level the search is for finding a way out of the quagmire of the most basic needs like food, shelter, etc., at the deeper level it is for finding solutions to the question of identity.

1568. Bald, Suresh Renjen. "Politics of a Revolutionary Elite: A Study of Mulk Raj Anand's Novels." *Modern Asian Studies* 8 (1974) : 473-89.

1569. Bande, Usha. "Gauri-Myth and Reality." Ram, *Mulk Raj Anand : A Home Appraisal.* 60-75. ref. : 1542.
Studies Anand's *Gauri* in the light of myth and reality : the protagonist, Gauri, as a representative of Sita, Shakti and Mohini (as chaste, the powerful and the charming

force) as well as a woman looked at from the new angle of reality as humans with self-esteem, rights, dreams, desires, weaknesses and strength.

1570. Banerjee, Surabhi. "Irony as a Stylistic Device : A Note on the Opening Chapter of Anand's *Across the Black-Waters*." *Journal of Literature and Aesthetics* 2.2-3 (1982) : 63-66.

A brief stylistic analysis of the text of the opening chapter of *Across the Black Waters* to throw light on some of the features of Anand's technique such as his narrative stance, his use of linguistic variables of omniscient narrative mode and of irony.

1571. Berry, Margaret. "Purpose in the Novels of Mulk Raj Anand." *Mahfil* 5 (1969) : 85-90

1572 ——. "India : A Double Key." *Journal of Indian Writing in English* 6.1(1978) : 31-38.

See 634.

1573. Bhaskaran, Gautam. "Writer as a Town Planner : Anand, M.R." *Statesman* 29 Nov. 1983 : 5.

1574. Bhatnagar, K.C. "Mulk Raj Anand: Poetic Realism and Protest." Bhatnagar, K.C., *Realism* 131-169. ref. : 218. Rpt. in Bhatnagar, O.P. *Essays* 131-169. ref. : 221.

Examines Anand's novels chronologically to suggest the presence of different shades of poetic realism.

1575. Bhatt, Sanjay. "The Lost Child." *Kakatiya Journal of English Studies* 2.1 (1977) : 219-222. Also in Dhawan, *The Novels of Mulk Raj Anand* 123–125. ref. : 1525.

A note on the narrative technique and the related symbolic pattern in "The Lost Child".

1576. Bhattacharya, B.K. "*Two Leaves and a Bud* : Truth and Fiction." *Kakatiya Journal of English Studies* 2.1 (1977) : 39-47.

Discusses the novel, *Two Leaves and a Bud,* as "a testament of man's inhumanity to man."

1577. Boparai, H. Singh "The Adamic Myth and *Two Leaves and a Bud.*" Ram, *Mulk Raj Anand : A Home Appraisal* 43-59. ref. : 1542.

Shows how Anand using archetypal images of Heaven and Hell transforms the social reality into mythic and psychic reality.

1578. Brown, J. "Mulk Raj Anand : Prophet of Revolution." *Bharat Jyoti* 15 Dec. 1945.

Discusses the element of prophecy in Anand's novels especially in relation to the proletarian revolution.

1579. Burra, Edward "Three Views on *Coolie.*" *Kakatiya Journal of English Studies* 2.1 (1977) : 226-227 Rpt. in Dhawan, *The Novels of Mulk Raj Anand* 82-83 ref. : 1525.

Considers *Coolie* as a work which is picaresque in its whole manner and construction, except that this hero is no rogue himself but victim of the world's rogueries."

1580. Carter, D. "Probing Identities : *Untouchable, Things Fall Apart* and *This Earth My Brother.*" *Literary Criterion* 14.3 (1979) : 14-29.

Analyses three novels from the New Literature in English including Anand's *Untouchable* to show how individual identity can be seen as a pointer towards national identity, thereby signifying a multi-levelled cultural dimension. In each of these novels, the novelist forges a unique artistic identity of his own with national identity.

1581. Chakravorty, D.K. "Gauri and Anasuya : Two Faces of Indian Womanhood." Chakravorty 1-5. ref. : 230.

A brief account of the two novels *Gauri* and *The Song of Anasuya* (Uma Vasudev's) to show how the protagonists of the two novels represent two completely divergent faces of Indian womanhood. Gauri, the village woman, with her untold suffering and humiliation belongs to the poor and Anasuya with her sheltered life and her pre-occupation with the manifold pleasures of life belongs to the rich aristocratic class.

1582. Chandra, Suresh. "Social Conscience in the Novels of Mulk Raj Anand." *English Studies in India* (April, 1985) : 137-143. Rpt. as "Mulk Raj Anand: A Sarvodaya Saint." Chandra 22-36. ref. : 231.
Considers Anand as one of the "Sarvodaya Saints" like Gandhi who, though obsessed with the well-being of the sub-humans — the sweepers, coolies, serfs and the like — has not turned a blind eye to the crises of the privileged and the possessor. Finds his novels advocating a balanced approach of sympathy for the needy and a willing sacrifice on the part of the possessor.

1583. Chatterjee, Debjani. "Gandhi's Influence on Anand and His Fiction." *Kakatiya Journal of English Studies* 2.1 (1977) : 149-162. Rpt. in Prabhakar 84-93. ref. : 433.
Traces the impact of Gandhi on Mulk Raj Anand through a study of his works and shows that it is Gandhian humanism rather than his ideology that has influenced Anand.

1584. Chaudhury, Jasbir. "Images of Women in the Novels of Mulk Raj Anand." *Panjab University Research Bulletin* (Arts) 16.2 (1985) : 47-56.
Examines the place a woman occupies in the general scheme of Anand's universe and the contribution she makes towards his humanistic ideology. Also hints at Anand's concept of the New Woman "who must rise and take what is rightfully hers in society."

1585. Chetan, Karnani. "Mulk Raj Anand — The Novelist as a Social Chronicle." *Thought* 24 August 1974 : 19-20.

1586. Chellappan, K. "The Child Archetype in the Commonwealth Short Stories : Katherine Mansfield, Janet Frane, and

Mulk Raj Anand." Dhawan, *et al. Recent Commonwealth Literature* Vol. 1, 60-68. ref. : 260.
A comparative study of the archetypes of childhood in the short stories of some New Zealand Writers and of Anand's. Argues that Anand's use of the archetype is to show the process of alienation in the modern world and how it stands as a metaphor for the eternal quest of man.

1587. Chew, Shirley. "Fictions of Princely States and Empire." *Ariel* 17.3 (1986) : 103-107.
See 681

1588. Chinneswara Rao, G.J. "Anand's *Private Life of an Indian Prince* and Malgonkar's *The Princes* : A Comparison." *Journal of Indian Writing in English* 4.1 (1976) : 15-20.
Argues that Malgonkar's approach is chronological and objective in projecting the image of the Maharaja as a man of stupendous courage swayed by external forces, whereas Anand's portrait of the Maharaja stands for an intensely realised human agony, a more engrossed figure projected through "a certain personal involvement."

1589. Cowasjee, Saros. "Anand's Princes and Proletarians." *Literary Half-Yearly* 9.2 (1968) : 83-104. Rpt. in *Journal of Commonwealth Literature* 5 (1968) : 52-64.
Considering it as a Dostoevskian novel on a grand scale, the author remarks that though his later novels are fine "they do not possess the energy and sweep of *The Private Life of an Indian Prince*."

1590. —. "Princes and Politics." *Literary Criterion* 8.4 (1969) : 10-18.
A comparative study of the novels by Anand and Malgonkar to show the diversity of points of view shown in them regarding contemporary politics. Argues that the major flaw of the novel, *The Princes,* is that

'politics' impinges on literature standing out against the development of character, while in *The private Life of an Indian Prince,* 'politics' fuses itself with the content of the story, presenting the emotional picture of the characters, thereby giving coherence and wholeness to the novel as a work of art.

1591. ——. "Mulk Raj Anand and His Critics." *Banasthali Patrika* 12 (1969) : 57-63.
Defends Anand from the accusation that Anand is a propagandist, by quoting from reviews and letters of the most outstanding British novelists and critics who have praised Anand.

1592. ——. "Mulk Raj Anand : A Profile." *Illustrated Weekly of India* 4 May 1969.

1593. ——. Afterword. *Untouchable* by Mulk Raj Anand. Delhi : Orient Paperbacks, 1970.

1594. ——. "Princes and their Collaborators." *Blitz* 1970.

1595. ——. "Mulk Raj Anand's *Coolie* : An Appraisal." *Banasthali Patrika* 8.19 (1972) : 8-19. Also in Dhawan, *The Novels of Mulk Raj Anand* 66-77. ref. : 1525. Also in Cowasjee, *Studies* 50-67. ref. : 236.
Fair assessment of the novel. Sketches tne salient features of Anand as a writer including his literary creed.

1596. ——. "Mulk Raj Anand : The Early Struggle of a Novelist." *Journal of Commonwealth Literature* 7.1 (1972) : 49-56.
Narrates the traumatic experiences of the author when he tries to 'break into print' and the disappointments and frustrations that lie beneath the story of success.

1597. ——. "Mulk Raj Anand and the B.B.C." *Indian and Foreign Review* 10.10 (1973) : 19-20.

1598. ——. "Anand's Literary Creed." *Journal of Indian Writing in English* 1.1 (1973) : 66-71. Also in Dhawan, *The Novels of Mulk Raj Anand* 13-18. ref. : 1525.

Discusses the positive and negative aspects of Anand's literary creed and argues that there is "no significant change in Anand's theory or attitude to the novel form" from the time he first began writing fiction as pronounced by Margaret Berry in her study, *Mulk Raj Anand : The Man and the Novelist.*

1599. ——. "Anand's *Two Leaves and a Bud.*" *Indian Literature* 16.3-4 (1973) : 134-147.

Argues that Anand fails as an artist due to the documentary nature of his work.

1600. ——. "Mulk Raj Anand's *Untouchable :* An Appraisal." *Literature East and West* 17. 2-4 (1973) : 199-211. Rpt. in Sharma, K.K., *Indo-English Literature* 87-100. ref. 501. Also in Sharma, K.K., *Perspectives on Mulk Raj Anand* 27-38. ref. : 1546.

Considers the novel as a tragedy — "a tragedy of a large section of mankind condemned to pariahdom of which there is no parallel in human history."

1601. ——. "*The Big Heart :* A New Perspective." *ACLALS Bulletin* 4.2 (1975) : 83-86. Rpt. in *Kakatiya Journal of English Studies* 2.1 (1977) : 85-92.

A critical analysis of the novel to show the growth of Anand's vision of maturity, the perceptive treatment of the complex Indian problems and his craftsmanship in comparison to his earlier novels — *Coolie, Untouchable* and *The Sword and the Sickle.*

1602. ——. "*The Big Heart :* A Note." Dhawan, *The Novels of Mulk Raj Anand* 140-144. ref. : 1525.

A modified version of the essay "*The Big Heart* A New Perspective."

See 1601.

1603. ——. "Mulk Raj Anand." *Encyclopedia of World Literature*

in 20th Century. Wolfgang Bernard Fleischamann. New York : Ungar, 1985.
A short biographical note.

1604. ——. "Mulk Raj Anand's *The Sword and the Sickle*." *World Literature Written in English* 14.1 (1975) : 267-277.
Finds the novel as an impressive achievement even though it is a 'lesser' work than *Untouchable* and *The Private Life of an Indian Prince :* It "presents a great historical story in fine detail, searching out every grain of truth as it goes."

1605. ——. "Mulk Raj Anand : A Hard Road to Fiction." Dwivedi, *Studies in Contemporary Indian Fiction* 82-96. ref. : 269.
A biographical sketch with an emphasis on the making of Anand as a literary artist.

1606. ——. "The Princes in Indian Fiction." *Kakatiya Journal of English Studies* 2.1 (1977) : 48-70.
A revised and enlarged version of the article, "Princes and Politics." Discusses the predicament of an Indian Princes as portrayed in Anglo-Indian (J.R. Ackerley's *Hindoo Holiday* and Forster's *The Hill of Devi)* and Indian English novels (Anand's *The Private Life of an Indian Prince)* against the background of Indian politics.
See 1590.

1607. ——. "Mulk Raj Anand : The Fusion of History and Fiction." McLeod *Subjects Worthy Fame:* 17-26. ref. : 357. Also in Cowasjee, *Studies* 96-108. ref. : 236.
Discusses the social problems and political and historical events that figure in the novels of Anand and shows how they are intricately woven into a design.

1608. Das, J.P. "Novels of Mulk Raj Anand." *Indian and Foreign Review* 31 June 1985 : 28-29.

1609. Das, G.K. "Between Two Heritages : A Note on Mulk Raj

Anand's *Confession of a Lover." Indian Literary Review* 1.2 (1978) 16-20.
Discusses *Confession of a Lover* as an expression of Anand's dilemma — as to his identity between two heritages, European and Indian.

1610. Dayal, B. "Mulk Raj Anand : A Spokesman of the Time." Dayal 25-94. ref. : 247.
A general survey of the short stories of Anand to assess his artistic achievement. Comments that "all the burning problems of his age have got expression in Anand's short stories through humour and satire and through tragi-comedies and grim tragedies."

1611. Devarajan, Padmini. "'Sadharanikarana' Elucidated in Anand's *The Bubble.*" *Littcrit* 36 & 37, 19. 1-2 (1993) : 101-116.
Discusses the novel applying the concept of Sadharanikarana (the principle of universalisation) and shows how Anand achieves this by reconciling the subjective-objective polarities.

1612. Dhar, T.N. "*The Big Heart* : Anand's Novel of Ideas." *Indian Literary Review* 5.3 (Oct. 1987) : 33-38.

1613. ——. "Dream, Nightmare, Alternative : The Dialectics of Form in Coolie." Ram, *Mulk Raj Anand : A Home Appraisal* 18-33. ref. : 1542.
Examines the structural aspects of the novel, *Coolie,* to show Anand's skill in arranging the action in a linear manner with shifts in time and place thereby building up a dialectical pattern by alternating the protagonist's (Munoo's) dreams with what they ultimately turn into his nightmares. Also points out that this specific design makes the novel acquire "the solidity and mass of a purposeful work of fiction."

1614. ——. "Conscious Raising in a Cultural Frame : The Fiction of Mulk Raj Anand Before 1947." Kaul and Jaidev 135-145. ref. : 319.

Considers Anand's novels, particularly pre-independence novels, as social and cultural debates intended to raise consciousness towards history and social change within the context of Indian culture and heritage.

1615. Dhatwalia, H. R. "*The Bubble* : A Study." Ram, *Mulk Raj Anand : A Home Appraisal* 127-138. ref. : 1542.
A mere thematic study of the novel. Sees the novel as Pointer towards understanding the psychological, mythical, historical, and biographical perspectives of Anand's vision.

1616. Dhawan, R.K. "Mulk Raj Anand : *Coolie*." Pradhan 1-22. ref. : 434. Rpt. as "The Thirties movement and Coolie" in Dhawan, *The Novels of Mulk Raj Anand* 54-65. ref.: 1525.
Considers Coolie as "an intensely realised and credible narrative that is both political thesis and absorbing fiction."

1617. ——. "*The Barber's Trade Union* : An Appraisal." *Rajasthan Journal of English Studies* 13 & 14 (1981): 14-19. Rpt. in Bhatnagar, *Essays* ref. : 221. Also in Dhawan, *The Novels of Mulk Raj Anand* 118-122. ref.: 1525.
An evaluation of the story in the light of Anand's literary and philosophical creed.

1618. Dommergues, A. "An Interpretation of Mulk Raj Anand's *Untouchable*." *Commonwealth : Essays and Studies* (France) 8.2 (1985) : 14-23.
A critical appreciation of the novel. Demonstrates the absurdity of the Hindu doctrine which assimilates high castes with moral excellence and outcastes, more particularly untouchables, with turpitude and depravity.

1619. Dinesh, Kamini. "Gauri : Connotations and Eponyms." Kaur 179-186. ref. : 320.
"A *Kali* in her fury, Gauri is a *Parvati* in her singleminded devotion to her husband."

1620. Dover, Cedric. "The Significance of Anand." *United Asia* 3.6 (1952).

1621. Dulai, Surjit Singh. "Practice Before Ideology : Mulk Raj Anand's *Untouchable.*" *Journal of South Asian Literature* 27.2 (1992) : 187-208.
Discusses the place of ideology in *Untouchable* and shows that the novel is not a documentation of progressive ideology or Marxist assumptions, but a powerful artistic portrayal of experience — the felt attitude and convictions of Anand.

1622. Dutt. Prabhat Kumar. "Mulk Raj Anand in Relation to Tagore, Premchand and Sarat Chatterjee." *Contemporary Indian Literature* Nov.-Dec. 1965.

1623. Dwivedi. S.C. "Existentialism in Anand's *Across the Black Waters.*" Pathak, *Indian Fiction in English* 25-37. ref.: 422.
Considers "loneliness and strange sense of fellowship" as "the twin modes of the hero's (Lalu Singh's) authentic existence, for which *Across the Black Waters* is a brilliant metaphor."

1624. Fisher, Marlene. "Mulk Raj Anand : The Novelist as Novelist." *Panjab University Research Bulletin* (Arts) 4.1 (1973) : 257-267. Rp. in Coppola 117-130 ref. : 235. Also in *Occasional Paper Series* (Michigan) (Win. 1974) 257-269.
Argues against the general view that Anand is a social realist and proves through the analysis of his novels. Anand is more a novelist with humanistic base than 'socialist realist writer' : "His novels are not handmaidens to a given social or philosophical doctrine. They are rather works of fiction, each with an integrity of its own."

1625. ——. "The Shape of Lostness : Mulk Raj Anand's Short Stories." *Journal of Indian Writing in English* 2.1 (1974) : 1-11.

Treatment of the theme of 'lostness' in Mulk Raj Anand's short stories and Anand's skill and craftsmanship in handling the theme.

1626. ——. "Mulk Raj Anand's Confessional Novels." *Journal of Indian Writing in English* 4.2 (1976) : 39-45.

1627. ——. "Mulk Raj Anand : A Study of His Confessional Novels." Dwivedi, *Studies in Contemporary Indian Fiction in English* 97-106. ref. : 269.
An extended version of the essay "Mulk Raj Anand's Confessional Novels." The discussion includes the other two novels of Anand. *Confession of a Lover* and *The Bubble.*

1628. ——. "On Being Seventy Years Young." *Youth Times* 2 Apr. 1976 : 10-11.

1629. ——. "Confession of a Lover." *Kakatiya Journal of English Studies* 2.1 (1977) : 107-118.
Analyses the protagonist's struggle towards the emergence of "a unified self." Traces the protagonist's adolescent struggles towards finding his identity.

1630. ——. "The Art of Self and the Self of Art : Mulk Raj Anand's *Confession of a Lover : Language Forum* 7.1-4 (1981-1982) : 90-100. Rpt. in Dhawan, *Explorations* 90-110. ref. : 253. Also in Dhawan, *The Novels of Mulk Raj Anand* 182-192. ref. : 1525.
Discusses the novel, *Confession of a Lover,* from the point of view of Anand's compulsion for emotional honesty (the art of self) and poetic imagination and authentic autobiographical experience (the self of art).

1631. ——. "Mulk Raj Anand." *Littcrit* 20 & 21, 11.1-2 (1985) : 1-10.
Reports his interview with Anand.

1632. ——. "*The Bubble :* Lightning of the Flame of Life." Dhawan, *The Novels of Mulk Raj Anand.* 216-218. ref.: 1525.

A brief note on the protagonist's journey to self-discovery and self-creation.

1633. ——. "Apology for Heroism : Autobiography and Anand." Dhawan, *The Novels of Mulk Raj Anand* 193-202. ref. : 1525.

"Shows how Anand's autobiographical works have a marked influence on his novels and how his novels are demonstrably autobiographical," achieving this metamorphosis through characters and the use of first person narrative.

1634. ——. "Mulk Raj Anand as Autobiographer." Yaraventelimath *et al.* 177-187. ref. : 558.

1635. Gandhi, Lingaraja. "Excursion to continental Grave Yard : A Reading Ananad's *Across Blackwaters.*" *Literary half-yearly* 38-1(1999) : 119-129.

1636. Garcia, Irene Santamaria. "Mulk Raj Anand : *'Coolie'* Romulo Gallegos : "Canaima:" *Hispanic Horizon* 13 (win 1989).

1637. Gautam, G.L. "Indian Renaissance and Reformation : A Comparative Study of Premchand's *Godan* and Mulk Raj Anand's *The Village.*" *New Quest* 95, Sep.-Oct. 1992.

Discusses the changing values of affirmation in Prem Chand's *Godan* and Anand's *The Village.* Also shows how radicalism and scientific humanism have shaped the portrayal of the major characters in the two novels.

1638. ——. "Kashmir : Bonds of unity." *Patriot* 29 July 1990. An article based on *Death of a Hero.*

1639. Gemmill, Janet P. "The City as Jungle in the Indo-English Novel." Noble and Dutt, 45-67 ref. : 408. See 737.

1640. Gilman, Marvin "Mulk Raj Anand's Critical Reception : A Reassessment." *Littcrit* 42, 22.1 (1996) : 58-68.

1641. Gowda, Anniah H.H. "Mulk Raj Anand." *Literary Half-Yearly* 6.1 (1965) : 51-60. Rpt. as "Mulk Raj Anand : A Committed Writer" in Prabhakar 69-77. ref. : 433.
A brief consideration of the novels, *Coolie, Untouchable* and *Two Leaves and a Bud* to show the achievement (virtues as well as defects) of Anand as a novelist — his political ideals, narrative technique and social realism. Finds Anand a committed writer whose novels "are propaganda novels which have considerable merits."

1642. Goyal, Bhagwat. "Mulk Raj Anand : The Writer as Humanist." Goyal, *Culture and Commitment* 70-73. ref.: 281.
Against the detractors who criticise Anand's novels as propagandist literature and as sociological tracts, argues that they are the expressions of comprehensive humanism based on the teachings of Gandhi, Tagore, The Buddha and others: *Untouchable* is "an attack on a whole order", a "reaction against the symbolic slap on the face of one man" and his *Coolie* "a total novel of human experience. His *Private Life of an Indian Prince* suggests "the inner process of the shift of classes."

1643. Gupta, G.S. Balarama. "*Untouchable* : A Study." *Contemporary Indian Literature* 7.4 (1967) : 12-13.

1644. ——. "The Humanism of Mulk Raj Anand." *Contemporary Indian Literature* 7.3 (1967) : 6-8.

1645. ——. "*Coolie* — A Prose Epic of Modern India." *Journal of Karnatak University* (Humanities) 12 (1968) : 92-99.
A review article. An appraisal of the novel which emphasizes Anand's capacity to evoke various scenes and situations and different men and moods.

1646. ——. "Woman in Anand's Shorter Fiction." *Journal of Karnatak Unviersity* (Humanities) 13 (1969) : 188-193.
Discusses some of the short stories to show Anand

as a humanistic writer who champions the cause of women. Comments that Anand's stories complement his novels, particularly those where woman is central to the theme.

1647. ——. "Anand's *Big Heart* : A Study ." *Banasthali Patrika* 13 (July 1969) : 37-43.
Analyses the novel from a humanist perspective.

1648. ——. "Anand's *Old Woman and the Cow* in Human Perspective." *Journal of Karnatak University* (Humanities) 14 (1970) : 143-149.
Considers *Old Woman and the Cow* as an expression of Anand's humanism which finds amplification in his strong plea for the recognition and acceptance of women's rights.

1649. ——. "Dr. Mulk Raj Anand's Prose Poem." *Contemporary Indian Literature* 11.3 (1971) : 14 -15.

1650. ——. "Towards a Closer Understanding of Anand." Sharma K.K., *Indo-English Literature* 113-120. ref. : 501. Also in Sharma K.K., *Perspectives on Mulk Raj Anand* 9-15. ref. : 1546.
A brief study of Anand's philosophy of humanism and its relevance to his work. Suggests that one has to take into consideration the whole work of Anand — his various other books and articles on fine arts, culture, education, politics and so on — to understand him fully.

1651. ——. "Anand in Letters." *Kakatiya Journal of English Studies* 2 (1977) : 210-218.
Attempts to provide "intimate insights into Anand, the man and Anand, the humanist by reproducing excerpts from the novelist's letters written to him during 1968-73.

1652. ——. "Mulk Raj Anand's *Untouchable* : The Dialectics of Self-Affirmation." Naik, *Perspectives* 13-20. ref. : 381.
Considers *Untouchable* as a "little classic" which "exemplifies the fiction of human condition of the

Promethean struggle for self-definition amidst conditions of existential isolation and alienation."

1653. Gupta, Rameshwar. "The Gandhi in Anand." Sharma K.K., *Perspectives on Mulk Raj Anand.* 77-83. ref. : 1546.
Traces not merely the influence of Gandhi on Anand which is "percolated through most of his work," particularly in his *Untouchable,* but also reads behind the lines to show how much Gandhi is in him.

1654. Gupta, Sangeeta. "The Nature of Brother-Sister Relationship : *Untouchable, A Bend in the Ganges* and *A Situation in Delhi*." Dhawan, *et al. Recent Commonwealth Literature* Vol. 1. 153-169. ref. : 260.
Examines the nature of brother-sister relationship bordering on incest in the context of Hindu household as depicted in the novels — *Untouchable, A Bend in the Ganges* and *A Situation in Delhi* and shows that the motif of brother-sister incest is not uncommon and can be traced to the oldest records of Indian Literature — the *Rig Veda.*

1655. Guruprasad, Thakur. "Experimentation with Language in Indo-Anglian Fiction : A Note Towards Definition of Traits in the Works of Mulk Raj Anand." Desai, *Experimentation* 33-80. ref. : 249.
Comments on the linguistic innovations made by Anand, particularly in *Untouchable* and *The Road,* to determine which ones of the innovations bear the marks of originality and which ones those of eccentricity.

1656. Habibullah, E. *Across the Black Waters* : A Novel about Army life." Dhawan, *The Novels of Mulk Raj Anand* 137-139. ref. : 1525.
A brief note on the novel. Finds it a revelation of social ties and the psychology of the Indians, particularly of the army men during the first quarter of this century.

1657. Harrex, S.C. "Mulk Raj Anand." Harrex, *The Fire and the Offering,* 69-146. ref. : 287.

1658. ——. "Quest for Structures : Form, Fable and Technique in the Fiction of Mulk Raj Anand." Sharma K.K., *Perspectives on Mulk Raj Anand* 153-168. ref. : 1546. Rpt. as "Western Ideology and Eastern Forms of Fiction : the Case of Mulk Raj Anand" in Amirthanayagam, *Asian and Western Writers* 142-158. ref. : 186.
Considers Anand's fiction as a "social-political-messianic novel". Discusses the formal and technical aspects of Anand's fiction and their correlation with the moral-social questions as a basis for his fictional matrix and shows how Anand in his quest for structures "has Indianised literary political models derived from the West and Westernized traditional Indian values."

1659. Henderson, Philip. "Mulk Raj Anand." The Novel Today." London: Bodley Head, 1936.

1660. Hemenway, Stephen Iqnatius. "Mulk Raj Anand." Hemenway Vol. 2. 3-18. ref. : 290.
Discusses the relationship between theory and practice of Anand's work illustrating from Coolie, Untouchable and in The Big Heart.

1661. Hirst, Mary Hooper. "Mulk Raj Anand." *New Circle* (England) 19.9 (May 1973) : 41.

1662. Inamdar, F.A. "Twice Born Ananta : *The Big Heart.*" Ram, *Mulk Raj Anand : A Home Appraisal* 34-42. ref. : 1542.
Studies the significance of the bull, cat and crow in *The Big Heart* as related to Ananta, a Christ-figure and also to Anand's basic theme in the novel "man's inhumanity to man."

1663. ——. "The Artist and His 'Beloveds' in Mulk Raj Anand's *Morning Face.*" *Commonwealth Review* 6.1 (1994-95): 146-154. Rpt in Bande, *Mothers and Mother Figures* 119-127. ref. : 205. Also in Dass, *Feminism and Literature* 146-155. ref. : 244.

Discusses the role of the mother and mother figures like Devaki, Mumtaz and Draupadi in the development of the protagonist, Krishan from a child to a man and in arousing his creative impulses as an artist.

1664. Iyengar, K. R. Srinivasa. "Mulk Raj Anand." Iyengar, *Indian Writing in English* 331-357 ref. : 297.
Considers Anand a 'committed writer' who can be described as a "veritable Dickens for describing the inequities and idiosyncrasies in the current human situation."

1665. ——. "Morning Face." *Kakatiya Journal of English Studies* 2.1 (1977) : 239-243.
Describes the novel "not as the life history of an individual alone, but that of a people, of a society."

1666. ——. "*The Bubble* : Not a Routine Work." Dhawan, *The Novels of Mulk Raj Anand* 219-221. ref. : 1525.
A letter written to Mulk Raj Anand incorporating his reactions to the novel. Finds the novel prodigious.

1667. Jaganmohana Chari, A. "Outside the Magic Circle : A Study of Anand's *Untouchable.*" *Kakatiya Journal of English Studies* 9 (1988-89) : 20-38.
Traces Bakha's quest for identity and his growth from being a helpless sacrificial animal to his emergence of a thinking articulated individual.

1668. Jha, Pashupati. "The Psychology of Superiority and Expression of Anger in Mulk Raj Anand." *Language Forum* 21.1-2 (1995) : 56-63. Rpt. in Singh, R.K., *Anger in Action* 56-63. ref. : 512.
Analyses *Untouchable* and *The Old Woman and the Cow* to show how the psychology of social/moral/educational superiority guides the discourse of anger in Anand; and also examines to what extent Anand has been successful in assimilating Indian anger and abuse into English expression adopted by him.

1669. ——. "Symbol and the Significance : Anand's *Untouchable* and *The Old Women and the Cow.*" Srivatsava, R.K., *Symbolism* 50-62. ref. : 527.

1670. Jha, Rama. "Mulk Raj Anand: The Champion of Gandhian Humanism." Jha 55-86. ref. : 306.
Discusses the nature of Anand's absorption of Gandhian thought and the way it has conditioned various aspects of his novels.

1671. Joshi, Krishnanand and B. Shyamala Rao. "Mulk Raj Anand as a Novelist." Joshi and Rao 90-99 ref. : 307.
A brief note on Mulk Raj Anand as a novelist of social concern. The whole essay is a collection of comments by critics.

1672. Jung, Anees & Dieter Rimenschnider. "Mulk Raj Anand's *Death of a Hero." Indian Book Chronicle* Mar. 1995: 20.

1673. Kalinnikova, Elena J. "The Big-Heart of the Humanist : Mulk Raj Anand." Kalinnikova, *Indo-English Literature : A Perspective* 97-110. ref. : 316.
Traces through some biographical details the personality of Anand and his philosophy of life that have gone into making of a novelist and shows how his works "are an important step on the path of development of realism and humanistic thought in Indian literature."

1674. ——. "Leo Tolstoy and Mulk Raj Anand." *Soviet Land* 35.2 (1982) : 43.

1675. ——. "Gorkay's Influence on the Creative Work of Mulk Raj Anand." Galik 119–205. ref. : 273.

1676. Kandaswami, S. and V. N. Bhat. "Mulk Raj Anand's Short Stories on Children" *Dyotana* 5.2 (1986) : 25-32.

1677. Karnani, Chetan. "Mulk Raj Anand : The Novelist as Socialist Chronicler." *Thought* 24 Aug. 1974 : 19-20.

1678. Kaul, Jagan Nath. "Mulk Raj Anand : A Study." *Literary Studies* (Kashmir) 1947 : 60-73.

1679. Kaushik, R. K. "From Potter's Wheel to Dragon's Teeth." *Mahfil* 6 (1970) : 17-32.
An unfavourable note on Anand's methods of Characterization. Comments that in Anand's fiction "character has been subordinated to purpose and the individual has been reduced from 'an organic integer of cosmos' to a mere quantitative factor of the collective man."

1680. —. "Red, Brown and Grey — Ideological Commitment in Mulk Raj Anand's Novels." Sharma, K.K., *Indo-English Literature* 101-113. ref. : 501. Rpt. in Sharma K.K., *Perspectives on Mulk Raj Anand* 16-26. ref. : 1546.
Finds Maxim Gorky's ideology in Anand's fiction.

1681. Kher, Indernath. "Mulk Raj Anand : Encounter with Dark Passion." *Journal of Indian Writing in English* 11.2 (1983) : 3-8.
Revised and enlarged version of a paper read at the Annual meeting of the Philological Association of the Pacific Coast, held at San Jose, California.
Finds *The private Life of an Indian Prince* "a brilliant analysis of human personality enmeshed in the web of sexuality which is neither sacramental nor fulfilling."

1682. Klaus, H. Gustav. "Zum Beispiel "Coolie" Ein Vorschlag Zur Eimbeziehung Indo-Englischer Romane in die Betrachtung der. Englischen Literatur des zo Jahrhunderts." *Germanisch romanische Monatschrift* 28, 453-67.

1683. Kohli, Suresh. "Anand Sensitive... But Lovable." *National Herald, Sunday Herald* 27 Dec. 1981 : V.

1684. ——. "Appetite for Words : Mulk Raj Anand." *Link* 4 July 1982 : 38.

1685. ——. "*The Road :* A Fresh Reappraisal." Dhawan, *The Novels of Mulk Raj Anand* 209–210. ref. : 1525.
A brief note on the novel. Considers *The Road* as an

extension of *Untouchable* and finds it mature and a superior work of the two.

1686. Kothari, Sunil. "Mulk Raj Anand : A Shining Splendour of Human Life ." *Economic Times* 16 Dec. 1979 : 4.

1687. Kulshrestha, Chirantan. "The Hero as Saviour : Reflections on Anand's *Untouchable." Journal of Literary Studies* 2.2 (1979) : 50-56. *World Literature Written in English* 19.1 (1980) : 84-90.
Untouchable negates the unrealistic and transparent optimism found in Tagore's *Gora*. Favourably comments on the problematic ending of the novel. Attempts to locate the terms of reference of the aesthetic framework for an adequate appreciation of the novel and to explain the success and popularity of the novelist.

1688. Kumar, Amarendra. *"The Bubble :* A New Form of Fiction." Paniker, *Contemporary Indian Fiction in English* 34–52 ref. : 418.
Considers Anand's *The Bubble* as a colossal experimental epic of the self which is cast in "a bifocal form of drama" and "the first genuine experiment with the novel form in India."

1689. Kumar, Kesaraju. "Narrative Technique in *Untouchable* and *Coolie* : A Reading." *Kakatiya Journal of English Studies* 13 (1993) : 104-112.
Studies the methods of narration such as point of view, tone, flash-back, etc. in the novels *Coolie* and *Untouchable* as conceptual variables in explicating the theme of exploitation and shows how they add depth and dimension to the social and political reality of the novels while drawing the reader's recreative sympathy.

1690. Kumar, Shiv K. "Gandhi on Stage *: Little plays of Mahatma Gandhi."* Dhawan, *The Novels of Mulk Raj Anand* 225-226. ref. : 1525.

A short note on Mulk Raj Anand's *Little Plays of Mahatma Gandhi,* a novel in dramatic dialogues. It is the first part of the epical novel in progress *And So He Plays His Part* in which the author deals with the theme, the progressive conversion of K.C. Azad (an alter ego of Anand himself) from his brown babuism to Gandhian Humanism.

1691. Kurmanadhan, K. "Women Characters in Dr. Anand's Novels." *Contemporary Indian Literature* 6.11-12 (1966) : 26-27.

1692. ——. "The Novels of Dr. Mulk Raj Anand." *Triveni* 36.3 (1967) : 50-57.

A general survey of Anand's novels. Studies particularly *Untouchable, Coolie, The Road, Gauri, Death of a Hero* to show that they are mainly concerned with bitter suffering and cruelty of humanity at different levels... and finds that the indomitable spirit, the spiritual upsurge of man is the real hero and the plea for universal love is the real theme of his novels and illustrates the same through the study of the characters Bhikku, Gauri and others.

1693. Latha, K.S. "Rural ethos in Indian Novels : Kamala Markandaya's *Nectar in a Sieve,* Raja Rao's *Kanthapura*, Mulk Raj Anand's *The Village.*" *Triveni* 61.2(1992) : 53-56.

See 4611.

1694. Laxmana Murthy, S. "Bakha : An existential Analysis." *Kakatiya Journal of English Studies* 2.1 (1977) : 163-175.

A study of *Untouchable* as a powerful evocation of alienation through Bakha as a "sensitized outsider."

1695. Lindsay, Jack. "Mulk Raj Anand : Novelist of Changing India." *Our Time* 5.2 (1945). Rpt. as "Mulk Raj Anand : A Study" in *Contemporary Indian Literature* 5 (1965).

1696. ——. "Mulk Raj Anand." *Kakatiya Journal of English Studies* 2.1 (1977) : 1-4.
Traces "the elements of deep human feeling and large scale vision" in the novels of Anand and shows how they form the essential ingredients of Anand's art.

1697. Mallick, R.P. "Mulk Raj Anand in Prince-Land." *Frontier* 29 Dec. 1979 : 10-12.

1698. Mathur, O. P. "An Approach to the Problem of National Integration in the Novels of Mulk Raj Anand." Sharma K.K., *Perspectives on Mulk Raj Anand* 115-125 ref. : 1546. Rpt. in Mathur, *The Modern Indian English Fiction* 52-65. ref. : 351.
A brief study of some of the main characters of Anand's fiction such as Bakha, Munoo, Krishna Chandar, Azad and Bhikhu in the context of their surroundings to show "how far the sources of their vitality lie in their efforts at becoming, at acquiring a personality integrated within itself by growing vision which synthesises and interprets...the complex forces which bewilder and crush them."

1699. ——. "Mulk Raj Anand's *Untouchable* and Richard Wright's *Bigger Thomas* : A Comparative Study in Social Protest and Affirmation." *Literary Half-Yearly* 29.2 (1978) : 115-128. Rpt. in Mathur, *The Modern Indian English Fiction* 30-41. ref. : 351.
Studies the similarities between the types of protest embodied in the works of Anand and Wright and the terms on which their protagonists arrive at a relative acceptance of life or death.

1700. ——. "The Hero Between : A Comparative Study of Ngugi's Waiyaki and Anand's Lalu." Narasimhaiah, *Commonwealth Literature* 116-126. ref. : 391. Also in Mathur, *The Modern Indian English Fiction* 42-51. ref. : 351.
A study of Ngugi's *The River Between* and Anand's *The Village* to show that in spite of obvious

differences in the political, cultural and religious backgrounds both Anand and Ngugi deal with similar situations, portray similar impasses in the native cultures, offer similar solutions to the problem of adjustment with the European milieu.

1701. ——. "Narayan's *The Dark Room* and Anand's *The Old Woman and The Cow* : Two modern versions of Sita Myth." *Journal of Commonwealth Literature* 21.1 (1986) : 16-25. Rpt. as *Two Versions of Sita Myth* : Narayan and Anand." in Mathur, *The Modern Indian English Fiction* 66-77. ref. : 351.
Discusses the treatment of Sita myth by Narayan *(The Dark Room)* and Anand *(The Old Woman and the Cow)* and the significant points of similarity and difference in reinterpreting the myth in its modern context.

1702. Mathur, O.P. and G. Rai. "The Early Anand : An Existential Approach." *Rajasthan Journal of English Studies* 13 & 14 (1981) : 1-3 Rpt. as "Indian Fiction in English." Bhatnagar's *Essays* ref. : 221.
A study of Anand's *Untouchable* and *Coolie* to focus on the existential dimensions of Anand's humanism.

1703. Mehta, P. P. "Mulk Raj Anand : The Novelist of the Underdog" Mehta, P.P. 139-175. ref. : 359.
A survey of Anand's fiction.

1704. Mehta, M. L. "Anand's *Gauri :* A Study in Feminine Sensibility." *Punjab Journal of English Studies* 5 (1990) : 37-52.
Finds Gauri a complex living character "at once female, feminine, and feminist in her sensibility in as much as she quivers with the hidden desire for her man, craves for motherhood, and protests against the wrongs of the cultural milieu."

1705. ——. "The Exploited Peasant in Indo-English Novel : A Study of Anand's Village Trilogy, Markandaya's *Nectar in a Sieve* and Reddy's *The Vultures."* Awasthi 132-146. ref. : 199.

Examines the treatment of the contemporary rural reality and the theme of exploitation of the peasant in the novels of Anand, Markandaya and Reddy. Finds in Anand and Reddy the emphasis on the role of human agency and the tainted milieu in the exploitation of the peasantry while in Markandaya the role played by the inscrutable forces of nature thwarting the peasant's dream of a better tomorrow is underscored.

1706. Melwani, Murali Das. "Approaches to Anand's Short Stories." *Kakatiya Journal of English Studies* 2.1 (1977) 119-124. Rpt. as "A Study in Different Approaches to Anand's Short Stories." in Dhawan, *The Novels of Mulk Raj Anand.* 50-53. ref. : 1525.

Outlines various, probable approaches to Anand's stories, as no single criterion is adequate.

1707. Mishra, M.L. "Indo-Anglian Literature : Mulk Raj Anand's *Two Leaves and a Bud." Modern Review* 143.6 (June 1979) : 376-81.

A brief critical evaluation of the novel : the significance of the title, plot, characterization, the author's descriptive power, theme, atmosphere and style. Finds that the theme of the novel is similar to that of Forster's *A Passage to India.*

1708. Mukherjee, Arun P. "The Exclusive of Post-Colonial Theory and Mulk Raj Anand's *Untouchable :* A Case Study." *Ariel* 22.3 (1991) : 27-48.

Suggests "through a reading of Mulk Raj Anand's *Untouchable* that the constitutive categories of postcolonial theory perform several homogenizing functions which produce an essentialized "native" who is devoid of race, gender, class, caste, ethnic and religious markers." Further argues "that post-colonial theory's exclusive concern with this essentialized native's "resistance" to "the colonizer", another essentialized construction, is politically retrogressive in so far as it occludes, on the one hand, this resisting native's own ideological agendas and, on the other, the heterogeneity of voices in post-colonial societies."

1709. Mukherjee, Dhurjati. "Indo-Anglian Writers : Anand and Bhattacharya." *Society and Commerce* 2.2 (Apr. 1973) : 104 -105.

1710. Mukherjee, Meenakshi. "Beyond *The Village* : An Aspect of Mulk Raj Anand." Naik *et al.*, *Critical Essays* 236–245 ref. : 377.
A study of Anand's triology — *The Village, Across the Black Waters* and *The Sword and the Sickle* — "to examine the success or failure of his novels in terms of the artistic realization of his intentions."

1711. ——. "The Tractor and the Plough : The Contrasted Vision of Sudhin Ghose and Mulk Raj Anand." *Indian Literature* 13.1 (1970) : 88-101. Rpt. in Mukherjee, *Considerations* 111-121. ref. : 370. Narasimhaiah, *Indian Literature for the past fifty years* 121-122. ref. : 389.
By analysing Anand's trilogy with Sudhin Ghose's tetralogy shows that while Anand is "a committed writer who uses art as a means to an extra-literary end," Sudhin Ghose belongs to the category of writers who have "no commitment save perhaps, to art itself."

1712. ——. "Who is an Indian Writer ? (Anita Desai and Mulk Raj Anand)." *Indian Express* (Mag) 22 Aug. 1982. 111-118.

1713. Muller , Majan S. "Grimm's "Sneewittchen' and Mulk Raj Anand's "The Son of Seven Blind Mothers : Ein Vergleich." *Journal of Karnatak University* (Humanities) 30 (1986) : 259-264.

1714. Murti, K. V. S. "Theme of Salvation : Mulk Raj Anand and R.K. Narayan." *Triveni* 34 (1965) : 50-59. Rpt. in Murti 112-123. ref. : 372.

Contends that both Anand and Narayan, though treating the same old theme, present it in two distinctly different ways — in Anand's case the spiritual advancement shown in his characters manifests itself externally, whereas in Narayan it is internal : "Anand takes up a pure and innocent character representing the soul and concentrates much on showing society as the external evil leading the spirit... Narayan taking the grown up man as the hero symbolizing the spirit, presents the various developing phases — the hero's evil life, repentance, self-awareness, regeneration and finally salvation.

1715. ——. "The Motif of Virtue in Dr. Mulk Raj Anand's Novels." *Contemporary Indian Literatures* 6.1 (Jan. 1966).

1716. ——. "Mulk Raj Anand: Chronology." *Contemporary Indian Literature* 5.11-12 (1965) : 42-47.

1717. —— "Literature as Soul-Search : A Note on Mulk Raj Anand's Novels:" *Journal of English Studies* (Warangal) 4.2 (1972) : 272-280. Rpt. in Murti 93-103. ref. : 372. Considers Anand's novels as "fictional experimentation in truth" about "life, death and reality" and search for "universal harmony." They are studies of 'body-soul drama.'

1718. ——. "Nautchization : Mulk Raj Anand's Novel Technique." *Triveni* 45.2 (1976) : 25 : 31. Also in Murti 104-111 ref. : 372.
Considers Anand's art of fiction as "an attractive modulation of colour and sound, music and rhythm, movement and sensation, idealistic and expressionistic, pervaded by the pathos of crushed life and broken spirit."

1719. ——. "*Seven Summers* : Anand's Fictional Matrix." *Kakatiya Journal of English Studies* 2.1 (1977). Also in Murti 82-92. ref. : 372.

Treats the novel, *Seven Summers* as the microcosm of the macrocosm of Anand's fictional world. It is a prologue which contains "all his themes and techniques, images, and symbols, and ideals...in embryonic forms."

1720. Nahal, Chaman. "Indian Political Novel : Mulk Raj Anand, Bhabani Bhattacharya and Nayantara Sahgal". Nahal 134-151. ref. : 376.
See 952.

1721. ——. "The Dancers in the Ring : *Little Plays of Mahatma Gandhi*" Dhawan, *The Novels of Mulk Raj Anand* 227-229. ref. : 1525.
A brief note on the *The Little Plays of Mahatma Gandhi* which is a part of Anand's auto-biographical saga, *And So He Plays His Part,* dealing with Krishna Chandar Azad's encounter with Gandhi.

1722. Naik, M. K. "The Plough and the Tractor : The Short Stories of Mulk Raj Anand." *Journal of Karnatak Unviersity* (Humanities) 16 (1972) : 91-106
A general assessement of Anand as a short story writer. Discusses Anand's theory of short story as the combination of Indian short story form with neo-psychology, lyrical awareness and compassionate sense of humour and his art of story telling. Also points out how his stories express both the strength and limitations of traditional Indian way of life and a rich understanding of the impact of modernity on it. This later becomes one of the chapters of Naik's book *Mulk Raj Anand* published by Arnold Heinemann, 1973, 130-151.

1723. ——. "The Achievement of Mulk Raj Anand." *Journal of Indian Writing in English* 1.1 (1973) : 41-50.
Assesses Anand's artistic achievement *vis-a-vis* his artistic credo.

1724. ——. "The Political Novel in Indian Writing in English." *ACLALS Bulletin* 4th Ser. 2 (1975) : 33-42.
See 956.

1725. ——. "Infinite Variety : A Study of the Short Stories of Mulk Raj Anand." Sharma K.K., *Perspectives on Mulk Raj Anand* 39-51. ref. : 1546.
Sees Anand's stories "as a museum of human nature and have a wide range and ample variety of mood and tone."

1726. Narain, Iqbal and Asha Kaushik. "The Democratic Experiment and Social Change in India : Some Perceptions from Mulk Raj Anand." Narain and Luthur 61-77. ref. : 385.
Brings into focus the socio-political radicalism present in Anand's works : Anand's aesthetic political criticism is intended to resurrect human dignity, a preclude to genuine democracy in India : a democracy in all its aspects — social, political and economic."

1727. Narasimhaiah, C. D. "Mulk Raj Anand : The Novel of Human Centrality." Narasimhaiah, *The Swan and the Eagle* 106-134 ref. : 388.
An assessment of the nature of Anand's achievement — his powers and weaknesses as a novelist, focusing on the great gifts of the mature artist.

1728. Narayan, Shyamala A. "Mulk Raj Anand." *Contemporary Novelists* 37-40. ref. : 234.

1729. Nasimi, Reza Ahmad. "*Untouchable* : Anand's Language of Compassionate Objectivity." Nasimi 5-28. ref. : 400.
Describes how Anand "wrestles with language which accounts for the interesting innovative tensions it generates to create the form of fiction."

1730. Nath, Suresh. 'The Element of Protest in Mulk Raj Anand's Fiction." Sharma K.K., *Perspectives on Mulk Raj Anand* ref. : 1546.
A discussion of the protest elements in Anand's fiction and the major causes that lead to alienation particularly in *Untouchable* and *Coolie.*

1731. Niranjan, Shiva. "The Nature and Extent of Gandhi's Impact on the Early Novels of Mulk Raj Anand and Raja Rao." *Commonwealth Quarterly* 3.2 (1979) 36-66.
Remarks that the unseen Gandhi in *Kanthapura* is a far more living person than the Gandhi who appears as character in Anand's novel and argues on the merits of truth and non-violence. In *The Serpent and The Rope* Gandhi "is more than a mere character. He is a pervasive force."

1732. Niven, Alastair. " Mulk Raj Anand : The Poetry of Protest." *Planet* 8 (Oct.-Nov. 1971) : 21-25.

1733. ——. "The Lalu-Trilogy of Mulk Raj Anand." *Literary Half-Yearly* 13.1 (1972) : 31-49. Rpt. in *Kakatiya Journal of English Studies* 2.1 (1977) : 17-38. Also in Walsh, *Readings* 11-26. ref. : 547.
Describes Lalu as "an embodiment of the spirit of India's masses who becomes in the course of action conscious of the ideas of a common cause, of a national destiny and of a collective history.

1734. ——. "Myth to Moral : Mulk Raj Anand's *The Old Woman and the Cow*." *ACLALS Bulletin* 4th ser. 3 (1975) : 30-38. Rpt. in *Kakatiya Journal of English Studies* 2.1 (1977) : 93-106.
Analyses the novel showing how Anand makes use of the epic tale and alters it for his own creative end. Discusses the changing perspectives of Anand's fictional art from political consciousness to the mythical and moral consciousness in the novel, *The Old Woman and the Cow.*

1735. Noorusan Bah Begum. "Anand's Short Stories." *Contemporary Indian Literature* 12.4 (Oct.-Dec. 1972) : 6-11.

1736. Orwell, George. "They Throw New Light on India." *Manchester Evening News* 9 Aug. 1945.

1737. ——. "Letter to an Indian." *Tribune* 19 March 1943.

1738. ——. "Selected Notice." *Horizon* (July 1942).

1739. Pachori, Satya S. "Anand's *Untouchable* : Bakha's Journey to a Sense of Self-hood." MLA Session on South Asian Literature. Utah : East-West Centre, 1976. Rpt. in *Commonwealth Novel in English* 2.2 (1983) : 141-149.
Traces Bakha's journey towards attaining a heightened consciousness and a freedom from ancestral servility through his emotional reaction to the social and religious rhythms forbidden to the low caste section of the society.

1740. Packham, Gillian. "Mulk Raj Anand and the Thirties Movement in England." Sharma K.K., *Perspectives on Mulk Raj Anand* 52-63. ref. : 1546.
Assesses "the importance of some of the intellectual influences Anand encountered in Europe" and explores "the elements which have led his particular synthesis of Marxist and humanist thought."

1741. ——. "Mulk Raj Anand's New Myth." *New Literary Review* 8 (1980) : 45-53.

1742. Pallan, Rajesh K. "Encounter with the Self : A Study of the Confessional Mode in Mulk Raj Anand's *The Bubble*." Kirpal, *The New Indian Novel* 11-23. ref. : 330
Considers *The Bubble* as an apogee of human development from being to becoming. Analyses the protagonist's encounter with his self from all the convexities and concavities of the mirror of experiences and shows how he recovers himself from the ravages of illusions and discovers "the wisdom of heart."

1743. ——. "The use of Myth in Mulk Raj Anand's *Morning Face*." Ram, *Mulk Raj Anand : A Home Appraisal* 86-100 ref. : 1542.
Anand successfully adopts and modifies the Krishna myth in *Morning Face* to our changed "cash-nexus society". Finds Krishna Chandar as anti-hero shown

through several contrasts between the traditional Krishna and his modern counterpart in order to suggest a social conscience in his hero.

1744. Pant, M.C. "Mulk Raj Anand : The Man." *Contemporary Indian Literature* 5.11-12 (Nov.-Dec. 1965).

1745. Parry, Graham, "Anand, Orwell and The War." *Language Forum* 7.1-4 (1981-1982) : 80-89. Rpt in Dhawan, *Explorations* 80-90. ref. : 243. Rpt. in Dhawan, *Common wealth Fiction* Vol. 1. 112-121. ref. : 256. Also in Dhawan, *The Novels of Mulk Raj Anand* 30-39. ref. : 1525.

Focuses on certain similarities between Orwell and Anand in their approach to social problems and accounts for their resemblance to the particular social conditions of the thrities both in India and England. Draws attention particularly to *Across The Black Waters.*

1746. Pathak, S. N. "Unusual Collocations and Compounds in *Coolie*." Diploma Paper, Central Institute of English and Foreign Languages (Hyderabad), 1973.

1747. Paul, Premila. "Anand's *Lament on the Death of a Master of Arts* : A Thematic Analysis." *Journal of Indian Writing in English* 6.2 (1978) : 70-76.

"Lament...is an emphatic illustration in fictional terms of the horrid consequences of such a system of education."

1748. ——. "Anand's Awakened Woman: Gauri." *Journal of Annamalai Unversity* (Humanities) 31 (1982) : 1-8.

1749. ——. "Major Themes in the Novels of Mulk Raj Anand." Naik, *Perspectives* 1-12 ref. : 381. Rpt. in Dhawan, *The Novel of Mulk Raj Anand* 19-29. ref. : 1525. Also in Prabhakar 78-83. ref. : 433.

A general evaluation of the thematic concerns of Anand's novels.

1750. Pontes, Hilda. "The Education of a Rebel : Mulk Raj Anand." *Literary Half Yearly* 27.2 (1986) : 105-123.

Documents Anand's experiences as a student and his antagonism towards the British system of education revealed through his own writings, both creative and non-creative works. Excerpts from *Morning Face, The private Life of and Indian Prince* and *Seven Summers* are given as illustrations.

1751. ——. "Anand's *Untouchable* : A Classic in Experimentation of Theme and Technique." Gupta, *Studies* 128-141. ref. : 285.

Considers the novel as a systematic exposition of Anand's philosophy of humanism.

1752. Prasad, Madhusudan. "Conflict in the *The Village*." Ram, *Mulk Raj Anand : A Home Appraisal* 101-110. ref. : 1542.

Discusses the nature and purpose of the several types of conflicts ideological, religious, social and personal — that are central to *The Village.*

1753. Prasad, R. Narendra. "Pollution in *Untouchable* and *Scavenger's Son." Littcrit* 11, 6.2 (1980) : 32-39.

Treatment of the problem of untouchability and the idea of pollution in the novels, Anand's *Untouchable* and Thakazi's *The Scavenger's Son.*

1754. Prasad, Shaikeswar Sati. "*Death of a Hero* : Maqbool Sherwani : The Secular Martyr." Bande, *Victim Consciousness* 17-16. ref. : 206.

1755. Pritchett, V. S. "The Art of Mr. Anand." *London Mercury* 24. 202 (1936).

1756. Raizada, Harish. "Ethics and Aesthetics of Mulk Raj Anand." Sharma, K.K., *Perspectives on Mulk Raj Anand* 115-128. ref. : 1546.

Comments on Anand's philosophy of comprehensive historical humanism and his technique of poetic realism as reflected in his novels.

1757. Rajagopalachari, M and K. Sampath. "History and Art in

Anand's *Private Life of an Indian Prince." Language Forum* 23.1-2(1997) 79-85.

1758. Rajan, C. K. "Myth in Mulk Raj Anand's *Gauri." Littcrit* 17.1-2 (1991) : 44-55.
Shows how the mythical base of *Gauri* serves more than a mere convenient structural device. If the 'Sita-Rama' myth provides a structural base to the novel the Shiva-Pravathi myth explicates the full import of the novel.

1759. Rajan, P. K. "*Untouchable* and *Coolie* : A Study in Theme and Form." *Rajasthan Journal of English Studies* 13 & 14 (1981) : 89-109. Rpt. as "Theme and Form in Mulk Raj Anand's Early Novels" in Bhatnagar, *Essays in criticism,* ref. : 221. Also in Rajan, *Studies* 11-31 ref. : 1540.
Explains the basic ambivalence between Anand as humanist and as realist in terms of the theme-form dialectics.

1760. ——. "Patterns of Cultural Orientation in the Approach to Indian Reality : A Study Based on the Writings of V.S. Naipaul, E.M. Forster, Nirad C. Chaudhari and Mulk Raj Anand." *Littcrit* 15, 8.2 (1982) : 68-109. Rpt. in *Journal of South Asian Literature* 8.1-2 (1982) : 121-135. Also in Rajan, *Studies* 68-93. ref. : 1540.
Examines the currents and cross-currents of similarities and variations discernibly in the diverse approaches to Indian reality in the writings of four major writers — Naipaul's *Area of Darkness,* Forster's *A Passage to India,* Nirad Chaudhari's *The Continent of Circe,* Anand's *The Big Heart* and observes an interesting polarisation in terms of cultural propensities in the case of four writers.

1761. ——. "Conflict and Resolution in 'The Tractor and the Corn Goddess'." *Littcrit* 17, 9.2 (1983) : 32-38. Rpt. in Rajan, *Studies* 32-38. ref. : 1540.

Discusses "The Tractor and the Corn Goddess" as a representative story of Anand's fictional matrix — a satirical commentary on the social life of pre-capitalist Indian village. Examines the story in depth and shows how exactly the social conflict (the conflict between tradition and modernity) is resolved through its form and how the artist's psychological make up is revealed in this mode of resolution.

1762. ——. " 'The Lost Child' as an Expression of Ambivalent Humanism." Rajan, *Studies* 1-10 ref. : 1540.
Presents the story as a symbolic expression of the artist's ambivalent humanism arising out of his own social ostracism.

1763. ——. "Conflict of Cultures and Creative Tension in Mulk Raj Anand : A Study Based on Lalu Trilogy." Breitinger and Sarder. 163-170. ref. : 218. Rpt. in Rajan, *Studies* 39-55. ref. : 1540.
Considers Lalu's trilogy as an epitomization of the conflicts and contradictions of a specific historical phase of India's national revolutionary movement and discusses the serious artistic problems and creative tensions that the novelist encounters in fictionalising the same.

1764. ——. "Anand's *Lalu Trilogy* and Thakazhi's *Kayar* as Saga Novels." Paniker, *Contemporary Indian Fiction in English* 58-67. ref. : 396. Also in Rajan, *Changing Traditions in Indian English Literature* 50-58. ref. : 449.
Though Anand's Lalu trilogy and Thakazhi's *Kayar* are great works written in the epic tradition, with their distinctive divergences in form and narrative technique, they fall short of communicating the essence of reality in fictional terms.

1765. ——. "Psychology of Aggression in Golding's *Lord of Flies* and Anand's *Untouchable.*" Rajan, *Studies* 56-62. ref. : 1540. Also in Dhawan, *The Novels of Mulk Raj Anand* 105-109. ref. : 1525.

While Golding dramatizes an aggressive human condition and its resultant savagery, Anand portrays the transformation of the psyche of the protagonist due to an aggressive external situation.

1766. ——. "The Theme of the Untouchable in Asan, Anand and Thakazhi." Rajan, *Studies* 63-67. ref. : 1540. Also in *Malayasam Literary Survey of India* 9.2 (1987) : 30-23.

Shows how the same theme of untouchability demands different responses from three major Indian writers.

1767. ——. "Three Heroines : Indurlekha, Sita and Gauri : A Study in Feminine Consciousness." *Indian Literature* May-June 1987 : 109-118. Rpt. as "Indurlekha, Sita and Gauri : A New Feminist Consciousness." Radha 1-10. ref. : 442.

Discusses the pervading socio-cultural parameters that determine the importance of feminine consciousness in contemporary creative thinking with the aid of three novels — Chandra Menon's Indulekha, Kumaran Asan's *Chintavishtayaya* Sita and Anand's Guari — written over a span of seven decades.

1768. ——. "Author as Hero : A Study of *Morning Face.*" Dhawan, *The Novels of Mulk Raj Anand* 153-166. ref.: 1525. Also in *Commonwealth Quarterly* 17.43 (1991): 17-38.

Considers the novel as a synthesis of the historical autobiographical truthfulness with a moralised aesthetic vitality. In this synthesis the critic traces the growth of Krishna Chandar, the protagonist, as "a true hero both like Anand and beyond Anand."

1769. ——. "The Two Voices in *The Old Woman and The Cow.*" *Journal of South-Asian Literature* 26.1(1991) : 277-292.

"The materialist and the spiritualist strains that co-exist in uncertain balance in Anand's humanism find their best expression" in the novel.

1770. Ram. Atma. "Mulk Raj Anand... The Novelist of Rural Life." *Tribune* 12 Dec. 1976.

1771. ——. "Dr. Anand : The Novelist of Protest." *Tribune* 11 Dec. 1977.

1772. ——. "Folk Elements in Anand's Novels." Ram, *Essays.* 1-7. ref. : 454.
Identifies some folk motifs in Anand's novels to show how they influence the peasant characters in his novels.

1773. ——. "Anand's Prose Style : An Analysis." Sharma, K.K., *Pespectives on Mulk Raj Anand* 169-176. ref. : 1546.
Studies Anand's prose style in the light of his own observations.

1774. ——. "Mulk Raj Anand : The Dozen of Novelists." *Nagpur Times* 6 Jan. 1979.

1775. ——. "Mulk Raj Anand : A Novelist of Revolt." *Tribune* 8 Dec. 1985.

1776. ——. "Some Studies on Mulk Raj Anand." Ram, *Essays* 67-78. ref. : 454.

1777. ——. "Anand and the emergence of Indian English." *Advance* May-June 1987 : 9-11.

1778. ——. "Mulk Raj Anand : Chronology." *Mulk Raj Anand : A Home Appraisal* 177-230. ref. : 1542.

1779. ——. "Anand : An Artist of Integrity and Vision." *Advance* Dec. 1989 : 19-21.

1780. ——. "The Linguistic Devices in Indian English of Raja Rao and Mulk Raj Anand." Ram, *Essays* ref. : 454. See 6562.

1781. ——. "The Humanist in Mulk Raj Anand." *Morality in Tess and Other Essays* 55-57. ref. : 456.
Praises Anand as "a writer of great integrity and enviable conviction."

1782. Ramakrishna, D. "Anand's Idea of the Novel." *Kakatiya Journal of English Studies* 2.1 (1977) : 190-199.

Traces the gradual evolution of the idea of the novel in Anand through an examination of his letters, essays and lectures.

1783. Rao, A.V. Krishna. "Mulk Raj Anand and the Novel of Protest." Rao, A.V. Krishna, *The Indo-English Novel.* ref. : 463.

Traces the development of Anand's art from *Coolie* to *The Private Life of an Indian Prince* and points out the attitudinal ambivalence of the latter which is attributed to the novelist's commitment to a particular philosophy.

1784. Rao, B. Damodar. "Orwell's *Burmese Days* and Anand's *Two Leaves and a Bud* : A Comparative Study." Narasimhaiah, *Commonwealth Literature* 185-202. ref.: 391.

A comparative study of George Orwell's *Burmese Days* and Mulk Raj Anand's *Two Leaves and a Bud* to show "how the social and political preoccupations of these writers are shaped into fiction in related but not identical ways."

1785. ——. Afterword. *Untouchable* by Mulk Raj Anand. Mysore : Geetha Book House, 1978.

1786. Rao, M. Madhusudan. "Anand's Tragic Destinies : An Indian View" Ratnam 38-43. ref. : 443.

Examines the evolution of Bakha's psyche from Indian "metaphysical point of view and comments that the destinies of Anand's heroes "are comic."

1787. Rao, E. Nageswara. "Dialogue in Forster and Anand: A Contrastive Analysis." *Kakatiya Journal of English Studies* 2.1(1977) : 176-189. Rpt. in *Approaches to E.M. Froster : A Centenary Volume.* Ed. V. A. Shahane, Delhi : Arnold Heinemann, 1981. 138-147. Rpt. as "The Dialogue Is a Thing : A Contrastive Analysis of Fictional Speech in E.M. Forster and Mulk Raj Anand." Rao, E. Nageswara 127-136. ref. : 464.

A contrastive analysis of the fictional dialogues in Forster's *A Passage to India* and Anand's *Untouchable* to show how Forster attempted to reproduce the peculiar features of Indian English while Anand merely translated certain typical expressions and usages from Indian Languages into English.

1788. Rao, M. Subba. "The Art of Mulk Raj Anand." Rao, M. Subba 141-153. ref. : 467.
Considers Anand's work as "an important step on the path of the development of realism and humanistic thought in Indian literature."

1789. ——. "Mulk Raj Anand and the Human condition." Rao, M. Subba 167-183. ref. : 467.
Assess the nature of Anand's achievement, his power as well as his weakness, by focusing attention on the novels, *Untouchable, Coolie* and *The Big Heart.*

1790. ——. "*Two Leaves and a Bud* : An Empathetic Study." Rao, M. subba 184-195. ref. : 467.
Examines the authenticity of the facts portrayed in the novel and considers it as a social document in the nature of propaganda.

1791. Rao, P. Raghavendra. "Mulk Raj Anand." Raghavacharyulu, *The Two-Fold Voice* 88-98. ref. : 445.
A critical comment on Anand's achievement as a novelist through the analysis of his novels — *Untouchable* and *Coolie.* Treats Anand as a novelist of social protest working for a classless society.

1792. Reddy, K.Venkata. "Anand's *Lament on the Death of a Master of Arts* : A Study." *Journal of Indian Writing in English* 5.2 (1977) : 28-35. Rpt. as "In the Great Crisis of Life *Lament on the Death of a Master of Arts"* in Reddy, K.Venkata, *Major Indian Novelists* 25-35. ref. : 475.
A close study of the novel to show how it describes

the gross limitations of human life and touches on the philosophical implications of human suffering.

1793. ——. "Cruelty of Man to Man : Mulk Raj Anand's *Two Leaves and a Bud.*" *Kakatiya Journal of English Studies* 8 (1987-88) : 49-59. Rpt. in Reddy, K. Ventaka, *Major Indian Novelists* 16-24. ref. : 475.
Against the charge that the novel is a crude piece of propaganda the author argues that *Two Leaves and a Bud* is dramatic with its tragic clash of interests and destinies. It portrays the protagonist's "wild urge to live" and his tragic death as a result of "man's cruelty to man."

1794. ——. "Why Don't I Die ? : *Coolie.*" Reddy, K. Venkata, *Major Indian Novelists* 7-15. ref. : 475.
Describes Anand's *Coolie* as a powerful social tragedy in which the author gives the artistic treatment of the cruel, inhuman social forces of poverty and exploitation.

1795 Reddy, T. Vasudeva. "Expression of Anger in Mulk Raj Anand's *Two Leaves and a Bud.*" *Language Forum* 21-1-2 (1995) : 75-80.
Discussing the theme of exploitation in the novel, comments that while humanism generates Anand's anger and the narrative organises it, "it is irony, frequently coupled with a note of fatalism, that both sustains the anger and sublimates it."

1796. Renuka, E. "Three Women at the Cross-roads : A Note on Man-Woman Relationship in Three Indian Novels [R.K. Narayan's *The Dark Room,* Anand's *Gauri* and Ranganayakamma's *Janaki Vimukthi* (Telugu)]" *Kakatiya Journal of English Studies* 17 (1997) : 103-110.

1797. Rickwood, Edgell. "Mulk Raj Anand." *Socialist* 2.8 (1937).

1798. ——. "Three views on *Coolie.*" *Kakatiya Journal of English Studies* 2.1 (1977) : 223-225. Also in Dhawan, *The Novels of Mulk Raj Anand* 78-79. ref. : 1525.

A short note on *Coolie*. Considers the novel as Anand's fine achievement as it presents "a most vivid panorama of life in India today" and a poetic view of life.

1799. Riemenschneider, Dieter. "An Ideal Man in Mulk Raj Anand's Novels." *Indian Literature* 10.1 (1966) : 29-51.
Argues that each of Anand's novels portrays the conflict between the individual and society in which the central 'problem' is that of "individual's self-realization." Traces the growth of maturity in the protagonists of the novels by discussing them in a chronological order.

1800. ——. "The Function of Labour in Mulk Raj Anand's Novels." *Journal of the School of Languages* (1976): 1-20. Rpt. in Nagarajan, *et al.* 67- 83. ref. : 374.
Discusses the character of human labour and the various forms of alienation caused by specific historical conditions and determines the relationship between man and labour and shows how Anand presents these aspects in an aesthetically convincing manner.

1801. ——. "Mulk Raj Anand: *Confession of a Lover.*" *World Literature Written in English* 16.1 (1977) : 105-109. Also in *Indian Author* 2.1 (1977) : 73-76.
Considers *Confession of a Lover* as "a documentation of the intellectual history of Western educated Indians."

1802. ——. "*Death of a Hero.*" *Kakatiya Journal of English Studies* 2.1 (1977) : 235-238. Rpt. as "*Death of a Hero :* The Problem of the Meaning of life." in Dhawan, *The Novels of Mulk Raj Anand* 222-224. ref. : 1525.

1803. ——. "'Alienation' in the Novels of Mulk Raj Anand." Sharma, K.K., *Perspectives on Mulk Raj Anand* 94-114. ref. : 1546.
Examines Anand's work in the light of Marx's definition of human labour.

1804. ——. "Mulk Raj Anand." *Edition Text und Kritix.* Munchen : 4 Nig, 1984 : 17.

1805. ——. "Mulk Raj Anand" Bock and Wertheim 173-189. ref.: 226.

1806. ——. "Mulk Raj Anand, Anita Desai, G.V. Desani, P. Lal, Kamala Markandaya, R.K. Narayan, Raja Rao, Salman Rushdie and Khushwant Singh." *Lexikon der Weit Literatur.* Dortmund : Harenberg Kommunikation, 1988.

1807. ——. "*Untouchable, Coolie, The Old Woman, and the Cow.*" *Kindlers Literatur Lexikon,* Vol. I, Munchen : Kindler Verlag, 1988.

1808. ——. "*The Bubble* : A Literary Achievement." Dhawan, *The Novels of Mulk Raj Anand* 211-215 . ref. : 1525. Finds the novel in the "bildungsroman tradition" and as the best achievement of Anand as a novelist.

1809. Robertson, R. T. "*Untouchable* as an Archetypal Novel." *World Literature Written in English* 142. (1975) : 239-245. Rpt. in *Kakatiya Journal of English Studies* 2.1 (1977) : 5-16. Also in Dhawan, *The Novels of Mulk Raj Anand* 98-104. ref. : 1525.
Considers *Untouchable* as the best example in Commonwealth literature of an individual representing a community (or a tribe) pitted against a whole society.

1810. S.K.R. "The Garden Coolie." *New Statesman and Nation* 14 (1937) ms. 332.

1811. Sahay, Vikas Mohan. "Social Prophetism in Anand's *Untouchable.*" *Orbit. Journal of Literature in English (*Gaya, Bihar) 1997 : 83-87.

1812. Sanjay. "The Lost Child" An Appreciation." *Mother India* Aug. 1973 : 648-649.

1813. Sanyal, S.C. "Mulk Raj Anand : His Stylistic Devices." Sanyal, *English Language in India* 69-77. Appendix. ref. : 492.

Examines Anand's experimentation with English language and stylistic devices and remarks that in spite of the defects in his use of language, Anand has established the novel "as a favoured medium of Indo-Anglian" and should be given credit for deflecting this literature from a worn-out romantic poetising into the more vigorous forms of realistic prose-fiction.

1814. Saxena, O.P. "M.R. Anand : Art Critic and Novelist." Saxena *Glimpses* Vol. 3. 159-171. ref. : 497.
Finds Anand a better art critic than a creative writer: "what he lost as a novelist, he has made up considerably by serving the course of art criticism in India."

1815. Sethi, Vijay Mohan. "The Theme of the Idiocy of Feudal Lords in Anand's Shorter Fiction." Ram, *Mulk Raj Anand : A Home Appraisal* 139-148. ref. : 1542. Rpt. in Sethi 81-92. ref. : 1545.
Examines one particular aspect of Anand's short fiction — the idiocy of feudal lords which contributes considerably to the suffering of the common people. The stories selected are "A Pair of Mustachios," "The Signature," "A Kashmir Idyll," "The Maharaja" and "The Tortoise" and "The Man who Loved Monkeys More Than Human Beings".

1816. ——. "The Lost Child : Anand's Stories at a Glance." Sethi 71-76. ref. : 1545.
Traces the motif of "lostness" in the stories — "Lajwanti", "Birth," "The Dark Night" — and discusses in terms of human predicament

1817. ——. "Mulk Raj Anand and Silent Sufferers." Sethi 7-12. ref. : 1545.
Reveals Anand's deep concern for the plight of Indian women whom he calls silent sufferers. Discusses in terms of fictional characters (Lajwanti, Naina, etc.) how woman has been reduced to a "sex-symbol" and working machine and remarks that her redemption lies with in herself..."

1818. ——. "A Lesson in Compassion." Sethi 77-80. ref. : 1545.
Narrates in Anand's own words the meaning of 'compassion' : "Compassion is not just a feeling of sentimental pity, but total understanding of the situation."

1819. Sharma, Ashok Kumar. "Native Consciousness in Anand's Short Stories." *Language Forum* 19.2 (1993) : 151-159.
Examines Anand's experimentation with language in his short stories, particularly the recurrence of words, idioms and images drawn from indigenous sources.

1820. Sharma, Atma Ram. "Folk Elements in Anand's Novels." *Kakatiya Journal of English Studies* 2.1 (1977) : 200-209.
See 1772.

1821. Sharma, I.K. "*Untouchable: Lava of Love.*" *Language Forum* 21.1-2 (1995) : 70-74.
Studies the nature and function of anger in the novel to show how it is "a book of angry love" initiated by "a moral vision, held tenaciously by moral anger and directed finally toward the centre of love."

1822. Sharma, K.K. Introduction. Sharma, K.K., *Perspectives on Mulk Raj Anand* IX-XXXI. ref. : 1546.
Presents Anand as a fiction writer who "has contributed not only to the growth of the Indian English novel but also to the novel as a literary genre."

1823. ——. "My Hunches about the Novel : Mulk Raj Anand's Theory of Fiction," *Kakatiya Journal of English Studies* 3 (1978) : 225-252.
Evaluates Anand's theory of fiction systemizing his views on the craft of fiction as expressed in his prefaces, letters, articles, addresses, conversations, etc.

1824. Sharma, Govind N. "Anand's Englishmen: The British Presence in the Novels of Mulk Raj Anand." *World Literature Written in English* 21.2 (1982) : 336-341.

Argues that Anand sees the English as catalytic agents who encouraged Indians to fashion themselves in the British image, thus making the British presence a basic principle in portraying his philosophical and moral concerns.

1825. Sharma, Sudharshan. "Gandhian Ideology and Mulk Raj Anand." Sharma Sudharshan, *The Influence of Gandhian Ideology* 21-42. ref. : 504.

1826. Sharma, Tara Chand. "Bakha's Struggle in *Untouchable.*" Ram, *Mulk Raj Anand : A Home Appraisal* 1-17, ref.: 1542.
Considers *Untouchable* as a protest novel — protest against anti-human forces and the spiritual decay of the caste Hindus in regard to untouchability and shows how the novel presents Anand's vision of spiritual and moral uplift of man as suggested by the protagonist, Bakha.

1827. Shepherd, Ron. "Alienated Being : A Reappraisal of Anand's Alienated Hero" Sharma, K.K., *Perspectives on Mulk Raj Anand* 139-152. ref. : 1546.
Examines the novels — *The Sword and the Sickle, Death of a Hero* and *The Private Life of an Indian Prince* — to bring out "the qualities belonging to Anand's alienated hero, paying particular attention to the sort of character which emerges from the 'psychological' novels.

1828. Shivpuri, Jagadish. "Tagore and Anand." Sharma, K.K., *Perspectives on Mulk Raj Anand* 84-93. ref. : 1546.
A brief study of the personalities of Tagore and Anand, their vision of life and art.

1829. ——. "*The Village :* The Emergence of a Hero." Dhawan, *The Novels of Mulk Raj Anand* 110-117. ref. : 1525.
Shows how the novel provides the background against which Lal Singh, the protagonist of his trilogy, has grown.

1830. ——. "*Across the Black Waters* : The Hero Crosses the Muteness of Obedience." Dhawan, *The Novels of Mulk Raj Anand* 126-136. ref. : 1525.
Tracing the fate of Lalu in the Lalu trilogy, rather disconnectedly, the author tries to show how his (Lalu's) instinct for tenderness shapes his humanity, even after suffering a million betrayals.

1831. ——. "*The Sword and the Sickle* : The Dynamic of Favourable Circumstances." Dhawan, *The Novels of Mulk Raj Anand* 167-181. ref. : 1525.
A review article on *The Sword and the Sickle* in which the author finds the hero "engaged in a quest for justice."

1832. ——. "Mulk Raj Anand's *The Road* : An Interpretation" *Littcrit* 22 & 23 12.1-2 (1986) : 19-26. Also in Dhawan, *The Novels of Mulk Raj Anand* 203-208. ref. : 1525.
Finds the novel *The Road* as an extension of *Untouchable*. "If *Untouchable* is a novel of struggle, *The Road* is a novel of achievement, in more senses than one: the construction of the road despite obstructions, the humiliation of high-caste Hindus, and the coming of a new sense of direction."

1833. ——. "*The Big Heart* : The Gathering of the Crows." *Kakatiya Journal of English Studies* 3 (1978) : 213-224. Also in Dhawan, *The Novels of Mulk Raj Anand* 144-152. ref. : 1525.
A critical analysis of the novel *The Big Heart*.

1834. Singh, Amarjit. "Why are Anand's Later Novels Unsuccessful?" *Commonwealth Quarterly* 4.13 (1979) : 68-70.
Examines the style of Anand's three novels — one each from the early, middle and later periods — *Untouchable* (1935), *Seven Summers* (1951), and *Morning Face* (1968) — and illustrates that it is Anand's lack of

attention to his style both in the structure of scenes as well as in the construction of sentences which has made his later novels unsuccessful.

1835. ——. "*The Private Life of an Indian Prince* as a Novel of Protest." *Commonwealth Quarterly* 13.37 (1988) : 1-16.
Considers *The Private Life of an Indian Prince* as an expression of protest against the arbitrary authority of corrupt and oppressive rulers whose tyranny and despotism ruined the people.

1836. Singh, Manmohan. "Marxian View of the British Raj in Anand." Srivastava, R.K., *Colonial Consciousness* 95-106 ref. : 526.
Discusses Anand's novels *Coolie, The Big Heart, Untouchable, Two Leaves and a Bud* as a presentation of Marxian view of history and society drawing attention to the disastrous socio-economic consequences of the Raj as well as the "regenerating role" that the British Raj played in India by dissolving village communities and laying foundation of India's industrial development and her ultimate emancipation.

1837. Singh, Mina Surjit. *"Female Perspective in the Fiction of Mulk Raj Anand "* Singh, Sushla 147-153. ref. : 517.
Studies the shorter fiction of Anand and the Novel, *Gauri,* to analyse womanhood in the specific context of woman in her social trappings, the woman-woman relationship and man-woman relationship which hold special focus and woman's attempts at emancipation.

1838. Singh, R. Bhagwan. "Victim Consciousness in the Early Novels of Mulk Raj Anand." Bande, *Victim Consciousness* 1-6. ref. : 206.

1839. Singh, R. S. "From Resentment to Social Protest : Mulk Raj Anand." Singh, R.S. *Indian Novel in English.* 38-54. ref. : 513.

A general assessment of Anand as a protest novelist as important as Gide, Malraux, Dos Passos. Commending Anand as a novelist of social consciousness, regrets that "his later novels are weak variations of the same theme."

1840. Singh, Satyanarain. "Yoke of Pity : The Poet in Anand's Novels." *Kakatiya Journal of English Studies* 2.1(1977) : 125-148.

Explores the poetics underlying Anand's fiction.

1841. Singh, Sunaina. "Protest in the Novels of Mulk Raj Anand." *Osmania Journal of English Studies* 17.1 (1981) : 123-134.

Discusses the vital element of Anand's protest (the misery and disaster caused by evil in the body-politic) and reveals his insight into the roots of suffering.

1842. Singh, Tajinder. "Elements of the Bildungsroman in *Coolie.*" *Punjab Journal of English Studies* " (1986) : 115-127.

Traces the growth and education of the central character, Munoo and his gradual but distinct progress from innocence into experience to show that the novel contains elements of the Bildungsroman and it constitutes the fictional form of the novel.

1843. Singh, Veera, "The Slave Rebel : A Closer Look at Untouchability." *Indian Literature* Sep.-Oct.1982 : 123-133.

Studies the problem of untouchability as dealt with in three creative works — Anand's *Untouchable,* Karanth's *Choma's Drum* and Thakazhi Pillai's *The Scavenger's Son* and shows how each writer discusses the problem from a different angle and a different consciousness. While Anand and Pillai take up the problem at a social level, Karanth considers it mainly from individual level and succeeds in making a metaphorical statement.

1844. Sinha, K.N. "Existentialism in Mulk Raj Anand's *Lament on the Death of a Master of Arts*" Sinha, *Indian Writing in English* 10-18. ref. : 518.

Discusses *Lament on the Death of a Master of Arts* as a novel of profound insight and exploration of the limitations of human life — the very nature of pain that is central to existence.

1845. ——. "The Mythic Parallel : A Study in Anand's Later Fiction." Prasad, Hari Mohan *Response* 63-79. ref. : 436.

A brief study of the three novels of the later phase — *The Old Woman and the Cow, The Road* and *Death of a Hero* — to show how myth and archetype, metaphor and symbol, irony and satire are used by Anand to highlight the essential identity of all human effort.

1846. Sinha, Ravinandan. "Expression of Anger in Anand's *The Sword and the Sickle*." *Language Forum* 21.1-2 (1995) : 64-69. Rpt. in Singh, R.K. *Anger in Action* 64-69. ref. : 513.

Examines the varied forms of anger expressed in the novel and shows how Anand uses them as "a motivating force that impels all struggle for achieving human dignity." Comments that in Anand's novels anger is both a response to the fundamental injustice of the Indian situation and a device to focus attention on the injustice and deprivation that characterize the life of the multitudes.

1847. Sivadasan, C.P. "Mulk Raj Anand's *Untouchable* and Thakazhi's *The Scavenger's Son :* Some Similarities." Paniker *Contemporary Indian Fiction in English* 53-57. ref. : 418. Rpt. as "Two Proletarian Novels" in *Indian Literature* 30.3 (1987) : 119-124.

Brings into focus certain similarities both in context and characterization in the two novels and comments that though social commitment is the hallmark of these two novels. Thakazhi's *The Scavenger's Son* is of a different kind as it resorts to armed rebellion for changing the existing social order, while *Untouchable* suggests peaceful remedies.

1848. Sood, S.C. "The Other Side of *Untouchable*." *Creative Forum* 1.1 (1989) : 13-27.
Traces the degenerating effect of Anglomania on Bakha. "Bakha the young untouchable, a Hindu outcaste," grows to be an "untouchable" in the other sense of the word, *viz.* "unapproachable," beyond the reach of alien influence.

1849. ——. "The Return of the Prodigal: A Reading of Mulk Raj Anand's *Untouchable*." *Commonwealth Quarterly* 14.39 (1989) : 34-49.
Traces the growth of Bakha, the protagonist, reeling under Anglomania, slowly returning to wisdom under Gandhi's influence.

1850. Srinath, C.N. "Pariah at Cross-Roads : Image as Symbol of Regeneration." Srinath, 70-84. ref. : 523.
See 1214.

1851. Steinvorth, Klaus. "Mulk Raj Anand's *Private Life of an Indian Prince* and Manohar Malgonkar's *The Princes*." *Literary Half-Yearly* 14.1 (1973) : 76-91.
Discusses the similarities and contrasts in the treatment of the subject of the Maharajas in both the novels and the presentation of exotic India.

1852. Stilz, Gerhard. "Experiments in Squaring of the Ellipsis : A Critical Reading of the Autobiographies of Gandhi, Nehru, Chauduri and Anand "Yaranintelimath *et al.* 162-176. ref. : 558.

1853. Sudhakar, Premila Paul. "Major Themes in the Novels of Mulk Raj Anand." Naik, *Perspectives* 1-12. ref. : 381.
See 1749

1854. Sundaram, P.S "Single and Double Vision : Anand, Raja Rao, and Narayan." *Rajasthan University Studies in English* 7 (1974) : 68-78.

1855. Tagore, Leo. "Social Justice in Anand's *Coolie* and Achebe's *Things Fall Apart*." Dhawan, *The Novels of Mulk Raj Anand* 84-97. ref. : 1525.
Studies Anand's *Coolie* and Achebe's *Things Fall Apart* to show the varying perspectives of the novelists on the question of social injustice and liberation.

1856. Tarinayya, M. "*Untouchable* : An Analysis." *Journal of Mysore University* (Arts) 26 (1969); 22-45.
Analyses the treatment of untouchability in the novel.

1857. Tasneem, N.S. "Mulk Raj Anand and New Humanism." *Advance* Dec. 1985 : 6-7, 9.

1858. Tharu, Susie. "Decoding Anand's Humanism." *Kunapipi* 4 (1982) : 30-42.
A deconstructive reading of Anand's *Untouchable* by demonstrating the secret languages which connote the notions of change and progress.

1859. ——. "Reading against the Imperial Grain : Inter-τexuality, Narrative structure and Literal Humanism in Mulk Raj Anand's *Untouchable*." *Jadhavapur Journal of Comparative Literature* 24 (1986) : 60-71.
In a close reading of Anand's *Untouchable* Ms. Tharu tries to look at the novel from the point of view of inter-textuality : "What happens when nationalism" makes "its alliances with liberal imperialism". She believes that by "reincarnating an ideology designed to suppress and destroy us and by manipulating us in such a way that we accept its designs uncritically." The problem Anand poses has distorting effects designating the result of our writing and thinking in English.

1860. Thomas, O.J. "The Enslaved and the Unsolved : The Characters of Anand and Anita Desai." *Quest* (Ranchi) 12.1(1998) : 39-43.

1861. Thomas, T.K. "The Hindu Ethos — A Novelist's Perspective." *Religion and Society* 20.4 (Dec. 1973) : 54-71.

1862. Tupikova, Y. "Mulk Raj Anand." *Soviet Literature* 9 (1953).

1863. Vakeel, Hilda, "Three views on *Coolie.*" *Kakatiya Journal of English Studies* 2.1 (1977); 228-231. Also in Dhawan, *The Novels of Mulk Raj Anand* 79-81. ref. : 1525.
Considers *Coolie* as a masterpiece which reveals Anand's "peculiar sense of what one might term the humanness of human beings."

1864. Varalakshmi, P. "Mulk Raj Anand's *Lament on the Death of a Master of Arts* : An Analysis." *Journal of Indian Writing in English* 7.2 (1979) : 82-87.
Interprets the novel in terms of the "existential panorama of life", the futility of life and the terrible reality of death or "the essential horror." Remarks that both in theme and technique it is modelled on a Greek Tragedy.

1865. Varma, Ravi S. "Hindustani Words in Mulk Raj Anand." A paper presented at XI All India Conference of Dravidian Linguists, 5-7 June 1981. Dept. of Linguistics, Osmania University, Hyderabad.

1866. Venugopal, C.V. "The Short Stories of Mulk Raj Anand : A Study." *Journal of Karnatak University* (Humanities) 15 (1971) : 145-156.
An evaluation of Anand's short stories to show him as the supreme master of that art.

1867. ——. "Munoo and Mrs. Mainwaring : A Note on the Last Chapter of *Coolie*." *Journal of Karnatak University* (Humanities) 29 (1975) : 110-116.
Argues against the detractors on the relevance of the final chapter of the novel to the totality of its structure.

1868. ——. "Bakha's Deliverance : A Consideration of the Last Part of Anand's *Untouchable.*" *Journal of Karnatak University* 21(1977) : 106-110.
Discusses the artistic triumph of the novel *Untouchable* showing the relevance of the last chapter to the rest

of the book. Argues against the detractors that the last chapter, in fact, suggests the solution for the problem of untouchability.

1869. Verghese, C. Paul. "Raja Rao, Mulk Raj Anand, Narayan and Others." *Indian Writing Today* 3.1 (1969) : 31-38.

1870. ——. "The Proletarian Humour of Mulk Raj Anand." Verghese, *Problems* 127-132 , ref. : 541.
Considers Anand as a proliterian novelist whose avowed purpose of writing is social legislation and shows through a comparison with another novelist, Thakazhi, Pillai, how his heavy emphasis on the didactic quality of art stands in the way of his attainment as a novelist.

1871. Verma, K.D. " 'Understanding Mulk Raj Anand.' An Introduction." *South Asian Review* 15.12 (July, 1991) : 1-11.

1872. ——. Ideological Confrontation and Synthesis in Mulk Raj Anand's *Conversations in Bloombury." Journal of South Asian Literature* 28.1 (1995) : 181-204.

1873. ——. "Mulk Raj Anand : A Reappraisal." *Indian Literature* 72, Mar.-Apr. 1996 : 150-165.

1874. Verma, Urmila. "Thematic Concerns and Artistic Devices in *Morning Face"* Ram, *Mulk Raj Anand : A Home Appraisal* 76-85. ref. : 1542.
A sketchy appraisal of the novel dealing with its themes, technique, imagery, the use of language, etc.

1875. Walsh, William. "Mulk Raj Anand." *Contemporary Novelists* 5th ed. 37-40. ref. : 225.

1876. ——. "Some Observations on Mulk Raj Anand's Fiction." Sharma, K.K., *Perspective on Mulk Raj Anand* 177-180, ref. : 1546.
A general estimation of Mulk Raj Anand as a novelist. Considers Anand as belonging to the fictional tradition of the nineteenth century : "He (Anand) writes in an

angry reformist way, like a less humorous Dickens and a more emotional Wells, of the personal sufferings induced by economics."

1877. Wasi, Jehanara. "The Big Heart at Eighty." *Link* 15 Dec. 1985 : 33-34.

1878. ——. "Focus on Two Writers." *Economics Times* 2 Oct. 1988 : 4.

1879. Weir, Ann Lowry. "Style and Range in New English Literatures (re : R.K. Narayan, Mulk Raj Anand and V.S. Naipaul)." Kachru 283-293. ref. : 313.
See 1276

1880. Williams, Haydn Moore. "Mulk Raj Anand : Realism and Politics." *Miscellany* 55, Feb. 1972 : 9-42. Rpt. in Williams, *Studies* 1.19-52 ref. : 551.
A general discussion of Mulk Raj Anand's contribution to Indian-English fiction. Discusses the post-romantic attitude in his works and relates Anand's socio-political concerns to the newly emerging medium of realism. Contains discussion and evaluative assessment on Anand's major novels.

1881. Xavier, M.J.N.A. "L 'humanisme de Mulk Raj Anand, Dans Ses Romans." *Journal of Karnatak University* (Humanities) 14 (1970) : 197-206.

1882. Zaheer, Sajjad. "Mulk Raj Anand." *Contemporary Indian Literature* 5. 11-12 (1965).

1883. ——. "The Future of the PWA Movement (Mulk Raj Anand)." *Contemporary Indian Literature* 7.1 (1967).

V. Reviews

1884. "All Men are Brother." Rev. of *The Sword and the Sickle, Times LIterary Supplement* 3 Jan, 1942 : 4.

1885. Asnani, Shyam M. Rev. of *Across the Black Waters, Commonwealth Quarterly* 9. 28 (1984) : 46-49.

1886. Bandopadhyay, Manohar. Rev. of *Untouchable. Patriot* 18 Apr. 1982 : 2-3.

1887. Bartholomew, R. L. "A Disappointing Autobiography." Rev. of *Seven Summers. Thought* 17 May 1952 : 15-16.

1888. Berry, Margaret. "Bhikhu and Kabir : The Untouchable and the Saint." Rev. of *The Road. CRNLE Review Journal* (Winter), 1988.

1889. Brown, F.J. Rev. of *The Big Heart. Life and Letters Today* XLVII. 99, 1945.

1890. Burra, Edward. Rev. of *Coolie. Kakatiya Journal of English Studies* 2.1 (1977) : 226-227. Notes, Rpt. from *Spectator* 5635 (1935).

1891. Calder-Marshall. Rev. of *Two Leaves and a Bud. Left Review* 3.1 (1931).

1892. ——. Rev. of *Across the Black Waters. Life and Letters Today* 28.4 (1941).

1893. Chander, K.M. Rev. of *Panorama : An Anthology of Indian Short Stories. Literary Criterion* 23.4 (1988) : 95-97.

1894. Clare, Tullis. Rev. of *The Sword and the Sickle. Time and Tide* 33.17 (1942).

1895. Collis Maurice. Rev. of *Across the Black Waters. Time and Tide* 21.48 (1940).

1896. Cowasjes, Saros. Rev. of *Morning Face. Indian Literature* 13.1 (1970).

1897. ——. Rev. of *Two Leaves and a Bud. Indian Literature* 16.3-4 (1973).

1898. ——. Rev. of *The Sword and the Sickle. World Literature Written in English* 14.2 (1975) : 267-277.

1899. ——. Rev. of *Confession of a Lover. International Fiction Review* 4.1 (1977). Also in *Journal of Commonwealth Literature* 12.1 (1977) : 75-76.

1900. Das, Kamala. Rev. of *Confession of a Lover. Youth Times* Sep. 1976.

1901. Davies, Rhys. Rev. of *The Village. Life and Letters Today* 21.22 (1939).

1902. Dewsbury, Ronald. Rev. of *Coolie. Life and Letters Today* Vol. XV, No. 5. 1936.

1903. Dhawan, R.K. Rev. of *The Barber's Trade Union. Rajasthan Journal of English Studies* 13 & 14 (1981). 14-19.

1904. Dobree, Bonamy. Rev. of *Across the Black Waters. Spectator* 22 Nov. 1940.

1905. Dover, Cedric. Rev. of *Coolie. Congress Socialist* 1.35 (1936).

1906. Duncan, Margaret. "Boy-Man Complexities" Rev. of *Morning Face. Times* 2 Mar. 1969 : V. "Weekly Review."

1907. "Eastern Apporaches". Rev. of *The Private Life of an Indian Prince. Times Literary Supplement* : Aug. 21 (1953). 533.

1908 "English and Indian." Rev. of *Two Leaves and a Bud. Times Literary Supplement* 15 May 1937 : 379.

1909. Fisher, Marlene. Rev. of *Confession of a Lover. Books Abroad* 50.4 (1976) : 953.

1910. ——. Rev. of *Between Tears and Laughter. World Literature Today* 16.3 (1992) : 581-582.

1911. Gandhi, Lingaraja. "Did the Sun Shine in Heaven Also." Rev. of *Betweeen Tears and Laughter. Literary Half-yearly* 35.1 (1994) : 162-164.

1912. Gupta, G.S. Balarama. Rev. of *Morning Face. Journal of Karnatak University* (Humanities) 13 (1969) : 204-206.

1913. Gupta, L.N. Rev. of *Confession of a Lover. Hitvada* 7 Mar. 1976.

1914. Hawkins, Desmond. Rev. of *Across the Black Waters. New Statesman and Nation* 20.509 (n.s.) (1940).

1915. "India At War" Rev. of *Across the Black Waters. Times Literary Supplement* 7 Sep. 1946 : 456.

1916. "Indian Childhood" Rev. of *Seven Summers. Times Literary Supplement* 28 Dec. 1951 : 833.

1917. Iyengar, K. R. Srinivasa. "We Belong to Suffering..." Rev. of *Coolie. Deccan Herold* 5 Nov. 1952.

1918. ——. Rev. of *Confession of a Lover. Journal of Indian Writing in English* 4.2 (1976) : 75-78.

1919. ——. Rev. of *Morning Face. Kakatiya Journal of English Studies* 2.1 (1977) 239-243.

1920. ——. "Unusual Achievement." Rev. of *The Bubble. Indian Literature* Jan.-Feb. 1985 : 113-119.

1921. Jacob, Jessica. "Touching Humdrum." Rev. of *Between Tears and Laughter. Times of India* July 1973 : 11.

1922. 1922 Kapadia, Novy. Rev. of *Across The Black Waters. Link* 19 Apr. 1981 : 40.

1923. Kapur, Kamala. "From the Complex to the Simple." Rev. of *The Village. Times Literary Supplement* 18 Sep. 1977 : 1010.

1924. ——. Rev. of *The Village. Times of India* 18 Sept. 1977 : 10

1925. Kaushik, R.K. "Indian Princes Again." Rev. of *The Private Life of an Indian Prince. Literary Half-Yearly* 12.1 (1971) : 107-112.

1926. Khare, Randhir. Rev. of *Two Leaves and a Bud. Indian P.E.N.* 41 (Feb. 1975) : 24-25.

1927. Kohli. Suresh. Rev. of *Morning Face. Indian and Foreign Review* 7.23 (1970) : 20-21.

1928. Krishna, Francine. "Love in the Twenties." Rev. of *The Old Woman and the Cow. Quest* 99, Jan.-Feb. 1976 : 90-91.

1929. Malhotra, Indu. Rev. of *Confession of a Lover. Times of India* (Mag) 9 Dec. 1976 : 10.

1930. McDowell, Judith H. Rev. of *Morning Face. World Literature Written in English* 9 (1970).

1931. Mehta, Boman, Rev. of *Untouchable. Scrutiny* 4.1 (1935).

1932. Melwani, Murali Das. Rev. of *Between Tears and Laughter. Journal of Indian Writing in English* 2.2 (1974) : 62-64.

1933. Menon, K.P.S. "Ennoblement via Tragedy". Rev. of *The Private Life of an Indian Prince. Times of India* 21 Feb. 71 : 10.

1934. Murti, K.V.S. Rev. of *Confession of a Lover. Triveni* 46.1 (1977) : 130-132.

1935. N.G.M. Rev. of *The Old Woman and the Cow. Indian P.E.N* 27, June 1961.

1936. Nahal, Chaman. Rev. of *Confession of a Lover. Indian literature* 20.1 (1977) : 90-83.

1937. Naik, M.K. Rev. of *Between Tears and Laughter. Littcrit* 38, 20.1 (1994) : 94-97.

1938. Naikar, Basavraj S. Rev. of *Between Tears and Laughter. Century* 4 May 1974 : 13-14

1939. Nandakumar, Prema. Rev. of *The Bubble. Journal of Indian Writing in English* 13.1 (1985) : 103-106.

1940. ——. "Many-Layered Exuberance". Rev. of *The Bubble. Indian Literary Review* 3.2 (1985) : 80-83.

1941. Niven, Alastair. "A Modern Indian Intellect." Rev. of *Morning Face and The Private Life of an Indian Prince. Journal of Commonwealth Literature* 6.1 (1971) : 129-131.

1942. ——. "Commitment to Humanity." Rev. of *The Bubble. Book Review* Jan.-Feb. 1985 : 14-15.

1943. ——. "A Novel of Self-Revelation : Anand's Enduring

Bubble." Rev. of *The Bubble. Indian Book Chronicle* Jan. 1991 : 3-4.

1944. O'Brien, Kate. Rev. of *The Sword and the Sickle. Spectator* 5938 (1942).

1945. ——. Rev. of *The Village. Spectator* 5783 (1939).

1946. Orwell, George. Rev. of *The Sword and the Sickle. Horizon* (1942). Rpt. in *The Collected Essays, Journalism and Letters of George Orwell* 11. Eds. Sonia Orwell and Ian Angus. London: Secker & Warburg. 1968.

1947. Pandit, Manorama. Rev. of *The Road. World Literature Written in English* 14.2 (1975) : 421.

1948. Palmer, Arnold. "Mr. Anand's Novel." Rev. of *Two Leaves and a Bud. London Mercury* May 1937.

1949. Perles, Alfred. Rev. of *The Barber's Trade Union and Other Stories. Life and Letters Today* XLII (1944).

1950. Pritchett, V. Rev. of *Coolie. Commonwealth Review* 6.1 (1994-95) : 173-174.

1951. Quennell, Peter. Rev. of *Coolie. New Statesman and Nation* 12.28 (n.s.) 1936.

1952. Raina, M.L. Rev. of *Confession of a Lover. Indian Book Chronicle* Jan. 1977 : 40.

1953. ——. "A Search for form." Rev. of *The Bubble. Indian Book Chronicle* 1 May 1984 : 161.

1954. Rees, Goronwy. Rev. of *Two Leaves and a Bud. Spectator* 5679 (1937).

1955. Reuben, Elizabeth. *Rev. of Panorama. Indian Express* 5 July 1987 : 11.

1956. Rev. of *Untouchable. Times Literary Supplement* 2 May 1935 : 289.

1957. Rev. of *The Village. Times Literary Supplement* 15 Apr. 1939 : 215.

1958. Rev. of *The Sword and the Sickle*. *Times Literary Supplement* 2 May 1942 : 221.

1959. Rev. of *Coolie*. *Times Literary Supplement* 20 June 1936 : 520.

1960. Rev. of *The Barber's Trade Union and Other Stories*. *Times Literary Supplement* 1 July 1944 : 317.

1961. Rickword, Edgell. Rev. of *Coolie*. *Kakatiya Journal of English Studies* 2.1 (1977) : 223-225. "Notes." Rpt. from *New Indian Literature* (London) 1935.

1962. Riemenschneider, Dieter. Rev. of *Confession of a Lover*. *World Literature Today* 16.1 (1977) : 105-109.

1963. Rev. of *The Bubble*. *Littcrit* 18, 10.1 (1984) : 62-65.

1964. S.D. "Fancy and Fact." Rev. of *The Private Life of an Indian Prince*. *Thought* 10 Apr. 1954 : 12.

1965. S.M. Rev. of *Gauri*. *Democratic World* 18 July 1976 : 16.

1966. Singh, Khushwant. "A Delightful Autobiography." Rev. of *The Bubble*. *Illustrated Weekly of India* 19-25 (1984) : 34-35.

1967. ——. "Good Guys, Bad Guys and Mulkees." Rev. of *Morning Face*. *Times of India* 13 July 1969 : IV.

1968. Singh, Madhu. Rev. of *The Tractor and the Corn Goddess and Other Stories*. *Indian Book Chronicle* Nov.-Dec. 1987 : 305.

1969. ——. Rev. of *Death of a Hero*. *Indian Book Chronicle* July 1988 : 177-78.

1970. Singh, Narendra Pal. "A Punjabi Response." Rev. of *Across the Black Waters*. *Indian Literary Review* No. 10 (1978-79) : 34-36.

1971. Stoll, Dennis Gray. Rev. of *The Barber's Trade Union*. *Aryan Path* Jan. 1945 : 36.

1972. Spender, Stephen. Rev. of *Two Leaves and a Bud*. *Life and Letters Today* 14.8 (1937).

1973. Sunderarajan, P.K Rev. of *Coolie. West Coast Review* 7.2 (1972).

1974. "Tales of Indians." Rev. of *Across the Black Waters. Times Literary Supplement* 7 Dec. 1940 : 619.

1975. Vakeel, Hilda. Rev. of *Coolie. Kakatiya Journal of English Studies* 2.1 (1977) 228-231. "Notes." Rpt. from *Free Press Journal* 1938.

1976. Venugopal, C. V. Rev. of *Confession of a Lover. Journal of Karnatak University* (Humanities) (1977) : 189-190.

1977. Verghese, Paul. "Self-Portrait." Rev. of *Morning Face. Quest* 63, Aug. 1973 : 103-104. Rpt. in Verghese, *Essays* 35-49. ref. : 506.

1978. West, Anthony. Rev. of *The Village. New Statesman and Nation* 27.425 (n.s.) 1939.

1979. Zuckerman, Ruth Van Horn. Rev. of *Lament on the Death of a Master of Arts. Books Abroad* 42.2 (1968) : 487.

VI. Dissertations

1980. Agarwal, Balaram Prasad. "Mulk Raj Anand : A Study of Miseries, Struggles and Splendours in his Fiction." Ravishankar U, 1980.

1981. Agnihotri, Gopinath. "On the Treatment of Indian Life and Problems in the Novels of M.R. Anand, Raja Rao and R.K. Narayan." Meerut U, 1973. Meerut : Shalabh Book House, 1984, 1993.

1982. Ahmad, Reja. "Fictional Structures : A Stylistic study of the Fiction of R.K. Narayan, Mulk Raj Anand and Anita Desai." U of Bihar, 19?.

1983. Badve, V. V. "Narrative Techniques in Indian Fiction in English with Particular Reference to the Work of Raja Rao, R.K. Narayan, M.R. Anand and Manohar Malgonkar." Shivaji U, 1979.

1984. Balaram, Chaswal. "The Stylistic Development of Mulk Raj

Anand." Central Institute of English and Foreign Languages (Hyderabad). 1973.

1985. Bamezai, Geeta. "Social and Moral Concerns in the Journalistic and Creative Writings of Mulk Raj Anand." Banaras Hindu U, 1989.

1986. Bhaskaran, V.H. "The Theme of Social Justice in the Novels of Mulk Raj Anand and Bhabani Bhattacharya." U of Madurai, 1989.

1987. Bhat V. Nithanatha. "Themes and Techniques in the Short Stories of Mulk Raj Anand, Raja Rao and R.K. Narayan." Calicutt U, 1988.

1988. Bhatt, P.N. "A Thematic Study of the Novels of R.K. Narayan, Mulk Raj Anand, Manohar Malgonkar." Surashtra U, 1978.

1989. Chowdhury, Beni Madhav. "Political Strain in the Novels of Mulk Raj Anand." Bihar U, 19?.

1990. Damodar Rao, B. "Social and Political Awareness in the Novels of Mulk Raj Anand and George Orwell." U of Mysore, 1980.

1991. Dayal, Barameshwar. "Critical Study of the Themes and Techniques of the Indo-Anglian Short Story Writers with Special Reference to Mulk Raj Anand, R.K. Narayan and K.A, Abbas." Magadh U (Bodh Gaya), 1984. Ranchi : Jubilee Prakashan, 1985.

1992. Desai, Achala Arun Kumar. "The Autobiographical Novels of Mulk Raj Anand : A Study." Karnatak U, 1990.

1993. Devasia, S. D. "Indian English and the Indian Spirit : Analysis of Three Novelists : R.K. Narayan, Raja Rao and Mulk Raj Anand." Diss. (M.A.). U of Calicut, 1979.

1994. George, C.J. "The Artist as Social Critic. A Study of Mulk Raj Anand's Major Novels." North Eastern Hill U, 1983.

1995. Gulati, Vinod Bhusan. "Mulk Raj Anand's Novels : A Study in Narrative Technique." Meerut U, 1983.

1996. Gupta, Balarama. "The Artist as Humanist: A Study of M.R. Anand's Fiction." U of Karnatak (Dharwad), 1970.

1997. Gupta, Shravan Kumar. "Tradition and Modernity in the Novels of Mulk Raj Anand." Meerut U, 1982.

1998. Jacob, Susan. "Women in Mulk Raj Anand's Fiction." Diss. (M.Phil.). U of Annamalai, 1982.

1999. Juneja, Om Prakash. "Colonial Consciousness in Recent Black American, Indian and African Fiction with Special Reference to the Novels of Richard Wright, Ralph Ellison, James Baldwin, Raja Rao, R.K. Narayan, M.R. Anand, Chinua Achebe, T.M. Aluko and James Ngugi." Maharaja Sayaji Rao U of Baroda, 1980.

2000. Kaushik, Raj Kumar. "Mulk Raj Anand — A Committed Artist." U of Delhi, 1968.

2001. Kaur, Matania Din, "Moral Vision in the Novels of Mulk Raj Anand" Diss. (M.Phil). Punjab U, 1992.

2002. Khan, S.A. "The Novel of Commitment : A Study of Mulk Raj Anand." U of Marathwada (Beed), 1988.

2003. Kulothungan. "Anand's *Gauri,* and Narayan's *The Dark Room :* A Comparative Study." Diss. (M.Phil). Annamalai U, 19?.

2004. Kumar, Birendra. "Social Conflict in the Novels of Mulk Raj Anand." Magadh U, 1988.

2005. Mehar, Amarjit Singh. "Artist as Rebel : Protest in Mulk Raj Anand's Novels." Punjab U, 1983.

2006. Mishra, D.S. "Novels of Mulk Raj Anand : A Reappraisal." Kashi Vidyapith, 19?.

2007. Misra, Lalji, "The Impact of Gandhi on Indian English Fiction with Special Reference to M.R. Srivastava, R.K. Narayan, Anand and Raja Rao" Diss. (D.Phil) Gyanpur, 1992.

2008. Narlikar, Arun. "An Examination of Mulk Raj Anand's

Novels with Particular Reference to His Themes, Characterization and Techniques." Saugar U, 1980.

2009. Oberoi, Narenda Kumar. "Sociology of Indo-English Novel with Special Reference to the Novels of Mulk Raj Anand, R.K. Narayan, Raja Rao." Punjab U, 1980.

2010. Periyanyaki, Premila. "The Novels of Mulk Raj Anand: A Thematic Study." Annamalai U, 1981.

2011. Perkins, Susan Havard. "Reflections of Modern Culture in Indo-Anglian Literature : Illustrations from the Novels of R.K. Narayan and Mulk Raj Anand." U of California, 1957.

2012. Prasad, Shaileshwar Sati. "Social Realism in the Novels of Mulk Raj Anand." Patna U, 1981.

2013. Rajan, C.K. "Language of Fictional Writings of Mulk Raj Anand." Kerala U, 1987.

2014. Rajan, P.K. "Humanistic Ambivalence in the Novels of Mulk Raj Anand : A Dialectical Approach." Kerala U, 1990.

2015. Rao, A.V. Krishna. "The Inod-Anglian Novel and the Changing Tradition : A Study of the Novels of M.R. Anand, Kamala Markandaya, R.K. Narayan and Raja Rao." U of Mysore, 1964. Rao and Raghavan, 1972.

2016. Rao, M. Prathapa. "Mulk Raj Anand's Trilogy : A Study." Diss. (M.Phil). Nagarjuna U, 1983.

2017. Reeta. "Woman Charaters in Mulk Raj Anand's Novels : A Psychological Interpretation." U of Himachal Pradesh, 1990.

2018. Ruebeling, Heinrich. "Die Stellung des Romans *Private Life of an Indian Prince,* in Gesam Twerk des Autors Mulk Raj Anand." Diss. (M.Phil). U of Johann Wolfgang Grethe Universtat, 1984.

2019. Satyanarayana N. "New Morality in Indian English Fiction with Special Reference to Anand, Narayan and Arun Joshi." Kakatiya U, 1989.

2020. Sethi, Vijay Mohan. "Short Stories of M.R. Anand : A Critical Study." U of Himachal Pradesh. 1989. New Delhi; Ashish Publishing House, 1990.

2021. Sharma, A. Kumar. "The Theme of Exploitation in the Novels of Mulk Raj Anand." Meerut U, 1986. New Delhi : H.K. Publishers, 1990.

2022. Sharma, T.C. "Mulk Raj Anand : The Art of Characterization." Himachal Pradesh U, 1985.

2023. Shepherd, Ronald. "Aspects of Identity in the Indo-English Novel : A Study of Three Novelists : Raja Rao, R.K. Narayan, and M.R. Anand." U of Adelaide, 1974.

2024. Singh, Jaipal, "Themes and Techniques in the Novels of Mulk Raj Anand." Rohilkhand U, 1988.

2025. Singh, M. "Mulk Raj Anand: A Study of the Malcontents in His Novels." Banaras Hindu U, 1985.

2026. Subhana, Asma. "A Comparative Study of Fictional Speech in E.M. Forster. M.R. Anand, Robin White and Alan Pafoti." Diss. (M.Phil). Osmania U 1988.

2027. Suresh Kumar, A.V. "Non-Indian Characters : Anglo-American and European in the Novles of Mulk Raj Anand, Raja Rao, R.K. Narayan, B. Rajan, Markandaya and Anita Desai." Osmania U, 1991.

2028. Suryanarayana Murti, K. V. "*The Sword and the Sickle* : A Study of Mulk Raj Anand's Novels." Andhra U, 1972. Mysore; Geeta Book House, 1983.

2029. Swarup, Hem Lata. "Mulk Raj Anand : A Critical Survey." U of Agra, 1970.

2030. Tara Chand, "Protest in the Five Novels of Mulk Raj Anand." Himachal Pradesh U, 1985.

2031. Thakur, V.R. "East and West : Indo-Anglian Novel with Special Reference to Mulk Raj Anand, Kamala Markandaya, Manohar Malgonkar." Bombay U, 1985.

2032. Upvinder Kaur, "Patterns of Linguistics Variation in Social Context in Mulk Raj Anand's *Coolie.*" Punjabi U, 1990.

PARO ANAND

Pepper, The Capuchirs and other stories., New Delhi, Indus, 1992.

Little Bird : A Modern Fable. New Delhi : Indus, 1993.

SAYAPAL ANAND

Life 's a Tale. Calcutta : Writers Workshop, 1991.

U. ANAND

Be Prepared. New Delhi : National Book Trust, n.d.

ANANDA

1747 : Dawn of the Raj. London : Lewis Book Guild, 1988.

VICTOR ANANT

A. Primary Sources

The Revolving Man. London : Macgibbon and Kee, 1961.

Sacred Crow. Delhi : Penguin Books, 1996.

B. Secondary Sources : Critical Works

I. Research Article

2033. Narayan, Shyamala A. "East-West Encounter in Raja Rao's *The Serpent and the Rope* and Victor Anant's *The Revolving Man.*" *Indian Literary Review* 1.5-6 (1978) : 50-55.

INDIRA ANANTAKRISHNAN

Nivedita's New Home and Other Stories. New Delhi : Publications Division, 1992.

M. ANANTA NARAYANAN

A. Primary Sources

The Silver Pilgrimage. New York : Criterion Books, 1961. Delhi :

Arnold Heinemann, 1975. New Delhi: Penguin Books, 1993.

B. Secondary Sources : Critical Works

I. Research Article

2034. Kothandaraman, Bala. "Philosophy in a Lighter Vein : *All About H. Hatterr* and *The Silver Pilgrimage*." Rao, A. Ramakrishna and Sivaramkrishna 81-97. ref. : 466. See 3083.

2035. Paranjape, Makarand R. "Indian Thought in *The Silver Pilgrimage*." Rao, A. Ramakrishna and Sivaramkrishna 68-80. ref. : 466.
Traces the change and the manner of the change wrought in the prince by the journey — both physical and mental — the mental sojourn moving from statecraft, medicine and philosophy to erotics, cookery and the occult, all these being based on Indian thought, science and culture.

2036. Ramachandra, R. "*The Silver Pilgrimage* : A Belated Response." *Literary Criterion,* 14.1 (1979) : 73-78.
An Appreciative evaluation of the novel, dealing with the significance of the title, the story telling method, the comic mode and the appropriateness of the conclusion.

2037. Srinath, C.N. "Journey into the Eternal City : M. Ananta Narayanan's *The Silver Pilgrimage.*" Srinath 312-339. ref. : 523.
Considers the novel as a modern classic and traces the journey of the protagonist from knowledge to experience and wisdom, and so categorizes it as a spiritual journey.

2038. Venugopal, C.V. "*The Silver Prigrimage* : A Study in Religious Discipline." *Journal of Karnatak University* (Humanities) 20 (1976) : 252-256.

Studies the novel as a treatise on religious discipline and comments that the pilgrimage of the protagonist is a process of learning to see everything in its proper perspective thereby leading him to true understanding of life and his duty towards humanity.

II. Reviews

2039. Lamba, B.P.S. Rev. of *The Silver Pilgrimage. Indian Book Chronicle* 1.2 (1976) : 46-48.

2040. Palakeel, Thomas. Rev. of *The Silver Pilgrimage. World Literature Today* 68.4 (1994) : 883-884.

2041. Ramanthan, Suguna. "A Distorting Metaphor." Rev. of *The Silver Pilgrimage. Indian Review of Books* 14 Feb.–15 Mar 1994 : 27.

KENNETH ANDERSON

Fires of Passion. Bombay : Jaico Publications, 1969.

KUSUM ANSAL

A. Primary Sources

I. Novels

Travelling with a Sunbeam. New Delhi : Vikas Publishing House, 1983.

Sing Me No Song : A Novel. New Delhi : Vikas Publishing House,1985.

Sheltering Shadows : A Novel. New Delhi : Har Anand Publications, 1992.

B. Secondary Sources : Critical Works

I. Research Article

2042. Tewari, R.P. "*Travelling with a Sunbeam,* : The Quest for Love and Identity." *Language Forum*, 18.1-4 (1992) : 157-177. Rpt. in Pathak, *Indian Fiction in English* 170-177. ref. : 422. Also in Pathak, *Quest for Identity* 170-177. ref. : 423.

Considers *Travelling with Sunbeam* a novel with a social purpose : a plea for the liberation of both men and women from the slavery of every kind — social, moral, and sexual.

LALITHAMBICA ANTHARJANAM

Agnisakshi. Trichur : Kerala Academy, 1980.

ANJANA APPACHANA

A. Primary Sources

I. Short Stories

Incantations and other stories. London : Virago, 1991 New Delhi: Penguin Books, 1991. New Brunswick (NJ) : Rutgers University Press, 1992.

Listening Now. New Delhi : Indian Ink, 1998.

B. Secondary Sources

I. Reviews

2043. Holmstrom, Lakshmi. "A Web of Lives." Rev. of *Listening Now.* Indian Review of Books. Apr.-May. 1999 : 5-6.

2044. Parameswaran, Uma. Rev. of *Incantations. World Literature Today* 67.2 (1993) : 444-485.

2045. Ponappa, Kaveri. Rev. of *Incantations. Times of India* 25 Aug. 1991 : V.

NIRMALA ARAVIND

A Video, a Fridge and a Bride. New Delhi : Rupa & Co, 1995.

JAGADISH ARORA

Senorita Said So. Varanasi : Swati Publications, 1964.

V.N. ARORA

A. Primary Sources

I. Novels

Sons and Fathers. New Delhi : Savitha Prakashan, 1983.

B. Secondary Sources : Critical Works

I. Research Articles

2046. Trika, M. "V.N. Arora's *Sons and Fathers,* : A Brief Study." *Journal of Indian Writing in English* 13.1 (1985) : 59–63.
Considers the novel an autobiographical one.

II. Reviews

2047. Begum, A. Jameela. Rev. of *Sons and Fathers. Littcrit* 18,10.1(1984) : 66-68.

2048. Cruden, Robert M. "Coming of Age." Rev. of *Sons and Fathers. Indian Book Chronicle,* 9.1-2 (1986) : 6.

BALAN ARSU

O Campers. Calcutta : Writers Workshop, 1994.

JAYA ARSU

Where Love was Folly and Other Stories. Bangalore : Up Pals Publications, 1975.

ASHA

Promotion. Secunderabad : Good News Literature Centre, 1956.

UPENDRANATH ASHK

Sorrows of the Snows. Calcutta : Writers Workshop, 1971.

GIRIJA RANI ASTHANA

Stormy Adventure and Other Stories. New Delhi : Publications Division, 1992.

IKBAL ATHAR

The years of Their Lives. London : Macdonald and Jones, 1976.

SALLY ATHOGIAS

Gold in the Dust : A Novel of Rural India. Bombay : Jaico Publicationa, 1958, 1960.

SRI AUROBINDO

A. Primary Sources

Conversations of the Dead. Pondicherry : Sri Aurobindo Ashram, 1951.

Collected Plays and Short Stories. Pondicherry : Sri Aurobindo Ashram, 1971.

B. Secondary Sources : Critical Works

I. Research Article

2049. Naik, M. K. "Idylls of the Occult : The Short Stories of Sri Aurobindo." Naik, *Aspects,* 150-161. ref. : 378.

Comments that though the short stories of Aurobindo, with the exception of 'The Phantom Hour', lack the rounded finish of his major poems and plays yet reveal "glimmerings of tantalizing artistic possibilities."

AIYLAM SUBRAMANIER PANCHAPAKESA AYYAR

A. Primary Sources

I. Novels

Baladitya : A Historical Romance of Ancient India. Bombay : Taraporevala, 1930. Banglore : P.T.I. Book Depot, 1954.

An Indian in Western Europe. Bangalore : R.C.S. Maniam, 1929.

Three Men of Destiny. Madras : C. Coomaraswamy Naidu & Sons, 1939.

The Story of Manimekalai. Vellore : K.V. Press, 1943.

The Legions Thunder Past. Madras : Rochouse & Sons, 1947.

Chanakya and Chandragupta : A Historical Novel. Madras : Ramaswamy Sastrulu, 1951.

II. Short Stories

Indian After-Dinner Stories. 2 vol. Bombay: Taraporevala, 1925.

Sense in Sex and other stories of Indian Women. Madras :

Teachers' Publishing House, n.d. Bombay : Taraporevala, 1929. 2nd ed. 1948.

The Finger of Destiny and other stories. Kumbhakonam : G.V.K. Swamy, 1932. Madras : Alliance & Co., n.d.

The Royal Jester or Tenali Rama. Vellore: K.V. Press, 1943. Rpt. as *Tenali Rama.* Madras : Alliance & Co, 1947.

Tales of Ind. Kumbhakonam : G.V.K. Swamy & Co, 1944.

Jolly Old Tales of India. Vellore : K.V. Press, 1945.

Life is one Long Sacrifice. Madras : Alliance & Co, 1947.

Three Famous Tales. Kumbhakonam; G.V.K. Swamy & Co. 1947.

Kovalan and Kannaki. Madras: C. Coomara Swamy Naidu & Sons, 1947.

Gripping Tales of India. Tenali : Orient Publishing & Co. 1948.

Famous Tales of India. Madras : Ramaswamy Sastrulu, 1954.

Selected Indian After Dinner Stories. Bombay : Taraporevala, 1948. Madras : Teachers' Publishing House, 1958.

Musician Shut the Gate : Stories. Madras : Alliance & Co., n.d.

Poorman's Son and Other Stories. Madras : V. Ramaswamy Sastrulu & Sons, 1963.

III. Non-Foction

Rambles in Literature, Art, Law and Philosophy. Madras : The Madras Law Journal Office, 1958.

B. Secondary Sources : Critical Works

I. Books

2050. Menon, K.P.K. *A.S.P. Ayyar,* Kerala Writers in English Series. Madras : Macmillan 1980.

This monograph evaluates the major works of A.S.P. Ayyar which include poetry, plays, novels, short stores religious works, travelogues, etc. The first chapter sketches briefly the life and works of the writer and the following chapters discuss his works genre-wise, describing briefly the achievement of A.S.P. Ayyar as a writer and his contribution to Indian English literature. Finds Ayyar as a competent master of the English language.

II. Research Articles

2051. Gupta, C.S. "A Note on Ayyar's short stories." *Contemporary Indian Literature,* 3 (1971) : 86-87.

2052. Gupta, G.S. Balarama. "A.S.P. Ayyar's : *Sense of Sex* : A Study." *Journal of the Karnatak University* (Humanities) 15 (1971) : 122-128. Rpt. in Gupta, *Essays* 75-81 ref. : 284.
An evaluation of the work, *Sense of Sex.*

2053. ——. Ayyar's *After Dinner Stories.* Gupta, *Essays* 82-90 ref. : 284.
An assessment of *After Dinner Stories.*

2054. Parameswaran, Uma. "Nostalgia : The Historical Romances of T. Ramakrishnayya and A.S.P. Ayyar." Parameswaran, *A Study of the Representative Indo-English Novelists* 5-41. ref. : 420.

CHANDRA SEKHAR SUBRAMANYA AYYAR
(Pseud. KUMARA GURU)

Life's Shadows,. 2 Vols. Bombay : Taraporevala, 1938 : Vol. 2. Is published as *A Daughter's Shadow.* Madras : by the Author, 1943.

BACH

Grand Trunk Road from the Front Seat. New Delhi : Indus Harper, 1993.

BACHINT KAUR

Draupadi. New Delhi : Enkay Publishers, 1990.

The Embers : A Collection of Stories. Delhi : Enkay Publishers, 1990.

ANITA RAU BADAMI

A. Primary Sources

Tamarind Men. Delhi : Penguin Books, 1996.

B. Secondary Sources

I. Reviews

2055. Banerji, Jaya. "The Razor's edge." Rev. of *Tamarind Men. Indian Book Chronicle* 16 Nov.-15 Dec. 1996. 40-41.

ASOKA K. BAGCHI

Tales from a Small Town. Delhi : Konark Publishers, 1993.

DESMOND BAGLEY

Fly Away. New Delhi : Rupa & Co., 1978.

H. BAHADUR

The Case of a Sprightly Widow. New Delhi : Sterling Paperbacks, 1977.

K.P. BAHADUR

Story of Rama. Allahabad : Indian Press, 1962.

The Curse of the Poisoned Cat. New Delhi: Sterling Publishers, 1973.

The Wiles of Women. Delhi : Hind Pocket Books, 1973.

Murder in the Delhi Mail. New Delhi : Sterling Publishers, 1976.

TEJANI BAHADUR

Day After Tomorrow. Nairobi : East African Literature Bureau, 1971.

UMRAO BAHADUR

Love and Its Charms. Delhi : Indraprastha Vedic Library, 1924.

Freaks of Fate. Delhi : Indraprastha Vedic Library, 1929.

Janaki. Delhi : Indraprastha Vedic Library, 1931.

The Unveiled Court : The Story of a Prince's Court Life. London : Arthur H. Stockwell, 1932.

The Curse of Society. Delhi : Printing and Stationery Depot, 1933.

Destiny. Delhi : Printing and Stationery Depot, n.d.

Tears of Sorrow. N.P. : n.p., 1949.

Paths of Life. Delhi : Rajkamal Publishers, 1950.

Nemesis. N.P. : n.p., n.d.

ANIRUDDBA BAHAL

A Crack in the Mirror. Calcutta : Rupa & Co., 1991.

P.N. BAHL

The Wheel of Time. New Delhi : Har Anand Publication, 1996.

KAVERI H. BAI

Meenakshi Memoirs : A Novel of Christian Life in the South. Madras : G.A. Natesan, 1937.

TARA ALI BAIG

A. Primary Sources

I. Novels

The Moon in Rahu : An Account of the Bhowal Sanyasi Case. Bombay : Asia Publishers, 1968.

B. Secondary Sources : Critical Works

I. Research Articles

2056. Rama Rao, Vimala. "The Craft of Truth-telling : Tara Ali Baig's *The Moon in Rahu.*" *Kakatiya Journal of English Studies* 9 (1988-89) : 39-50. Rpt. in Dhawan, *Indian Women Novelists* Set III. Vol. 4, 115-124. ref. : 257.

An appreciative evaluation of the novel. Considers the novel an excellently crafted book, remarkable both in terms of subject matter and treatment.

2057. ——. "Tell My Story" : The Feminist Theme in *The Moon in Rahu.*" Radha 1-4. ref. : 416. Rpt. in

Commonwealth Review 6.1 (1994-95) : 159-162. Also in Dass, *Feminism and Literature* 159-163. ref. : 244. Also in Dhawan, *Indian Women Novelists* Set III. Vol. 4. 110-114. ref. : 257.

Focuses on the aspects of Feminism implicit in the theme — the deadly struggle the woman waged alone to preserve her privacy.

II. Reviews

2058. Rao, K.S.N. Rev. of *The Moon in Rahu. Books Abroad* 44.4 (1990) : 708.

2059. Rev. of *The Moon in Rahu. Statesman* 10 May 1976 : 11.

YAWAR BAIG

Holycat : Sufi and Other Stories. New Delhi: Orient Longman, 1994.

CHANDRAKANT BAKSHI

Lost Illusions : A Novel. New Delhi : Sterling Publishers, 1989.

K.P. BALAJI

A. Primary Sources

I. Novels

Abhimanyu. Madras : Sangam Books, 1978. Bombay : Disha Books, 1992.

B. Secondary Sources

I. Reviews

2060. Anjeneyulu, D. Rev. of *Abhimanyu. Economic Times* 30 July 1978 : 4.

T.L. BALAKRISHNA

The Love of Kusuma : An Eastern Love Story. London : T. Werner Laurie, 1910.

PURASU BALAKRISHNAN

A. Primary Sources

I. Short Stories

The Gold Bangles and Other Stories. Bombay : Bharatiya Vidya Bhavan, 1966.

B. Secondary Sources

I. Reviews

2061. Ramachandra, Rajini. Rev. of *The Golden Bangles and Other Stories. Literary Criterion* 8.3 (1968) : 104-105.

V. BALAKRISHNAN and LEELA BAI

A. Primary Sources

I. Novels

Blue Jasmine. New Delhi : Sterling Publishers, 1979.

B. Secondary Sources

I. Reviews

2062. Ram, K.S. Rev. of *Blue Jasmine. Literary Criterion* 26.1 (1981) : 79-80.

NALAPPAT BALAMANI AMMA

Mother. Bombay : International Book House, 1950.

MALLIKA BALARAMA

Home Life in Bengal : An Account of the Every day of a Hindu Home at the Present Day. Calcutta : N. Newman, 1985.

SUJATHA BALASUBRAMANIAM

A. Primary Sources

I. Short Stories

The House in the Hills and Other Stories. New Delhi : Arnold Heinemann, 1973.

B. Secondary Sources

I. Reviews

2063. Dhruva Kumar, A. Joshi. Rev. of *The House on the Hills and Other Stories*. *Indina P.E.N.* 39.8 (1973) : 21-22.

D. BALA SUBRAMANIAN

Cats Have Nine Lives. Madras : Wiley Eastern, 1994.

AMARNATH BALI

Laughs at Life. Delhi : Indian Book & Co, 1967.

BALDWIN, SHAUNA SINGH

English Lessons and Other Stories. New Delhi. Harper Collins, 1998.

MAYA BALSE

A. Primary Sources

I. Novels

Just a Matter of Mistresses. Bombay : Bell Books, 1972. Bombay : Jaico Publications, 1974.

The Sensuous Saint. New Delhi : Sterling Publishers, 1975.

The Singer. Bombay : Jaico Publications, 1975.

Indiscreet. New Delhi : Orient Paperbacks, 1977, 1992.

The Stranger. Bombay : Bell Books, 1977. New Delhi : Vikas Publishing House, 1977.

The Cannibal. New Delhi : Hind Pocket Books, 1982.

B. Secondary Sources : Critical Works

I. Research Articles

2064. Singh, P.K. "Mayah Balse's *Just a Matter of Mistresses* : A Voyage Within." Dhawan, *Indian Women Novelists* Set II. Vol. 3. 246-252. ref. : 257.
"It is not just a satire on sex but a tragic work of art embodying strong undercurrent of high seriousness and

a streak of religiosity unravelling the complexities of the inner recesses of human consciousness."

II. Reviews

2065. Datta, Eua. "Unappealing Mistresses." Rev. of *Just a Matter of Mistresses. Times of India* 15 Apr. 1973 : 11.

2066. Kaul, Rupa. "The Network." Rev. of *Just a Matter of Mistresses. Thought* 31 Mar. 1973 : 18.

2067. Rao, Raj. "Blood and Thunder." Rev. of *Cannibal. Indian Express* 16 Apr. 1983 : 8.

V. BALU

Day Dreams. Mysore : J. Nanumal & Sons, 1964.

R.P. BAMBI

The Crusaders of Tibet. Dalhousie : Khampa Pocket Books, 1960.

M.M. BANAJI

Sublime Though Blind : A Tale of Parsi Life : Men and Manners. Bombay : published by the Author, 1923.

GAUTAM SHANKER BANERJEE

Indian Hippies : A Novel. Trivandrum : Indian Fine Arts Bureau, 1996.

H.C. BANERJEE

An English Girl in Bengal and Other Stories. Calcutta : Datta Bose and Co., 1928.

JULIETTE BANERJEE

The Boy Friend and Other Stories. Calcutta : Writers Workshop, 1978.

RANGIN BANERJI

A Black Paddy. Calcutta : Writers Workshop, 1995.

S.B. BANERJEE

Misunderstood and other sketches of Indian Life. Calcutta : S. Bandyapadya, 1907.

Adventures of Mrs. Russell : Stories of Mystery from India. London : Stockwell, 1909.

Tales of Bengal. Ed. Francis Henry Skrine. London : Longmans, Green and Co., 1910.

Indian Detective Stories. London : Gay and Hancock, 1911.

SAMERENDRANATH BANERJEE

Offering. Ambala Cantonment : By the Author, 1950.

Step Mother. New Delhi : By the Author, 1964.

SARA BANERJI

A. Primary Sources

I. Novels

Cobweb Walking. London : Victor Gollancz, 198?.

The Wedding of Jayanthi Mandal. London : Victor Gollancz, 1987.

The Tea Planter's Daughter. London : Victor Gollancz, 1987. London : Arrow Books, 1991.

Shining Agues. London : Victor Gollancz, 1990.

B. Secondary Sources : Critical Works

I. Research Articles

2068. Simon, Irene. "Truth and Semblance of Truth in Sara Banerji's *The Wedding of Jayanthi Mandal.*" Maes-Jelink 203-212. ref. : 344.

Analyses the novel to show how "the adequacy of the narrative procedure (the point of view of the actor narrator and the two-fold view of the scene) reflects the ambiguity of the central theme without impairing the fairy tale aspect of the story."

ASHOK BANKER

A. Primary Sources

Iron Bra. New Delhi : Rupa & Co, 1993.

Byculla Boy . New Delhi : Penguin Books, 1994.

B. Secondary Sources

I. Reviews

2069. Alikhan, Anvar. "Five Go Off the Psychiatrist." Rev. of *Byculla Boy. Indian Review of Books* 16 Dec.-Jan. 15. 1995 : 32.

ACHALA BANSAL

Once a Year It Is March and Other Stories. New Delhi : National Publishing House, 1991.

SARALA BARNABAS

A. Primary Sources

I. Novels

The Promise of Spring : A Novel. Aurangabad : Parimala Prakashan, 1989.

Sakshi. Calcutta : Writers Workshop, 1993.

Anjolie. Calcutta : Writers Workshop, 1993.

Nayantara. Calcutta : Writers Workshop, 1993.

Dark Passion : *A Novel.* New Delhi : Prestige Books, 1997.

B. Secondary Sources : Critical Works

I. Research Articles

2070. Dnyate, Ramesh "Guilt and Reconciliation in Sarala Barnabas's *The Promise of Spring.*" Dhawan, *Indian Women Novelists* Set III. Vol. 4. 193-222. ref. : 257. Traces the causes of guilt in Akbar Khan and Marcus Huntleigh and their ultimate happiness through reconciliation to the changing conditions in their lives.

2071. Patil, Z.N. "Sarala Barnabas's *The Promise of Spring* : A Socio-Pragmatic Analysis." Dhawan, *Indian Women Novelists* Set III. Vol. 4. 210-222. ref. : 257.
Examines the role of politeness strategies in the establishment and maintenance of interpersonal relationships in the novel and shows how "the study of these devices is an integral part of socio-pragmatics.

2072. Puranik, Vijay. "Sarala Barnabas's *The Promise of Spring* : A Study." Dhawan, *Indian Women Novelists* Set III. Vol. 4. 201-202. ref. : 257.
A general appraisal of the novel discussing the appropriateness of the title and the situations.

2073. Rathi, Vineydeep. "Sarala Baranbas's *Sakshi* Aspects of Womanhood." Dhawan, *Indian Woman Novelists* Set III. Vol. 4. 223-226. ref : 257.
Shows how the novel *Sakshi* depicts womanhood through many perspectives : from a middle class working woman to a woman separated from her husband.

2074. Simon, G.D. "The Sins of the past and the Lessons of the Present : A Study of Sarala Barnbas's *Nayantara.*" Dhawan, *Indian Women Novelists* Set III. Vol. 4. 227-236. ref. : 257.
Examines the nature of sin and its impact on succeeding generations, taking the example of Nayantara.

2075. Sarkar, Mitakida and R.K.Singh. "Sarala Barnabas : A Foursome Search for co-existence." *Language Forum* 24.1-2 (1998) : 91-98.

II. Reviews

2076. Ramachandra, Ragini. Rev. of *The Promise of Spring. Journal of Indian Writing in English* 19.1 (1991) : 47-50.

INDERJIT KAUR BARTHAKUR

So Full So Alive : Short Stories. New Delhi : Allied Publishers, 1994.

J.A.G. BARTON (Pseud.)

See Soshee Chunder Dutt

HEM BARUA

The Red River and The Blue Hills. Gauhati : Lawyer's Book Stall, 1962.

MOHAMMED VAI KHAN BASHEER

Poovan Banana and Other Stories. New Delhi : Orient Longman, 1994.

LAL BAHADUR BASNET

His Majesty's Paying Guest. Gangtok : Privately published, 1982.

ZEBA BASHIRUDDIN

Ripples. Hyderabad : Mahati Publications, 1967.

ARINDAM BASU

Picaro or Me. Calcutta : Writers Workshop, 1972.

ALU BASU

A. Primary Sources

Thy Will Be Done. New Delhi : Rupa & Co, 1994.

River Beneath the River. Bombay : Megna Publishing Company, 1996.

B. Secondary Sources

I. Reviews

2077. Thomas A.J. "A Bumpy Adventure." Rev. of *Thy Will Be Done. Indian Review of Books* 16 Feb.-Mar. 15. 1995. 33-34.

ROMEN BASU

A. Primary Sources

I. Novels

A House Full of People. Calcutta : G.C. Ray, 1968. Also by Navana, 1968.

Your Life to Live. Calcutta : Firma K.L. Mukopadya, 1972.

A Gift of Love. Calcutta : Writers Workshop, 1974. New Delhi : Sterling Publishers, 1976.

The Tamarind Tree : A Novel of Bengal. Calcutta : Writers Workshop, 1975.

Candles and Roses. New Delhi : Sterling Publishers, 1978.

Portrait on the Roof. New Delhi : Sterling Publishers, 1980.

Sands of Time. New Delhi : Sterling Publishers, 1985.

Out-Caste : A Novel. New Delhi : Sterling Publishers, 1986.

House Before Dawn : A Novel. New Delhi : Sterling Publishers, 1989.

Black Stone : A Novel . New Delhi : Sterling Publishers, 1989.

The Surrendering Self. New Delhi : Sterling Publishers, 1990.

The Street-Corner Boys : A Novel. New Delhi : Sterling Publishers, 1992.

My Own Witness : A Novel. New Delhi : Sterling Publishers, 1993.

In Silence. New Delhi : Sterling Publishers, 1995. New York : Facet Books International, 1995.

Torn Apart : A Novel. New Delhi : Sterling Publishers,1997.

II. Short Stories

Canvas and the Brush. Calcutta : Firma K.L. Mukopadya. 1971.

Rustling of Many Winds. New Delhi : Sterling Publishers, 1982.

Reflections. New Delhi : Sterling Publishers, 1989.

III. Non Fiction

"The Novel as a Document of the Human Condition." *Littcrit* 39, 20.2 (1994) : 5-9.

B. Secondary Sources : Critical Works

I. Books

2078. Somnath, P. *Romen Basu : His Vision and Art.* New Delhi : Sterling Publishers, 1995.

II. Research Articles

2079. Burns, Isabella. "Romen Basu : A Profile." *Indian Book Industry* 28.6 (1983) : 41.

2080. Prasad, K.T. Krishna. "Romen Basu." Prasad, Madhusudan, *Indian English Novelists* 172-180. ref. : 437.
A general assessment of Romen Basu as a novelist of social milieu of changing India.

2081. Ranilall, Rama. "The Many Worlds of Romen Basu." *Indian Book Chronicle* May 1989 : 106-107.
Considers Romen Basu as a deeply committed humanitarian writer and comments on his novels and stories in a general way.

II. Reviews

2082. Bose, Meera. Rev. of *Outcaste. Literary Criterions* 22.1 (1987) : 76-78.

2083. Darkar, Imtiaz. "Correct Conclusions." Rev. of *Your Life to Live. Times of India* 25 Mar. 1973 : 11.6.

2084. Daruwalla, Keki. Rev. of *Outcaste. Hindustan Times* 26 Apr. 1987 : 8.

2085. Jaidka, Manju. Rev. of *Rustling of Many Winds. New Quest* 43, Jan.-Feb. 1984 : 61-62.

2086. Jakhar, Sunita. "A Search for Happiness. Rev. of *Candles and Roses. Indian Book Chronicle* Dec. 1991 : 20.

2087. Lago, Mary. Rev. of *The Tamarind Tree. World Literature Today* 51.2 (1977) : 332.

2088. M.D. "Romance and Realism." Rev. of *The House Full of People. Hindustan Times* (Mag) 19 Jan. 1969 : 111.

2089. Narasimhan, Shaukuntala. "Shadows in the Country." Rev. of *Outcaste. Indian Express* 5 Apr. 1987 : 5.

2090. Paniker, Ayyappa. "A Minor Talent." Rev. of *Rustling of Many Winds. Indian Book Chronicle* May 1984 : 165-167.

2091. Rao, D.S. Rev. of *Portrait on the Roof. Indian Literature* July-August. 1981 : 156-162.

2092. Rev. of *Outcaste . Tribune* (Sunday) 18 Jan. 1987 : 2.

2093. Rev. of *Black Stone. Tribune* (Mag) 1 Oct 1989 : 2.

2094. Saha, Murari. Rev. of *Sands of Time. Link* 1 Dec. 1985 : 39.

2095. Saraiya, Indu. Rev. of *Candles and Roses. Indian P.E.N* July-Aug. 1979 : 20-21.

2096. Sharma, P.P. Rev. of *A Gift of Love. Journal of Indian Writing in English* 5.2 (1977) : 68-69.

2097. Singh, Veena. Rev. of *Outcaste. Indian Book Chronicle. May*-June 1987 : 151-152.

2098. Stuckert, Klaus. Rev. of *Portrait on the Roof. Journal of Indian Writing in English* 10 : 1-2 (1982) : 78.

2099. Wasi, Jehanara. Rev. of *Rustling of Many Winds*. Link, 7 Apr. 1985 : 40.

S. BASU

Man in the Red Maruthi and Other Stories. Calcutta : Writers Workshop, 1994.

SUBODH BASU

The City of New Moghals. Calcutta : S.C. Bose, 1947.

SHAKTI BATRA and S.P. SINDHU

ed. *Choice of Short Stories.* Delhi : Oxford University Press 1986.

SATISH BATRA

A. Primary Sources

I. Short Stories

The Quest and Other Stories. Delhi : Enkay Publishers, 1987.

B. Secondary Sources

I. Reviews

2100. Merchant, Naina. Rev. of *The Quest and Other Stories. Literature Alive* 2.2 (1985) : 42-44.

IQBAL S. BAWA

The Gully Slave. Delhi : Frank Bros & Co., 1979.

P.S. BAWA

A. Primary Sources

Memories of the Raj. New Delhi : Hind Pocket Books, 198?.

B. Secondary Sources

I. Reviews

2101. M.B. Rev. of *Memories of the Raj. Financial Express* 4 July 1982 : 5.

H.E. BEAL

Indian Ink. Bombay : Orient Longman, 1947.

GURUMUKH SINGH BEDI

Emerging Worlds : Short Stories. Delhi : Atma Ram & Sons, 1980.

KISHAN SINGH BEDI

The Fear of Retribution. Chandigarh : by the Author, 1970.

DEEPCHAND BEEHARRY

A Touch of Happiness. Port Louis : editions Nationales, 1966.

That Others Might Live. New Delhi : Orient Paperbacks, 1976.

The Road Ahead. Port Louis : Ashley Printer, n.d.

HAMID BEY

A. Primary Sources

Small Town Stories. Gauhati : Barna Agency, 1974.

B Secondary Sources

I. Reviews

2102. Futehally, Shama. "Small Stories." Rev. of *Small Town Stories. Quest* May-June, 1975 : 96-98.

LAKSHMI NATH BEZBAROA

Tales of a Grand Father from Assam. Bangalore : Indian Institute of Culture, 1955.

MANJUL BHAGAT

A. Primary Sources

The Search and Other Stories. Calcutta : Writers Workshop, 1952.

B. Secondary Sources

I. Reviews

2103. Futehally, Shama. Rev. of *The Search and Other Stories. Indian Book Chronicle* 16 Oct. 1982 : 333.

DURGA NARAYAN BHAGWAT

Romance in Sacred Lore (short stories). Allahabad : Kitab Mahal, 1946.

LEELAWATI BHAGWAT

Trip to Heaven and Other Stories. New Delhi : National Book Trust, 1990.

ALOK BHALLA

ed. *Stories About the Partition of India.* 3 Vols. New Delhi : Harper Collins, 1994.

CHHOTE BHARANY

Salvation Prison : A Novel. New Delhi : Sterling Publishers, 1992.

Games of Life. New Delhi : Sterling Publishers, 1993.

PERIN BHARUCHA

The Fire Worshippers. Bombay : Strand Book Stall, 1969

SHAKUNTALA BHARVANI

Lost Directions. Bombay : Orient Longman, 1996.

A. BHASKAR RAO

The Secret. New Delhi : Sterling Paperbacks, 1978.

SUDHAKAR BHAT

Holier Than Thou. New Delhi : Sterling Paperbacks, 1978.

MARGARET DELANCY BHATIA (Pseud. J. Rana)

Alien There is None. London : Hodder & Stoughton, 1960.

GAUTAM BHATIA

Malana Dreams and Other Visions of Architecture. New Delhi : Penguin Books.1996.

Punchtantra : Parables for the 21st Century. New Delhi : Penguin Books,1997.

A Short History of Everything. Delhi : Harper Collins,1998.

RITU BHATIA

A. Primary Sources

Gurus and Other Stories. New Delhi : Har Anand Publications, 1996.

B. Secondary Sources

I. Reviews

2104 Gopinath, Ratan. "Neurotic Urbania." Rev. of *Guru and Other Stories. Indian Review of Books* 16 Nov.-15 Dec. 1996. 41-42.

PRAMOD BHATNAGAR

Zoramthangi : Daughter of the Hills. New Delhi : Vikrant Press, 1982.

KAVERY BHATT

The Truth (almost) About Bharat. New Delhi : Penguin Books, 1991.

S.C. BHATT

The Jagmohan Millions. Calcutta : Writers Workshop, 1982.

SUJATHA BHATT

Monkey Shadows. New Delhi : Penguin Books, 1993.

JYOTSNA BHATTACHARJEE

Shadows in the Sunshine. Calcutta : Alpha Beta Publication, n.d.

BASUDEB BHATTACHARYA (Pseu. Pandit Acharya and Sree Basudeb)

The Saffron Veil. Nyack (New York) : Prana Press, 1953.

BHABANI BHATTACHARYA

A. Primary Sources

I. Novels

So Many Hungers. London : Victor Gollancz, 1947. Bombay : Hind Kitabs, 1947. Bombay : Jaico Publications, 1964. New Delhi : Orient Paperbacks, 1978.

Music For Mohini. New York : Crown Publisher, 1952. London : Angus and Robertson, 1959. New Delhi : Orient Paperbacks, 1952, 1984. Bombay : Jaico Publications,1964. Serialized in *The Illustrated Weekly of India* in 1950.

He Who Rides a Tiger. New York : Crown Publishers, 1952. London : Agnus and Robertson, 1959. Bombay : Jaico Publications, 1954. New Delhi : Hind Pocket Books, 1955. New Delhi : Arnold Heinemann, 1977.

A Goddess Named Gold. New York : Crown Publishers, 1960. Delhi : Orient Paperbacks, 1960. Delhi : Hind Pocket Books, 1967.

Shadow from Ladakh. London : W.W. Allen, 1967 (Awarded Sahitya Akademic Prize for 1967). New York : Crown Publishers, 1966. Delhi : Hind Pocket Books, 1966, 1970.

A Dream in Hawaii. Delhi : Macmillan, 1978. Delhi : Vision Books, 1983.

II. Short Stories

Steel Hawk and Other Stories. Delhi : Hind Pocket Books, 1968.

ed. *Contemporary Indian Short Stories*. Series II New Delhi : Sahitya Akademi, 1967.

III. Non-Fiction

A. Books

The Golden Boat (Translations from Rabindranath Tagore). London : Allen & Unwin, 1930. New York : Macmillan, 1930. Bombay : Jaico Books, 1955.

Some Memorable Yesterdays. Patna : Pusthak Bhandar, 1942. *Indian Cavalcade* (Some Memorable Yesterdays). Bombay : Nalanda Publications, 1948.

Towards Universal Man. Bombay : Asia Publishing House, 1961. *Gandhi the Writer : The Image as it Grew*. New Delhi : National Book Trust, 1969.

Mahatma Gandhi. New Delhi : Arnold Heinemann, 1977, 1982.

Socio-Political Currents in Bengal : A Centruy Perspective. New Delhi : Vikas, Publishing House, 1980.

B. Essays

"Europe Behind the Veil." Series of articles in *Hindu* 1930.

"In London Today." Bi-weekly feature in *Hindu* (Madras) 1930.

"This Week in History." Weekly feature in *Hindu* Madras 1935-36.

"Literature and Social Reality." *Aryan Path* 26.9 (1955). Rpt. in Srivasta, Ramesh K., *Perspectives on Bhabani Bhattacharya.* Ghaziabad : Vimal Prakashan, 1982.1-6.

"Indo-Anglian." *The Novel in Modern India.* Bhakhtiyar 45-58. ref. : 186.

"Baseless Prejudice Against Indian Writing in English." *Statesman* (New Delhi) 20 Apr. 1968.

"Hollow Arbiters of the Writer's Destiny." *Statesman* (New Delhi) May 1968.

"How I Wrote *So Many Hungers.*" *Letteraturnaya Gazetta* (Moscow) 1951.

"Tagore as a Novelist." *Rabindranath Tagore 1861-1961 : A Centenary Volume.* New Delhi : Sahitya Akademi, 1961.

"The People of the Village Change their Theme." *Times* (London) 23 Jan. 1961.

"Life Long Dynamism. " (Article on Tagore) *Hemisphere* (Sydney) 1961.

"A Bridge Between the People." *India and South- East Asia,* (Proceedings of a Seminar). New Delhi : Indian Council for Cultural Relations, 1968. 99-101.

"The Nature of Wisdom." *Abbottempo.* North Chicago : Abbott Universal Ltd.1970.

"Women in My Stories." *Journal of Indian Writing in English* 3.2 (1975). 1-6.

V. Interviews

Coppola, Carlo. An Interview. *Mahfil* V. 1-2 (1968-69) : 43-48.

Gemmill, Janet P. An Interview. *World Literature Written in English* 14.2 (1975) : 300-309.

Joshi, Sudhakar. "An Evening with Bhabani." *Sunday Standard* 27 Apr. 1969.

Srivastava, Ramesh K. "Bhattacharya at Work : An Interview." *Perspectives on Bhabani Bhattacharya.* Ghaziabad : Vimal Prakashan, 1982. 218-238.

B. Secondary Sources

I. Bibilographies

2105. Grover, Malta. "Bibliography." *Bhabani Bhattacharya as a Novelist of Social Conscience.* Meerut : Shalabh Prakashan, 1991 : 147-160.

2106. Rai, G. "Bibliography." *Bhabani Bhattacharya : A Study of His Novels.* New Delhi : B.R. Publishing Corporation, 1995. 115-119.

2107. Sharma, K. K. "Select Bibliography." *Bhabani Bhattacharya : His Vision and Themes.* New Delhi : Abhinav Publications, 1979 : 153-156.

2108. Srivastava, Ramesh K. "Select Bibliography." *Perspectives on Bhabani Bhattacharya.* Ghaziabad : Vimal Prakashan, 1982. 239-248.

2109. ——. "Selected Bibliographies." *Six Indian Novelists.* Amritsar : Guru Nank Dev. University, 1987. 343-346.

II. Books

2110. Bhatnagar, M.K. *Political Consciousness in Indian English Writing* (A Study of Manohar Malgonkar, Nayantara Sahgal and Bhabani Bhattacharya). New Delhi : Bahri Publications, 1991.

See 4313.

2111. Chandrasekharan, K.R. *Bhabani Bhattacharya. New* Delhi : Arnold Heinemann, 1974.

The book, an Arnold Heinemann's publication, surveys the works of Bhabani Bhattacharya and evaluates his limitations and achievements. Finds Bhattacharya a vigorous campaigner against anti-life forces seen in the traditional way of life who pleads for a synthesis of values of the past and the present.

The book consists of nine chapters among which five are devoted to individual works while others deal with his other Writings, use of language, his vision of life and art.

2112. Desai, S. K. *Bhabani Bhattacharya.* New Delhi : Sahitya Akademi, 1995.

2113. Grover, Malta. *Bhattacharya as a Novelist of Social Conscience.* Meerut : Shalabh Prakashan, 1991.
An exploration of the novelist's outraged conscience, of the prevalent wrongs and evils of society as expressed in Bhattacharya's works. Finds in his fiction a synthesis between moral and aesthetic concerns.
Among other things the book deals with the biographical details of the novelist, influences on him and his responses to contemporary social issues as well as his use of language and stylistic details.

2114. Rao, B. Shyamala. *Bhabani Bhattacharya and His Works.* Bareilly : Prakash Book Depot, 1982.

2115. Rai, G. *Bhabani Bhattacharya : A Study of His Novels.* New Delhi : B.R. Publishing Corporation, 1995.
The book critically examines the main features of Bhabani Bhattacharya as a novelist — his realism, his humanism and his fictional craft. The first chapter, while throwing light on his life and influences, explains his views of the art of the novel and his major concerns as a novelist. The other chapters deal with the social aspects of realism, his humanistic vision of life and his technique of fiction. Concludes that "Bhattacharya's discussion of the nature and function of art, his organization of the narrative, his portrayal of fully realized characters, his use of wit, humour, irony, satire, images, symbols, allegory and linguistic experiments clearly show that he is a conscious artist of the first water."

2116. Sharma, K.K. *Bhabani Bhattacharya : His Vision and Themes.* New Delhi : Abhinav Publications, 1979.

Studies the dominant themes in the novels of Bhabani Bhattacharya and assesses his vision as a novelist, especially in terms of his concern for social reality. Considers his novels as artistic embodiments of his affirmative vision of life, through a discussion of the various social, political and economic themes with a conclusion as to how there is a synthesis in Bhattacharya's theory and practice of fiction.

2117. Sharma, K.K., ed. *Bhabani Bhattacharya : Some Points of View*. Delhi : K.K. Publications, 1995.
The book is an anthology consisting of fifteen articles written by different scholars on several aspects of Bhattacharya's creative genius. While the first ten articles are devoted to his fictional work, at least one article is on each of his novels, the other five articles focusing on his creative background, world view, socio-political ethos, Gandhian influence and his fictional intent.
See 2137, 2156, 2157, 2160, 2176, 2178, 2182, 2188, 2191, 2211, 2212, 2216, 2221, 2234, 2237.

2118. Shimmer, Dorothy B. *Bhabani Bhattacharya*. Boston : Twayne Publishers, 1975.
This book, one of Twayne's World Author Series, ably touches upon the essential elements of his life and works within the limited compass.
The book consists of one chapter each on the five novels (except *A Dream in Hawaii)* on the short stories and non-fiction.

2119. Sorot, Balaram S. *The Novels of Bhabani Bhattacharya*. New Delhi : Prestige Books, 1991.
Discusses Bhattacharya's novels and short stories with a focus on the theme of modernity and tradition and the contribution the novelist makes to the technique of fiction writing. While making an assessment of Bhattacharya the author compares him with R. K. Narayan.

2120. Srivastava, Ramesh K., ed. *Perspectives on Bhabani Bhattacharya.* Ghaziabad : Vimal Prakashan, 1982.

The book is an anthology of critical essays presenting a Kaleidoscopic view of the various aspects of Bhabani Bhattacharya as a novelist. In addition, the book includes an essay by Bhattacharya "Literature and Social Reality", and an informative interview which offers the novelist's own views on the craft of fiction.

The other articles evaluate his work and achievement basing their argument on the novelist's theory and practice of fiction.

The book consist of 17 essays out of which some of them are general articles taking up the whole oeuvre in their span and others devoted to an examination of one particular novel in detail providing multi-lateral perspectives.

See 653, 2141, 2148, 2153, 2154, 2158, 2162, 2169, 2175, 2190, 2199, 2215, 2218, 2219, 2220, 2225, 2226, 2227.

III. Research Articles

2121. Agnihotri, H.L. "Traces of Gandhi in Bhabani Bhattacharya." *Kurukshetra University Research Journal* (1980-91) : 14-15.

2122. Ameeruddin, Syed. "Social Commitment in Bhattacharya's Novels." *Littcrit* 7, 4.2 (1978) : 20-30.

As a novelist with a purpose Bhattacharya's novels are a protest against the deep rooted social evils of our country.

2123. Arulandram, H.G.S. "Social Consciousness in the Novels of Bhabani Bhattacharya." *Mirror* Feb. 1970 : 96-97.

2124. ——. "Prostitution : Bhattacharya's Observations." *Century* July 1975 : 20-21.

2125. ——. "Bhabani Bhattacharya's Concept of Novel Writing." *Thought* 14 June, 1975 : 17-19.

2126. ——. "Marriage Reforms : Bhattacharya's Suggestions." *Century* July 1976 : 28-29.

2127. ——. "Bhabani Bhattacharya : A Social Reformer." *Rajasthan Journal of English Studies* 1.2 (1975) : 36-38.
Considers Bhattacharya a committed writer who directs his energies in exposing the various social evils of modern India.

2128. ——. "Tagore's Impact on Bhabani Bhattacharya." *Indian Literature* 18.4 (1975) : 27-31. Rpt. in *Journal of English Studies* (Warangal) 8.1 (1976) : 517-520.
Shows how Bhabani Bhattacharya's novels reflect Tagore's philosophy of joyousness and a synthesis of diverse values.

2129. ——. "Bhabani Bhattacharya's Novels : A Note on Theory and Practice." *Banasthali Pathrika* 9.21 (1976) : 10-15.
Evaluates Bhattacharya's novels to show how they illustrate his own theory of the novel.

2130. ——. "Bhabani Bhattacharya's Novels." *Triveni* 46.3 (1977) : 68-73.
Discusses Bhattacharya's credo, in terms of his practice as a novelist.

2131. ——. "A Note on Bhabani Bhattacharya's Medium of Expression." *ELT Forum* 4 (1982) : 21-26: 5.1 (1982) : 25-29.
Discusses Bhattacharya's views on the medium of expression and his experimentation with language and comments that Bhattacharya, like Anand and Raja Rao, attempts "to evolve a kind of idiom to suit to the Indian sensibilities."

2132. ——. "Literary Genius : A Note on Bhabani Bhattacharya." *Dvotana* Apr. 1983 : 20-24.

2133. ——. "Bhabani Bhattacharya's World View." *Commonwealth Novel in English* 2.1 (1983) : 37-64.
Presents Bhattacharya's world view as that of building up of world community with man as its central focus.

2134. ——. "Man and Religion in *A Dream in Hawaii.*" *Literary Half-Yearly* 26.2 (1985) : 27-36. Rpt. in Nagarajan, *et al.* 102-108. ref. : 374.
An analysis of the novel to show how Bhattacharya envisions a man-centred religion : "a religion which measures all values and actions in relation to human personality."

2135. Asnani, Shyam, M. "Form, Technique and Style in Bhattacharya's Novels." *Littcrit* 8 5.1(1979) : 28-41.
A general estimation of Bhattacharya as a novelist with special reference to his thematic and technical complexities.

2136. ——. "The Theme of Famine and Hunger : Bhabani Bhattacharya and Kamala Markandaya." Asnani, *New Dimensions* 11-38. ref. : 197.
Considers Bhabani Bhattacharya and Kamala Markandaya as 'committed' novelists whose concern is social reality as the novels deal with the problems of poverty, pestilence, traditionalism and casteism.

2137. Aston, Natham M. *"He Who Rides A Tiger :* A Stylistic Analysis." Sharma, K.K., *Bhabani Bhattacharya : Some Points of View* 40-52. ref. : 2117.
Discusses certain stylistic tendencies — different strategies of nativisation such as Indianization, literal translations of words, idioms, proverbs and syntax in the novel and shows how they help in establishing author-reader relationship in the novel

2138. ——. "Modes of Address among the Cowhouse Five in Bhabani Bhattacharya's *A Goddess Named Gold." Commonwealth Review* 5.2 (1993-94) : 113-120. Rpt. in Dhawan, *Indian Literature Today* 113-120. ref. : 258.

Studies the modes of addresses and how they modify and establish interpersonal relationships in the novel.

2139. Badal, R.K. "Bhabani Bhattacharya and His Novels." *Literary Half-Yearly* 12.2 (1971) : 71-85.
An assessment of Bhattacharya as a novelist of social reality whose novels reveal a curious blend of horror and pathos.

2140. Bhatt, P. N. "The Impact of Gandhi on Dr. Bhabani Bhattacharya's Novels." *Indian P.E.N.* Jan.-Feb. 1984 : 19-21. Rpt. in *Triveni* 54.3 (1985) : 83-86.
A documentation of Bhattacharya's novels to show the influence of Gandhi and Tagore.

2141. Boparaj, Harcharan Singh. "The Achievement of Bhabani Bhattacharya." Srivastava, R.K. *Perspectives on Bhabani Bhattacharya* 200-217. ref. : 2120.
Considers Bhattacharya a world-class novelist whose "achievement does not lie in the portrayal of life alone, it lies in the vision of life which he conveys through it."

2142. ——. "Bhabani Bhattacharya's Response to Colonialism in India." Srivastava, R.K. *Colonial Consciousness* 113-126. ref. : 526.
Examines Bhabani Bhattacharya's response to the colonial rule in India with special reference to the Gandhian movement between 1930-44 as evidenced in his novels *So Many Hungers* and *He Who Rides a Tiger.*

2143. Chakravartee, Moutashi. "Political Freedom and Creative Response : A Study of *So Many Hungers* and *Azadi.*" Dinesh and Joshi 52-57. ref. : 263.
Discusses *So Many Hungers* and *Azadi* as two creative responses to political unrest, nationalist upsurge and partition and comments that political freedom may cost many things yet there is a fresh resurgence of human dignity.

2144. Chakravorty, D.K. "An Approach to the Short Stories of Bhabani Bhattacharya." Chakravorty 56–62. ref. : 230.

An explication of the bond of kinship of various shades and significance in some of the short stories of Bhattacharya ("Pilgrims in Uniform", "The Faltering Pendulum", "The Quack" & "Steel Hawk") to show that this bond of kinship with the people and the objects around the fictional characters provide a key to understand and evaluate the stories better.

2145 ——. "The Novel as a document : An Approach to Bhabani Bhattacharya's *So Many Hungers."* Chakravorty 24-29. ref. : 230.

Describes the novel as "a powerful document of the great national calamity" — the fight for independence and the great Bengal famine.

2146 ——. "The Pursuit of Obscure Salvations : An Approach to Indian Novels in English." Chakravorty 69-76. ref. : 230.

See 669.

2147. —— "Of Gods and Demons : A Study of Bhabani Bhattacharya's *A Goddess Named Gold."* Chakravorty 16-23. ref. : 230.

Describes the novel as one depicting the fight between good and evil forces.

2148. Crawford Cromwell. "Bhabani Bhattacharya : A Mediating Man." Srivastava, R.K., *Persectives on Bhabani Bhattacharya* 7-20. ref. : 2120.

A study of the man behind the letters. An illumination of Bhattacharya's personality depicting him as a mediating man between East and West.

2149. Dayal, B. "Minor Indo-Anglian Short Story Writers : Kaleidoscopic View." Dayal 220-234. ref. : 257.

An assessment of Bhattacharya as a short story writer and his contribution to Indian short story in English.

See 700.

2150. Desai, S.K. "Bhabani Bhattacharya : The Writer Who Rides a Tiger." Naik, *Perpectives* 119-134. ref. : 381.
Traces Bhattacharya's development as a novelist and comments that Bhabani Bhattaharya "has come a long way from poetry (in *So Many Hungers)* to irony and satire (in *A Dream in Hawaii*).

2151. Dhar, T.N. "Bhabani Bhattacharya's *He Who Rides a Tiger :* The Role Playing Matrix." *English Studies in India* (1983) : 26-36. Rpt. in Gupta, *Studies* 93-103. ref. : 285.
Discusses the role-playing of Kalo as a key to the structuring of the novel's fictional experience.

2152. ——. "The Image of Woman in Bhattacharya's Fiction." Radha 1-10. ref. : 442.
Against the critics like Marlene Fisher who consider that women hold a significant place in Bhabani Bhattacharya's novels argues that Bhattacharya denies to the woman her aspiration to be herself.

2153. Dhawan, R. K. "Bhabani Bhattacharya's Narrative Technique." Srivastava, R.K., *Perspectives on Bhabani Bhattacharya* 185-199. ref. : 2120.
Evaluates the various devices of story telling employed by Bhattacharya to reveal his "complete assimilation of technical knowledge in the act of unfolding the story."

2154. Fisher, Marlene. "The Women in Bhattacharya's Novels." *World Literature Written in English* 11.1 (1972) : 95-108. Rpt. in Srivastava, R.K., *Perspectives on Bhabani Bhattacharya* 66-82. ref. : 2120.
Focuses on Bhattacharya's treatment of women both as individuals and as symbols in his fiction and shows that the significant content of a given novel and its artistic centre of interest lie in the women characters.

2155. ——. "Personal and Social Change in Bhattacharya's Novels." *World Literature Written in English* 12.2 (1973) : 288-296.

Shows how Bhattacharya's novels deal "with the efforts of human beings to forge and to fulfil workable and communal ideals and, perforce, with the struggle to reconcile individual and social goals."

2156. Gaur, Rashmi. *"So Many Hungers* : Restructuring of Society and Human Personality." Sharma, K. K., *Bhabani Bhattacharya: Some points of View* 1-10 ref. : 2117.

Finds two distinct strains in Bhattacharya's novels in general and in *So Many Hungers* in particular — the realistic and the idealistic. Claims that the novel attempts to reproduce the truth in terms of the reality and also insists on "a commitment to social restructuring" (to motivate the people towards recognition of the ills prevalent in the society).

2157. Gautam, G.L. "*So Many Hungers* : A Single Dimensional View of Reality." Sharma K.K., *Bhabani Bhattacharya: Some Points of View* 11-17. ref. : 2117.

Evaluates critically to show how far Bhattacharya has succeeded in presenting a true picture of contemporary reality.

2158. Goyal, Bhagwat S. "The Sensuous and the Sublime: Bhabani Bhattacharya's *A Dream in Hawaii.*" Srivastava, R.K., *Perspectives on Bhabani Bhattacharya* 179-184. ref. : 2120.

Considers the novel as an expression of the philosophic — cultural duality of the East and the West — the fusion of the sensuous and the sublime.

2159. ——. "Bhattacharya's *A Dream in Hawaii.*" Goyal, *Culture and Commitment* 119-123. ref. : 281.

Presents the novel as an artistic achievement of Bhattacharya: "it breaks new ground in structural vitality and an intimacy of suggestiveness that function together to invest the novel with a deeper philosophical, cultural and social significance."

2160. ——. "The Metaphysics of Absence and the Seductions of Phallogo-centric Discourse: A (Mis) Reading of Bhattacharya's *A Dream in Hawaii.*" Sharma K.K., *Bhabani Bhattacharya : Some Points of View* 92-102. ref. : 2117.
Examines how the phallo-centric and logo-centric concerns are blended into the novel's structured corporeality and spirituality to show how the narrative logic of the novel "is surcharged with a rigorously subversive potential."

2161. Gupta, G.S. Balarama. "Bhabani Bhatacharya's *So Many Hungers* : A Study." Naik, *Aspects* 209-221. ref. : 378.
Discusses the significance of the title to the novel's major concerns and illustrates how "contemporary history can be transformed by a socially conscious artist into fiction of permanent relevance to mankind."

2162. ——. "*Steel Hawk and Other Stories* : An Evaluation." Srivastava, R.K., *Perspectives on Bhabani Bhattacharya* 166-178. ref. : 2120.
An evaluation of Bhattacharya's short stories to emphasize the merits of Bhattacharya as a short story writer. Though the stories reveal Bhattacharya's varied interests and his keen sense of observation, the lack of technical perfection hampers his recognition on a top-ranking short story writers.

2163. Gupta, L.N. "Bhabani Bhattacharya: A Bridge between India and the West." *Hitavada* 29 March 1969.

2164. Harrex, S. C. "Bhabani Bhattacharya." *Contemporary Novelists.* 2 ed., 153-157. ref. : 234.

2165. Hemenway, Stephen I. "Bhabani (sic) Bhattacharya." Hemenway. 36-45 ref. : 290.
A general assessment of Bhabani Bhattacharya as a novelist drawing attention to his merits and demerits.

2166. Iyengar, K.R. Srinivasa. "Ideal and Real in Bhabani Bhattacharya's Novels." *Swarajya* 13 (1968) : 13 -14.

2167. ——. "Bhabani Bhattacharya and Manohar Malgonkar." Iyengar, *Indian Writing in English* 412-434. ref. : 297.

2168. Jain, Jasbir. "Coming to Terms with Gandhi: *Shadow from Ladakh." Journal of Indian Writing in English* 3.2 (1975) : 20-22.
Analyses *Shadow from Ladakh* to show how it explores the meanings of Gandhian thought in human terms. While discussing Gandhian ethics, their validity and relevance in the post-Independent India and placing Gandhi in the true perspective the author finds Bhaskar (one of the characters of the novel) as "New Gandhi" against Satyajit (another character of the same novel) who is believed to be "the true Gandhi."

2169. ——. "Human Dimensions of Stasis and Growth." Srivastava, R.K., *Perspectives on Bhabani Bhattacharya* 52-65. ref. : 2120.
An exploration of the various dimensions of individual freedom in Bhattacharya's novels to show that the basic issue central to his fiction "is one of an integral vision which can only grow out of a living understanding and compassion, not out of the imposition of a philosophy or an ideology and definitely not out of a static tradition...."

2170. Jha, Rama. "Bhabani Bhattacharya : The Novelist of Gandhian Social Realism." Jha 153-174. ref. : 306.
Discusses the ethical, moral and social aspects embedded in the novels of Bhabani Bhattacharya particularly in *So Many Freedoms*, and shows how they have been drawn from the Gandhian vision of life.

2171. Jha, K.S. "Bhabani Bhattacharya : The Humanist — A Critical Study of His Novels." *Indian Journal of English Studies* 22 (1982-1983) : 139-151.
Analyses Bhattacharya's first five novels *(So Many Hungers, Music for Mohini, He Who Rides the Tiger, A Goddess Named Gold* and *Shadow From Ladakh)* to

show that they are novels of 'human centrality,' dealing with the themes of hunger (various dimensions of hunger) and freedom (different kinds of freedom).

2172. Juneja, Punim. "The East-West Theme: *Some Inner Fury, The Serpent and the Rope* and *A Dream in Hawaii.*" Dhawan, *Commonwealth Fiction.* Vol.1. 178–197. ref.: 256.
Examines the novels to show the difference in the treatment of the East-West theme by the three writers. Finds Bhattacharya's positive approach to the problem of East-West of encounter as an enlightening one.

2173. Kalinnikova, E.J. "Ob ideinoi napravlenoste ramà Bhabhani Bhattacharya 'Boginiazoloto' (About the ideological direction of the novel of Bhabani Bhattacharya, *A Goddess Named Gold*)." *Akademija Nauk* SSSR (Moscow) 80 (1965) : 50-56.

2174. ——. "The Winner of Evil Forces: Bhabani Bhattacharya." Kalinnikova 87-96. ref. : 316.
Points out some of the peculiarities in the development of critical realism in Bhattacharya's works.

2175. ——. "The Problems of Bhabani Bhattacharya's Novels: A Survey." Srivastava, R.K., *Perspectives on Bhabani Bhattacharya* 101-110. ref. : 2120.
A survey of Bhattacharya's novels to show how Bhattacharya has dealt with the social, political and psychological problems and the solutions he offered. Traces Bhattacharya's essential ideas to Gandhism.

2176. Kansal, S.M. "The Eternal Conflict: Patterns of Struggle in Bhattacharya's Novels." Sharma, K.K., *Bhabani Bhattacharya : Some Points of View* 110-117. ref. : 2117.
Shows how the different types of struggles (within and outside) are various facets of the eternal struggle between good and evil, which, in Bhabani Bhattacharya, reveals itself in the portrayal of social reality.

2177. Krishnaswamy, Shanta. "Bhabani Bhattacharya: The Pure Woman as Victim." Krishnaswamy 60-82. ref. : 334.
Traces Bhattacharya's concept of the innocent victimised women as a motif running through all his novels and shows that these victims are pure women who reform society and redeem mankind.

2178. Kusum Lata. "The Background to Bhabani Bhattacharya's Fiction." Sharma, K.K., *Bhabani Bhattacharya . Some Points of View* 136-149. ref. : 2117.
A brief discussion of the major events in Bhattacharya's life and the influences on him that moulded his mind and art.

2179. Lal, P. *"Shadow from Ladakh :* A Note." *Language Forum* 7.1-4 (Apr. 1981- Mar. 1982) : 51-50. Rpt. in Dhawan, *Explorations* 169-171. ref. : 253.
While "there are parts which are brilliant in their sensitive handling of feeling and relationship," the tone and texture of the novel are weak and the stylistic naivete and over-simplification hamper the flow of the story which is a strong point in Bhattacharya's novels.

2180. Mahashabde, Ashok. "Victim Consciousness in the Early Novels of Bhabani Bhattacharya." Bande, *Victim Consciousness* 67-73. ref. : 206.

2181. Marshal, Prem Kumari. "The Global village in Ruby Wiebe's *Peace Shall Destroy Many* and Bhabani Bhattacharya's A *Dream in Hawaii." Literary Half-Yearly* 36.1 (1995): 80-93.
Analyses Wiebe's *Peace Shall Destroy Many* and Bhattacharya's *A Dream in Hawaii* in the light of global concerns such as peace, religion, humanism and universal values.

2182. Mishra, A. K. "The Gandhian Overtone in the Novels of Bhabani Bhattacharya." Sharma, K.K., *Bhabani Bhattacharya : Some Points of View* 103-109. ref. : 2117.

Tracing the Gandhian ideals of truth, love, chastity etc. in Bhattacharya's novels, pleads for a synthesis between asceticism and modern technology for the resurgence of India.

2183. Mukherjee, Dhurjati. "Indo-Anglian Writers : Anand and Bhattacharya." *Society and Commerce* 2.2 (Apr. 1973): 104-105.

2184. Nahal, Chaman. "Indian Political Novel: Mulk Raj Anand, Bhabani Bhattacharya and Nayantara Sahgal." Nahal 134-151. ref. : 376.

2185. Narayana, T. "Writer with a Social Purpose." *Hindu* 20 Nov. 1988, vii. "Literature".

2186. Pandia, Mahendra N. "Relevance of Bhattacharya's Fiction. An obituary note." *Indian P.E.N.* 50.10-12 (1989) : 6-10.
Discusses briefly some of the novels of Bhattacharya — *So Many Freedoms, He Who Rides the Tiger, Shadow from Ladakh* and *A Dream in Hawaii* and their social and political relevance to the times.

2187. Pandeya S. M. (in collaboration with T.N. Dhar). "Bhattacharya's *Shadow From Ladakh.*" Pandeya 217-251. ref. : 413. Rpt. in Prabhakar 233-247. ref. : 433.
Discusses "the dual structure" of the novel, uniting the story of Satyajit and his Gandhian mask. Also deals with the structure of the novel from the point of view of Indian poetics (especially that of *Vibhava*) and also the novel's technical complexities.

2188. Pathak, R.S. "Human Predicament and Bhabani Bhattacharya's Integrated vision." Sharma K. K., *Bhabani Bhattacharya : Some Points of View* 118-128. ref. : 2117.
Designating Bhabani Bhattacharya as a practical idealist, traces the message of synthesis in his novels.

2189. Raizada, Harish. "Bhabani Bhattacharya : Novelist of Social

Ferment." *Language Forum* 7.1-4 (Apr. 1981-Mar. 1982) : 157-168. Rpt. in Dhawan, *Explorations* 157-168. ref. : 253. Also in Prasad, H.M., *Response* 127-149. ref. : 436.

Treats Bhattacharya's novels as "allegories of the revolutionary sensibility needed for the building up of new forms of life."

2190. ——. "Fiction as Allegory : Novels of Bhabani Bhattacharya." Srivastava, R.K. *Perspectives on Bhabani Bhattacharya* 83-100. ref. : 2120.

Shows how Bhattacharya made use of the allegorical mode to analyse contemporary society and to signify deeper moral values needed for the reconstruction of a new India.

2191. ——. "Symbolism in Bhabani Bhattacharya with reference to *Music for Mohini.*" Sharma, K.K., *Bhabani Bhattacharya : Some Points of View* 18-33. ref. : 2117. Also in Srivastava, R.K., *Symbolism* 72-87. ref. : 527.

Explicates the symbolic configuration beneath the realistic details and shows how Bhattacharya by using symbolic perception creates a new technique of "symbolic realism" in his novels to reveal his world view and express the hidden recesses and motives of human heart citing *Music for Mohini* as an example.

2192. Ram, Atma. "The Theme of Hunger in *So Many Hungers.*" *Rajasthan Journal of English Studies* 14 (1984) : 69–73. Rpt. in Ram, *Essays* 51-56. ref. : 454.

Examines the structural unity for the novel in terms of the theme of hunger.

2193. ——. Bhabani Bhattacharya : A Novelist of Humanity." *Advance* Feb. 1990 : 38-40. Rpt. in Ram, *Morality in Tess and Other Essays* 58-61 ref. : 456.

A brief assessment of Bhattacharya as a novelist.

2194. Ramachandraiah, P. "The Short Stories of Bhabani

Bhattacharya." *Literary Endeavour* 6.1-4 (1985) : 68-82.
Considers the stories as richly imaginative showing the ingenuity of the artist.

2195. Ramakrishna, D. "Academies and Yogies : Reflections on the Recent Indian English Fiction." *Journal of Indian Writing in English* 7.2(1979) : 89-96.
See 1096.

2196. ——. "Bhabani Bhattacharya's *A Dream in Hawaii* : A Study in Postcolonial Spirituality." *Kakatiya Journal of English Studies* 18(1998) : 45-52.

2197. Rani, T. Asoka. "Nationalism in Bhabani Bhattacharya's *So Many Hungers* and *Shadow from Ladakh.*" *Revaluations* 1.3 (1995) : 86-93.
Traces the nationalistic concerns delineated in the novels and comments that *So Many Hungers* upholds Gandhian ideals of non-violence and passive resistance whereas *Shadow from Ladakh* questions the validity of the very ideals of Gandhi in the changed context of post-independence scenario.

2198. Rao, A.V. Krishna. "*Shadow from Ladakh* : A Critical View Point." *Literary Endeavour* 1.2 (1979) : 77-80.
Shadow from Ladakh is viewed as a symbolic illumination of the deterministic patterns of life in modern India under the impact of a multifaceted change.

2199. ——. "*He Who Rides a Tiger* : A Study." Srivastava, R.K., *Perspectives on Bhabani Bhattacharya* 141-148. ref. : 2120. Rpt. in Prabhakar 225-232. ref. : 433.
He Who Rides a Tiger "is an authentic artistic attempt at revealing ironically and imaginatively the complex relationship between the mask and identity in the web of circumstances."

2200. Rao, B. Shyamala. "Bhabani Bhattacharya as a Novelist."

Triveni 40.1 (Apr. 1971) : 35-40.
A general assessment.

2201. ——. "Bhabani Bhattacharya as a Short Story Writer." *Century* 15 Aug. 1971 : 27-28; 21 Aug. 1971 : 15.

2202. Ray, Lila. "Bhabani Bhattacharya : A Profile." *Indian Literature* 11.2 (1968) : 73-76.
A brief survey of Bhattacharya's works to explain his world-view. Illustrates his constructive and purposeful outlook on life which reveals abundant humour.

2203. Reddy, K. Venkata. "An Approach to Bhabani Bhattacharya's *So Many Hungers.*" *Journal of South Asian Literature* 22.2 (1987) : 43-48. Rpt. as "Man's Inhumanity to Man : *So Many Hungers.*" in Reddy, K. Venkata, *Major Indian Novelists* 60-68. ref. : 475.
Considers the novel as a "sincere and artistic embodiment of Bhatacharya's affirmative vision of life."

2204. ——. "A Legend to Inspire and Awaken : *He Who Rides a Tiger.*" Reddy, Venkata *Major Indian Novelists* 69-77. ref. : 475.
Considers *He Who Rides a Tiger* Bhattacharya's masterpiece for its appeal is manifold : as a moral fantasy, as a type of "rasa-inspired art work", and so on.

2205. ——. "Bhabani Bhattacharya : A Writer with a Social Purpose." *Triveni* 62.1 (1993) : 31-33.
Traces the development of Bhattacharya as a novelist, especially in terms of the quest motif.

2206. Reddy, T. Vasudeva. "Tradition *Versus* Modernity in Bhattacharya's *Music for Mohini.*" *Rajasthan Journal of English Studies* 9 (1988) : 21-29.
Considers *Music for Mohini* as a novel which analyses the conflict between tradition and modernity in all its phases — ideological, sociological, ethnological and psychological.

2207. Roy, Ashutosh. "Bhabani Bhattacharya : *A Goddess Named Gold.*" *Quest* (Ranchi) 9 & 10.1-2 (1995) : 47-52.

2208. "Rural World of Bhabani." *Enlite* 14 Sep. 1968 : 3, 27-30.

2209. Sandhu, Ramandeep S. "Bhabani Bhattacharya." Dwivedi *Studies in Contemporary short stories* 63-76. ref. : 271.

2210. Sarma, S. Krishna and V. Rangan. "What is in a Dream? A Critical Appraisal of Bhabani Bhattacharya's *A Dream in Hawaii." Literary Endeavour* 1.3 (1980) : 85-96.
A critical evaluation of the novel. Though *A Dream in Hawaii* is a novel with many facets and layers of meaning, the novel does not signify Bhattacharya's advancement in the art.

2211. Savita, J.P. *"Music for Mohini :* A Note." Sharma, K.K., *Bhabani Bhattacharya : Some Points of View* 33-39. ref. : 2117.
Finds the novel as something different from all the other novels of Bhattacharya and gives reasons for its uniqueness. Considers it as a novel of character which in turn is a study in psychology.

2212. Sharma B.D. "The Gandhian Resistance in the Crucible in *Shadow from Ladakh."* Sharma K.K., *Bhabani Bhattacharya : Some Points of View* 64-71. ref. : 2117.
Discusses the novel in terms of Gandhian ideology — the technique of passive resistance — and shows how far this technique has been useful in solving the problems posed in the novel.

2213. Sharma, Jayanti. "The Mother in Bhabani Bhattacharya's *So Many Hungers."* Bande, *Mothers and Mother Figures* 128-133. ref. : 205.
Explores the role played by Kajoli's mother and shows how her chaste ways of life create a healthy influence on her family.

2214. Sharma, K.K. "Bhabani Bhattacharya's *So Many Hungers :* An Affirmative Vision of Life." Sharma, K.K., *Indo-English Literature* 201-214. ref. : 501. Rpt. as "The Everlasting Yea : Bhabani Bhattacharya's View of Life" in Dwivedi, *Studies in Contemporary Indian Fiction* 191-212. ref. : 269.

Finds *So Many Hungers* an artistic presentation of Bhattacharya's affirmative vision of life.

2215. ——. "Bhattacharya's Aesthetics." Srivastava, R. K., *Perspectives on Bhabani Bhattacharya* 28-40. ref. : 2120.

An evaluation of Bhattacharya's mind and art through an examination of his thoughts on art, literature and fiction.

2216. ——. "*Shadow from Ladakh :* The Ideal of Integration and Synthesis." Sharma, K.K., *Bhabani Bhattacharya : Some Points of View* 72-82. ref. : 2117.

Shows how the novel gives expression to an integration between the conflicting issues of "steel civilization" and Gandhian asceticism.

2217. Sharma, P. P. "Bhabani Bhattacharya : A Novelist with Social conscience." *Rajasthan Journal of English Studies* 13 & 14 (1981) : 52-61.

Shows how Bhattacharya as a novelist of social conscience has expressed his tolerance and understanding of different segments of society in his novels.

2218. ——. "Bhabani Bhattacharya : Artist/Propagondist?" Srivastava, R.K., *Perspectives on Bhabani Bhattacharya* 41-51. ref. : 2120.

Illustrates that the artist and propagandist in Bhattacharya are kept in perfect poise and in a delicate balance.

2219. Sharma, Som P. "Mohini and the Quaternio of the Feminine Prinicple." Srivastava, R.K., *Perspectives on Bhabani Bhattacharya* 127-140. ref. : 2120.

Analyses the character of Mohini the heroine of Bhattacharya's *Music for Mohini* from different angles

— as mother, companion or *hetaira,* Amazon and medium of the feminine Prinicple.

2220. ——. "Gandhian Influence on the Writings of Bhabani Bhattacharya." *South Asian Review* 5.2 (1981) : 74-81. Srivastava, R.K., *Perspecives on Bhabani Bhattacharya* 21-27. ref. : 2120.
A brief study of Bhattacharya's novels to show the influence of Gandhi and Tagore on his writings.

2221. Singh, Kh Kunjo. "Socio-Cultural and Politico-Economic Reflections in the Novels of Bhabani Bhattacharya." Sharma, K.K. *Bhabani Bhattacharya : Some Points of View* 129-135. ref. : 2117.
Shows how Bhattacharya's novels reflect both the positive and negative aspects of Indian life and culture.

2222. Singh, R.S. "Bhabani Bhattacharya : A Novelist of Dreaming Wisdom." *Banasthali Patrika* 13 (1969) : 60-75.
Discusses how Bhattacharya heightens our awareness of the undercurrents of history based on his own evaluation of human society.

2223. ——. "From Social Criticism to Utopianism : Bhabani Bhattacharya." Singh, R.S., *Indian Novel in English.* 96-117. ref. : 513.
A general assessment of Bhattacharya as a novelist, comments that while Bhattacharya's novels not only give expression to the socio-political situation in India but also become pointers to the possibility of creating a better world inculcating faith in man and his future.

2224. Sircar, Arjya. "Duplicity in Saffron Robes : A Contrastive Study of *The Guide, He Who Rides a Tiger* and *Putul Nacher Itikatha." New Quest* 33, May-June 1982 :163-168.
A contrastive study of the theme of duplicity in saffron robbed men in R. K. Narayan's *The Guide,* Bhattacharya's *He Who Rides a Tiger* and Manik Bandopdhaya's *Putul Nacher Itikatha* which points out

the differences in the use of irony that operate at different levels in the three novels : at the personal level in *The Guide,* at the social level in *He Who Rides a Tiger,* and at the moral level in *Putul Nacher Ithikatha.*

2225 Srivastava, Narsingh. "Symbol and Allegory in *A Goddess Named Gold." Rajasthan Journal of English Studies* 13 & 14 (1981) : 106-126. Rpt. in Srivastava, R.K., *Perspectives on Bhabani Bhattacharya* 149-165. ref. : 2120. Also in Bhatnagar, *Essays.* ref. : 221. Also in Srivatsava, R.K., *Symbolism* 88-102. ref. : 527.
A comprehensive analysis of the allegorical pattern of *A Goddess Named Gold* to show that it is "a powerful allegory of the meaning and purpose of freedom as well as of its failure besides being the pursuit and worship of the gold goddess."

2226. Srivastava, Ramesh K. "Bhabani Bhattacharya's Prose Style." Srivastava, R. K., *Perspectives on Bhabani Bhattacharya* 111-126. ref. : 2120. Rpt. in Srivastava, R.K., *Six Indian Novelists* 254-271. ref. : 525.
Brings into focus the variety in and experimentation of Bhattacharya's style which will reflect his broad outlook, his vision and maturity.

2227. ——. "Introduction." Srivastava, R.K., *Perspectives on Bhabani Bhattacharya* ref. : 2120.
A critical introduction comprising an account of the novelist's life and worldview, his theory and practice of fiction, treatment of various themes, symbolism and allegory, characterization and narrative technique.

2228. ——. "The Theme of Hunger in Bhattacharya and Kamala Markandaya." *Language Forum* 7.1-4 (Apr. 1981– Mar. 1982) : 172-183. Rpt. in Dhawan, *Explorations* 192-83. ref. : 253. Also in Srivastava, R.K., *Six Indian Novelists* 223-238. ref. : 525.
A comparative study of Bhattacharya's *So Many Hungers* and Markandaya's *Nectar in a Sieve* to show

the similarities and differences in their treatment of the theme.

2229. ——. Bhattacharya's *Shadow from Ladakh* : A Study." Pradhan 155-173. ref. : 434. Rpt. in Srivastava, R.K., *Six Indian Novelists* 239-253. ref. : 525.
A critical appreciation of the novel both at its thematic and structural levels. Against the detractors the author justifies Bhattacharya's use of contemporary material in a literary work and shows didacticism as a part of Bhattacharya's concept of the novel.

2230. Swain, S.P "Self and Society : A Study in Bhabhani Bhattacharya's *So Many Hungers.*" *Journal of Indian Writing in English* 25.1-2 (1997) : 97-105.

2231. Tarinayya, M. "Two Novels : Bhabani Bhattacharya's *So Many Hungers* and Khushwant Singh's *Train to Pakistan.*" *Indian Literature* 13.1 (1970) : 113-121. Rpt. in Narasimhaiah, *Indian Literature of the Past Fifty Years* 177-202. ref. : 389.
Considers the two novels as transcreations of history the events of which have a bearing on our national life.

2232. Tamilarasan, C. "Bhabani Bhattacharya's *Music for Mohini*: A Study." *Literary Endeavour* 2.4 (1981) : 35-43.
A study of the treatment of the theme of tradition *versus* modernity in *Music for Mohini*.

2233. Tripathi, Bimalesh Kumar. "Bhabani Bhattacharya's *He Who Rides a Tiger* : Socio-Economic Study." *Quest* (Ranchi) 1.1 (1987) : 11-21.
Examines the personal problems of man in the light of the larger socio-economic conditions and political situations and their effect on the individual psychology as is evidenced in the characters of *He Who Rides a Tiger*.

2234. Tripathy, J.P. "*A Goddess Named Gold* : A Study in Structure and Texture." Sharma, K. K., *Bhabani*

Bhattacharya : *Some Points of View* 53-63. ref. : 2117.

Deals with the dramatization of conflict between the human welfare ideal and man's selfishness, between altruism and egoism as evidenced in the novel achieved through several structural devices.

2235. Varma, R.V. "The Breakdown of Village-Community in Indo-Anglian Fiction." Varma 14-31. ref. : 539. Rpt. in Saxena, *Glimpses* Vol. 2. 174-191. ref. : 497. See 1249.

2236. Vinoda, T. "*Music for Mohini* : A Classic of Flawed Perspective." *Kakatiya Journal of English Studies* 13 (1993) : 13-22.

Delineates Mohini as an emerging new woman struggling for self-fulfilment at the beginning and transforms herself into another Sita or Savithri, contented with the enslaving career of motherhood and house-wifery later.

2237. Viswas, Asha. "Structure of Desire in Bhabani Bhattacharya's Short Stories." Sharma K.K., *Bhabani Bhattacharya: Some Points of View* 83-91. ref. : 2117.

Studies some of the short stories and describes them as "maieutic" as they bring forth hidden human desires.

2238. Weir, Ann Lowry. "Courtesans and Prostitutes in South Asian Literature (re. R.K. Narayan, Bhabani Bhattacharya and others)." *The Image of the Prostitutes in Modern Literature.* Eds. Pierre L. Horn and Mary Bath Pringle. New York : Frederick Ungar, 1984.

2239. Yadagiri, K. "Spiritualism *Vs.* Materialism in Bhabani Bhattacharya's *A Dream in a Hawaii." Triveni* 64.3 (1995) : 36-40.

Discusses how neither strict asceticism (represented by Neeloy Mukherjee) nor rank materialism (represented by Stella Gregson) achieve meaning in the lives of the characters.

IV. Reviews

2240. Archer, Rosanne. "Tragi-Comedy in India, 1947." Rev. of *A Goddess Named Gold. New York Herald Tribune Book Review* 28 Aug. 1960 : 11.

2241. Arulandram, H.G.S. Rev. of *A Dream in Hawaii. Commonwealth Novel in English* (1982).

2242. Boyle, F.A. Rev. of *He Who Rides a Tiger. Library Journal 79,* 15 Sep. 1954 : 1588.

2243. Brandel, Sarah Ensley. Rev. of *Shadow From Ladakh. Literature East & West* 11 (1967) : 209-10.

2244. Coppola, Carlo. Rev. of *A Dream in Hawaii. World Literature Today* 58.3 (1984) : 472.

2245. Forbes, Harriet. Rev. of *Music for Mohini. Library Journal* 77, 1 June 1952 : 1011.

2246. Geevak. Rev. of *A Dream in Hawaii. Surya India* 3.7 (Apr. 1979) : 36-37.

2247. ——. Rev. of *A Dream in Hawaii. Book Review* May-June 1979 : 30-31.

2248. Goyal, Bhagwat S. "No Dream is for Sale." Rev. of *A Dream in Hawaii. Humanastic Review* 1.1 (1979) : 34-37.

2249. Grindly, F. H. Rev. of *A Goddess Named Gold. Christian Science Monitor* 8 Sep. 1960 : 7.

2250. "Heightened Perceptions." Rev. of *Music for Mohini. Times Literary Supplement* 29 May 1959 : 326.

2251. Hitrec, Joseph. "Indian Path-finder." Rev. of *He Who Rides a Tiger. Saturday Review* 37, 20 Nov. 1954 : 34.

2252. ——. "Magic Alone Could not Do the Trick." Rev. of *A Goddess Named Gold. New York Times Book Review* 21 Aug. 1960, Sec. 7 : 4

2253. "Holding By the Neck." Rev. of *He Who Rides a Tiger. Times Literary Supplement* 5 Feb. 1960 : 86.

2254. Holsaert, Eunice. "Astride Two Worlds." Rev. of *Music for Mohini. New York Times Book Review* 15 June 1952, Sec. 7 : 16.

2255. Lask, Thomas. "Rolling Hills and Hunger Strikes." Rev. of *Shadow from Ladakh. New York Times.* 1 June 1966.

2256. M.D. "Three Indian Novels." Rev. of Thakazhi's *Two Measures of Rice,* Menon Marath's *The Sale of an Island,* Bhattacharya's *Shadow from Ladakh. Hindustan Times* (Mag) 12 Jan. 1969 : 111.

2257. Mann, C.W. Rev. of *A Goddess Named Gold. Library Journal* 85, 1 Sep. 1960 : 2955.

2258. Nandakumar, Prema. "The Amulet Gandhiji Gave." Rev. of *A Goddess Named Gold. Swarajya* 28 July 1962.

2259. Narayan, Shyamala A. "Music and Philosophy." Rev. of *Music for Mohini. Times of India* 23 May 1976 : 10.

2260. Parvathi. Rev.of *So Many Hungers. Commonwealth Quarterly* 3.12(1979) : 99-100.

2261. Parton, Margaret. "He Rode a Lie as if It were a Tiger." Rev. of *He Who Rides a Tiger. New York Herald Tribune* (Book Review) 24 Oct. 1954 : 20.

2262. ——. Rev. of *A Goddess Named Gold. Saturday Review* 43,3 Sep.1960 : 20.

2263. Payne, Robert. Rev. of *Music for Mohini. Saturday Review* 35, 28 June 1952 : 12.

2264. ——. Rev. of *He Who Rides a Tiger. New York Times Book Review* 24 Oct. 1954 : 5.

2265. Prasher, Madhu. "More Telling Than Showing." Rev. of *A Dream in Hawaii. Indian Literary Review* 1.12 & 2.1 (1979).

2266. Prescott, Orville. "Books of the Times." Rev. of *He Who Rides A Tiger. New York Times* 28 Dec. 1954.

2267. Rao, K.S. Narayana. Rev. of *Steel Hawk and Other Stories. Books Abroad* 44 (1970) : 355-356.

2268. Rev. of *Music for Mohini. New York Herald Tribune* 3 Aug. 1952 : 8.

2269. Rev. of *Music for Mohini. Kirkus* 20, 1 Aug. 1952 : 234.

2270. Rev. of *Music for Mohini. Book List* 48, 1 July 1952 : 360.

2271. Rev. of *He Who Rides a Tiger. Kirkus* 22, 1 Sep. 1954 : 591.

2272. Rev. of *He Who Rides a Tiger. Book List* 51, 15 Nov. 1954 : 132.

2273. Rev. of *A Goddess Named Gold. Kirkus* 28, 15 July 1960 : 570.

2274. Rev. of *A Goddess Named Gold. Booklist* 57, 1 Oct. 1960 : 87.

2275. Sharpe, Patricia L. Rev. of *Shadow from Ladakh. Mahfil* 5. 1-2 (1968-69) : 134-138.

2276. Snyder, M.B. Rev. of *Music for Mohini. Chicago Tribune* (Sunday). 10 Aug. 1952 : 4.

2277. Sohi, Harinder. Rev. of *A Dream in Hawaii. Indian Book Chronicle* 16 Oct. 1979 : 343-344.

2278. Stock, A.G. "Kinds of Dedication." Rev. of *Shadow from Ladakh. Journal of Commonwealth Literature* 5 (1968) : 124-125.

2279. Sundaram, P.S. Rev.of *A Dream in Hawaii. Hindustan Times* 29 July 1979 : IV.

2280. Sweeny, Mary K. "More Than Glitter." Rev. of *A Goddess Named Gold. America* 8 Oct. 1960.

2281. Towle, Lawrence. "A Changing World." Rev. of *Shadow from Ladakh. Courant Magazine* 21 Aug. 196[illegible]

2282. Tucker, Gretchen. Rev. *Contemporary Short Stories. Mahfil* 5.1-2 (1968-69) : 133- 134.

2283. Wood, Percy. "Story of an Indian Village The Best in Years." Rev. of *A Goddess Named Gold. Chicago Tribune* 25 Sep. 1960 : 5.

V. Dissertations

2284. Ananta Rao, Kambhampati. "Bhabani Bhattacharya: His mind and Art." Nagpur U, 1977.

2285. Arulandram, H. G. S. "Humanism in the Works of Bhabani Bhattacharya." Madras U, 1981.

2286. Aston, N.M. "Stylistic Analysis of Bhabani Bhattacharya's Novels." U of Poona, 1986.

2287. Bachchan, Ashok K. "The Theme of Integration in the Novels of Bhabani Bhattacharya." L.N. Mithila U, 1993.

2288. Baskaran, V.H. "The Theme of Social Justice in the Novels of Mulk Raj Anand and Bhabani Bhattacharya." Madurai U, 1989.

2289. Bhatnagar, Manmohan. "Political Consciousness in Indo-Anglian Fiction : A Study of Bhabani Bhattacharya, Manohar Malgonkar and Nayantara Sahgal." Dayanand U, (Rothak), 1988.

2290. Dagar, Dharam Veer. "Bhabani Bhattacharya : The Novelist as a Social Historian." Kurukshetra U, 1983.

2291. Dubey, S.K. "Bhabani Bhattachrya *His Mind and Art.*" Magadh U (Bodhgaya), 199?.

2292. Grover, Malta. "Bhabani Bhattacharya as a Novelist of Social Conscience." Roorke U, 1987.

2293. Kaul, Indra. "A study of Bhabani Bhattacharya and Manohar Malgonkar as Novelists with Speical Reference to Some Selected Works." Diss. (M. Phil.). U of Kashmir, 1989.

2294. Jha, Vinita. "Rebel Characters in the Novels of Bhabani Bhattacharya." Bihar U, 19?.

2295. Madhubatta. "Bhabani Bhattacharya as a Novelist." Awadesh U, 1986.

2296. Mehta, J.P. "Thematic study of the Novels of Bhabani Bhattacharya." Saurashtra U, 1980.

2297. Moolls, Yusuf Mohamed. "An Evaluation of the Contribution of Bhabani Bhattacharya to English Fiction." Diss. (M.A.). U of South Africa, 1975.

2298. Paul, Ram. "Quest for identity in the novels of Kamala Markandaya and Bhabani Bhattacharya." Himachal Pradesh U, 1985.

2299. Ray, Shukla. "Bhabani Bhattacharya : The Bengàli Ethos in His Novels." Banaras Hindu U, 1984.

2300. Shrivastava, Rajni. "The art of Bhabani Bhattacharya." Dr. H.S. Gour U, 19?.

2301. Singh, Balram. "Blending of the Traditional and Modern Values in the Novels and Short Stories of Bhabani Bhattacharya." Meerut U, 1983.

2302. Singh, Mahima. "Human Suffering in the Novels of Bhabani Bhattacharya." Meerut U, 1989.

2303. Singh, Narendra Pratap. "Social Criticism in the Novels of Bhabani Bhattacharya." Banaras Hindu U, 1987.

2304. Sudhakar, D. John. "The Bengal Famine in Bhabani Bhattacharya's Novels." Diss. (M.Phil.). U of Hyderabad, 1988.

2305. Shyamala Rao. "Bhabani Bhattachrya : A Study." Andhra U, 1980.

2306. Tamilarasan, C. "Novels of Bhabani Bhattacharya : A Study." Annamalai U, 1985.

JOY DEEP ROY BHATTACHARYA

The Gabriel Club New Delhi : Penguin Books, 1998.

KERON BHATTACHARYA

The Pearls of Coromandal. London : Robert Hale, 1996.

NALINAKSHI BHATTACHARYA

Item and Maxine. London : Jonathan Cape, 1996.

A Fistful of Desire : A Novel. New Delhi : Penguin Books, 1997

R. BHATTACHARYA and DHARMARAJAN

Katha Prize Stories. New Delhi : Rupa & Co., 1991.

VIVEK RANJAN BHATTACHARYA

A Scoop from Heaven. New Delhi : Enkay Publications, 1990.

Item and Maxine. London : Jonathan Cape, 1996.

MARGARET R. BHATTY

The Evil of Empire. New Delhi : Penguin Books,1992.

Little Old Women. New Delhi : National Book Trust,1993.

KISHORE BHIMANI

A. Primary Sources

The Cocktail Insurgency. Calcutta : Writers Workshop, 1989.

B. Secondary Sources

I. Reviews

2307. Rev. of *The Cocktail Insurgency.* Hindustan Times (Mag) 15 Apr. 1990 : 5.

2308. Sharma, Aparna. "After the Party." Rev. of *The Cocktail Insurgency. Indian Book Chronicle* 16 June 1991 : 11.

O.S. BHONDI

Man and God : A Novel. Jullunder City : Raj Rattan Press, 1970.

Mysterious Mansion and Other Stories. Palampur (Himachal Pradesh) : Unico Publishing House, 1970.

BHARAT BHOOSHAN

From the Roof Top. Delhi : Goyal, 1992.

MATHURAM BHOOTHALINGAM

Sons of Pandu. Madras : Dotton Publishers, 1966.

The Nectar of the Gods. New Delhi : By the Author, 1969.

Stories of Vikramaditya. New Delhi : Publications Division, 1983.

V.N. BHUSHAN

ed. *The Earthen Bowl : An Anthology of Short Stories.* Bombay : Padma Publishers, 1940.

Magic Shadow. Bombay : Educational Publishing House, 1942.

LAKSHMI NIVAS BIRLA

A. Primary Sources

Sultan and Nihalda. Calcatta : Grantham, 1964.

Folk Tales of Rajasthan. Bombay : Asia Book House, 1964.

The Curse of Padmini. Bombay : Bharatiya Vidya Bhavan, 1971.

One Heart and Two Swords : Saga of Rajput Chivalry. Bombay : Bharatiya Vidya Bhavan, 1973.

For Love and Freedom. Bombay : Bharatiya Vidya Bhavan, 1977.

That Atom of Sand. Bombay : Bharatiya Vidya Bhavan, 1981.

B. Secondary Sources

I. Reviews

2309. Rev. of *The Curse of Padmini. Swarajya* 22 July 1972 : 19-20.

2310. Rev. of *One Heart and Two Swords. Teacher Today* 19.3 (1977) : 97.

VANDANA BIST

Ticket to Home and Other Stories. New Delhi : Indus Harper, 1994.

ANIL CHANDRA BISWAS

Stories of Indian Life. New Delhi : Amrit Book Depot, 1964.

Through Sunlight and Gloom. New Delhi : Amrit Book Depot, 1964.

Trials of Glory. New Delhi : Amrit Book Depot, 1966.

K.K. BISWAS

Stories of Rural Bengal. Calcutta : Purvasa, 1944.

SUBODH BISWAS

Glare in Gloom. Calcutta : Bhawanipore Press, 1962.

RUSKIN BOND

A. Primary Sources

I. Novels

The Room on the Roof. London : Deutsch, 1956. Bombay : Wilco Books, 1958. Middlesex . Penguin Books, 1987. New Delhi : Penguin Books, 1988.

An Axe for the Rani., Delhi : Hind Pocket Books, 1972.

Love is a Sad Song. New Delhi : Orient Paperbacks, 1975.

The Blue Umbrella., Calcutta : Rupa & Co., 1992.

Strangers in the Night (Two Novellas). New Delhi : Penguin Books, 1996.

Ruskin Bond : The Complete Stories and Novels. New Delhi : Penguin Books, 1996.

II. Short Stories

The Neighbour's Wife and Other Stories. Madras : Higginbothams, 1967.

My First Love and Other Stories. Bombay : Pearl Publications, 1968.

The Last Tiger. New Delhi : Publications Division, 1971.

The Man-Eater of Manjari. New Delhi : Sterling Publishers, 1973.

A Girl from Copenhagen. New Delhi : India Paperbacks, 1977.

A Flight of Pigeons. Bombay : Indian Book House, 1980.

The Young Vagrants. Bombay : India Book House, 1981.

Ghost of a Hill Station. Bombay : India Book House, 1985.

The Night Train at Deoli and Other Stories. New Delhi : Penguin Books, 1988.

Time Stops at Shamli and Other Stories. 1989, New Delhi : Penguin Books, 1990.

Tales and Legends from India. New Delhi : Rupa & Co, 1990.

Panther's Moon and Other Stories. New Delhi : Puffins Books, 1991.

Our Trees Still Grow in Dehara and Other Stories. New Delhi : Penguin Books, 1991. Awarded by Sahitya Akademi in 1992.

Island of Trees : Nature stories and poems. Delhi : Raina Sagar, 1992.

Road to the Bazzar. New Delhi : Rupa & Co, 1993.

Quakes and Flames. New Delhi : National Book Trust, 1994.

Family Ghosts and Other Stories. New Delhi : Frank Bros, 1995.

Thief and Other Stories. New Delhi : Frank Bros, 1995.

III. Children Booka

Grandfather's Private Zoo. Bombay : India Book House, n.d.

The Hidden Pool. New Delhi : Children's Book Trust, 1966.

Once Upon a Monsoon Time. New Delhi : Orient Longman, 1974.

Angry River. Calcutta : Rupa & Co., 1992. Harmondsworth (Middle sex) : Puffin Books, 1994.

The Penguin Book of Indian Ghost Stories. New Delhi : Penguin Books, 1993.

The Penguin Book of Indian Railway Stories. New Delhi : Penguin Books, 1994.

Delhi is Not Far : The Best of Ruskin Bond. New Delhi : Penguin Books, 1994.

Ruskin Bond : Children's Omnibus. New Delhi : Rupa & Co, 1995.

Tigers Forever (A Collection of poems and stories...). Delhi : Ratna Sagar Pvt. Ltd., 1996.

When the Tree Walked and Other Stories. Madras : Chandamama Publications, 1996.

IV. Interviews

"To Be or Not to Be a Writer." *Times of India* 6 Dec. 1987 : 4. "Sunday Review."

"I am Not Dying; This is a Dress Rehearsal." Interviewed by Sujit Chakraborty. *Debonair* Nov. 1982 : 8-10, 15-18.

V. Non-Fiction

"First Strokes of Pan." *Sunday Herald* 4 Aug. 1996 : 1.

B. Secondary Sources : Critical Works

I. Books

2311. Singh, Prabhat K, ed. *The Creative Contours of Ruskin Bond : An Anthology of Critical Writings*. New Delhi: Pencraft Publications, 1995.

II. Research Articles

2312. Banerjee, Victor. "Ping, Pong and Ruskin Bond : A Profile." *Deccan Herald (Sunday)* (Banglore) 6 Dec. 1992.

2313. Khanna, Namita. "From Ruskin with Love" *Sunday* 10 Nov. 1991 : 75-77.

2314. Lal, Anand. "Ruskin Bond." Prasad, Madhusudhan, *Indian English Novelists*. 153-171. ref. : 437.
An assessment of Ruskin Bond as a novelist. Traces how his flair for short stories influences his fictional technique by pruning and by evoking the atmosphere. Similarly susceptibility to children's literature influences the content of his novels.

2315. Melwani, Murali Das. "Ruskin Bond." *Writers Workshop Miscellancy* 49, Feb. 1972 : 40-44. Rpt. as "The Gentle Voice of Indo-Anglian Literature" in *Thought* 28 Aug. 1971 : 15-17. Also in Melwani *Critical Essays* 36-41. ref. : 361.
An assessment of Ruskin Bond as a short story writer.

II. Reviews

2316. Bhatt, Kaveri. "Too Simple for the likes of us." Rev. of

Ruskin Bond's *The Room on the Roof* and *Vagrants in the Valley.*" *Indian Review of Books* 16 July-Aug. 1994 : 32-33.

2317. Dhar, T.N. "Tender and Authentic." Rev. of *The Night Train at Deoli and Other Stories. Indian Literature* Jan.-Feb. (1989) : 153-156.

2318. Futehally, Laeeq. Rev. of *An Axe for Rani. Quest* 81, Mar.-Apr. 1973. 99-102.

2319. Gour, Neelam Saran. "Of Human Bondage." Rev. of *The Complete Stories and Books. Indian Review of Books* 16 Aug.-15 Sep. 1996. 53-54.

2320. Karunakaran K. "Nostalgic Talks With a Rural Flavour." Rev. of *Time Stops at Shamli and Other Stories. Deccan Chronicle* 17 Dec. 1989 : 3.

2321. Zutshi, Urmilla. Rev. of *The Young Vagrant. Hindustan Times* (Mag) 8 Dec. 1981 : 4.

R.M. BORGONKAR

A. Primary Sources

I. Short Stories

A Paradise of Sinners. Banglore : Shanta Publications, 1975.

B. Secondary Sources

II. Reviews

2322. Rao, Damodar. "Variety Only." Rev. of *A Paradise of Sinners. Literary Half-Yearly* 17.1 (1976) : 141-142.

2323. Sahridaya. Rev. of *A Paradise of Sinners. Triveni.* 47.1-2 (1978) : 94-95.

IRENE BOSE

Totaram, The Story of a Village Boy in India. New York : Macmillan, 1933.

The Monkey Tree. New York : Dodd Mead, 1956.

S.S. BOSE

Humourous Sketches. Allahabad : Pioneer Press, 1903.

REMIGIO BOTELHO

On a Goan Beach : A Novel. Panjim : Star Types, 1994.

SASTHI BRATA

A. Primary Sources

I. Novels

Confession of an Indian Women-Eater. London : Hutchinson, 1971. Rpt. as *Confession of an Indian Lover*. New Delhi : Sterling Publishers, 1973.

She and He. Delhi : Orient Paperbacks, 1973.

A Search for Home. New Delhi : Orient Paperbacks, 1975.

The Sensuous Guru (The Making of a Mystic President). New Delhi : Sterling Publishers, 1980.

II. Short Stories

Encounters. New Delhi : Orient Paperbacks, 1978, 1980.

III. Non-Fiction

My God Died Young. London : Hutchinson, 1968. New Delhi : Orient Paperbacks, 1967.

IV. Interviews

R.S. "The Confession of Sasthi Brata : An Interview." *Times Weekly* 11.

B. Secondary Sources : Critical Works

I. Research Articles

2324. Kohli, Suresh. "Writings of Sasthi Brata." *Patriot* (Mag) 21 March 1983 : 3.

2325. Narayan, Shyamala A. "Sasthi Brata." *Contemporary Novelist* 5th ed. 136-138. ref. : 225.

2326. Pathak, R. S. "The Stories of Sasthi Brata." Dwivedi, *Studies in Contemporary Indian Short Stories* ref. : 271.

2327. ——. "Sasthi Brata 's *Encounter* with a Fictional Form." Singh, Avadesh 54-69. ref. : 507.

Evaluates Sasthi Brata as a short story writer and comments that his stories "though done on a small canvass, are commendable achievements in modern Indian fiction in English."

2328. Sarma, G.P. "Sasthi Brata." Prasad, Madhusudan, *Indian Novelists in English* 188-200. ref. : 437.

Discusses autobiographical nature of Sasthi Brata's novels — an iconoclast who is over-jealous of breaking the old order in the Indian Society.

II. Reviews

2329. Chaddah, R.P. Rev. of *A Search for Home. Thought* 21 June 1975 : 17.

2330. Kumar, Sharwan. "Panty Party." Rev. of *Confession of Indian Women-Eater. Thought* 2 Oct. 1971 : 66-77.

BRIJ MOHAN

Stranger Than Fiction : A Collection of Credible Supernatural Stories. Delhi : Anupama Publications, 1993.

RAMESH BUCKTAWAR

Sting of the Wasp : A Novel. Delhi : Ajanta Publications, 1994.

AHMED BUNGLOWALA

Midnight Blue. Poona : Falcon Books, 1990.

K.M. PTALITH BUTT

Some Indian and Other Stories. Calcutta : Newsman, 1897.

SANJEEV CANAKAPALLI (Pseud. Sanjeev)

Buds and Blossoms. Madras : Higginbothams, 1974.

GEET U. CANPAPEE

The Amulet Mystery. Calcutta : Writers Workshop, 1996 (for children).

SHYAM BEHARI CAPOOR

A. Primary Sources

A Woman's Tears and Other Stories. New Delhi : Sterling Publishers, 1977.

B. Secondary Sources

I. Reviews

2331. Melwani, Murali Das. Rev. of *A Woman's Tears and Other Stories. World Literature Today* 52.2 (1978) : 341.

ARSHAD ANWAR CASHMIRI

Shy Guy and Other Stories. Calcutta : Writers Workshop, 1995.

K.V. CHACKO

A. Primary Sources

I. Short Stories

Man and Woman. Calcutta : Writers Workshop, 1981.

B. Secondary Sources

I. Reviews

2332. Futehally, Shama. Rev. of *Man and Woman. Indian Book Chronicle* 16 Oct. 1982 : 333-334.

2333. Khemani, T. G. Rev. of *Man and Woman. Illustrated Weekly of India* 23 Jan. 1983.

2334. Melwani, Murali Das. Rev. of *Man and Woman. Indian Book Chronicle* 16 Oct. 1982. : 333.

2335. Nagarajan, S. Rev. of *Man and Woman. CRNLE Review Journal* 1 (1954) : 83-84.

NARINDER CHADHA

The Drop Out. New Delhi : Young Asia Publications, 1972.

JAIDEEP SINGH CHADHA

Vinculum. Madras : Acme Books, 1992.

B.C. CHAKRABORTY

Stories of Heroism. New Delhi : Allied Publishers, 1995.

SAIBAL CHAKRABORTY

Boats with Wings and Other Stories. New Delhi : Rupa & Co., 1994.

HARIPADA CHAKRAVARTI

Man in a Million. Nabagram : by the Author, 1969.

KEDARNATH VIDYA BINOD CHAKRAVARTI

The Liberation : A Highclass Devotional Novel (Ethical and Philosophical). Calcutta : Bejay Gopal Chakravarti, 1924.

KHETRAPAL CHAKRAVARTI

Sarala and Hingama : Talks Descriptive of Indian Life. Calcutta : Basu Mitra & Co, 1875. 2nd ed. 1899.

S.M. CHAKRAVARTI

The Call (short stories). London : Stockwell, 1936.

MEIRA CHAND

House of The Sun. New Delhi : Penguin Books, 1998.

ANIL CHANDRA

Hakim's Commitment and Other Stories. New Delhi : Har Anand Publications, 1995.

Thanedar of Lakhanpur and Other Stories. New Delhi : Har Anand Publications, 1996.

JAGADISH CHANDRA

The Broken Bridge. New Delhi : Vikas Publishing House, 1975.

SURESH CHANDRA

Baba's Tribe : A Novel. Nagpur : Bahri Publications, 1989.

VIKRAM CHANDRA

A. Primary Sources

First Fictions. London : Faber & Faber, 1995.

Red Earth and Pouring Rain. New Delhi : Penguin Books, 1995. London : Faber & Faber, 1995.

Love and Longing in Bombay : Stories. Boston Little Brown, 1997. New Delhi : Penguin Books, 1997.

B. Secondary Sources : Critical Works

I. Research Articles

2336. Kaur, Charanjit. "*Red Earth and Pouring Rain* : A Study in Dislocation and Assimilation." Kirpal, *Postmodern Indian English Novel* 215-222. ref. : 331.
Explores various aspects of dislocation, displacement and the process of assimilation on cultural, individual and philosophical levels in the novel and shows how it fits into post-modernist tradition as it fuses in its framework the fragment of history, myth, family and legend.

2337. Padmanabhan, Mukund. "Drenched in Dejavu : Vikram Chandra's *Red Earth and Pouring Rain.*" *Indian Review of Books* 16 June-15 July 1995 : 2-3 "In Focus."

II. Reviews

2338. Bhaskaran, Nandini. "The Novel in 70 mm." Rev. of *Red Earth and Pouring Rain. Times of India* 7 May 1995.

2339. De, Shobha. Rev. of *Red Earth and Pouring Rain. Indian Review of Books* 16 June-15 July 1995.

2340. Ramlal Agarwal. Rev of *Love and Longing in Bombay; Stories. World Literature Today.* 72.1(1980) 206-207.

MAYA CHANDRASEKHARAN

Janaki's First Term. Calcutta : Writers Workshop, 1993.

B. CHANDRIKA AND AYYAPPA PANIKER, ed.

Best Loved Stories. Madras : Anuchitra Publications, 1991.

BALWINDER, CHATHA

The Dexters. New Delhi : Enkay Publications, 1991.

BANKIMCHANDRA CHATTERJEE

A. Primary Sources

I. Novels

Rajmohan's Wife. Calcutta : R. Chatterjee, 1935. Calcutta : Bangiya Sahitee Parishad, 1940. New Delhi : Ravi Dayal, 1996. First published serially in *The India Field* (Weekly) Calcutta in 1864.

Bankin Rachanavali. Ed. Jogesh Chandra Bgal. Calcutta : Sahiya Sansad, 1969.

B. Secondary Sources : Critical Works

I. Research Articles

2341. Mishra, Ganeswar. "The Indian Narrative Tradition and Bankim Chandra's *Rajmohan's Wife*." *Journal of Literary Studies* 4.1 (1981) : 55-78. Rpt. in Mishra 1-17. ref. : 364.

Analyses the novel to show the nature of transition of the traditional folk form of India into the Western form and comments that "it is not in the theme as much as in the treatment of the Theme that Chatterjee's novel is traditional and closer to the folk-tale."

DEBIDAS CHATTERJEE

The Imperfect Journey : A Fantasia. N.P. n.p. n.d.

HARI SADHAN CHATTERJEE

The Traveller. Vol. 1-3. Calcutta : Writers Workshop, 1995. Vol. 1996.

JAYABROTO CHATTERJEE

Last Train to Innocence. New Delhi : Penguin Books, 1995.

JAYASREE CHATTERJEE

A. Primary Sources

Where Oleanders Don't Grow. Calcutta : Writers Workshop, 1981.

One Step Ahead. New Delhi : Arnold Heinemann, 1985.

B. Secondary Sources : Critical Works

I. Reviews

2342. Subramaniam, S. Rev. of *Where Oleanders Don't Grow. Illustrated Weekly of India.* 1 April 1982 : 51.

2343. Williams, H.M. Rev. of *Where Oleanders Don's Grow. CRNLE Review Journal* 2 (1983) : 83.

MARGARET CHATTERJEE

At The Homeopath's and Other Stories. Calcutta : Writers Workshop, 1973.

The Sound of Wings. New Delhi : Arnold Heinemann, 1978.

The Rimless World. Delhi : B.R. Publishing Corporation, 1986.

SAYAN CHATTERJEE

A Bureaucrat's Yarns (Short Stories). New Delhi : Har Anand Publications, 1995.

A Slice of Delhi. New Delhi : Bookwise Private Ltd., 1998.

SEETA CHATTERJEE

The Knight Errant. Calcutta : R. Chatterjee, 1924.

SEETA CHATTERJEE AND SANTHA

Tales of Bengal. London : Oxford Press, 1922. Calcutta : R. Chatterjee, 1936.

UPAMANYU CHATTERJEE

A. Primary Sources

I. Novels

English, August : An Indian Story. London : Faber & Faber, 1988. Madras : East-West Books, 1988. Calcutta : Rupa & Co., 1992.

The Last Burden. New Delhi : Penguin Books, 1993.

II. Interviews

Matto, Amitabh. "Magic Realism Isn't My Kind of Stuff." Interview With Upamanyu Chatterjee. *Illustrated Weekly of India* 31 July-6 Aug. 1993 : 28-29.

B. Secondary Sources : Critical Works

I. Research Articles

2344. Aiyer, Savita, "*English, August :* What Life is All About." *Literary Journal of Stella Maris College* (Madras) Feb. 1990. 16-17.
A general evaluation of the novel. Finds that Upamanyu Chatterjee displays an uncanny ability to point out the incongruities of life.

2345. Hema, M.S. "Upamanyu Chatterjee's *The Last Burden.*" Kirpal, *Postmodern Indian English Novel* 49-58. ref. : 331.
Analyses the novel to show how it focuses on the visceral reality of life today — the depravity of human relationships, the consequent trauma of dispossession and migration.

2346. Kerr, David. "History and the Possibilities of Choice : A Study of Anita Desai's *Baumgartner's Bombay,* Chatterjee's *English, August,* and Shashi Deshpande's *That Long Silence.*" Dhawan, *Indian Women Novelists* Set I. Vol. 1. 129-138. ref. : 257.
See 2696.

2347. Kumar, Sanjay. "The Nowhere Man : The Exiled Self in Upamanya Chatterjee's *English August : An Indian Story.*" *Creative Forum* 8.1-2 (1998) : 105-108.

2348. Kumar, T. Vijay. "I Can't Get No Satisfaction." : Upamanyu Chatterjee's *English, August.*" Kirpal, *The New Indian Novel* 169-178. ref. : 330.
Traces the characteristic trends of the Indian novel in English of the 1960s and 1980s and considers *English, August* a recognisably contemporary novel embodying in itself both the trends : the concern with the unrooted self of the former (1960s) and the hybrid idiom of the latter (1980s)."

2349. Prasad, Murari. "Society in Upamanyu Chatterjee's *English, August.*" *Indian Journal of English Studies* 33 (1994-95) : 68-75.
Shows how the novel gives expression to the complex reality of Indian society through the observations of a sensitive individual, Agastya and through the depiction of the small town, Madna, a microcosm of India.

2350. Ramanam, Mohan. "Upamanyu Chatterjee's *The Last Burden.*" Dass and Dhawan, *Fiction of the Nineties* 98-101. ref. : 243.
Considers *The Last Burden* as "a troubling and troublesome book," only "remotely concerned with Indian life, middle class life, and explores that life with a rare linguistic brilliance and wryness."

2351. Rayakar, Meenakshi. "The Intellectual in a State of "Anomy" : Achebe's *No Longer at Ease* and Chatterjee's *English, August : An Indian Story.*" *New Quest* 92, Mar.-Apr. 1992 : 109-111.
In spite of the differences in locales and value systems Achebe's *No Longer at Ease* and Upamanyu Chatterjee's *English August* discuss the intellectual state of "anomy" in a decolonized world.

2352. Sengupta, C. "Upamanyu Chatterjee's *English August* : Metaphor of Contemporary Youth's Quest for Self-Realization." *Commonwealth Review* 5.1 (1993-94) : 110-121. Rpt. in Dhawan, *Indian Literature Today* 110-121. ref. : 258.
Discusses the novel in terms of its title — "English, August" and as the protagonist's odyssey of self-discovery and as an "Indian Story."

2353. Singh, A.K. "Upamanyu Chatterjee's Agastya : A New Voice of August." *Language Forum* 18.1-4(1992) : 163-170. Rpt. in Pathak, *Quest for Identity* 163-170. ref : 423.
Basing his arguments on Frye's concept of the hero's power of action and the quest myth, comments that" beneath Agastya's action and elusive quest rages a highly sceptical mind facing a crisis of self-confidence that reveals the perils of disillusionment and a sense of dissatisfaction — which surfaced to a good measure in the 1980's."

2354. ——. "*English August : An Indian Story* : A Critical Appraisal." Pathak, *Recent Indian Fiction* 82-103. ref. : 424.
An appraisal of the novel focusing on the ideological stances of the novelist on subjects like postcolonial Indian bureaucracy, development, politics, language and education, and on its technique which follows the postmodern meta-fictional literary tradition.

2355. Trikha, Pradeep. "Emotional Bonds in Upamanyu Chatterjee's *The Last Burden*." *Commonwealth Review* 5.1 (1993-94). Rpt. in Dhawan, *Indian Literature Today* 122-127. ref. : 258.
Examines the plot, theme, narrative sequence, flashback technique and characterization to show how they help to explore the dark side of kinship and family ties and evoke and sustain the intensity of "emotional bonds."

II. Reviews

2356. Advani, Rukun. "All's Not Well at the Collectrate." Rev. of *English, August. Indian Express* 31 July 1988 : 5.

2357. Basu, Ranjita. Rev. of *English, August. Literature Alive* 3.2 (1988) : IV.

2358. Dayal, Ravi. "A Burden Well-carried." Rev. of *The Last Burden. Indian Express* (Sunday Magazine) 21 Nov. 1993.

2359. Doctor, Geetha. Rev. of *English, August. Literature Alive* 3.2 (1989) : 18-19.

2360. ——. "Adventures in Slobland." Rev. of *The Last Burden. Indian Review of Books* 16 Oct.-15 Nov. 1993 : 51-52.

2361. Ezekiel, Nissim. Rev. of *English, August. Indian Post* 21 Aug. 1988.

2362. Rama Rao, Vimala. Rev. of *English, August. Literary Criterion* 27.4 (1992) : 78-79.

2363. Rev. of *The Last Burden. Economic Times* 3 Aug. 1993 : 13.

2364. Roy, Navkala. Rev. of *English, August. Seminar* 384, Aug. 1991 : 7-18.

2365. Sethi, Rumina. "All Dressed Up and Nowhere to Go." Rev. of *The Last Burden. New Quest* 104, Mar.-Apr. 1994 : 127-128.

2366. Tejpal, Tarun. "The Literary Babu." Rev. of *The Last Burden. India Today* 15 Aug. 1993 : 124-125.

2367. Viney Lal. "Enjoyable Reading." Rev. of *English, August. Indian Literature* May-June 1990. 155-161.

2368. Williams, Elaine. "Driven by Distraction." *Times Literary Supplement* 15-21 July, 1988.

UPENDRANATH CHATTERJI

Behula or Adventure of a Hindu Satee (From Padma Purana in Bengal). Calcutta : Published by the Author, 1914.

VEERA CHATTERJEE

A. Primary Sources

All This is Ended : The Life and Times of H.H. The Begum Samroo of Sardhana. New Delhi : Vikas Publishing House, 1979.

B. Secondary Sources

I. Reviews

2369. Daruwala, Rusi J. Rev. of *All This is Ended. Financial Express* 8 Apr. 1979 : 4.

2370. Pestonji, Meher. Rev. of *All This is Ended. Eve's Weekly* 21 July 1979 : 35.

PRADYOT CHATTERJI

A Passage to London. Calcutta : Writers Workshop, 1991.

SHOMA A. CHATTERJI

Yes! and Other Stories. Calcutta : Writers Workshop, 1987.

HARINDRANATH CHATTOPADHYAYA

The Queen's Parrot and The King's Ape. Bombay : India Book House, 1968.

Lotte : The Power of Love : The Life Story of Lotte Nivelli. Delhi : B.R. Publishing Corporation, 1991.

RAMESH CHANDRA CHATTOPADHYAYA

The Sorrows of a Sub-Post Master : A Story from Life. Calcutta : Book & Co., 1927.

PADMA CHATURVEDI

Beyond Self. Delhi : Sterling Publishers, 1976.

BHAGWAT SWARUP CHATURVEDI

Face to Face with Criminals. Delhi : Hind Pocket Books, 1970.

AMIT CHAUDHARI

A. Primary Sources

A Strange and Sublime Address. London : Heinemann, 1971. A Novella and nine short stories.

Afternoon Raag. London : Minerva, 1994.

Freedom Song. London : Picador, 1998.

II. Interviews

Sen, Mandira. Author at Work. *Times of India.* 22 Sep. 1991 : VIII.

Doctor, Geetha. "Master Craftsman : Face to Face with Amit Chaudhuri." *Indian Review of Books* 16 Jan.-15 Feb. 1999.

B. Secondary Sources : Critical Works

I. Research Articles

2371. Bose, Devika. "The Novels of Amit Chaudhari : Stories without Beginnings, Middles or Ends." Kirpal, *Postmodern Indian English Novel* 94-104. ref. : 331.

Evaluates Chaudhari's novels as novels of a different kind from the conventional ones both in their subject and technique for they highlight subjects that are traditionally considered 'drab' and 'undramatic' while deviating from the accepted pattern with a beginning, a middle and an end.

2372. Dey, Esha. "The Instant Made Eternity : Amit Chaudhuri's *A Strange and Sublime Address.*" *Commonwealth Review* 5.1 (1993-94) : 103-109. Rpt. in Dhawan, *Indian Literature Today* 103-109. ref. : 258.

Discusses how the banal occurrences of day-to-day life and inconsequential encounters possess a depth of life and finds in the novel "a fine sense of proportion, almost classical in its control," steering "the delicate theme, the shapeless contingency of life into the intended destination of an equivalent form in art."

2373. Doctor, Geetha. "In the Land of the Irish Eaters : *Freedom Song*." *Indian Review of Books.* 16 Jan.-15 Feb. 1999 : 6. "In Focus."

2374. Ramakrishnan, E.V. "'Children of a Free State' : Amit Chaudhari's *Afternoon Raag* Amitav Ghosh's *Shadow Lines* as Novels of Growing up." *Critical Practice* 4.1 (1997) : 1-8.

2375. Sengupta C. "Amit Chaudhari's *A Strange and Sublime Address*." Pathak, *Recent Indian Fiction* 219-234. ref. : 424.

Analyses the novel to show "the skilful manner in which the novelist juxtaposes the simple joys of childhood...against the complicated world of the grown-ups.

II. Reviews

2376. Kaul, R. K. Rev. of *A Strange and Sublime Address. Indian Book Chronicle* June 1995 : 2-3.

2377. Paranjape, Makarand R. "Giving us style." Rev. of *A Strange and Sublime Address. Indian Review of Books* Dec. 1991 : 26.

2378. Ponnapa, Kaveri. "Dislocation Sensibilities." Rev. of *A Strange and Sublime Address. Times of India* 22 Sep. 1991.

2379. Prasad, G.J.V. "Gifted Miniaturist." Rev. of *Afternoon Raag. Indian Review of Books* Dec.-Jan. 1994 : 35.

BHABES CHANDRA CHAUDHARI

Rural Ghost. Calcutta : Alpha Beta, 1966.

JAGAT PRAKASH CHAUDHRY

Jungle Providence. Delhi : J.P. Publications, 1972.

C.S. CHELLAPPA

A. Primary Sources

I. Short Stories

Satyagrahi (Stories of the Gandhian Era). Madras : Ezhutthu Prachuram, 1964.

B. Secondary Sources

I. Reviews

2380. Doraiswamy, T. K. "Gandhian Idealism Appraised." Rev. of *Satyagrahi. Thought* 30 Jan. 1965 : 15.

GOVINDA KRISHNA CHETTUR

The Ghost City. Manglore : Basel Mission Bookshop, 1932.

SANKAR KRISHNA CHETTUR

Muffled Drums and Other Stories. Madras : n.p., 1927.

The Cobras of Dharmashevi and Other Stories. Madras : Higginbothms, 1940.

Bombay Murder. Banglore : Higginbothms, 1940.

The Spell of Aphrodite and Other Stories. Bombay : Jaico Publications, 1957.

Mango Seed and Other Stories. Madras : Jupiter Press, 1974.

CHIMPU and DEVIL

Blue Cave. New Delhi : Dimond Pockets, 1985.

JESUDASEN CHINNADURAI

Sugirtha : An Indian Novel. London : Hulbert Publishing Company, 1929. Rpt. London : Heath Cranton, 1938.

ARDESHIR F.J. CHINOY AND A.T. DENABAI CHINOY

Pootli (A Story of Life in Bombay). London : T. Werner Laurie, 1915.

V.V. CHINTAMANI

Vedanatam : The Clash of Traditions. London : Heath Cranton, 1928.

S.K. CHIRIMAR

Traveller and His Flower. Calcutta : Writers Workshop, 1967.

VENU CHITALE (Pseudo Leelabai Ganesh Khare)

A. Primary Sources

I. Novels

In Transit. Bombay : Hind Kitabs, 1958.

B. Secondary Sources : Critical Works

I. Research Articles

2381. Dardinski, M. "India in Transition : A Political Literary View." *Mahfil* 8.2-3 (1972) : 215-22.
Shows how the novelist detailedly accounts for the changing attitudes of the individuals of a Maharastrian family in the wake of the twentieth century.

CHITTAPROSAD

Kingdom of Rasagolla and Other Stories. Bombay : Echo, 1968.

AFTAB CHOPRA

Sundance : Into the Heart of Espionage. New Delhi : A'N'B Publishers, 1995.

DEEPAK CHOPRA

The Return of Merlin. London : Century, 1995. London : Random House, 1995.

GAUTAM CHOPRA

Child of the Dawn : A Magical Journey. New Delhi : Viking/ Penguin 1997

PREM N. CHOPRA

The Destiny. Delhi : Hind Pocket Books, 1991.

Salaam New York — A Novel. New Delhi : Sterling Publishers, 1993.

Lorita : A Novel. New Delhi : Sterling Publishers, 1997.

SUNEET CHOPRA

A. Primary Sources

I. Short Stories

Transactions and Other Stories. New Delhi : Amar Prakashan, 1984.

B. Secondary Sources

II. Reviews

2382. Panwar, Purabi. "In Flesh and Blood." Rev. of *Transactions and Other Stories. Link* 16 Sep. 1984.

2383. Rahi, R.P. "Craftsmanship in Short Story." Rev. of *Transactions and Other Stories. Patriot* 11 Nov. 1984.

CHANDRAHAS CHOUDHURY

Retreat and Other Stories. New Delhi : Indus Harper, 1994.

D.S. CHOWDHURY

The Last Encounter and Other Stories. Jalandhar : by the Author, 1987.

O.S. CHOWDHARY

The Burning Night and Other Stories. New Delhi : Metropolitan Books, 1983.

PRATAP CHANDRA CHUNDER

A. Primary Sources

Job Charnock and His Lady Fair. Delhi : Himalaya Books, 1978.

B. Secondary Sources

II. Reviews

2384. Jha, Rama. "Job Well Done." Rev. of *Job Charnak and His Lady Fair. Indian Literary Review.* June 1978 : 48-49.

ISMAT CHUGATAI

The Quilt and Other Stories. New Delhi : Kali for Women, 1990.

Two Novellas. Calcutta : Kali for Women, 1993.

KAKU CHUNOGUCHI

Raja Griha. New Delhi : Allied Publishers, 1992.

SORABJI CORNELIA

Love and Life Behind Purdah. London : Freemanth, 1901.

Sun Babies. London : John Murray, 1904.

Between the Twilights. London/New York : Harper & Co., 1908.

Indian Tales of Great Ones. London : Blackie & Son, 1916.

Shubala : A Child Mother. Calcutta : Baptist Mission Press, 1920.

SAROS COWASJEE

A. Primary Sources

I. Novels

Goodbye to Elisa. London : Bodley Head, 1974. Toronto : New Press, 1974. Delhi : Orient Paperbacks, 1975.

II. Short Stories

Stories and Sketches. Calcutta : Writers Workshop, 1970.

Nude Therapy. New Delhi : Orient Paperbacks, 1978.

Suffer Little Children. New Delhi : Allied Publishers, 1981. Rpt. as *The Assistant Professor.* Toronto (Canada) : TSAR, 1996.

Stories from the Raj : Selected and Introduced. New Delhi : Harper Collins, 1992.

Last of the Maharajas (A film script to Mulk Raj Anand's Novel). Calcutta : Writers Workshop, 1980.

SAROS COWASJEE and K.S. DUGGAL, eds.

When the British Left : Stories of the Partition of India. Delhi : Arnold Heinemann, 1987.

Orphans of the Storm : Stories of the Partition of India. New Delhi : UBSPD Publications, 1995.

SAROS COWASJEE and SHIV K. KUMAR

Modern Indian Short Stories. Delhi : Oxford Books, 1987.

III. Interviews

Mathur, O.P. An Interview with Saros Cowasjee. *Journal of Indian Writing in English* 15.2 (1987) : 21-25

B. Secondary Sources : Critical Works

I. Research Articles

2385. Mathur, O.P. "Saros Cowasjee." *Encyclopaedia of Indian Literature* Vol. 1. New Delhi : Sahitya Akademi.

2386. Narendra Kumar, V.L.V.N. "Reverse Odyssey : Saros Cowasjee's *Good Bye to Elisa.*" *Quest* (Ranchi) 9.1 (1995) : 10-15.

II. Reviews

2387. Arulandram, H.G.S. Rev. of *Good-bye to Elisa. Rajasthan Journal of English Studies* 2.1 (1976) : 44-45.

2388. Bhaskaran, M.P. Rev. of *Stories and Sketches. Literary Half-Yearly* 12.2 (1971) : 124.

2389. Birandralall, Samuel. Rev. of *Good-bye to Elisa. Littcrit* 8, 4-2. Dec. 1978 : 52-54.

2390. Chellaram, Raju. Rev. of *Stories from the Raj. Economic Times.* 24 Apr. 1983 : 6.4.

2391. Colomer, John. Rev. of *Stories from Raj. CRNLE Review Journal* (1983) : 24.

2392. Das, Manoj. Rev. of *Stories from the Raj. Hindu* 13 July 1982.

2393. De Souza, Eunice. "Messiah Indeed." Rev. of *Good-bye to Elisa. Times of India* 27th July 75 : 8.

2394. Imam, Zinat. Review of *Nude Therapy. Hindustan Times* 10 Sep. 1978 : IV.

2395. Jesudasan, Tony. "Of the Partition and the Raj." Rev. of *When the British Left : Stories on the Partition of India 1947. Hindustan Times* 15 Nov. 1987 : 8.

2396. Kabir. "The Wish to Shock." Rev. of *Suffer Little Children. Patriot* 25 April 1982 : 2.

2397. Kumar, Manjushree S. Rev. of *Orphans of the Storm. Literary Criterion* 31.3 (1996) : 88-89.

2398. Mason, Philip. Rev. of *Stories from the Raj. Times Literary Supplement.* 6 Aug. 1982 : 863.

2399. Nagpal, Jagjit Kaur. "Vivid Portrayal of Confusion." Rev. of *Suffer Little Children. Hindustan Times* (Mag) 8 Aug. 1982 : 4. Also in *Overseas Hindustan Times* 28 Oct. 1982 : 1-2.

2400. Rahaman, Tariq. Rev. of *Orphans of the Storm. World Literature Today* 70.4 (1996) : 1031-32.

2401. Ravindran, Vanaja. "Heart Rendering Tales." Rev. of *Orphans of the Storm. Indian Review of Books* May-June 1995 : 34.

2402. Rodrigues, Eusebio L. Rev. of *Goodbye to Elisa. Books Abroad* 49.1 (1975) : 184-185.

2403. Rutherford, Anna. Rev. of *Goodbye to Elisa. World Literature Written in English* 14.2(1975) : 427. Also in *Literary Half-Yearly* 26.2(1975) : 174-175.

2404. Shahane, V.A. Rev. of *Goodbye to Elisa. Osmania Journal of English Studies* 11.1 (1974-75) : 69-72.

2405. Singh, Rajendra. Rev. of *Goodbye to Elisa. Journal of Indian Writing in English* 4.2 (1976) : 78-80.

2406. Wasi, Jehanara. Rev. of *Stories from the Raj. Link* 28th Apr. 1985 : 40.

GEMMA M. D'CUNHA

Middling Tales. New Delhi : Sterling Publishers, 1994.

NISHA DA CUNHA

A. Primary Sources

Old Cypress. New Delhi : Penguin Books, 1991.

The Permanence of Grief. New Delhi : Penguin Books, 1993.

B. Secondary Sources : Critical Works

I. Research Articles

2407. Saxena, Alka. *"Old Cypress* : Contrary Perspectives." Dass, *Feminism and Literature* 183-191. ref. : 244.

II. Reviews

2408. Doctor, Geeta. "Good Grief." Rev. of *Permanence of Grief. Indian Review of Books* 16 Aug.-15 Sep. 1993 : 21-22.

2409. Khanna, Namita. "Going Public." Rev. of *Old Cypress. Sunday* 4 Aug. 1991 : 72-73.

2410. Sanghvi, Vir. "Haunting Voice." Rev. of *Old Cypress. Sunday* 4 Aug. 1991. 73-74.

2411. Singh, Madhu. Rev. of *Old Cypress. Indian Book Chronicle* Aug.1996 : 19.

NERGIS DALAL (Pseud. ARIES)

A. Primary Sources

I. Novels

Minari. Bombay : Pearl Publications,1967. Bombay : India Book House, 1967.

Never a Dull Moment. Madras : Orient Longman, 1970.

The Sisters. Delhi : Hind Pocket Books, 1973.

The Inner Door. New Delhi : Hind Pocket Books, 1975. New Delhi : Orient Paperbacks, 1977.

The Girl from Overseas. Delhi : Hind Pocket Books, 1979.

II. Short Stories

The Nude. New Delhi : Orient Paperbacks, 1977.

III. Non-Fiction

"On How I Became a Writer." Dhawan, *Indian Women Novelists* Set III. Vol. 5. 9-14. ref. : 257.

B. Secondary Sources : Critical Works

I. Research Articles

2412. Barnabas, Sarala. "Nergis Dalal's *The Girl from Overseas* and Jhabvala's *A Backward Place* : A Matter of Survival." Dhawan, *Recent Commonwealth Literature* Vol. I. 194-217 ref. : 260. Rpt. in Dhawan, *Indian Women Novelists* Set III. Vol. 5. 82-108. ref. : 257.
Deals with the predicament of foreign women who married Indians and their struggle for survival.

2413. ——. "A Study of Nergis Dalal's *Minari* and *The Sisters.*" Dhawan, *Indian Women Novelists* Set III. Vol. 5. 38-68. ref. : 257.
Analyses the novels to show Dalal's achievement and artistic skill as a novelist and deplores that "all these achievements have not served to win her critical attention, let alone claim."

2414. Bharucha, Ferheiz C. "Nergis Dalal's *The Girl from Overseas* : A Cultural Encounter and Existential Query." Dhawan, *Indian Women Novelists* Set III. Vol. 5. 107-109. ref. : 257.
Regards the novel as the novelist's attempt to study ethno psychology — the study of the psychology of races and peoples.

2415. Bhatnagar, O. P. "A Study of Nergis Dalal as a Novelist." *Commonwealth Quarterly* 3.39 (1978) : 57-70. Rpt. in Prasad, Madhusudan, *Indian Novelists* 130-152 ref. : 437.
Analyses Nergis Dalal's novels to show that their artistic merit lies in portraying the two modes of reality — "an Indian Westernised way of looking at Indian life and the Indian way of looking at Indian life."

2416. Kapadia, Novy. "The Theme of Selfhood in Nergis Dalal's *Minari* and *The Inner Door.*" Dhawan, *Indian Women Novelists* Set III. Vol. 5. 14-37. ref. : 257.
Shows how the quest for selfhood and all its subtle ramifications become the core of the novels — *Minari* and *The Inner Door.*

2417. ——. "The Dilemma of Marriage in Nergis Dalal's *The Sisters.*" Dhawan, *Indian Women Novelists* Set III. Vol. 5. 69-81. ref. : 257.
Discusses Nergis Dalal's use of the essential Parsee paradox — the dilemma of identity — to explore the attitudes to marriage and social relationship in the novel *The Sisters.*

2418. Rajeshwar, M. "The Oedipus Configuration in Nergis Dalal's *The Inner Door.*" *Kakatiya Journal of English Studies* 12 (1993) : 113-119.
Traces the narcissistic character of Rahul and his Oedipal relationship with his mother and shows that his renunciation of the world and pursuit of *moksha* are his unconscious responses to his Oedipal problems — "a means of escape from psychic anxieties originating in his unequal relations with powerful personalities."

2419. Sharma, D.R. "The Creative Art of Nergis Dalal." *Journal of Indian Writing in English* 5.1 (1977) : 17-22.
Traces the growth of Nergis Dalal as a novelist and shows her *Inner Door* as her *tour-de-force*, "an enduring piece of creative exploration."

2420. Srivastava, Ramesh K. "From Caterpillar to Butterfly : Stages in Rahul's Metamorphosis to Sainthood." Prasad, Hari Mohan, *Response* 265-273. ref. : 436.
Traces the transformation of Rahul, the protagonist *(The Inner Door)* from a handsome dreamy boy to a real swami in three stages corresponding them to the last three stages of the butterfly.

II. Reviews

2421. A.S.N. Rev. of *The Inner Door. Democratic World* 20 July 1975 : 16-12.

2422. Arulandram, H.G.S. & Joseph Pandian. Rev. of *The Inner Door. Rajasthan Journal of English Studies* 6 (1977) : 59.

2423. Contractor, Behram. "Guns, Gutters and Gurus." Rev. of *The Inner Door. Times of India* 27 July 1975 : 8.

2424. Dutta, Ajit Kumar. Rev. of *The Girl from Overseas. Indian Foreign Review* 15 July 1980 : 25.

2425. Geivak. Rev. of *The Girl from Overseas. Surya India* 8 May 1929 : 41.

2426. Nimbkar, Jai. "Tell a Good Story." Rev. of Nergis Dalal's *The Sisters. Quest* 85, Nov.-Dec. 1973 : 92-93.

2427. Potter, Nancy. Rev. of *The Sisters. World Literature Written in English* 14.2 (1975) : 423.

2428. Rev. of *Never a Dull Moment. Triveni* 41.1 (1972) : 94.

2429. Sethi, H.S. Rev. of *The Girl from Overseas. Indian Express* 10 Feb. 1980 : 6.

2430. Sharma, D.R. Rev. of *The Inner Door. Indian P.E.N.* Mar.-Apr. 1976 : 17-18.

JAYAWANT DALWI

Chakra. Bombay : Orient Longman, 1973.

ARJUN DANGLE

A Corpse in the Well. Bombay : Disha Books, 1992.

PAUL HARRIS DANIEL

Red Tea. Madras : Higginbothams, 1969.

Sister. Delhi : Hind Pocket Books, 1973.

MICHAEL CHACKO DANIELS

A. Primary Sources

I. Novels

That Dawn Romantic Fool : A Story of Narayanan and Joseph. Calcutta : Writers Workshop, 1972.

Anything Out of Place is Dirt. Calcutta : Writers Workshop, 1971.

B. Secondary Sources : Critical Works

I Research Articles

2431. Dwivedi, A.N. "Michael Chacko Daniels." Prasad, Madhusudan *Indian English Novelists* 117-129. ref. : 437. Also in Dwivedi, *Indian Writing in English* 106-117. ref. : 257.

Considers Daniels a novelist with potentialities who has not exploited them to the maximum.

SHOURI DANIELS (Pseud. Molly Ramanujan)

A. Primary Sources

I. Novels

The Salt Doll. New Delhi : Vikas Publishing House, 1978.

II. Short Stories

The City of Children and Other Stories. New Delhi : Chanakya Publications, 1986.

B. Secondary Sources : Critical Works

I. Research Articles

2432. Chaddha, R. P. *"The Salt Doll." Commonwealth Quarterly* 3.9 (1978) : 186-187.

A Review article. A brief note of appreciation of the novel. Feels that with *The Salt Doll* Shouri Daniels deserves a ranking with the front line female fiction writers — Ms. Jhabvala, Ms. Sahgal, and Ms. Markandaya.

2433. Dey, Esha. "Woman as object : The Feminine Condition in a Decadent Patriarchal Society." (Raja Rao's *The Serpent and the Rope* and Shouri Daniels's *The Salt Doll). Literary Criterion* 20.4 (1985) : 9-19. Also in Narasimhaiah, *Women in Fiction* 9-19 ref : 392.
See 714.

2434. Ezekiel, Nissim. "An Image of India in Shouri Daniels's *A City of Children.*" Pandey and Raj Rao 135-140. ref. : 412.
Describes the novel as a projection of the pleasant and unpleasant realities of Indian life in post-Independence India.

2435. Katamble, V.D. "*The Salt Doll* : An Experimentation with Existentialist Writing in Indo-Anglian Fiction." *Littcrit* 9.2 (1983) : 32-39.
Considers the novel with its first person narrative technique, as a bold experimentation in the introspective and psychoanalytical of man-woman relationship.

2436. Kumar, Sukrita Paul. "*The Salt Doll* : Evolving a New Identity." Dinesh, *Between Spaces* 41-46. ref : 262.
"*The Salt Doll* then, is a creative delineation of a woman's psyche oscillating between tradition and modernity and evolving into a new identity through an alert self-awareness."

2437. Mukherjee, Meenakshi. "Towards Liberation : Four Recent Novels of India." *Westerly* 28.4 (1983) : 66-72.
See 933.

2438. Swain, S.P. "Forbidden Stream : Shourie Daniels's *The Salt Doll.*" Dhawan, *Indian Women Novelists* Set III. Vol. 3. 199-207. ref. : 257.
Explores the stream of consciousness technique used by Daniels in the novel.

II. Reviews

2439. Erry, Uma. Rev. of *The Salt Doll. Indian P.E.N.* Sep.-Oct. 1978 : 18-19.

2440. Kulshrestha, Chirantan. Rev. of *The Salt Doll. World Literature Written in English* 20.2 (1981) : 350-352.

2441. Mukherjee, Meenakshi. Rev. of *A City of Children. Indian Express* 4 June 1986.

2442. Rev. of *A City of Children and Other Stories. Tribune* (Sunday) 15 Feb. 1987 : 6.

2443. Singh, Yashoda N. Rev. of *The Salt Doll. Osmania Journal of English Studies* 17.1 (1981) : 135-137.

KEKI W. DARUWALLA

A. Primary Sources

Sword and Abyss : A Collection of Short Stories. New Delhi : Vikas Publishing House, 1979.

The Minister for Permanent Unrest and Other Stories. Delhi : Ravi Dayal, 1996.

B. Secondary Sources : Critical Works

I. Research Articles

2444. Chakravorthy, D. K. "The Short Stories of Keki N. Daruwalla." Chakravorthy 63-68. ref. : 230.
An assessment of the short stories of Keki N. Daruwalla. Finds them having a "radiance of a well-written lyric."

II. Reviews

2445. Anand, M.R. Rev. of *Sword and Abyss. Indian Horizons* 2.9 (1980) : 59-60.

2446. Banerjee, Purabi. Rev. of *Sword and Abyss. Book Review* Nov.-Dec. 1978 : 41.

2447. Dutta, A.K. Rev. of *Sword and Abyss. India Today* Apr. 1979 : 83.

2448. Gondal, Joseph. Rev. of *Sword and Abyss. Hindustan Times* 4 Nov. 1979 : IV.

2449. Hashmi, Alamgir. Rev. of *Sword and Abyss*. *Journal of South Asian Literature* 17.2 (1982) : 243-248.

2450. Naqvi, Aruna. Rev. of *Sword and Abyss*. *Indian Express* 25 Feb. 1979 : 6.

2451. Narasimhan, Maya. "World of Fiction." Rev. of *Sword and Abyss*. *Economic Times* 13 May 1979 : 4.

2452. Padhi, Bijhu. Rev. of *Sword and Abyss*. *Journal of Literary Studies* 2.2 (1979) : 170-172.

K.S. DARYANI

Shravan Kumar : A Hindu Mythological Story of a Youth's Devotion to Parents. Bombay : Mahinder, 1945.

ARVIND N. DAS

The Republic of Bihar. New Delhi : Penguin Books, 1992.

BIJOY DAS

Destination Good Hope and Other Stories. Calcutta : Writers Workshop, 1987.

BIMAL JYOTI DAS

The Rose and the Lily. Calcutta : Rupa & Co., 1973.

D.P. DAS

Untouchable Story. New Delhi : Allied Publishers, 1985.

Twenty First Century and Other Sullen Stories. Calcutta : Writers Workshop, 1988.

FRIEDA MATHILDA HAUSWIRTH DAS

Into the Sun. London : Dent, 1933

GANMOHAN DAS

Selected Short Stories. Calcutta : Rupa & Co., 1990.

GURUCHARAN DAS

A. Primary Sources

I. Novels

A Fine Family. New Delhi : Penguin Books, 1990.

II. Non-Fiction

"A Novelist's Faith." *Indian English Fiction 1980-90 : An Assessment.* Eds. Nilufer E. Barucha and Vilas Sarang. New Delhi : B.R. Publications, 1994. 1-3.

B. Secondary Sources : Critical Works

I. Research Articles

2453. Mathur, Malati. "Gurucharan Das's Vision of Reality in *A Fine Family.*" Kirpal, *Postmodern Indian English Fiction* 119-129. ref. : 331.
Shows how the kaleidoscope of historical events form a meaningful backdrop in shaping the life styles of the characters. Describes the sequence of events as the process of coming to terms with the realities of existence.

HARI DAS

A. Primary Sources

The Oddyssey. Calcutta : Writers Workshop, 1987.

B. Secondary Sources

I. Reviews

2454. Rahi, R.P. "Note Worthy Volumes of Fiction." Rev. of *Oddyssey, Patriot* 20 Dec. 1987.

J.P. DAS

Spider's Web and Other Stories. New Delhi : Vikas Publishing House, 1990.

Prostitute and Other Stories. New Delhi : Har Anand, 1995.

KAMALA DAS

A. Primary Sources

I. Novels

Alphabet of Lust. New Delhi : Orient Paperbacks, 1976.

Daughter of Immortality. New Delhi : S. Chand & Co 1985.

II. Short Stories

A Doll for the Child Prostitute. New Delhi : Indian Paperbacks, 1977.

Padmavathi, The Harlot and Other Stories. New Delhi : Sterling Publishers, 1992.

Sandal Tree and Other Stories. Hyderabad : Disha Books, 1995.

III. Non-Fiction

My Story : An Autobiography : New Delhi : Sterling Publishers, 1971.

IV. Interviews

Geetha, T.N. An Interview with Kamala Das." *Indian Women Novelists.* Ed. Dhawan. New Delhi : Prestige Books, 1995. Set II. Vol. 1. 93. ref. : 257.
"My Instinct, My Guru" (edited version of "Meet the Author" Programme organised by the Sahitya Akademi in New Delhi on 19th July 1990). *Indian Literature* 139, Sep.-Oct. 1990 : 155-162.

B. Secondary Sources : Critical Works

I. Books

2455. Kaur, Iqbal. *Unitying and Retying the Text : An Analysis of Kamala Das's My Story*. New Delhi : Bahri Publications, 1990.

2456. ——, ed. *Perspectives on Kamala Das's Fiction*. New Delhi : Intellectual Book Corner, 1995.

2457. Radha K. *Kamala Das.* Kerala Writers Series. Madras : Macmillan, 1987.

A monograph explicating Kamala Das's achievement as a writer makes a brief survey of her works-poetry, fiction *(Alphabet of Lust),* Short Story "A Doll for the Child Prostitute," autobiography as well as some miscellaneous writings including Malayalam works. Finds Das at her best in the short-story genre.

II. Research Articles

2458. Ahmed, Shafiuddin and Angela Gaewel. "The Politics of Money : Incomplete Feminism in *A Doll's House." Dalhousie Review* 70.2 (1992) : 170-190.

2459. Chandra, Subhash. "A Feminist Reading of *My Story."* Dhawan, *Indian Women Novelists* Set II. Vol. 1. 141-149. ref. : 257.

2460. Dwivedi, A.N. "Kamala Das's *Alphabet of Lust.*" Dwivedi, *Indian Writing in English* 118-125. ref. : 270.

2461. Elias, Mohmed. "Kamala Das and the Nayar Heritage." *Journal of Indian Writing in English* 6.2 (1978) : 15-24.

Traces the influence of Dravidian ethos in Kamala Das's work.

2462. ——. "The Short Stories of Kamala Das." *World Literature Written in English* 52.2 (1985) : 307-312. Rpt. in Rajan, *Changing Traditions* 30-37. ref. : 449.

This paper was originally entitled "Kamala Das : The Matriarchal Memsahib as a Dravidian Anglo-Phile" when it was presented at a seminar on "The Colonial and the Neo-Colonial Encounters in the Short Story of the Commonwealth" held in the University of Mysore, 16-18 Jan. 1984.

Attributes the decline of Dravidian India to the betrayed matriarch personified in the short stories.

2463. Geetha, T.N. "A Study of the Short Stories of Kamala Das." Dhawan, *Indian Women Novelist* Set II. Vol. 1. 175-195. ref. : 257.

Finds Kamala Das's short stories from the collection entitled *A Doll for the Child Prostitute* as "insightful studies in feminine psycho-social situation."

2464. Harish, Ranjana. "My Story." Jain, *Women's Writing* 213-222. ref. : 301

2465. Kanwadkar, M.M. "Motherly Sensibility in *My Story.*" Dhawan, *Indian Women Novelists* Set II. Vol. 1. 149-155. ref. : 257.

2466. Kaur, Iqbal. "Sexual Politics and Kamala Das." Dhawan, *Indian Women Novelists* Set II. Vol. 1. 102-140. ref. : 257.

2467. ——. "Colonial Anguish in *My Story.*" Dhawan, *Indian Women Novelists* Set II. Vol. 1. 156-169. ref : 257.

2468. ——. "Protest Against Sexual Colonialism : Kamala Das's *My Story.*" Jain, *Women Writing* 223-232. ref. : 301. Rpt. in Kaur 193-208. ref. : 320.

2469. Memon, I.U. "Amrita Pritam's *The Revenue Stamp* and Kamala Das's *My Story*." Dhawan, *Indian Women Novelists* Set III. Vol. 4. ref. : 257.

2470. Lall, Rama Rani. "Rebellion and Escape : Kamala Das's *My Story.*" Jain, *Women's Writing* 233-242. ref. : 301.

2471. Narayan, Shyamala A. "A Note on Kamala Das's *My Story*." *Commonwealth Quarterly* 3.9 (Dec. 1978) : 148-155. Also in Dhawan, *Indian Women Novelists* Set II. Vol. 4. 170-174. ref. : 257.

2472. Rahman, Anisur. "A Poet's Tale : *A Doll for the Child Prostitute*." Prasad, Hari Mohan, *Response* 274–284. ref. : 436.

Finds the short story "A Doll for the Child Prostitute" at times as an expression of the poet's self and at other times as a dramatic poem of the eventful life of the prostitutes, hence a poet's tale.

2473. Radha, K. "Common Ground Between the Poems of Kamala Das and Her Other Works in English." *ACLALS Bulletin* 6-7 Ser. 1986.

2474. ——. "The Short Stories of Kamala Das. An Analysis." Dhawan, *Indian Women Novelists* Set II. Vol. 1. 191-203. ref. : 257.
An assessment of Kamala Das as a short story writer.

2475. Shrivastava, K. C. "The Novels of Kamala Das : The Quest for Identity." Sinha and Sinha 117–122. ref. : 519. Rpt. in Dhawan, *Indian Women Novelists* Set II. Vol.1. 94-101. ref. : 257.
Studies the novels — *Alphabet of Lust* and *A Doll for the Child Prostitute* — to show how the quest for identity manifests itself as a theme both at emotional and intellectual levels. Discusses the autobiographical undertones of this theme.

2476. ——. "Political Spectrum in Kamala Das's *Alphabet of Lust*." Saxena, *Glimpses* Vol. 1. 124–130. ref. : 497.
Examines the nature of the political spectrum in Kamala Das's *Alphabet of Lust,* the question of its verisimilitude and its underlying suggestions of correct political values and ethics.

2477. Uma, Alladi. "What is in a Genre? Kamala Das's *My Story*." *Literary Criterion* 32.3 (1996) : 69-76.

2478. Usha, V.T. "Literary Paradigms of Matriliny : Kamala Das's *My Story*." *New Quest* 118, 1990 : 217-220.

Reviews

2479. Chhabra, Navroop. "Failure of Identification." Rev. of *A Doll for the Child Prostitute : Indian Literary Review* 1.12 & 2.1 (1979) : 88-91.

KISHORE CHARAN DAS

A. Primary Sources

I. Short Stories

Death of an Indian. New Delhi : Prachi Prakashan, 1984.

Midnight Moon and Other Stories. Delhi : B.R. Publishing Corporation, 1993.

Prayer Room and Other Stories. New Delhi : Sahitya Akademi, 1993.

B. Secondary Sources

I. Reviews

2480. Chander, K. M. Rev. of *Death of an Indian. Literary Criterion* 20.4 (1985) : 112-114.

MANMATH NATH DAS

Keep the Story Secret. Cuttack : Vidyapuri, 1968.

MANOJ DAS

A. Primary Sources

I. Novels

Cyclones : A Novel. New Delhi : Sterling Publishers, 1987.

Tiger at Twilight : A Novel. New Delhi : Penguin Books, 1991.

II. Short Stories

Song for Sunday and Other Stories. Madras : Higginbothams, 1967.

Short Stories. Madras : Triveni Publications, 1969.

The Crocodile Lady : A Collection of Stories. New Delhi : Sterling Publishers, 1975.

Fables and Fantasies for Adults. New Delhi : Orient Paperbacks, 1978.

Man Who Lifted the Mountain and Other Fantasies. London : Spectre Press, 1979.

The Vengeance and Other Stories. New Delhi : Sterling Publishers, 1980.

The Submerged Valley and Other Stories. London : Baston Books, 1986.

The Dusty Horizon and Other Stories. Delhi : B.R. Publishing Corporation, 1989. New World Series, 3.

Bulldozers and Fables and Fantasies for Adults. Delhi : B.R. Publishing Corporation, 1990.

The Miracles and Other Stories. New Delhi : Sterling Publishers, 1993.

Farewell to a Ghost (Short Stories and a Novelette). New Delhi : Penguin Books, 1994.

III. Chrildren Books

Books for Ever. New Delhi : National Book Trust, n.d.

Stories of Light Delight. New Delhi : National Book Trust, 1970.

Legends of India's Rivers. Bombay : India Book House, 1975.

IV. Interviews

Raja P. "Manoj Das : Compelling Tale-Teller." *Eastern Times* 4 Sep. 1983 : iv.

An interview on Manoj Das's Writing techniques.

——. "Manoj Das : A Significant Story-Teller." *Times of India* (Sunday) 18 May 1980 : III

An interview based article mainly about Manoj Das as a story teller.

——. "Manoj Das." *Hitavada* (Sunday), 15 June 1980 : 1.

An interview based article mainly on his characters and humour.

——. "Citizen of Two Worlds." *Deccan Herald* 20 March 1988 : 5.

An interview with Manoj Das about his bilingual writings.

——. An Interview with Manoj Das. *Literature Alive* 2.1 (1988) 25-27.

B. Secondary Sources : Critical Works

I. Books

2481. Raja P. *Many Worlds of Manoj Das*. Delhi : B.R. Publishing Corporation, 1993.
The book is the first full-length critical study on Manoj Das. Evalutes his short stories both thematically and technically and shows that his art and craft as something unique. Comments that he is the finest short story writer in India today. The book is a modified version of the Ph.D thesis of the author.

II. Research Articles

2482. Biswal, Jayant K. "The Still Sad Story of Humanity : A Study of Manoj Das's Short Stories." *Triveni* 51.3 (1982) : 50-52.
Examines how Manoj Das presents the complex human situation of agony and ecstasy under the facade of comedy.

2483. Padida, Sarat Chandra. "Short Stories of Manoj Das : A Brief Critical Study." *Triveni* 42.3 (1973) : 65-70.
Analyses some of Das's stories to show how he explores the deepest recesses of human mind, be it the psychological insights of a "mass mind" or a solitary individual.

2484. Raja, P. "An Authentic Story-Teller." *Bhavan's Journal* 27.22(1981) : 63-65.

2485. ——. "The Short Stories of Manoj Das." *Indian Literature* 25.5(1982) : 56-62.
Considers that the most noteworthy trait of Das's stories is his powerful penetration into the subtle realities of life.

2486. ——. "Fusion of Vision and Technique in Short Stories of Manoj Das." *Literary Endeavour* 2.2-3 (1980) : 15-20.

Discusses the total fusion of the author's technique and vision in the stories from the four collections.

2487. ——. "Indian Sensibility and the Fiction of Manoj Das." *Language Forum* 12.1-4 (1986) : 133-140. Also in Singh R.K. *Indian English Writing 1981–1985* : 133-146. ref. : 511.

Examines some of Manoj Das's short stories to show how they are steeped in Indianness and reveal Indian sensibility unobtrusively.

2488. ——. "Manoj Das's 'Shama and the Wonderful Lump' : A Study." *Triveni* 50.1 (1981) : 69-72.

A study of the novelette that appeared serially in *The Illustrated Weekly of India.* Considers the story as an allegory. Despite its fairy tale-like form it suddenly surprises us with a message that is of great relevance to our times.

2489. ——. "The Saga of Transition." *Indian and Foreign Review* 25.3 (1988) : 29.

A review article on Manoj Das's first novel, *Cyclones.*

2490. ——. "Manoj Das's *Cyclones :* Humour at the service of Realism." *Triveni* 59.2 (1990) : 20-28.

"The novel demonstrates successfully how humour can be an intrinsic aspect of realism, even when the level of realism is quite high and the message the work conveys is profound."

2491. ——. "Manoj Das's "The Owl : A Study." *Literary Criterion* 25.2 (1990) : 85-89.

A review article.

2492. ——. "The Ghost Stories of Manoj Das." *Language Forum* 18. 1-4 (1992) : 87-94. Also in Pathak, *Quest for Identity* 87-94. ref. : 423.

Analyses two of Manoj Das's stories "Farewell to a Ghost" and "The Dusky Horizon" to show Das's narrative skill and his use of the super-natural element, the latter quality serving on perfect "objective correlative" to the experiences communicated.

2493. Samuel, Sarbeswar. "Symbolic Overtones in the Stories of Manoj Das." *Ravenshaw Journal of English Studies* 4.1 (1994) : 77-94.

2494. ——. "Love and Romance in the Stories of Manoj Das." *Ravenshaw Journal of English Studies* 5.2(1995) : 49-57.

III. Reviews

2495. Chibber, V.N. Rev. of *Fables and Fantasies. Illustrated Weekly of India* 13 June 1980 : 10. Also in *Democratic World* 13 Jan. 1980 : 10.

2496. Coppola, Carlo. Rev. of *The Crocodile Lady : A Collection of Short Stories. Journal of Indian Writing in English* 5.1 (1977) : 67-68.

2497. Dhar, Somnath. Rev. of *Vengeance and Other Stories. Indian and Foreign Review* 15 Feb 1981 : 26-27.

2498. Mukherjee, Jugal Kishore. "Short Stories of Manoj Das." *Indian Literature* 14 : 1971 : 131-132.

2499. Narasimhan, Maya. Rev. of *Fables and Fantasies for Adults. Economic Times* Nov. 1978 : 7.

2500. Narayan, Shyamala. Rev. of *The Crocodile Lady. Times of India* 29 Feb. 1976 : 10.

2501. Prasad, G.J.V. "Quintessentially Indian." Rev. of *The Farewell to a Ghost." Indian Review of books* 16 May-15 June 1995 : 30-31.

2502. Ramachandra, Ragini. Rev. of *Cyclones. Literary Criterion* 22.2 (1987) : 65-66.

2503. ——. Rev. of *The Submerged Valley and Other Stories. Literary Criterion* 22.2 (1987) : 65-66.

2504. Rev. of *Farewell to a Ghost. Book Review* Oct. 1995 : 27-28.

2505. Sundaram, P.S. "A Storm Rages." Rev. of *Cyclones. Book Review* Sep.-Oct. 1987 : 48-49.

C.V. NARASIMHA DAS

The Stubble Under the Cloven Hoof. Cuttack : Sahitya Samsad, 1967.

SISIR DAS

The Last Lambada : A Novel. New Delhi : Sterling Publishers, 1998.

SUJATA DAS

The Queen is Dying. New Delhi : Heritage Publishers, 1987.

SIDDHARTHA DASA

The Accident and Seven Short Stories. Cuttack : Vidyapuri, 19?.

DIWAN JARMANI DASS

Maharaja. Delhi : Hind Pocket Books, 1970.

TRILOKYANATH DASS

Hirimba's Wedding. Midnapore : n.p., 1884.

D.H. DASTUR

Rajput Rani. Bombay : Ahura Printing, 1939.

A booklet containing the story of Rani Rajba of Rajputana.

K.K. DATEY

Your Heart and You. Bombay : Somaiya Publications, 1971.

DINESH CHANDRA DATTA

Matriculation : Short Stories. Jaipur : Asian Publishing House, 1948.

S. DATTA

World of Twilight and Other Stories. Bombay : Oxford University Press, 1970.